MOVIES
of the
THIRTIES

BD-K-2

MOVIES of the THIRTIES

EDITED BY ANN LLOYD
CONSULTANT EDITOR
DAVID ROBINSON

ORBIS PUBLISHING
LONDON

Many of the illustrations come from stills issued to publicize films made or distributed by the following companies: Aldrich and Associates, British and Commercial Gas Association, British Lion, CBS, Central Office of Information, Ceylon Tea Board, Charles Chaplin Corporation, Ciné-Alliance/Gray Films, Cinès, Constantin Film, Les Films du Cyclope, Daiei, Dino De Laurentiis, Cecil B. DeMille, © Walt Disney Productions, EMI, EPI-Club de l'Ecran, Ealing, Empire Marketing Board, FRD, First National, GB Instructional Films, GPO Film Unit, Gainsborough, Gas Light and Coke Co, Gaumont, Gaumont British, Samuel Goldwyn, Grand National, D.W. Griffith, Hepworth, Howard Hughes, Stanley Kramer, Leguan Films, Lenfilm, London Films, MGM, Mirisch, Mosfilm, Nero Film, Vicomte de Noailles, Nouvelles Editions Françaises, ORTF/Son et Lumière/RAI, Orion, Société des Films Osso, Films Marcel Pagnol, Panaria/Hoche Productions, Paramount, Paris Film, Pioneer Pictures, Carlo Ponti, Otto Preminger, RKO, Rafran/San Marco, Rank, Réalisation d'Art Cinematographique, Lotte Reiniger, Films Jean Renoir, Republic, Leni Riefenstahl, Hal Roach, David O. Selznick, Seven Arts, Shamley/Alfred Hitchcock, Sigma, Sincap, Film SOFAR, Elizabeth Taylor-Mead, Terra Films, Tobis, Tonfilm, 20th Century-Fox, Ufa, United Artists, Universal-Prod ENIE-Franco London Films, King Vidor, Volksdeutsche GmbH, Walter Wanger, Warner Brothers.

Acknowledgments: Atmosphère, Martyn Auty, Claude Beylie, Annette Brown, Kingsley Canham, Cinema Bookshop, Culver Pictures Inc, Československý Filmový Ústav-Filmový Archiv, Walt Disney Productions, Joel Finler Collection, Institut Français, Ronald Grant Archive, Bernard Happé, David Henry, David Hine, Robert Hunt Picture Library, David King Collection, Ray Kirkpatrick, Kobal Collection, Kodak Museum, Museum of Modern Art Stills Archive, National Film Archive, David Robinson Collection, Stiftung Deutsche Kinemathek, Talisman Books, Bob Willoughby.

Although every effort is being made to trace the present copyright holders, we apologize in advance for any unintentional omission or neglect and will be pleased to insert the appropriate acknowledgments to companies or individuals in any subsequent edition of this publication.

Facing title-page: Characteristic publicity portrait of Bette Davis, making no homage to glamorous extravagances

Abbreviations used in text

add: additional; **adv:** advertising; **anim:** animation; **art dir:** art direction; **ass:** assistant; **assoc:** accociate; **chor:** choreography; **col:** colour process; **comm:** commentary; **cont:** continuity; **co-ord:** co-ordination; **cost:** costume; **dec:** decoration; **des:** design; **dial:** dialogue; **dial dir:** dialogue direction; **dir:** direction; **doc:** documentary; **ed:** film editing; **eng:** engineer; **ep:** episode; **exec:** executive; **loc:** location; **lyr:** lyrics; **man:** management; **mus:** music; **narr:** narration; **photo:** photography; **prod:** production; **prod co:** production company; **prod sup:** production supervision; **rec:** recording; **rel:** released; **r/t:** running time; **sc:** scenario/screenplay/script; **sd:** sound; **sp eff:** special effects; **sup:** supervision; **sync:** synchronization; **sys:** system. Standard abbreviations for countries are used. Most are self-evident but note:
A = Austria; AUS = Australia; GER = Germany and West Germany after 1945; E.GER = East Germany.

Editor
Ann Lloyd
Consultant Editor
David Robinson
Editorial Director
Brian Innes

Deputy Editor
Martyn Auty
Chief Sub Editor
Maggie Lenox
Senior Sub Editors
Alastair Dougall, Graham Fuller
Editorial Assistant
Lindsey Lowe

Research Consultant
Arnold Desser
Picture Researchers
Dave Kent, Sue Scott-Moncrieff
Research
Kingsley Canham, Paul Taylor, Sally Hibbin

Designers
Ray Kirkpatrick, Richard Burgess

Printed and bound in Spain by Printer industria gráfica sa
Sant Vicenç dels Horts   Barcelona   D.L.B. 10551-1984

ISBN: 0-85613-523-2 (hardback)
         0-85613-660-3 (paperback)

CONTENTS

INTRODUCTION

In retrospect the Thirties appear as one of the most ominous periods in world history. In the Soviet Union the Stalin reign of terror was tightening; in Germany the Nazis assumed totalitarian power; Mussolini's new Italy was at its zenith; the reverberations of the Spanish Civil War and the Sino-Japanese war were felt throughout the world. With the memories of World War I hardly erased, a second and more dreadful war was already on its way.

Little of all these events, however, is reflected in the films of the time. Film-makers it seemed, in whatever country, saw their role to be that of heroic fiddlers, to provide a diversion from a reality that was crowding in too close. In the United States, out of the thousands of films made during the decade, not a dozen so much as touched upon the Depression, the Spanish Civil War or any of the cataclysmic developments in Europe. Germany developed an entertainment cinema of marvellous technical gloss and unashamed escapism. The Soviet Union enthusiastically adopted the newly stated tenets of 'socialist realism', which laid down that the duty of the artist is to show the world not as it is but as it ideally should be. Certainly the whiter-than-white heroes of the Revolution and the glowing, broad-backed peasants, full of smiles and songs, who peopled so many films of the period were far from the realities of life in that unhappy country.

In America this was the apogee of the studio era. Each studio had its own stars, style, signature and guarantee of quality. MGM, boasting 'more stars than there are in heaven', outran all the rest in glamour and spectacle. Paramount, under Ernst Lubitsch's artistic direction, had a special Continental sophistication. Warners excelled in gritty, economical narratives and the hyper-realism of their gangster films. Fox had John Ford, Shirley Temple and a tendency to sentiment. Columbia had Frank Capra. Universal was the home of horror though it occasionally made more evident excursions into art with films like Milestone's *All Quiet on the Western Front*.

The genres of film we now most readily remember from the period are the gangster films, making drama out of the news headlines; the musicals, in which Busby Berkeley and Astaire and Rogers were supreme; star comedies which have left us the icon images of Mae West, W.C. Fields and Laurel and Hardy; the daffy comedies initiated by Capra, which showed the fun of sexual relations and began to define a new and more liberated role for women; opulent re-creations of the past in MGM's literary adaptations or Warners' historical biographies.

It was an age of stars – Garbo, Dietrich, Davis and Crawford; Gable, Cagney, Robinson and Muni. It was an age too of star directors, men like Ford, Capra, King Vidor and Clarence Brown who had learned their craft in the silent period and reached their full maturity in the age of sound.

Despite the riches of its resources, the American cinema suffered its own delayed depression in the early Thirties, coincidentally with one of the British film industry's rare periods of prosperity and euphoria. With a measure of trade protection, production expanded, and two outstanding producers and an inspired director – Alexander Korda, Michael Balcon and Alfred Hitchcock – were ready to seize the opportunities. The decade saw the emergence of other figures, too, who were to be outstanding in British films, among them Carol Reed, Michael Powell and Anthony Asquith.

In France the decade began with the brilliance of René Clair's Parisian musicals and the incomparable, poetic creations of Jean Vigo, then passed through a time of deep depression and ended with the period of Jean Renoir's greatest works, *La Grande Illusion* and *La Règle du Jeu*, and that school of romantic fatalism which was for long afterwards to establish in the minds of foreign audiences a special impression of the French cinema.

Inevitably there were exceptions to the general rule of the cinema as escape and opiate. An artist like Renoir is always aware of the reality of his own times, and *La Règle du Jeu* is full of omens. Other film-makers approached reality more directly. The Thirties had seen the fulfilment of John Grierson's ideal of a documentary cinema that would not only reflect but help shape the reality of people's daily lives. The formative figures of the British documentary movement – Humphrey Jennings, Basil Wright, Arthur Elton, Edgar Anstey, Harry Watt, Paul Rotha –

were making an instrument which would be a valuable defensive weapon in the coming war; and they were in later years to leave a permanent influence on the direction of realist film-making every-where in the world.

The essays in this book show the cinema of the Thirties as standing between two worlds. The films of the time were the summation of the gathered experience of the cinema's first four decades. A few of them – the best – looked forward to the future.

DAVID ROBINSON

Cecil B. DeMille views the film that marked his successful return to the Western, The Plainsman *(1936), starring Gary Cooper and Jean Arthur and based on the life of Wild Bill Hicock and Calamity Jane*

THE COMING OF SOUND

By the mid-Twenties the movies had been moving for thirty years; now the race was on to find the best way to make them talk and sing

Films were fully thirty years old before they learned to speak – a surprising fact when you consider that Thomas Edison had first put his mind to the idea of motion pictures as an extension of his talking machines in the 1880s. Edison went so far as to equip some of his Kinetoscope peepshow machines with phonographs, for which he coined the name 'Kinetophone', but he was unsuccessful in matching sound to picture precisely enough to make the image of a person on the screen appear to be actually speaking or singing.

Even so, films of the 'silent cinema' era were rarely exhibited in silence. Back in 1897 the Lumière brothers engaged a saxophone quartet to accompany the Cinématographe at their theatre in Paris. The composer Saint-Saëns was asked to write a special score for the prestigious film production *L'Assassinat du Duc de Guise* in 1908, and after that it became customary for any major feature-length film to have a specially composed or compiled musical accompaniment. Music, therefore, was an important branch of the silent film business. It provided employment not only for the composers and music publishers, but also for the musicians who played at each performance.

But music was not the only type of sound associated with silent films, as a writer of 1912, Frederick Talbot, observed in his *Moving Pictures: How They Are Made and Worked*:

'When a horse gallops, the sound of its feet striking the road is heard; the departure of a train is accompanied by a whistle and a puff as the engine gets under weigh; the breaking of waves upon a pebbly beach is reproduced by a roaring sound. Opinion appears to be divided as to the value of the practice.'

To provide sound effects cinema owners could equip themselves with special machines that made all kinds of noises, from bird song to cannon fire. The drawback to these live accompaniments was that they depended so much on the availability and skill of the people making the noises – whether musical performers or mere machine operators. Frederick Talbot recalled an effects boy who 'enjoyed the chance to make a noise and applied himself with a vigour of enthusiasm which over-

stepped the bounds of common sense'.

The elaborate musical accompaniments devised by Joseph Carl Breil for the films of D.W. Griffith, or the musical 'suggestions' supplied as a matter of course by distributors in the Twenties, were one thing when the film was performed at Picture Palaces but quite another when it arrived at some backwoods fleapit with only a derelict piano.

Machine-made sound effects added drama to silent movies – or unwanted hilarity if the operator missed his cue

From an early stage, it was clear that a truly satisfactory sound accompaniment must be recorded and reproduced mechanically. The means, it seemed, were already at hand. A decade or more before movies, Edison's phonograph and Berliner's disc-gramophone had made mechanical reproduction possible. In the early stages these had the disadvantage that even with huge trumpet-like horns for amplification, the volume of sound they could produce was limited: but by the early Twenties electrical recording and reproduction had overcome this problem. The more persistent difficulty was to make the sound fit the image exactly.

As early as the 1890s a Frenchman, Auguste Baron, had taken out patents for several systems of synchronizing phonograph and projector. By 1900 at least three competing sound film systems were on show at the Paris Exposition. The most successful of them was the Phono-Cinéma-Théâtre of Clément-Maurice Gratioulet and Henri Lioret (who had earlier patented a cylinder recording device called the Lioretographe). First shown at the Exposition on June 8, 1900, the Phono-Cinéma-Théâtre offered one-minute talking or singing movies of eminent theatrical celebrities.

Another Frenchman, Léon Gaumont, exhibited a device called the Chronophone, which succeeded in synchronizing projector and phonograph but required the projectionist to adjust the film speed

Top: souvenir programme from the Phono-Cinéma-Théâtre announcing 'talking' films of theatrical celebrities – among them Sarah Bernhardt – as early as 1900. Above: as silent movie audiences demanded more than mere musical accompaniments, cinema owners bent over backwards to satisfy the craze for more 'realistic' sound effects. Right: wiring up a phonograph to a film camera inside Edison's 'Black Maria' studio in the 1890s

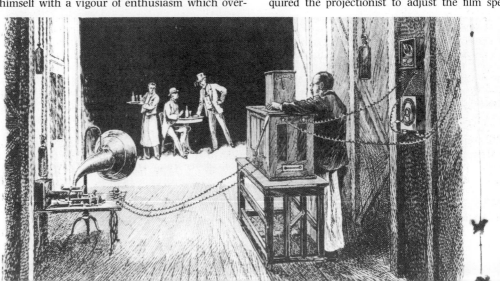

constantly. Gaumont developed his apparatus in competition with other commercial imitators, and enjoyed considerable success in the course of the decade. In America such systems were exploited by the Actophone Company, Camerafilm, and Edison's Cinemaphonograph. In Germany Oscar Messter, in Sweden Paulsen and Magnussen and in Japan the Yoshizawa Company all developed sound film devices. In Britain Hepworth's Vivaphone Pictures had a host of competitors with names like Cinematophone, Filmophone and Replicaphone.

But supposing that, instead of trying to match a separate disc recording to the film, the sound and image could be recorded on the same strip of film? The idea was explored: attempts were made at cutting a needle groove along the edge of the film, but such ingenious efforts to marry phonograph-style recording to film projection were not practicable. Other experiments, however, had shown that sound waves could be converted into electrical impulses and registered on the celluloid itself; the sound *track* (a narrow band running down the edge of the film) was printed on to the film. As the film was projected the process was reversed: variations of light on the track were translated back into sound again.

Soon after World War I, the development of radio greatly assisted engineers researching into sound projection. As sound film systems were patented, it was the giant electrical and radio companies who bought up the patents and moved in on the potential sound-film market. Through the early Twenties the General Electric Company was concentrating on a sound-on-film system, while Western Electric and Bell Telephone still favoured a sophisticated method of synchronized disc reproduction.

By 1923 Lee De Forest, who had been working independently on a sound-on-film system since 1919, was ready to demonstrate his Phonofilms. His first public show of short films was presented in April at the Rivoli Theatre in New York; and in 1924 it went on tour with some 30 theatres specially wired to play it. The repertory included not only songs and turns by vaudeville artists, but also newsreel-style interviews with President Coolidge and other politicians, a dramatic short – *Love's Old Sweet Song* – and musical accompaniments for James Cruze's epic *The Covered Wagon* (1923) and Fritz Lang's *Siegfried* (1924).

Phonofilms were a moderate success, though by no means a revolution. When De Forest demonstrated his system to the moguls of the American cinema, they showed no serious interest. Perhaps the recession that gripped the film industry in the mid-Twenties influenced their better judgment: certainly public interest was falling off; seat prices were rising; quality of the product was declining, and audiences were becoming more discriminating. Above all the new excitement of radio posed a serious threat – a big broadcast could empty cinemas for an evening (much as television can today). Had the Hollywood tycoons taken up De Forest's Phonofilms sooner, however, they might have won back their huge audiences. As it was they went for stop-gap solutions: vaudeville turns, potted light operas between films, Saturday night lotteries – in short, novelty at any price.

On the other hand, the big companies were no doubt shrewd enough to foresee the threat that talking pictures posed to their vested interests, should they permanently catch on with audiences. And the companies were proved right: when talkies arrived, the great studios and their equipment became obsolete overnight, along with backlogs of silent films and bevies of former stars whose talents were better suited to mime than to vocalization.

One company – Warner Brothers – decided to take the plunge with the Vitaphone sound-on-disc system. In later years there was a popular belief that – with nothing to lose by the risk – they had grasped at Vitaphone in a desperate bid to stave off imminent bankruptcy. Recently, however, Professor J. Douglas Gomery and others have shown that at this time Warner Brothers were, in fact, pursuing a policy of dramatic expansion.

Radio gave the American public talking Presidents, wise-cracking comics and instant music. Unless the movies could go one better, radio might put them out of business

In 1924 the company had sufficiently impressed Waddill Catchings, investment banker with the Wall Street firm of Goldman Sachs, to secure substantial investment. Catchings was apparently struck by Warners' rigid cost accounting system; and, with Harry Warner's approval, he devised a master-plan for long-term growth, similar to an earlier plan whereby he had helped transform Woolworths from a regional business to a national corporation. Early in 1925, Catchings accepted Warners' offer of a seat on the board of directors, and devoted his energies to securing more capital.

Thus financed, Warners embarked on a programme of major prestige pictures, set about acquiring cinemas and distribution facilities, modernized their laboratories, and developed their publicity and exploitation methods. At the same time they started a radio station. The consequence of such enormous capital outlay was that Warner Brothers went heavily, but calculatedly, into the red in 1926. The 'near bankruptcy' myth is based mainly on a misreading of annual accounts which showed, but did not explain, an abrupt fall from a $1,102,000 profit to a $1,338,000 loss between March 1925 and the end of the next fiscal year.

No doubt it was this expansionist mood that made the Warners receptive to Western Electric who, since 1924, had consistently failed to interest the major producers in their sound-on-disc system

of synchronization. In later years, having survived all his brothers, the youngest Warner, Jack, was inclined to claim credit for introducing sound pictures. In fact, however, it seems to have been Sam Warner who was mainly responsible, having perhaps had contact with sound through dealing with the affairs of the company's radio station.

In June 1925 the Warners built a new sound stage at the old Vitagraph Studio in Brooklyn and began production of a series of synchronized shorts. On April 20, 1926, the company established the Vitaphone Corporation, to lease Western Electric's sound system along with the right to sub-license. Sam Warner began to plan the launching programme for Vitaphone; his expenditure of some $3

Left: an explanatory and perhaps idealized drawing of how the Chronophone entertained audiences. Top: Hepworth's was a workable sound-film system on the market from 1909 but the pictures did not sing and talk synchronously. Centre: Lee De Forest's trade ad summed up his achievement but it was the big companies who profited from his work. Above: songsheet from the historic film-with-music Don Juan

Above centre: not the first sound film but the one that started it all. Above: within a year talkies were shot on location

Lindbergh, Coolidge and Mussolini; and in October 1927 Fox introduced a regular Movietone newsreel.

Any doubt that the future of the film industry was bound up with sound was removed by the triumph of *The Jazz Singer*, which had its premiere on October 6, 1927. The public had already seen films that talked and sang. What seems to have caught their imagination in this sentimental melodrama about a cantor's son who becomes a jazz singer, was the naturalness of the brief dialogue scenes that Jolson improvised, and the fact that he addressed the audience directly.

Warners stole a march on the industry by plunging into sound. The other moguls waited to see if they would sink or swim

Sound films could no longer be ignored, and the major companies had no intention of ignoring them. After the *Don Juan* premiere Adolph Zukor's Famous Players Company had begun negotiations with Warners and Vitaphone, but these had broken down. In December 1926 Zukor formed a committee representing most of the major companies – Famous Players, Loew's, Producers Distributing Corporation, First National, United Artists and Universal – who agreed upon joint research and united action in the matter of sound pictures.

For the next 15 months the committee received reports from technical experts on the various systems available to them: Vitaphone could be subleased from Warners; Fox's Movietone also attracted their interest; Photophone, developed at General Electric, was on offer from RCA; and Western Electric, although marketing their disc system, were busy developing a sound-on-film system. But the choice was still fairly evenly balanced between sound-on-disc and sound-on-film. The priority was to settle upon a system that would make all equipment compatible, thus avoiding the kind of wrangling and litigation over patents that had beset the early days of movies.

While the other studios analyzed tests and deliberated, Warners and Fox gained a brief but considerable advantage. Not until May 1928 did the six companies enter into an agreement with Western Electric to adopt their sound-on-film system; a year later several of the smaller Hollywood companies followed suit and subscribed to this agreement. Accordingly, although Warner Brothers invested extensively in sound-on-disc productions from 1927 to 1929, the writing was on the wall for the Vitaphone system less than a year after *The Jazz Singer*'s premiere, and Warners would soon follow the other studios in adopting sound-on-film (though retaining the name Vitaphone).

1928 was a year of transition, for the changeover could not happen overnight. It took time to re-equip the studios, and for many months sound films continued to be released in alternative silent versions; at the same time sound effects and music were patched on to silent films to prolong their commercial life. Nevertheless, the silent cinema, with all the art and sophistication it had perfected over the last three decades, had instantly become archaic. Some 80 features with sound were made in the course of 1928.

Warners held on to their lead, maintaining a regular output of silent films with synchronized music and effects, along with a prolific production of Vitaphone shorts. Between April and June 1928 they released three part-talkies – silent films with sound sequences hastily added: Michael Curtiz's

million on it is hardly consistent with the idea of a bankrupt studio.

The culmination of this feverish activity came on August 6, 1926 with the great Vitaphone premiere of *Don Juan* – the first film with a fully synchronized score. (It is important to remember here that it was musical accompaniment and not talking pictures that appealed to the film moguls.) The supporting programme consisted of a series of rather classy musical shorts, preceded by a stodgy filmed speech of introduction by Will Hays, president of the Motion Picture Producers' Association.

Don Juan is a variation on the theme of the great philanderer conquered by true love; and as a swashbuckler it still retains a great deal of attraction today. The title role is played by John Barrymore, in the athletic style of Douglas Fairbanks; and the heroine is the young and exquisite Mary Astor. The film was scripted by Bess Meredyth, and directed by Alan Crosland.

The first Vitaphone programme amply justified Warners' faith and investment – it ran in New York for well over half a year – and henceforth the brothers were wholeheartedly committed to sound. They announced that all their future releases would be provided with Vitaphone accompaniments, and began the process of equipping major cinemas throughout the country for sound. On October 6, 1926 Warners presented a second Vitaphone programme with Sydney Chaplin in *The Better 'Ole*, and some new short films of vaudeville material in contrast to the prestige shorts shown at the Vitaphone premiere two months earlier.

Although most of the major companies were still watching and waiting, behind the scenes William Fox's film company had bought rights in a sound system so close to De Forest's Phonofilm that it became the subject of lengthy litigation. Fox combined in his system elements from Phonofilm and the German Tri-Ergon system (whose American rights he owned), and launched Fox Movietone with a programme of shorts on January 21, 1927. In May he presented a synchronized version of Frank Borzage's *Seventh Heaven*. The supporting programme included a dialogue short – Chic Sale's sketch *They're Coming To Get Me*. In June a new Movietone programme included sound film of

Tenderloin was a gangster story; *Glorious Betsy* was an Alan Crosland costume spectacle; and Lloyd Bacon's *The Lion and the Mouse*, a melodrama, with a leading performance by Lionel Barrymore which confirmed the growing belief that stage-trained actors were what the talkies needed.

On July 8, 1928 Warners released the first all-talkie, *Lights of New York*, a simple tale of two country lads who come to New York and get mixed up with bootleggers. Directed by Bryan Foy, the film ran only 57 minutes, and was from all accounts banal and crude, with the actors shackled to the microphone and nervously delivering their lines in a halting monotone. For all that, it proved a box-office success. Later in the year Warners repeated the triumph of *The Jazz Singer* with a new Al Jolson vehicle, *The Singing Fool*.

Fox's Movietone News provided a major sensation with an interview with Bernard Shaw, in which the 72-year-old celebrity cunningly used the talking film to project his well-managed and much-publicized personality. For the most part Fox concentrated on putting out silent features with synchronized scores and effects. Their 1927–1928 output included a group of pictures made by the studio's star directors, veterans of the silents who would become major figures of the sound era: John Ford (*Four Sons; Mother Machree*), Raoul Walsh (*The Red Dance; Me, Gangster*), Howard Hawks (*Fazil; The Air Circus*) and Frank Borzage (*Street Angel*). Movietone newsreels had indicated the possibilities of shooting sound in the open air; and Ford and Walsh, fearless action directors, took their recording equipment on location, Ford for a short subject, *Napoleon's Barber*, and Walsh for a feature, *In Old Arizona*. Despite rather a lot of wind and an overgrowth of sage brush to hide the microphones, *In Old Arizona* was the first truly successfuly talking action picture.

By the end of 1928 Movietone had been adopted by some major studios including MGM whose sound projects in this transitional year were tentative. Synchronized scores and sound effects were added to Harry Beaumont's jazz-era drama *Our Dancing Daughters* and to King Vidor's delightful comedy *Show People*, starring Marion Davies; otherwise the company experimented with two part-talkies, W.S. Van Dyke's *White Shadows in the South Seas* (which was virtually a silent film) and a crime melodrama *Alias Jimmy Valentine* (1929).

'Talkies, squeakies, moanies, songies, squawkies . . . Just give them ten years to develop and you're going to see the greatest artistic medium the world has known' D.W. Griffith

---

For release in 1928 Universal added sound to their prestige pictures of the previous year: Paul Leni's *The Man Who Laughs*, and Harry Pollard's *Uncle Tom's Cabin*; they also, somewhat unnecessarily, provided dialogue sequences for Paul Fejos's admirable *Lonesome*. The studio's first all-dialogue film, A.B. Heath's *Melody of Love*, was poorly received: the public was sufficiently accustomed to sound films to reject a hasty run-up.

Paramount had tried an experiment with sound early in 1927, when *Wings* had been provided with a synchronized score and sound effects. After opting for Movietone, the company embarked seriously on a sound programme in 1928. They also concentrated on equipping their major silent pictures, such as Ernst Lubitsch's *The Patriot*, William Wellman's *Beggars of Life* and von Stroheim's *The*

Wedding March, with music and sound effects. The first Paramount picture to be conceived as a sound film was a part-talkie, *Warming Up*, a baseball drama of which it was said that the crack of the bat and the roar of the crowd did not match particularly well with the pictures. Their first full talking picture was *Interference* (1929), with Clive Brook, whose stage experience served him well.

Coincidentally, Brook also starred in *The Perfect Crime* which was the first sound venture of RKO (Radio-Keith-Orpheum). This new studio was formed in 1928 through the amalgamation of Joseph Kennedy's distribution network (FBO), the Keith-Albee-Orpheum cinema chain, and Rockefeller's Radio Corporation of America (RCA). The merger enabled RCA to apply its own Photophone sound system to the studio's product and begin production of talkies.

It was also a year of reorganization. First National Pictures was absorbed by Warner Brothers, and put out eight features in the course of 1928. The first was a part-talkie, *Ladies' Night in a Turkish Bath*, but the most successful was George Fitzmaurice's *Lilac Time* with Colleen Moore and Gary Cooper, and a synchronized music score provided by the company's own Firnatone system.

The full creative possibilities of sound were revealed by a mouse. Walter E. Disney had boldly taken the decision to marry sound to an animated cartoon. Mortimer, later known as Mickey Mouse, starred in *Steamboat Willie* which opened at the Roxy Theatre on the same day as *The Singing Fool*. The ingenuity and fluency with which Disney used sound in *Steamboat Willie* and the early 'Silly Symphonies' was greatly admired in the early years of the sound film.

By the close of 1928 every significant American studio had talking pictures in production. It was timely. Between 1927 and 1930 box-office takings, which had been falling unnervingly, shot up by 50 per cent. The renewal of interest in the movies, mainly attributable to the novelty of sound, must go far towards explaining the ability of the film business to ride out the storms of the great Crash and Depression that hit the USA as the Twenties gave way to the Thirties. Hollywood had reason to be grateful to the timing of the Warner Brothers' initiative in sound films.   DAVID ROBINSON

Top: talkies gave Joan Crawford her break into stardom as a Jazz Age flapper. Centre: Mickey Mouse talks – and the voice was Walt Disney's! Above: Clive Brook's classy English tones were heard for the first time in Paramount's debut talkie

THE STUDIO SYSTEM

Was the studio system an honest attempt to streamline Hollywood, or simply a mania for empire building by unscrupulous, power-mad movie moguls?

From the Thirties to the Fifties, American film production was utterly dominated by a handful of Hollywood film companies: Paramount, MGM, Warner Brothers, 20th Century-Fox and RKO Radio. Often referred to as the Big Five or the 'majors', they were not just production companies and international distributors of motion pictures but also owned massive cinema circuits, thus controlling the entire movie business from film-making through to exhibition.

In the second division of the studio league were two studios, Universal and Columbia, and a releasing company, United Artists. These companies differed from the majors in that they owned few or no cinemas. Without that measure of control they could not be guaranteed prime booking time for their films, but had to take what programme slots were left in the Big Five's cinemas or deal with independent exhibitors.

United Artists differed from all the others in one crucial respect: it was not a studio but a distribution company formed in 1919 by Mary Pickford, Douglas Fairbanks, Charlie Chaplin and D.W. Griffith in order to gain greater control over the marketing of their films.

Finally there was the group of minor studios, known collectively as 'Poverty Row', that specialized in B pictures. Of these only Republic and Monogram (later to become Allied Artists) lasted for any length of time or made much impression on film history. Their story is told in a future chapter.

The financing of motion pictures was based in New York. Wall Street had consolidated its hold on the big film companies during the financial crises of the late Twenties and early Thirties when the cost of equipping for sound and rapid acquisitions of theatres stretched the resources of most companies to snapping point. As the Depression set in, cinema audiences fell away by almost 50 per cent, and without the strong support of the East Coast finance houses some studios might well have gone under.

But it was on the West Coast that the flamboyant and legendary moguls who had built their dream factories in Hollywood created, through their individual enterprises, a superstructure that became known as the studio system. This system was an attempt to make films in the most efficient and orderly way possible. Studios not only had directors, actors, supporting players and writers on contract but also cameramen, art directors, special effects men, editors and composers, all of whom could be ordered about as it suited the studio, regardless of the wishes of the individual.

The few individuals who really mattered in this system were the old moguls and the young whizz-kids – MGM's Louis B. Mayer and Irving Thalberg, Warners' Jack L. Warner, Columbia's Harry Cohn and Darryl F. Zanuck at 20th Century-Fox.

At RKO the young David O. Selznick was appointed head of production in October 1931 and was promised a completely free hand to carry out the studio's merger with Pathé. But interference from one of RKO's backers soon caused Selznick to leave and join MGM. Even there, under the benevolent eye of his father-in-law, Louis B. Mayer, Selznick felt curbed and in 1935 he left to form an independent company. Later at RKO another production chief, Dore Schary, responsible for encouraging new talent like directors Robert Wise and Edward Dmytryk, was harried out of office by the studio's last owner, the eccentric millionaire Howard Hughes.

Universal's problems in the early Thirties stemmed largely from boss Carl Laemmle's practice of nepotism. As Universal's founder he gave his son the post of head of production for a twenty-first birthday present. Laemmle's faith in youth could be forgiven, for back in 1920 he had appointed the 20-year-old Irving Thalberg to run the studio but Thalberg had taken his estimable talent off to MGM and left Universal to the Laemmles. Carl Laemmle Jr initiated a memorable horror-film cycle with *Dracula* (1931) and *Frankenstein* (1931) but the company's output was not strong enough to withstand the ill winds of the Depression and both father and son were eventually forced out of office. At this time it was proved, in the words of a popular rhyme, that 'Carl Laemmle had such a large family', for over 70 relatives and dependents had found their way onto the studio payroll. Universal went through the next decade excessively dependent on the few major stars – Deanna Durbin, Abbott and Costello – it was lucky enough to discover.

More than anyone, Irving Thalberg at MGM refined the system of delegated responsibility that became a management blueprint for other studios. Louis B. Mayer handled the temperamental actors, looked for new talent, welcomed important guests, made big speeches; Thalberg, who abhorred publicity and declined any form of screen credit, chose the pictures and got them made.

He assigned each project to a supervisor (like Albert Lewin, Bernard Hyman, Hunt Stromberg or Lawrence Weingarten) who worked on the script with the writers and saw the film through production. Thalberg would keep an eye on the script but tended not to view the rushes during shooting. Believing, however, that 'Films aren't made, they're remade', he took a keen interest in audience pre-

Above: the signs of things to come – although a studio's films could often be recognized by visual style and subject matter. Left: David O. Selznick, founder of 20th Century Productions

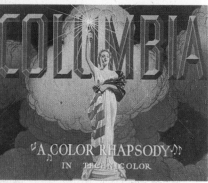

Above: the 'second league' studios Universal and Columbia and the independent distribution company United Artists, were to find their way into the big league after World War II: Republic Pictures, despite defying their 'Poverty Row' status with an eagle trademark, eventually abandoned production in the late 50s

views, recutting and even reshooting sections of a film until audience reaction satisfied him.

After Thalberg's early death in 1936, Mayer reigned supreme over the studio until 1948, and encouraged a committee system of decision-making, rather than allowing a single-handed production chief to dominate the studio. MGM was extremely well-funded and certainly the richest studio for talent: it had a regular staff of some 20 directors, 75 writers and 250 players on the payroll, and an annual profit that went from $4 million (in a bad year!) to $10 million in a good year.

Under Mayer's paternalistic rule MGM was jokingly said to stand for Mayer's *Ganz-Mispochen*, Yiddish for 'Mayer's whole family' and members who got out of line were brought to heel politely but firmly. Mayer believed, for example, that stars should behave like royalty and once criticized a performer for eating with a minor employee in the studio dining room. He prided himself on 'clean pictures' for family viewing.

Warner Brothers' Darryl F. Zanuck had been a screenwriter before his promotion to production chief. It was Zanuck who launched the gangster and musical cycles that carried Warners to success past the initial boost provided by Vitaphone talkies. Zanuck and Jack Warner understood each other, but Harry's meanness eventually led to Zanuck's resignation and Hal B. Wallis took over. Wallis kept Warners in the money with his shrewd choice of supervisors, directors and writers.

Everyone under contract was kept ferociously busy at Warners: a director like Michael Curtiz was responsible for five or six features annually in the early Thirties; a leading actor like George Brent was in as many as seven films in the course of 1932.

Cooped up in their office, the Warners' writers expended more ingenuity in circumventing Jack Warner's tiresome regulations than they did on shaping their plots. When Jack forbade his scribes to make outside phone calls from their office in an attempt to make them more industrious, the entire department formed one mighty queue in front of his eyes at the single pay-phone on the lot.

Jack Warner's workhorse regime provoked some famous quarrels. Stars like Bette Davis and James Cagney protested at the films they were being forced to make. Miss Davis hoped to make better films in Britain but was defeated in the courts. Cagney managed to make two independent films but both Davis and Cagney returned to Warner Brothers with the satisfaction of being offered better parts.

Another criticism of the studio system voiced by actors was the practice of adding time spent on suspension to the original expiry date of a contract. Olivia de Havilland, for example, took Warners to court on this issue – she had been suspended six times on a seven-year contract for refusing to make particular films – she won the case but it kept her off the screen for over a year while it was settled.

At Paramount creativity was given a freer hand. Indeed the company went so far as to appoint a major established artist, the producer-director Ernst Lubitsch, to run the studio. Unfortunately this was not a happy move and he soon returned to directing. In the late Thirties certain directors, like William Wellman and Mark Sandrich, were permitted to produce their own films. The studio also gave some writers the chance to direct. Preston Sturges made *The Great McGinty* (1940) and Billy Wilder began with *The Major and the Minor* (1942).

How well the studio system worked for RKO depended largely on who was running the 'shop'. When George Schaefer was appointed head of production, he brought in Orson Welles and his Mercury Players and gave them unprecedented

freedom. The result was *Citizen Kane* (1940).

Schaefer's policy failed, however, to produce profits. His successor, Charles Koerner, was the production chief who put an end to Welles's activities at the studio. Welles may never have been comfortable within any studio format but he suffered particular harassment from a production manager at Columbia named Jack Fier during the shooting of *The Lady From Shanghai* (1947). Welles walked off the set in protest and hung up a huge sign for his fellow-workers: 'You Have Nothing To Fear But Fier Himself'. Fier retaliated with a sign 'All's Well That Ends Welles'.

At its most rigid the system resembled a military regime: writers were locked into their rooms, productions went to the wall at a whim and actors were left to languish on suspension

---

Columbia studios were run by the notoriously foul-mouthed Harry Cohn. In the Thirties his hottest property was the director, Frank Capra, whose *Lost Horizon* (1937) was one of a string of films that conferred profits and prestige upon the studio. The success of the film served to attract other major film directors like John Ford, Howard Hawks and George Stevens.

In the Thirties the studio was desperately short of big stars: Cohn had to borrow Clark Gable from MGM and Claudette Colbert from Paramount for Capra's *It Happened One Night* (1934), and Edward G. Robinson from Warners for Ford's *The Whole Town's Talking* (1935). Fortunately Columbia developed some stars of its own in the Forties and Fifties, notably Rita Hayworth and Jack Lemmon. Whatever was said about Harry Cohn, he had picture-making in his blood; it was his penny-pinching brother Jack who brought about Capra's exit from Columbia when he refused to allow the director to make *The Life of Chopin* in colour.

Darryl Zanuck's status after he left Warners was sufficient for the money-man Joe Schenck to finance a wholly new company, 20th Century Productions. In the first place they simply produced films, releasing them through United Artists but in 1935 when they merged with the ailing Fox Film Corporation, the new 20th Century-Fox company made its own movies in its own studio and took care of its own releasing.

Down on 'Poverty Row' two studios stood out from the rest: Monogram made itself known for series films like the Charlie Chan mysteries (from an original story bought from 20th Century-Fox) and the Dead End Kids (taken over from Warners). Republic, on the other hand, had flirtations with the big time thanks to a contract they had with John Wayne. Having loaned him out for *Stagecoach* (1939), which made him a major star, Republic toplined him in *The Dark Command* (1940), even though they had to borrow a director (Raoul Walsh from Warners) and co-star (Walter Pidgeon from MGM) to ensure first-feature quality.

Republic's powerful boss Herbert J. Yates also had Western stars Gene Autry and Roy Rogers on contract, but Wayne's films made the really big money until Yates backed out of a deal to let Wayne make his cherished project *The Alamo* in 1951 and lost the star's services for good. Yates further handicapped Republic by insisting that Vera Ralston, later to become Mrs Herbert J. Yates, starred in the company's pictures even though her

box-office appeal was dubious. Veteran studio director Joseph Kane recalled:

'Republic was a public corporation owned by the stockholders, but Yates did as he pleased and the stockholders had about as much say as a native in Timbuktu.'

In the late Forties the Big Five came under government pressure to break up their monopolistic control of the film industry into smaller units. At the same time more stars and directors sought independent projects to work on. In these circumstances, and faced with the challenge posed by television, it was inevitable that the monolithic studio system should begin to fall apart. Production declined and it was no longer feasible to have so many artists on contract expecting to be paid weekly; it was better to hire them when necessary.

Only Universal kept to traditional procedures, turning out formula films as vehicles for its new generation of stars: Rock Hudson, Tony Curtis, Jeff Chandler and, after she left Warners, Doris Day.

United Artists passed into new management in 1951 after its surviving founders, Chaplin and Mary Pickford, sold out their interests. In the changing climate of production, United Artists reaped rewards from a large number of independent producers who brought their projects to them for additional finance and guaranteed distribution. Otto Preminger, who produced and directed *The Man With the Golden Arm* (1956) described United Artists' post-war set-up:

'Only United Artists has a system of true independent production . . . They recognize that the independent has his own personality. After they agree on the basic property, ie projected film, and are consulted on the cast, they leave everything to the producer's discrimination.'

After World War II, when the ownership of cinema chains had been divorced from the production side of the business, the roster of Hollywood studios reflected the loss of economic advantage held by the Big Five. Columbia, Universal and United Artists now ranked alongside the others; all were on an equal footing for the upcoming battle with television.

The studio system was never so rigid as to justify the 'factory production line' label sometimes attributed to it, but it is important to recognize a consistency in the product of each studio.

While it is true that Warners specialized in topical, tightly edited, realistic pictures in the early Thirties, that MGM made classy comedies and

musicals, that Paramount encouraged a Continental sophistication (in their Thirties films) and that Universal went from horror movies in the Thirties to Technicolored adventure films in the Forties, every studio also made films that ran counter to its prevailing image.

When a studio is said to have possessed a certain visual style, this often refers to the 'look' of a film as determined by the laboratory processing favoured by each individual studio. An experienced film editor might tell at a glance which studio had made the film according to the graininess of the black and white or the tones of the colour.

An easier although less reliable guide to the studio origins of a particular film lay in the recurrence of particular stars in one studio's movies: Tyrone Power, for example, was identified with 20th Century-Fox, Alan Ladd with Paramount, Gable with MGM, and so on down the list of supporting players and technicians.

The studios looked after their own: MGM even maintained its own police force, medical teams and lawyers. In return they expected unswerving devotion and total dedication

What is certain is that the studio system encouraged high standards of technical excellence. Most independently made films of the Thirties and Forties looked tatty by comparison, lacking the strong casts and lavish settings that the big studios could always provide. Goldwyn and Selznick certainly spent money on a scale equivalent to that of the majors, if not in excess of it, but other independents were usually either short of cash or keen to spend as little money as possible to get adequate results.

The studio system offered 'the safety of a prison', said Bette Davis. But good films were made, nonetheless, and every company permitted the occasional experiment. Paramount, Columbia and Republic, for example, all indulged the offbeat notions of the writer-director Ben Hecht. Orson Welles, however fiercely single-minded, was more productive while the big studios were flourishing than he has been ever since.

Increasing freedom of subject matter has been the only real advance – and a mixed blessing at that – since the studio system faded away. Even by 1960 one of Hollywood's leading directors, John Huston, a man with a strongly independent streak, could look back with some regret on the passing of the old Hollywood: 'I'm not sure I wasn't better then. Some of the worst pictures I ever made I've made since I've had complete freedom!'   ALLEN EYLES

Top: Marion Davies and director Mervyn LeRoy are visited, on the set of Page Miss Glory, *by Jack Warner and Hal B. Wallis. Below left: Howard Hughes, eccentric multi-millionaire and independent producer, with Warners star, Bette Davis. Centre: Universal's founder, Carl Laemmle, and son in earlier, happier days, and (above) Laemmle's ex-employee, whizz-kid Irving Thalberg, with his mogul boss at MGM, Louis B. Mayer*

Directed by Lewis Milestone, 1930
Prod co: Universal. **prod:** Carl Laemmle Jr. **sc:** Del Andrews, Maxwell Anderson, George Abbott, from the novel *Im Westen Nichts Neues* by Erich Maria Remarque. **dial:** Maxwell Anderson, George Abbott, C. Gardner Sullivan. **dial dir:** George Cukor. **titles:** Walter Anthony. **photo:** Arthur Edeson. **sp eff photo:** Frank H. Booth. **ed:** Edgar Adams, Milton Carruth, Maurice Pivar. **art dir:** Charles D. Hall, W. R. Schmitt. **sync/mus:** David Broekman. **rec sup:** C. Roy Hunter. **sd:** William W. Hedgecock. **sd sys:** Movietone. **ass dir:** Nate Watt. **r/t:** 138 minutes. New York premiere, 28 April 1930.
Cast: Lew Ayres (*Paul Baumer*), Louis Wolheim (*Katczinsky*), John Wray (*Himmelstoss*), George 'Slim' Summerville (*Tjaden*), Raymond Griffith (*Gerard Duval*), Russell Gleason (*Müller*), William Bakewell (*Albert*), Scott Kolk (*Leer*), Walter Rogers (*Bohm*), Ben Alexander (*Kemmerich*), Owen Davis Jr (*Peter*), Beryl Mercer (*Paul's mother* – sound version), ZaSu Pitts (*Paul's mother* – silent version), Edwin Maxwell (*Paul's father*), Harold Goodwin (*Detering*), Marion Clayton (*Paul's sister*), Richard Alexander (*Westhus*), G. Pat Collins (*Lieutenant Bertinck*), Yola D'Avril (*Suzanne*), Poupée Andriot, Renée Damonde (*French girls*), Arnold Lucy (*Kantorek*), William Irving (*Ginger*), Edmund Breese (*Herr Meyer*), Heinie Conklin (*Hammacher*), Bertha Mann (*Sister*), Bodil Rosing (*Wachter*), Joan Marsh (*poster girl*), Tom London (*orderly*), Vincent Barnett (*cook*), Fred Zinnemann (*man*).

Our bodies are earth and our thoughts are clay and we sleep and eat with death

Erich Maria Remarque wrote *Im Westen Nichts Neues* to free himself from his memory of the Great War and from 'my thoughts and those of my companions'. Like the leading character in the novel, the author was one of a class of 18-year-olds who enlisted in the infantry and suffered the brutalities of life in the trenches. The book was a best-seller. Soon after it appeared in the United States, the rights were snapped up by Carl Laemmle, head of Universal. Laemmle originally intended to use the story for a silent movie, and a silent version with synchronized music exists – running a reel longer than the complete talkie copy and with ZaSu Pitts in the role of Mrs Baumer instead of Beryl Mercer, who played the part in the sound film. (Perhaps Miss Mercer's stage experience was thought to fit her better for talkies.)

Lewis Milestone set himself uncompromisingly to reproduce the realism of the novel. It is arguable that no film – whether fiction or fact – has given so vivid an account of the physical actuality of World War I; and fragments of *All Quiet* have frequently turned up in later compilations, credited as documentary.

The battle scenes were shot on an area of almost 1000 acres on the Irvine Ranch, 69 miles south-east of Los Angeles. Over 5 miles of water pipes were laid to provide the authentic water-logged appearance of the battlefields. And 2 miles of road were built for the operation of Universal's high new camera crane which was assigned to the picture. In all, 35 different sets were built for the film – those representing frontline France being destined for destruction during filming.

Unerringly, Milestone reconciled the realism of the setting with the deliberately lyrical style of the dialogue: 'Our bodies are earth and our thoughts are clay, and we sleep and eat with death'. He also blended the extreme stylization of some performances with the easy naturalism of Louis Wolheim (Katczinsky) and Slim Summerville (Tjaden).

Milestone used his facilities with incomparable flair. He brought all the fluidity of silent films to the camera – which freely tracked and panned and soared over the battlefields or the little German town from which the hero and his schoolboy friends march out to war – and to the editing. At the same time Milestone imaginatively explored the possibilities of sound, from the beginning where the bellicose harangues of the schoolteacher are drowned by the noise of a band outside, to the haunting echoes of the battlefield as the cry of 'Mind the wire' goes down the line.   DAVID ROBINSON

At the outset of World War I a group of German boys leave their desks for the army, inspired by the marching soldiers in the streets (1) and by the uplifting rhetoric of their schoolmaster. Only one wavers but he too is eventually persuaded (2). Sent to the front, their illusions are shattered by the cynical stoicism of seasoned soldiers (3) and by their own first experiences under fire (4). They share the terror and exhaustion of constant fighting as well as the bewilderment of watching their schoolfriends die (5) on the battlefield.

The central character is Paul Baumer. His first experience of killing a man, face to face, is traumatic (6): in other circumstances the Frenchman could have been a friend and comrade rather than the enemy.

After being wounded, Paul is sent home on leave to find a world with which he now has little contact. False romantic ideas of war still persist in the school and among the belligerent old men in the beer cellars (7).

Almost with relief he returns to the front. A few old comrades are still alive in his unit but it is mostly filled with new recruits – as young and green as he was once, not so many months ago.

Some time later Paul is peering through the loophole of his trench (8) when he sees a butterfly. He reaches out to catch it (9). A French sniper takes aim. Paul's hand falls limp.

Across the corpse-strewn fields of France march columns of ghostly soldiers – accusation in their eyes (10).

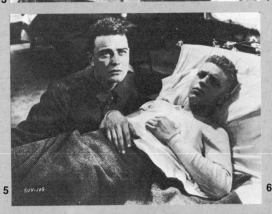

17

René Clair
The Poet of Paris

When René Clair made his first sound picture, *Sous les Toits de Paris* (*Under the Roofs of Paris*) in 1930, he had already gained an international reputation with silents like *Entr'acte* (1924) and *Un Chapeau de Paille d'Italie* (1927, *The Italian Straw Hat*). 'The most French of directors' did not particularly welcome the coming of sound. At the time he wondered if 'the voice does not take away more from elements of expression than it adds . . .' and even now thinks 'the silent film still had a great deal more to say, but I could not continue to battle alone'.

Clair's early sound films did not use speech in the dramatic sense; they were 'almost silent films' with little dialogue:

'I purposely avoided dialogue because I felt that it should be amalgamated with the conquests of the silent film, that is to say, be expressed essentially in images, the spoken word intervening only as a "reserve motor" to avoid certain lengthy visual explanations.'

This does not mean, however, that these films had no sound. He experimented with everyday noises, such as a factory siren, a policeman's whistle, a gramophone, and a banging window. The story of *Sous les Toits de Paris* concerns a street-singer who loses his girl when he is wrongfully arrested. A fight is accompanied only by the sound of a passing train; the final scene, when the hero tries to win his girl back, is shot from outside a window – so nothing is heard. Clair also explored the musical possibilities in his in-

novative use of song in his next film *Le Million* (1931, *The Million*).

The films of director René Clair identify him as one of the great artists of the French cinema. Born in Paris in 1898, Clair served as a volunteer ambulanceman in World War I. Invalided out, he became a journalist, then an actor and silent film-maker. When sound came along he handled the new medium with dexterity, but also with caution, in his charming studies of the ordinary people of Paris. Spells in Britain and America gained him a worldwide reputation as a director with a magic touch for comedy. Back in France after 1945, he explored a sadder vision in films which recalled his early Thirties classics like *Sous les Toits de Paris*. More than any other director Clair has been responsible for preserving on the screen the popular, romantic image of France.

Like *Un Chapeau de Paille d'Italie*, *Le Million* involves a chase – in this case after a missing lottery ticket – and, like *Sous les Toits de Paris*, it takes place in the world of shopkeepers and *petites gens* that Clair remembered from his youth in Les Halles.

Then came *A Nous la Liberté* (1931), filmed at the Epinay studios for the German company Tobis, and it too had songs instead of dialogue in the early sequences. Its story, '. . . about men's friendship', concerns two convicts who break jail and meet years later when one is owner of a gramophone factory and the other his employee. The owner eventually gives the factory to the workers and takes to the road with his friend:

'It was the time I was closest to the extreme Left. I wanted to fight the machine when it enslaves man rather than contributing to his happiness. I was wrong in using the operetta formula . . . I thought that the songs would give a satirical tone better than a realistic style.'

Tobis, under Goebbels, later sought to sue Charles Chaplin for plagiarizing *A Nous la Liberté* in *Modern Times* (1936). Clair stopped the suit, declaring 'We are all indebted to a man whom I admire and if he has been inspired by my film it would be a great honour for me'.

Quatorze Juillet (1932, *July 14th*), which followed, is a melodramatic comedy with the kind of triangular plot Clair loved: a taxidriver's affections are divided between a virgin and a vamp. Again the archetypal Parisians are admirably depicted.

These early sound pictures were made in the style Clair had developed in his silent period, full of wit and burlesque, handled with enchanting visual sparkle. Lazare Meerson's delightful sets, often tiny bars in cobbled streets overlooked by attic rooms inhabited by good-natured singers, tradesmen and lovers, are photographed with a fluent, unhampered camera. And whether or not Clair was happy with the *idea* of sound, he harnessed it with joyful ease to add to his cheerful, airy impression of low-life Paris.

In 1934 the French film company Pathé-Natan produced Clair's *Le Dernier Milliardaire* (The Last Multi-millionaire):

'Tobis didn't like the idea of a script . . . about an imaginary dictator. I had received offers from Pathé, so left Tobis, which was a good thing for them as the film was a catastrophe . . . it was a bad film. There was also the reason that it is a slightly political film, and at that time Mussolini was in power in Italy and Hitler in Germany. In Paris, opinion was very divided . . . the right-wing organizations fought anything that was not to the right, and the ridicule

Left: the noise of the street fight in Sous les Toits de Paris *is drowned by the sound of a passing train – seconds later the scene itself is obliterated by engine smoke*

of dictatorship offended them . . . certain French people wanted a dictatorship then, and the opposition to the film was not only violent in the press, but there were fights in the cinemas where it was shown.'

Under the roofs of London

'I had had a brilliant career until then, success after success; suddenly a disaster – and opinion changes immediately. I needed a change of air.'

Alexander Korda in England had the film rights of the story 'Sir Tristan Goes West', about a ghost that travels with a castle when it is removed stone by stone to America:

'I liked the idea and asked him to sell me the rights. He refused, adding, "If you want to

make it, come and do so for my company". So . . . I went to work for Alex.'

London Films' *The Ghost Goes West* (1935) emerged as a fanciful comedy, with Robert Donat playing both the spirit and his present-day descendant. Clair, as usual, wrote his own script:

'When talking films started, many writers thought the scripts should be their domain, the director having the same role as a director in the theatre. It was also the era of the producers' reign. Producers have always tried to divide the work so as to remain the masters. They couldn't stand anyone like Chaplin or me, who wanted to do everything . . .'

Break the News (1937), another British picture, had Jack Buchanan and Maurice Chevalier as down-and-out vaudeville artists.

'It was a sort of remake of a French film, *Le Mort en Fuite* (1936), Dead Man on the Run), with Michel Simon and Jules Berry. I had bought the film rights and readapted it . . .' Clair doubts that anyone would like the picture today, considering it silly and uninspired.

A Parisian in America

After a series of frustrated projects, Clair left wartime Europe for Hollywood where his first film was *The Flame of New Orleans* (1940):

'I had wanted to make a film with Deanna Durbin, a girl I much admired. She was under contract with Universal, who told me she had several other films waiting for her. They offered me this film with Marlene Dietrich, which didn't really appeal to me, but that's how things happen in Hollywood. The result was not happy.'

He replaced Hitchcock on a sketch in *Forever and a Day* (1943), made by British actors in Hollywood for the Red Cross. 'It's of no interest to me . . . I was considered an Englishman

Top: ex-jailbirds Emile (Henri Marchand) and Louis (Raymond Cordy) renew their friendship in A Nous la Liberté (*and left*). *Right: one of Clair's enchanting fantasies*

because I had been in England . . . It was the only time that I directed scenes I had not written.' Clair is uncredited as a scriptwriter on some of his British and American films, though he generally worked in close liaison with his writers. He says that he also edited all his films with the assistance of a cutter, but again took no credit.

In *I Married a Witch* (1942) Veronica Lake is a beautiful, naughty witch pestering, and then falling in love with Fredric March, an elegant politician whose ancestors had burned her at the stake. This film and *It Happened Tomorrow* (1944) – a tale of a reporter who can read tomorrow's news, and learns about his death in advance – appealed to the same taste for the magical that Clair's silents, *Paris Qui Dort* (1923, *The Crazy Ray*) and *Le Voyage Imaginaire* (1925, The Imaginary Voyage), had revealed:

'These . . . films saved me from American realism for which I did not feel gifted, because I wasn't American . . . *I Married a Witch* was almost a success . . .'

Clair still received offers but was disgusted at the prospect of making war films in wartime. Instead he bought the film rights of Agatha Christie's *Ten Little Niggers* and unenthusiastically made it into *And Then There Were None* (1945), independently produced, and co-written with Dudley Nichols, his collaborator on *It Happened Tomorrow*:

'We realized a strange thing as we worked. When you read a mystery story you believe it all. But when you adapt it for the cinema, which is more logical than a novel, you discover discrepancies . . . certain parts had to be reconstructed. Even that clever writer had made mistakes!'

Home is where the heart is

In 1945 Clair returned to France having stubbornly maintained independence in Hollywood – with only four films in five years:

'I was rather sad to see how much things had changed . . . I had missed a part of the life of my country, and of Paris . . . I had been away while the Germans were there . . . I felt like a stranger . . .'

Perhaps this feeling accounts for a change in Clair's later films. The technique is still perfect, the tone as elegant, but the humour has less sparkle and the satire less bite. *Le Silence Est d'Or* (1947, *Man About Town*) nostalgically echoes the old Parisian films but it seems Clair was trying to copy himself:

'[It] was a great success in Europe, but not in the Anglo-Saxon countries. Analyzing this, I decided it was because the film is only about love . . . It occurred to me that even in the English-speaking theatre there has been al-

Above: Gérard Philipe and Michel Simon, two great French stars, in La Beauté du Diable. *Below right: Philipe, centre of attention in another Clair film,* Les Belles de Nuit

most no treatment of love as a subject. If I say that, inevitably someone retorts: "And Romeo and Juliet?" It illustrates my point, there is no love intrigue. It is a duel between two families, whereas French theatre and literature . . . so often treat love as the main subject.'

In 1949 he met Gérard Philipe, who was to become one of France's leading male stars of the Fifties:

'When I thought of the Faust legend, which was the basis of *La Beauté du Diable* (1949, *Beauty and the Beast*), I immediately thought of Gérard Philipe, whom I did not then know . . . For the first time, I started looking for ideas or writing for an actor with whom I wanted to work.'

Clair and Philipe next worked together on *Les Belles de Nuit* (1952) and *Les Grandes Manoeuvres* (1955). In the second film, Philipe plays a philandering young officer in a provincial garrison who woos a milliner for a wager and discovers, too late, that he has fallen in love with her. It is an elegant and bitter-sweet comedy of errors.

Porte des Lilas (1957) was another story of mistaken friendship. It starred actor Pierre Brasseur, who recommended the original property, René Fallet's book *La Grande Ceinture*, to him. Clair recalls:

'I thought it was a subject for me, so Brasseur arranged it all. I wrote the script alone, and often quote it as an example of dramatic or realistic subjects being much easier than comedies. I wrote this script in a month, whereas I had taken eight months to write *Les Belles de Nuit*, which had so much more invention.'

A moral ending

In 1960 Clair became the first film artist to be elected to the distinguished French Academy. The same year he directed 'Le Mariage', a sketch in *La Française et l'Amour* (*Love and the Frenchwoman*), later contributing 'Les Deux Pigeons' (The Two Pigeons) to *Les Quatres*

Filmography
1920 Les Deux Gamines (actor only); Le Lys de la Vie (actor only). **'21** L'Orphéline (actor only); Parisette (actor only); Le Sens de la Mort (actor only). **'23** Paris Qui Dort (+sc) (GB: The Crazy Ray). **'24** Entr'acte (short) (adapt); Le Fantôme du Moulin Rouge (+sc). **'25** Le Voyage Imaginaire (+sc). **'26** La Proie du Vent (+sc). **'27** Un Chapeau de Paille d'Italie (+sc) (USA: The Horse Ate the Hat; GB: The Italian Straw Hat). **'28** Les Deux Timides (+sc); La Tour (short) (+sc). **'30** Sous les Toits de Paris (+sc) (USA: Under the Roofs of Paris). **'31** Le Million (+sc) (USA: The Million); A Nous la Liberté (+sc). **'32** Quatorze Juillet (+sc) (USA: July 14th). **'34** Le Dernier Milliardaire (+sc). **'35** The Ghost Goes West (GB). **'37** Break the News (+prod) (GB). **'39** Air Pur (unfinished) (+co-sc). **'40** The Flame of New Orleans (USA). **'42** I Married a Witch (+prod) (USA). **'43** Forever and a Day (co-dir; +co-prod) (USA). **'44** It Happened Tomorrow (+co-sc) (USA). **'45** And Then There Were None (+prod) (USA) (GB: Ten Little Niggers). **'47** Le Silence Est d'Or (+sc) (USA: Man About Town). **'49** La Beauté du Diable (+co-sc) (FR-IT) (USA: Beauty and the Devil; GB: Beauty and the Beast). **'52** Les Belles de Nuit (+sc) (FR-IT) (USA: Beauties of the Night); Le Rouge Est Mis (short on Les Belles de Nuit). **'55** Les Grandes Manoeuvres (+sc) (FR-IT) (USA: The Grand Maneuver). **'57** Portes des Lilas (+sc) (USA: Gates of Paris). **'59** La Grande Epoque (comm. sc. and narr. only) (USA: The Golden Age of Comedy, 1958). **'60** La Française et l'Amour *ep* Le Mariage (+sc) (FR-IT) (USA/GB: Love and the Frenchwoman *ep* The Marriage). **'61** Tout l'Or du Monde (+co-sc) (FR-IT) (USA/GB: All the Gold in the World). **'62** Les Quatres Vérités *ep* Les Deux Pigeons (+sc) (FR-IT-SP) (USA/GB: Three Fables of Love *ep* The Two Pigeons; shortened version of French film; En Compagnie de Max Linder (introduction only). **'65** Les Fêtes Galantes (+co-sc) (FR-RUM).

Vérités (1962; the English version dropped an episode and became *Three Fables of Love*).

Tout l'Or du Monde (1961, *All the Gold in The World*) deals with a simple farmer who refuses to sell his land to a real-estate promoter seeking to turn the village into a holiday camp. The film was notable for the performance of Bourvil, cast as a father and his three sons. But Clair was clearly less at ease with rustics than with his beloved Parisians:

'This film was inspired by a true story. Who was right and who was wrong? Those who, impressed by the money, agreed to sell land and houses, or the one person who preferred to spend the rest of his life with his apple trees and his well? I don't know. I have no taste for passing judgment and I don't think all tales should necessarily have a moral.'

Yet there was a kind of moral about his last film, *Les Fêtes Galantes* (1965), a Franco-Rumanian co-production filmed in Rumania and featuring Jean-Pierre Cassel. Clair had wanted for some time to make a film about the stupidity of war – he set this in the eighteenth century to avoid the kind of organized massacre he felt characterized his own century. The film was unsuccessful.

René Clair has since devoted himself to writing, his first love. His living room in Neuilly now no longer surveys trees, but instead looks out on the skyscrapers of the new town of La Défense. 'The view is not what it used to be', he remarks, 'but at night it is beautiful.'
ANNE HEAD

Based on an interview with René Clair, February 1979. With acknowledgments to: Mme Mary Meerson, Messrs Edgardo Cozarinsky, Louis Marcorelles, and Roger Régent for their kind assistance; L'Histoire du Cinéma by Georges Sadoul; René Clair by Barthélemy Amengual; The Cinémathèque Française; IDHEC.

CONTINENTAL SOUND

The struggle was on to control the world film market: multi-language films were produced in Europe to beat off the challenge from Hollywood

The Jazz Singer and the early talkies arrived in Europe in 1928. This new challenge from across the Atlantic affected the highly developed film industries of Germany and France in remarkably different ways. In this chapter we look at the struggle in these two countries to keep pace with the Americans.

The French film studios were totally unprepared for the introduction of sound, and the lucrative domestic market was consequently invaded by the better-organized American and German film companies. Yet in Germany too – although filmgoers had seen talking pictures as early as 1922 – the Americans were allowed to take the lead in exploiting sound, as a result of under-investment, lack of interest, and wasted opportunities on the part of German business.

The legal battles fought over the rights to sound film systems were not resolved until 1930 when a conference in Paris passed a worldwide patents agreement. This resolution went some way towards vindicating the work of a number of European sound-film pioneers whose claim to a place in cinema history might otherwise have been overshadowed by their American counterparts.

In 1918, three Germans, Hans Vogt, Joseph Massolle and Joseph Engl, patented a sound-film system they called Tri-Ergon ('the work of three people'). Theirs was a sound-on-film system (see Chapter 1) and was extremely advanced for its time. On September 17, 1922, Vogt, Massolle and Engl mounted the first public show of their invention at the Alhambra Cinema in Berlin. The audience saw – and heard – a two-hour film programme of musical numbers and recitations.

By all accounts the Tri-Ergon system scored an immediate hit with the public who were thrilled at the perfect synchronization of lip movements and sound. Under normal circumstances Tri-Ergon would have been ripe for commercial exploitation, but its inventors were to receive much the same kind of negative reaction from sponsors as the American De Forest had encountered for his Phonofilms. Furthermore, Germany had scarcely recovered from the devastation of World War I, and the economy was at its most inflationary.

For a crucial couple of years the ownership of Tri-Ergon sound-film patents passed from one company to another, with none of them succeeding in capitalizing on the system. Late in 1924 a contract was signed linking Tri-Ergon with Ufa (Universum Film Aktiengesellschaft), Germany's biggest film-making company, for the purpose of attempting a sound feature film. The result was *Das Mädchen mit den Schwefelholzern* (1924, also known as *Armes Kleines Mädchen*) which was based on Hans Christian Anderson's tale 'The Little Match Girl'. A studio with the necessary technical equipment was constructed and the film was shot at a breathtaking pace. Its premiere on December 20, 1925, however, was bedevilled with breakdowns and technical mishaps. As a result Ufa turned down the offer of world rights to the Tri-Ergon system.

Three months later, on a visit to Europe, the movie mogul William Fox purchased the American rights. The following year the first of Fox's Movietone Newsreels, showing Lindbergh's triumphal crossing of the Atlantic, was watched in Germany by enthusiastic filmgoers and red-faced Ufa executives who had finally realized their mistake in not taking up the option on the Tri-Ergon system.

As far as sound-film production was concerned, little progress had been made in the three years since the failure of *Das Mädchen mit den Schwefelholzern*, but the merger of the Tobis and Klangfilm companies signalled a combined attack on the European film markets.

Early in 1929 the Deutsches Lichtspiel Company gave a sneak preview in Berlin. Two popular stars of the silent screen – Harry Liedtke and Marlene Dietrich – were billed to appear in *Ich Küsse Ihre Hand, Madame* (1929, *I Kiss Your Hand, Madame*). The film was screened and, to everyone's surprise, Liedtke *sang* the title song to the film. Actually the voice was that of the famous tenor Richard Tauber, but the effect on the screen was totally believable: Liedtke had opened his mouth and sung; the German sound film had arrived.

By the end of the Twenties, then, German film producers were convinced of the future of sound films. As in America it had taken some time to persuade them. But having decided in favour of the optical sound solution, the German pioneers represented a genuine challenge to the American Vitaphone system. It is not surprising that when *The Singing Fool* was shown in Germany in the late Twenties, projection room doors were firmly locked to prevent industrial espionage. From this point on the production of German sound films began in earnest: Walter Ruttmann's *Die Melodie der Welt* (1929), a kind of travelogue with story sequences made by Tobis Studios for the Hamburg–American

Top: Pioneer inventor Hans Vogt. Above: 'The Victory of German Sound Films'. Below: Garbo makes the German version of Anna Christie *in Hollywood*

Top: Three Men and Lilian, *a contemporary musical comedy.*
Above: Lilian Harvey was just as popular in the more romantic musicals like Love Waltzes.
Below: Renate Muller and the chorus line of The Private Secretary *(1931) which she remade in England as* Sunshine Susie.
Below right: Westfront 1918

steamship line, is generally taken to be the first German sound feature.

During the transitional period of 1928–29, German producers tried to recapture the markets lost to the Americans at the time of the release of *The Singing Fool*. Typical of their efforts was *Das Land Ohne Frauen* (1929, *The Land without Women*), which was begun as a silent film but had music and some dialogue added before its release on September 30, 1929. This film was a spectacular production featuring love stories and stirring action, directed by the Italian Carmine Gallone, with Conrad Veidt in the leading role. Veidt had been a top box-office star in Germany since *Das Kabinett des Dr Caligari* (1919, *The Cabinet of Dr Caligari*), and his debut in talking pictures certainly did not disappoint audiences who had come to love his hypersensitive, full-blown acting style. As he ranged from outbursts of insanity, through quiet sobbing to hysterical laughter, audiences rose to their feet and applauded. A few critics were slightly more reserved, suggesting that the addition of sound to certain sequences in an otherwise silent film disrupted the style and continuity of the movie.

By another quirk of history the honour of making the first 100 per cent talking film went not to Ufa, Germany's biggest production outfit, but to Afa Film with a production called *Dich Hab'Ich Geliebt* (1929, *I Loved You*). The explanation for Ufa's delay in getting into sound production lies in the disputes over sound-film patents.

In sharp contrast to the preparations made in Germany, the French film industry was caught napping when the talkies arrived. The great Danish director Carl Dreyer was brought to Paris in 1928 to direct *La Passion de Jeanne d'Arc* (*The Passion of Joan of Arc*), a film he intended as a talking picture, only to discover that the studios were not equipped for sound, and so the film was shot silent. The same lack of sound facilities forced enterprising French producers to make the earliest French talkies in London; among these were *Les Trois Masques* (1929, *The Three Masks*) and two detective films starring Léon Mathot.

Not that there wasn't a vociferous demand for French-speaking films: when *Lights of New York* was shown in Paris late in 1928 the sound was drowned by angry cries of 'In French!' Part of the

problem was that the manufacturing end of the French film business was entirely foreign-owned. The German or American companies who controlled the means of production were therefore largely free to decide where and when to install sound-reproducing equipment in cinemas. Faced with two-sided domination, the French film companies Gaumont and Pathé combined, rather as Tobis and Klangfilm had done in Germany, to beat off the foreign challenge, and equip the home market themselves, albeit with foreign-made sound apparatus.

Back in Berlin Ufa had completed the building of four sound studios in the Babelsberg suburb, and were now fully geared up for sound production. The new head of production at Ufa was Erich Pommer, who had spent three years in Hollywood and was now assigned the task of promoting Germany's sound films both at home and abroad. Ufa's first full sound film was a prestige picture called *Melodie des Herzens* (1929, *Melody of the Heart*) premiered on December 13, 1929. In order to maximize its distribution, the film was shot simultaneously in German, English, French and Hungarian, and was thus an early example of the foreign-version, or 'multi-language', films discussed in Chapter 3.

As well as mounting an unprecedented export drive for their first sound feature, Ufa were keen to saturate the home market. Special spreads appeared in film magazines; the script of *Melodie des Herzens* was published in book form (another promotional novelty permitted by the introduction of dialogue in films). The stars of the film, Willy Fritsch and Dita Parlo, made public appearances to sign autographs and promote records of the film's hit songs. Ufa's massive advertising campaign hammered home the message 'The Victory of German Sound Films'.

A new transatlantic war had replaced the one fought over sound patents: the objective of American and German film producers was to sell their product to as many different countries (or 'territories', to use the film trade term) as possible. Foreign version films were expedient for this purpose though rarely successful in themselves. All too often the process of making them resembled a factory production line; untried directors were often assigned to them, and even where respected and experienced directors made foreign versions they rarely turned in work that was up to their normal standard.

In Hollywood, directors like the Belgian Jacques Feyder processed the German and Swedish versions of *Anna Christie* (retaining Greta Garbo in the title role), and the Hungarian Paul Fejos was responsible for the French and German versions of George Hill's big American hit *The Big House* (1930).

As far as the American companies were concerned the formula consisted in adapting a successful Hollywood scenario to what the company executives took to be a 'European mentality' or

'style'. It is hardly surprising, therefore, that most American-made versions misfired.

Of all the studios Paramount went in deepest: not content to make foreign versions in Hollywood, with expatriate actors and directors, they financed and built an entire multi-studio complex at Joinville, outside Paris, reported by one historian to look more like Hollywood than the real thing. Production chief Robert T. Kane was put in charge of this 'Hollywood-sur-Seine' which consisted of nine sound stages, laboratories and luxury accommodation for the stars. With the French film industry at a low ebb, Paris was ripe for colonization by the commercially stronger Americans and Germans; and at the same time as Paramount moved in, the German Tobis-Klangfilm set up a Paris office and shortly afterwards built a studio at Epinay. It was here that René Clair made his first sound film *Sous les Toits de Paris* (1930, *Under the Roofs of Paris*), as a German production, but in time these foreign-owned studios would pass into French hands.

The Germans were perhaps more sensitive than the Americans to the taste and needs of the European film market. Tobis pursued a policy of making specifically French films in Paris; everything, except the capital and a share of the profits, was French, and in this way *Sous les Toits de Paris* could legitimately be welcomed, by critic Georges Sadoul, as the first swallow of the new spring of French Cinema. Clair's next three films were made for Tobis at Epinay, but remained resolutely French. By 1934, however, Clair had run into problems with Tobis, now under the eye of Dr Goebbels, and was forced to take his film *Le Dernier Milliardaire* (The Last Millionaire) to another studio.

Studios became 'Towers of Babel' as movies were made in four or five different languages at once

Gradually, however, the French film industry caught up with their foreign competitors. A leading financier named Natan bought a sizeable shareholding in the pioneer firm of Pathé and set up a sound film programme bearing the name Ciné-romans. A parallel development from the equally famous Gaumont company resulted in there being two sound film combines in operation by 1930. Suddenly the indigenous French cinema had a new lease of life: in 1930 the output of talking pictures was double the previous year, and rose to 130 by 1931 and over 150 in 1932.

Production in Germany matched this trend: from 14 sound films made in 1929 the number climbed to 127 the following year and to 200 by 1931. During the production boom, melodramas and light-hearted operettas seemed to represent the most popular box-office fare. Fairytale escapism was predictably successful at the height of the economic depression.

Typical of the German musical genre was *Liebeswalzer* (1930, *Love Waltzes*), directed by Wilhelm Thiele, featuring the magical partnership of Lilian Harvey and Willy Fritsch, already a popular duo in silent films, who went on to become cult figures and wealthy stars. The story concerned a princess in a fictitious, small country who is supposed to marry a monarch, and instead falls in love with the son of an American automobile millionaire. Thiele's other famous musical-comedy of the same year was *Die Drei von der Tankstelle* (1930, *Three Men and Lilian*). Both films were made in several different language versions and were as

successful abroad as they were in Germany. The following year Erik Charrell made *Der Kongress Tanzt* (1931, *Congress Dances*), again in English and French, as well as in German, with the versatile Lilian Harvey appearing in all three versions. It became one of the best-known German films of the period and an effective challenge to the Hollywood musical revue film.

While film production increased, many cinemas in Germany were still waiting to be equipped for sound films. In the severe economic climate of the early Thirties independent exhibitors were naturally cautious about installing sound equipment. As late as the end of 1932, one in three German cinemas had no sound facilities. This delay meant that some genuinely silent films had a longer run for their money than might have been expected. But there was no question that sound was what the public wanted. Any lingering doubt on this matter was dispelled by the enormous success of *Der Blaue Engel* (1930, *The Blue Angel*). Directed by Josef von Sternberg – who had already made a talkie in America – and starring Emil Jannings and Marlene Dietrich, the film was undoubtedly the hit of the year. It was made simultaneously in English and has since gone on to become one of the all-time classic movies.

Perhaps more typical of the German filmgoers' taste, however, was an all-talking, all-singing film called *Die Privatsekretärin* (1931, *The Private Secretary*) starring Renate Muller as a clever country girl who comes to Berlin and gets a job as a secretary. On its appearance in America the New

"Caligari"

"Das indische Grabmal"

"Die letzte Kompanie"

"Lady Hamilton"

Above: magazine feature on Conrad Veidt on the occasion of an early German talkie 'The Last Company'. Photomontage serves to remind fans of his earlier silent movies: Lady Hamilton *(1921),* The Cabinet of Dr Caligari *(1919),* Above all Laws *(1921),* The Student of Prague *(1926). Below: Siodmak's social drama* Farewell *was notable for the camerawork of Eugen Schufftan and the script by Emeric Pressburger*

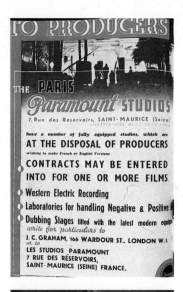

York Times critic commented, 'Miss Muller sings, dances and chatters her way through one and a quarter hours of gay music and comic situations. The theme song, "Today I feel so happy" sums up the mood.' As the Depression continued, the demand for light-hearted fairytale films increased. Titles like *Es Wird Schön Wieder Besser* (Things will soon get Better) and *Einmal Mocht' Ich Keine Sorgen Haben* (For once I'd like to have no Worries) or, more deceptively, *Man Braucht Kein Geld* (You don't need any Money), all appeared in 1931–1932.

More serious material established Robert Siodmak's reputation as a director and would launch him on a highly successful Hollywood career later in the Thirties. From his debut on the neo-documentary *Menschen Am Sonntag* (1929, People on Sunday) Siodmak had distinguished himself as a serious-minded and skilful director. His early work was in the harshly 'realistic' style known as *Neue Sachlichkeit* ('new objectivity'). His first sound film, *Abschied* (1930, Farewell), was set in Berlin's slums and recalled the urban 'street' films of Gerhard Lamprecht in the mid-Twenties. However worthy his films were, austerity was bad news at the box-office, and Ufa hastily tacked on a happy ending to try and salvage their investment. *Abschied* was not, however, without influence. Its treatment of social issues was reflected in films like Piel Jutzi's *Berlin Alexanderplatz*, Lupu Pick's *Gassenhauer* (Street Ballad) and Georg Klaren's *Kinder Vor Gericht* (Children Before the Courts) all made in 1931.

Undoubtedly the most significant social comment film of this period is *Kühle Wampe* (1932, Whither Germany?), famous not so much for what it said about the conditions of the German working class, but for how it put its message across. The film was the result of collaboration between the writer and dramatist Bertolt Brecht and the director Slatan Dudow and was sponsored by the Communist party who approved its radical style; even the Nazis could not overlook it.

Another director noted for his outspoken views, at least at the beginning of the decade, was Georg Wilhelm Pabst. His pacifist masterpiece *Westfront 1918* (1930) ranks alongside Milestone's anti-war classic, *All Quiet on the Western Front*, which was released in the same year. If his use of sound was not original in itself, it certainly enhanced the atmosphere of the film. Sound was to play a much

more important role in Pabst's next feature *Die Dreigroschenoper* (1931, *The Threepenny Opera*), where Kurt Weill's music was intended to carry a dramatic and political charge. The film, however, was subjected to a protracted court case after Brecht had seen and declared his objections to it. Pabst's other commercial success of the year was *Kameradschaft* (1931, Comradeship), the story of a pit disaster in Alsace-Lorraine where, in defiance of national frontiers, German miners came to the rescue of their French comrades.

By the time Fritz Lang's *M* was released in May 1931 sound films in themselves no longer surprised audiences. Lang's use of sound in *M* was nevertheless quite original: the voice of the mother calling her daughter over a shot of the child's empty chair, the tune whistled by the murderer which eventually gives him away, and the atmospheric roaring of the crowd conveying all the threat of the lynch mob. It is still surprising, however, that Lang uses very little direct sound – noise recorded on set at the time of filming – to heighten his effects, whereas Robert Siodmak's murder-hunt thriller *Voruntersuchung* (1931, Preliminary Investigation) clearly demonstrates how effective the dramatic use of direct sound could be.

M, the story of a mass murderer, and *Dreyfus*, an attack on anti-semitic purges, hinted at the shape of things to come; but after 1933 German films offered pure escapism

The attack on militarism implicit in Richard Oswald's *Dreyfus* (1931) is one of the earliest indications of the way films reflected the political events of the day. The direction the German cinema was taking at the beginning of the Thirties was made more politically explicit in the pre-Nazi films of Gustav Ucicky whose *Das Flotenkonzert von Sanssouci* (*The Flute Concert at Sanssouci*, 1930) was a portrait of Frederick the Great of Prussia. Ucicky's *Yorck* (1931) was a more aggressively militaristic, account of a Prussian general who rebels against his king (not Frederick) to represent the true Prussian spirit. The shape of things to come could be discerned at least two years before the Nazis took over.

In Paris, business had not been going well for Paramount; hand-me-down Hollywood simply wasn't popular with French audiences. The Joinville studios were run down, staff were dismissed and contracts were liquidated. But the studios did continue to function for dubbing purposes, and a number of French actors and actresses found work speaking their lines over the lip movements of famous Hollywood stars.

In order to prevent American-dubbed films swamping the market, the French government limited the number of foreign films – English, Italian, German as well as American – that could be shown in France. At last the French seemed to be gaining a measure of control over their industry, and, with Paramount pulling out of Joinville, they now had major production facilities to hand. The long-established firm of Pathé, now freshly financed as Pathé-Natan, took over Joinville.

After a late start in the sound film stakes, one of the richest periods of world cinema was about to begin: Vigo, Renoir, Carné, Feyder and Duvivier would soon be dazzling filmgoers in France and abroad with their talents. We return to their story in another chapter.

HERBERT HOLBA

Top: Paramount's costly multi-language studio in Paris was up for hire by 1932. Above: French actors dubbing an American film – the lines are written on rotating drums synchronized to the film projector. Below: powerful pacifist statement by G.W. Pabst was Kameradschaft

Ernst Lubitsch *the Paramount stylist*

Top: Emil Jannings and Dagny Servaes in The Loves of Pharaoh, *Lubitsch's last silent epic. Above: 'If the cap fits . . .' Lubitsch and Pola Negri on the set of* Forbidden Paradise, *their first American film together*

Ernst Lubitsch is one of the supreme stylists of the American cinema. The secret of his pre-eminence lies in the celebrated 'Lubitsch touch' – the inimitable, mischievous way he satirized the foibles of society, especially sex, in the series of frivolous 'European' comedies and musicals he directed in Hollywood.

In the Twenties and Thirties it was usually possible to tell from which Hollywood studio a film came, for each of the major studios had a distinctive individual style. Paramount pictures reflected a sophisticated, continental image, due largely to the studio's European stars and directors. Among the stars were Dietrich and Chevalier; the directors included Sternberg, Mamoulian and, above all, Lubitsch.

The chief difference between Lubitsch and other directors who worked under the studio system in Hollywood was that nobody ever told Lubitsch what he must do – what stories to film, which stars were to play in them, and who was to do the final cut of each film. With his first batch of American films, which included *The Marriage Circle, Forbidden Paradise* (both 1924), and *The Student Prince* (1927), he had established himself as a 'slick American director'. When sound came in, therefore, Paramount gave him *carte blanche* to make his first talkie, *The Love Parade* (1929).

Lubitsch had already shown that he did not need words to put witty dialogue across on the screen. His silent adaptation of Oscar Wilde's *Lady Windermere's Fan* (1925), using not a single Wildean epigram, proved that the silent screen did not need dialogue – nor even titles for that matter (there were very few in his

A. C. & R. C. BROMHEAD
present

'KISS
ME
AGAIN'

An
ERNST
LUBITSCH

SPECIAL
WARNER
PRODUCTION

Exclusively controlled by
THE GAUMONT
COMPANY, LTD.

Above: the long lost Kiss Me Again (1925) *was a formative Lubitsch sex comedy starring Marie Prevost, Monte Blue and Clara Bow*

silent films). But when he was given dialogue Lubitsch made it jump and stand on its head. He always took a hand in the screenplay, and Samson Raphaelson – who did the screenplays for *Trouble in Paradise* (1932), *The Shop Around the Corner* (1940) and several others – said that when he saw the finished films he couldn't tell which 'Lubitsch touches' were his and which were Lubitsch.

Touch of irony

The great period of 'the Lubitsch touch' was that of his American sound films, such as *The Love Parade*, *Monte Carlo* (1930), *The Smiling Lieutenant* (1931), *Trouble in Paradise* (his personal favourite), and *Ninotchka* (1939).

Where did it come from, 'the Lubitsch touch'? How did it start? Lubitsch traced it back to Berlin in 1918 and all the misery following Germany's ignominious defeat in World War I. He related a story, typical of those hard times, about a man so bereft of everything that he decided to kill himself. So he bought a rope to hang himself with, but the rope (like everything else in those days) was synthetic and broke. Taking this as a sign from heaven that he should live, he went to a café and bought himself a cup of coffee, but the coffee, too, was synthetic. It made him ill and he died. 'That' said Lubitsch, 'was my introduction to the dramatic virtue of irony, of which I became aware when I began making my own films in Berlin.'

Historical background

Lubitsch came to the cinema from the stage where he had been an actor. He was at first a technical apprentice; then, as the character Meyer, became the star of slapstick one-reelers – some of which he wrote and eventually directed. He achieved international fame,

Below: The Love Parade, *Lubitsch's first complete sound film, widened the scope of the hitherto stage-bound screen musical; it is a frothy Ruritanian romance with Maurice Chevalier and Jeanette MacDonald*

'The Lubitsch touch'

'The Lubitsch touch' is the most difficult thing in the world to define . . . It's just like asking what made Garbo Garbo or Marilyn Monroe Marilyn Monroe. It wasn't schooling, nor was it years at, let's say, the Swedish Academy. It was the element x. If we knew that we could sell it to manufacturers . . .

'The Lubitsch touch' was just elegance of mind; the original way he had of attacking a scene, or a moment, or a dialogue twist. I think the secret was that he involved audiences by giving them some hints so that they became his co-conspirators . . . In other words he never spelt out $2 + 2 = 4$, he would give them $1 + 3$ and they would add it up for themselves – that was the joy of it.

When I talk to students, to the American Film Institute, to young directors – to people who are interested in the art of cinema – about Lubitsch I say: 'Look, now; I'm going to give you the following project as homework. The plot is as follows: there is a king and a queen and a lieutenant in the king's army. I would like you to dramatize how the king finds out that his lieutenant is having an affair with his wife.' Now there are going to be thousands of permutations of this situation . . . but I would wager anything in the world that you would never come up with a better one than Lubitsch. Here's the way he dramatized it [in *The Merry Widow*, 1934]; he gave the audience an atmosphere of joy, built up laughter in a way that I don't think any other director could have done.

It starts off with the king and queen in bed in the morning, just before they are getting up. The king was George Barbier, a very heavy-set man. The queen was Una Merkel. There was a lot of kissing and stuff; then the king gets dressed and finally kisses his wife goodbye and leaves the bedchamber. There is a door outside, and standing guard at it is Chevalier [the lieutenant], wearing a sword which he raises [in salute] as the king goes by. The king salutes back and, smiling and laughing, starts down the steps. Chevalier now puts the sword back, looks after the king and enters the bedchamber. The door closes. Then the king stops; he realizes he forgot his sword and belt. He goes back up the steps. The suspense! He enters the bedchamber. The door closes again. Still we don't see [inside]. He comes out again with the belt and the sword, still smiling. [As he walks] he tries to put it [the belt] on but it is too small. [He goes back to the bedchamber and] now we go inside and see that he finds Chevalier under the bed . . .

After his funeral, William Wyler and I were walking away and I said 'My God! Lubitsch is gone', and he said 'Worse than that, not only no more Lubitsch but no more Lubitsch pictures!' It was a kind of lost art, like Chinese glass-blowing, you know; he took the secret with him to the grave . . . And all of us [who revered him] – Leo McCarey, Preston Sturges, William Wyler – when we came to some comical aspect in a picture . . . always thought 'How would Lubitsch have done it?'
BILLY WILDER
*From an interview with Adrian Turner,
Spring 1979*

however, with a series of costume pictures – *Madame Dubarry* (1919), *Anna Boleyn* (1920), *Das Weib des Pharao* (1922, *The Loves of Pharaoh*) – which combined magnificent spectacle with an ironic and realistic treatment of history. His stars included Emil Jannings, Ossi Oswalda and, above all, Pola Negri. In 1922 Mary Pickford invited him to Hollywood to direct her. The film they chose was *Rosita* (1923). Lubitsch and Pickford did not agree professionally about the film and shared three unhappy months making it. Nevertheless, *Rosita* was highly successful commercially and Warner Brothers then offered Lubitsch a five-picture contract.

Love and money

Lubitsch decided that if he were to remain in America he would have to make 'typically American' films, regardless of their setting (which was usually Continental Europe). 'Typically American' meant stories involving money and sex; these were the two commodities every American understood and knew the value of. In delineating them, 'the Lubitsch touch' began to flower.

George Bernard Shaw said 'If you want to tell people the truth, you'd better make them laugh or they'll kill you.' So Lubitsch told them

Filmography

1912 Das Mirakel (actor only); Venezianische Nächte (actor only). **'13** Meyer auf der Alm (actor only); Bedingung: Kein Anhang (actor only). **'14** Fräulein Piccolo (actor only); Die Firma Heiratet (actor only) (USA: The Perfect Thirty-Six); Der Stolz der Firma (actor only); Fräulein Seifenschaum (+sc; +act); Die Ideale Gattin (actor only); Serenissimus Lernt Tango (actor only); Meyer als Soldat (actor only); Rund um die Ehe (actor only). **'15** Arme Marie!/Arme Marie!: Ein Warenhauseroman (actor only); Robert und Bertram (actor only); Blinde Kuh (+act); Auf Eis Geführt (+act); Zucker und Zimt (co-dir; +co-sc; +act). **'16** Dr Satansohn (actor only); Leutnant auf Befehl (+act); Wo Ist Mein Schatz? (+act); Als Ich Tot War (+sc); Der Schwarze Moritz (+act); Schuhpalast Pinkus (+act); Der Gemischte Frauenchor (+act); Der GmbH Tenor (+act). **'17** Ossis Tagebuch (+co-sc); Der Blusenkönig (actor only); Wenn Vier Dasselbe Tun (+co-sc); Ein Fidelis Gefangnis (+act). **'18** Prinz Sami (+act); Der Rodekavalier (+act); Ich Möchte Kein Mann Sein (+co-sc); Der Fall Rosentopf (+act); Die Augen der Mumie Ma (USA: The Eyes of the Mummy Ma); Das Mädel vom Ballet; Carmen (USA: Gypsy Blood); Fuhrmann Henschel (attributed to Lubitsch). **'19** Meyer aus Berlin (+act); Meine Frau, die Filmschausspielerin (+co-sc); Schwabenmädel; Die Austerprinzessin (+co-sc); Rausch; Der Lustige Ehemann (sc. only); Madame Dubarry (USA: Passion); Die Puppe (+co-sc) (USA: The Doll). **'20** Kolheisels Töchter (+co-sc); Romeo und Julia im Schnee (+co-sc); Sumurun (+co-sc; +act) (USA: One Arabian Night); Anna Boleyn (USA: Deception). **'21** Die Bergkatze (+co-sc). **'22** Das Weib des Pharao (+co-prod) (USA: The Loves of Pharaoh). **'23** Die Flamme (+co-prod) (USA: Montmartre). *All remaining films USA:* **'23** Rosita. **'24** The Marriage Circle; Three Women; Forbidden Paradise. **'25** Kiss Me Again; Lady Windermere's Fan. **'26** So This is Paris. **'27** The Student Prince (some scenes reshot by John Stahl). **'28** The Patriot. **'29** Eternal Love; The Love Parade. **'30** Paramount on Parade (co-dir); Monte Carlo. **'31** The Smiling Lieutenant (French language version: Le Lieutenant Souriant, 1931). **'32** The Man I Killed (retitled Broken Lullaby, also GB title); One Hour with You; Trouble in Paradise (+prod); If I Had a Million *ep* The Clerk (+sc). **'33** Mr Broadway (short) (appearance only); Design for Living. **'34** The Merry Widow (French language version: La Veuve Joyeuse, 1934). **'36** Desire (sup. only). **'37** Angel. **'38** Bluebeard's Eighth Wife (+prod)' **'39** Ninotchka. **'40** The Shop Around the Corner (+prod). **'41** That Uncertain Feeling. **'42** To Be or Not to Be (+co-prod). **'43** Heaven Can Wait (+prod). **'45** A Royal Scandal (prod; +act) (GB: Czarina); Where Do We Go From Here? (actor only). **'46** Dragonwyck (prod. only); Cluny Brown (+prod). **'48** That Lady in Ermine (completed by Otto Preminger). *Lubitsch is uncredited on other films associated with him from 1913 to 1921.*

Above: Lubitsch directing Bluebeard's Eighth Wife *(1938) in which a 7-times divorced playboy (Gary Cooper) meets his match in wife No. 8 (Claudette Colbert). Written, like his next film* Ninotchka, *by Charles Brackett and Billy Wilder, this screwball comedy was the last film Lubitsch made for Paramount*

Below: in Lubitsch's first colour film, a deceased playboy recounts his life to the Devil, who eventually sends him up to heaven – meanwhile dropping a society lady through a trapdoor into hellfire. The background of Kansas and New York in the Naughty Nineties is delightfully satirized by Lubitsch

the truth: about royalty in *The Love Parade*, about sex and money in *Monte Carlo, Trouble in Paradise*, money alone in the Charles Laughton sequence of *If I Had a Million* (1932), and about communism and capitalism in *Ninotchka* – the film that gave him his long-awaited opportunity to direct Garbo. 'Ninotchka was the only time I had a great director in Hollywood,' she later said.

Paramount, to which he moved in 1929, was so impressed with Lubitsch's commercial success that in 1934 they made him chief of production. Paramount films tended to be light and frothy, and if anyone knew that recipe it

was Lubitsch. He was not happy as an executive, however, and returned to direction in 1937 with *Angel*, starring Marlene Dietrich.

Although the Thirties are considered Lubitsch's great years he made several splendid films in the Forties. There was *To Be or Not to Be* (1942), a brilliant anti-Nazi parody with Jack Benny and Carole Lombard; *Heaven Can Wait* (1943), his first film in colour; and *Cluny Brown* (1946) which is set in pre-war England and satirizes English manners.

Lubitsch the great

In 1947 Lubitsch started work on *That Lady in Ermine* (1948, finished by Otto Preminger), a comic ghost story, but his heart had been bad for several years and he died after a sixth heart attack. He was 56. No-one has replaced him as the arch-stylist of comedy. Many other directors have been influenced by his work: Mal St Clair, Frank Tuttle, Roy del Ruth, Frank Capra, Rouben Mamoulian, Preston Sturges, Lewis Milestone and Billy Wilder. His musicals and sound comedies – especially those made during the golden years at Paramount – are featherweight and frivolous on the surface, but sly, subtle and ironic underneath. They earned Lubitsch this tribute from Joseph L. Mankiewicz: 'He went head and shoulders above everyone in the field of sophisticated high comedy.'   HERMAN G. WEINBERG

THE GOLDEN TOUCH OF LUBITSCH

As great as it is brilliant . . . an event for the box-office . . . the nation's picturegoer . . . destined for every "Best Ten" list of the year!

An ERNST LUBITSCH PRODUCTION

HEAVEN Can WAIT

Gene TIERNEY and Don AMECHE

CHARLES COBURN
Marjorie Main
Laird Cregar
Spring Byington
Allyn Joslyn
Eugene Pallette
Signe Hasso

Produced and directed by ERNST LUBITSCH

'IN TECHNICOLOR

20th "HEAVEN" TO THE SHOW WORLD

FRITZ LANG

An evil mastermind, the blind fury of a lynch-mob, a psychopathic child-murder, the weary figure of Death – all are manifestations of the hostile forces that rule Lang's world, threatening the frail happiness of men and women with violence and chaos

'They all say I am dark and pessimistic. Some of my pictures show dark things about men and life, of course. Some of the later ones maybe even are a bit pessimistic. However, I think that all my pictures are portraits of the time in which they were made . . . I always made films about characters who struggled and fought against the circumstances and the traps they found themselves in. I don't think that is pessimistic.'

So Fritz Lang commented on the popular view of him – which could not be more misleading. He was a generous friend and an immensely intelligent companion with a highly developed sense of ironic humour not only about life in general, but, above all, about himself and his work.

His career as a director, which began in 1919 with the now lost *Halbblut* (The Half-Caste) and ended in 1961 with *Die Tausend Augen des Dr Mabuse* (*The Thousand Eyes of Dr Mabuse*), spans the greater part of history of the cinema. In his later years he often jokingly referred to himself as 'one of the last dinosaurs', claiming that students and others 'treat me like some sort of public monument'.

Lang was born in Vienna in 1890. His life and career show clearly that he was a man who would never acquiesce to circumstances that he found unacceptable. As a young man he endeavoured to please his parents by studying for a short time to be an architect like his father. Then, wishing to become a painter, he ran away from home to travel the world.

When war was declared in 1914, Lang returned to Austria and joined the army. While recovering from wounds in hospital, he met the film director Joe May, to whom he showed his sketches and a few short stories he had written. May immediately bought some of Lang's stories and hired him to write scenarios; thus, although his first love was painting, it was words that brought Lang into films.

Mystery and melodrama

The first Lang script known to have been filmed was Joe May's *Die Hochzeit in Exzentric Club* (1917, The Wedding in the Eccentric Club) – now lost without trace. Lang remembers being bitterly disappointed with the film, and deciding that in future he would have to direct films or leave film-making altogether.

Of the 40 films that Lang directed, 5 no longer exist. His earliest surviving film is *Die Spinnen* (*The Spiders*), a thriller in two parts made in 1919:

'Things in Germany were very depressing in 1919, so we made such things to escape. Later on I found that one could still use strong sensational elements and melodrama which would appeal to a broad audience and that I could still say things about their real lives and ideas which were important to me.'

Lang returned to the 'sensational thriller' throughout his career: the two-part *Dr Mabuse der Spieler* (1922, Dr Mabuse, the Gambler), *Spione* (1928, *The Spy*), *Das Testament des Dr Mabuse* (1932, *The Testament of Dr Mabuse*), *Der Tiger von Eschnapur* and *Das Indische Grabmal* (1959, released together in Britain as *Tiger of Bengal*) and *Die Tausend Augen des Dr Mabuse* (1961, *The Thousand Eyes of Dr Mabuse*). Although they vary in quality, all entertain with a series of strong, sensational adventures

and contain, to some extent, one of the themes recurring in his thrillers and other films – the possibility of the world being controlled by a tyrannical madman or group. Another of his themes is the redemptive power of romantic love, usually in the person of a beautiful, loving woman:

'Yes, I have always liked women. I have loved and been loved by a fair number of wonderful women who have also been my friends. I am Viennese and I can be sentimental about romance and love. However, be careful! Look at other pictures I did in which the

Above: The Testament of Dr Mabuse *was taken later to be a parable of Nazi terror methods. Below left: Death demands a child's life in* Destiny. Below: *The Wedding in the Eccentric Club,* Lang's first filmed script

Above: the death of Siegfried, hero of Lang's epic Die Nibelungen. Above right: Fritz Lang behind the camera. Below right: the Master of Metropolis and the inventor plot to replace Maria, the workers' leader with an evil robot

women are not so nice and who cause destruction and hatred: *Scarlet Street*, *Die Nibelungen*, *Beyond a Reasonable Doubt*, and probably *While the City Sleeps* and *Human Desire* as well.'

Certain motifs also occur with frequency: the underworld in its literal sense (caves, cellars, hidden underground corridors), mirror images, disguises, and the control of others through trickery and illusion.

Lang often spoke of the importance and planning that must be given to each detail in each frame of a film so as to create atmosphere and provide information:

'An audience learns more about a character from detail in the decor, in the way the light falls in a room, than from pages of dialogue.'

In order to get these details exactly as he wanted them, Lang was known to have spent a whole day 'composing' a pile of dirty dishes in a sink which would only appear in the background of a shot; to have spent hours rearranging Joan Bennett's negligée so that it would cast exactly the right shadow in *Scarlet Street*; and to have washed the set floor of that film himself so that the light would reflect exactly the way he wished it to. This perfectionism and attention to detail helped give his films that special Lang stamp and also gained him his Hollywood reputation as an 'impossible tyrant'.

Of all his films, one that he both counted a 'good' movie and cared about personally, was *Der Müde Tod* (1921, *Destiny*), the script of which was co-written by him and his future wife, Thea von Harbou. The film divides into three parts, all variations on the main theme. Death gives a woman three chances to have her lover returned to life – each chance introduces a story. The first is set in ancient Bagdad, the second in fifteenth century Venice, the third in ancient China. Each time the girl's efforts are in vain. Finally Death offers her one last chance – she must offer another life in

exchange for her lover's. She fails, but is allowed to join her lover in the afterlife. There are action-filled historical episodes packed with special effects, such as flying horses, scrolls that move alone, and a whole miniature army that marches out of a small box. Lang still delighted in these effects 50 years later:

'Douglas Fairbanks bought the film, put it on the shelf and proceeded to steal everything. They remade all the special effects in *Thief of Bagdad*.'

He was less fond of the epic *Die Nibelungen* (1924: Part 1, *Siegfried*; Part 2, *Kriemhild's Revenge*). The first part tells the legend of the Norse hero Siegfried. The second is the story of the havoc wrought by his widow Kriemhild after his murder, and it is a terrifying study of revenge and destruction.

'I never really liked Siegfried as a hero very much. He is a liar, a cheat, and he was also rather insipid. Yet it was wonderful at the time, working with all that, constructing whole forests and all the rest. It is still fine to look at, I

suppose, but I can't warm up to the whole first part. It is too sweet. It is also too Germanic. I was an absolute prince in the German cinema then, and maybe I was too carried away with giganticism.'

His next film, *Metropolis* (1927), depicts a city of the future where the exploited workers are on the verge of rebellion against their rulers. With the possible exception of *M* (1931), it is Lang's best-known film, but not one of his own favourites:

'I think the film is a bit silly and a bit naive, with all of that business about the heart being a link between capital and labour – or in seeing capital as the brain and labour merely as the hand. Well, I know more now. Mrs von Harbou and I took out whole sections about magic and science, which may have been an error because the film doesn't hang together well now.'

Through the eyes of exile

In 1933, Lang fled Hitler's Germany for Paris, where he filmed Ferenc Molnar's play *Liliom* in 1934, but the film was never a popular success. Following the outbreak of war, Lang decided to sign a contract with David O. Selznick, then at MGM, and move to the USA, although it would be two years before the studio gave him a property to direct.

In Hollywood he found himself part of a system which limited creative freedom. Yet, as he never signed a long-term contract with any studio, he was freer than many contract directors, and generally able to choose his projects. Thus his American work reveals a continuity of style and theme with his earlier German films. His continuing interest in justice, social criticism, the constant struggle

against circumstances and fate is clearly evident in such films as *Fury* (1936), *You Only Live Once* (1937), *While the City Sleeps* (1955) and *Beyond a Reasonable Doubt* (1956).

While many social problem films tend to date (particularly after such problems have faded from the public view) Lang's retain their freshness and power. He commented:

'Those films, like *Fury*, are not documentaries about America, but every so-called "social problem" in them comes out of newspaper stories – I made whole collections of clippings before I started shooting – so maybe they could be called "documented films". I tried always to tell strong, entertaining stories connected with the "problems". That way people were entertained, but they also had something to talk about. Most of them were popular with audiences because I tried to tell the stories from the point of view of the average man, who was always the central person, and that made them easy to identify with.'

Fury is about mob rule and lynching, with Spencer Tracy as Joe, an average man who is arrested and jailed for a kidnapping he did not commit. A mob burns down the jail, Joe is presumed dead, and various members of the mob are put on trial for his murder. It is only through the love of Katherine (Sylvia Sidney) that Joe reappears in time to save the lives of those who tried to kill him. In the false arrest and near lynching of Joe, as well as in the trial, complete with damning and 'certain' evidence of guilt, Lang calls into question not only standard ideas of how innocence and guilt might be determined, but the entire notion of absolute justice as well. He also returns to his

theme of the destructive power of revenge in his portrayal of Joe who, on the verge of insanity, becomes possessed of a blood lust every bit as strong as that of the mob; the regenerating power of romantic love also plays its part in Katherine's influence for good. Powerful as the film remains, and though Lang continued to like it, he saw its flaws clearly:

'Lynching in the American Thirties was directed against Negroes, but that was too strong for MGM, so the most I could do was to slip in a few Negroes almost in passing. The ending is terrible, but MGM insisted on having that fade-out kiss in the court between Tracy and Sylvia.'

You Only Live Once tells the story of three-time loser Eddie (Henry Fonda) who, after his parole, is hounded to death by a society that refuses to let him go straight. Lang is never quite as simple as that, however, and he makes us remain sympathetic towards Eddie, despite watching him kill (in mad desperation) a kindly prison priest. The moral ambiguities thus set up about innocence and guilt, the law

and the outlaw, continue long after Eddie is 'freed' through death.

Tales of murder and revenge

It is not surprising, in the light of Lang's exile, that he should have been one of the leaders in the making of anti-Nazi films like *Man Hunt* (1941) and *Hangmen Also Die!* (1943), nor that his view of humanity began to darken so that he was able to create some of the best films in the *film noir* category made in the USA, including *Woman in the Window* (1944) and the corrosive and violent *The Big Heat* (1953). In the latter film, the whole of society seems touched by corruption, greed and violence. Even the 'average man', honest cop Dave Bannion (Glenn Ford), who pursues the mob which runs the city, turns into a revenge-seeking man of violence after his wife is killed.

Lang thought that what was interesting was to examine what happens when 'good' society tries to rid itself of the 'bad', but becomes corrupted by using 'bad' methods.

Lang's Westerns, in which he took particular pleasure 'because they are so purely

Top left: The Woman in the Window – literally a nightmare of love and murder. Above: the lynch-mob gathers in Fury. *Below: Scarlet Street was a tragic tale of jealousy and retributive justice. Left: Eddie (Henry Fonda) and Joan (Sylvia Sidney) on the run from the law in* You Only Live Once

Filmography

1917 Die Hochzeit im Exzentrik Klub (sc. only); Hilde Warren und der Tod (sc + actor only). **'19** Halbblut (+sc); Die Frau mit den Orchideen (sc. only); Der Herr der Liebe; Totentanz (sc. only) (GER-A); Die Spinnen (Pt 1: Der Goldene See) (+sc) (USA/GB: The Spiders); Die Pest in Florenz (sc. only); Harakiri. **'20** Das Wandernde Bild (+co-sc); Die Spinnen (Pt 2: Das Brillianten Schiff) (+sc) (USA/GB: The Spiders); Vier um die Frau (+co-sc). **'21** Der Müde Tod (+co-sc) (USA: Between Two Worlds, re-edited and shown as Beyond the Wall in 1927, later titled Destiny; GB: Destiny); Das Indische Grabmal (Pt 1: Die Sendung des Yoghis; Pt 2: Das Indische Grabmal) (+co-sc) (USA: re-edited into single feature, retitled Mysteries of India/Above All Laws). **'22** Dr Mabuse der Spieler (shown in two parts: Pt 1: Dr Mabuse der Spieler; Pt 2: Inferno-Menschen der Zeit) (+co-sc). **'24** Die Nibelungen/Die Nibelungen: Ein Deutsches Heldenlied (Pt 1: Siegfried; Pt 2: Kriemhilds Rache, re-released as one film, Siegfrieds Tod 1933) (+co-sc) (USA: Pt 1: Siegfried; Pt 2: Kriemhild's Revenge). **'27** Metropolis (+co-sc). **'28** Spione (+prod; +co-sc) (USA: The Spy). **'29** Frau im Mond (USA: By Rocket to the Moon; GB: The Girl in the Moon). **'31** M/M: Dein Mörder Sieht Dich An/Mörder Unter Uns (+co-sc) (USA release version dubbed into English). **'32** Das Testament des Dr Mabuse (+prod; +co-sc) (USA: The Last Will of Dr Mabuse; GB: The Testament of Dr Mabuse) Les Testament du Dr Mabuse (French version). **'34** Liliom (+co-sc) (FR). *All remaining films USA unless specified:* **'36** Fury (+co-sc). **'37** You Only Live Once. **'38** You and Me (+prod). **'40** The Return of Frank James. **'41** Western Union; Man Hunt. **'43** Hangmen Also Die! (+prod; +co-sc). **'44** The Woman in the Window; The Ministry of Fear. **'45** Scarlet Street (+prod). **'46** Cloak and Dagger. **'48** Secret Beyond the Door (+prod). **'50** House by the River; American Guerrilla in the Philippines (GB: I Shall Return). **'52** Rancho Notorious; Clash by Night. **'53** The Blue Gardenia; The Big Heat. **'54** Human Desire. **'55** Moonfleet. **'56** While the City Sleeps; Beyond a Reasonable Doubt. **'59** Der Tiger von Eschnapur and Das Indische Grabmal (+co-sc) (GER-FT-IT) (USA, single feature: Journey to the Lost City/Tigress of Bengal; GB, single feature: Tiger of Bengal). **'61** Die Tausend Augen des Dr Mabuse (+prod; +co-sc) (GER-FR-IT) (USA/GB: The Thousand Eyes of Dr Mabuse). **'63** Le Mépris (actor only) (FR) (USA: Contempt).

American', reveal a similar darkening view, beginning brightly enough with his first colour film *The Return of Frank James* (1940) but ending with a tale of 'murder and revenge' – *Rancho Notorious* (1952).

Although he used colour subtly to underscore emotion and to create atmosphere, Lang had reservations about its use:

'It limits everything. You can't show a dirty street in colour; it turns out too pretty. It is difficult to compose with lines and shadows in colour. After experimenting, and having a bit of fun with it – like with the Indians in *Western Union* – I tried to make my colours more sombre. I think that worked best in *Moonfleet*.'

He was of divided opinion, too, about 're-

Above: Rancho Notorious tells of a cowboy's hunt for the killer of his fiancée. Below: Clash by Night was a drama of passion – with a happy ending. Below right: Lang turned to an Eastern setting for Tiger of Bengal

makes'. He never forgave Joseph Losey, who remade *M* in 1951, because that director made slighting remarks about the earlier version. Lang himself admitted that *Human Desire* (1954), his own remake of Renoir's *La Bête Humaine* (1938, *Judas Was a Woman*) was unsuccessful, but his other Renoir remake, *Scarlet Street* (1945), was one of his favourites.

Lang's final American films, *While the City Sleeps* and *Beyond a Reasonable Doubt*, are among his most interesting in their treatment of the ambiguities of 'moral' justice, capital punishment and the ethics of American society. The first film tells of a media tycoon who lures three friends into tracking down a murderer with the promise of promotion for the successful one. The second concerns a journalist who, ostensibly to show how a miscarriage of justice arises, cunningly diverts suspicion on to himself for a murder of which he is in fact guilty, while retaining bogus evidence designed to prove his innocence.

After these films, Lang realized that he could continue working in the USA only under the most strained conditions, particularly as he

was no longer a 'big money-making director':

'Anyway, they didn't seem to care for quality any longer; just make them fast, make them cheap. I got an offer to work on two films to be made in India, but produced by a German . . . I thought *Der Tiger von Eschnapur* and *Das Indische Grabmal* would do several things: they would demonstrate that I was still a box-office director, they would allow me to play a bit with the idea of a popular pulp thriller, and they would allow me to escape the rat race in Hollywood.'

Lang had mixed feelings about the results, but they were popular enough in Europe for the producer to persuade Lang to make another version of the Mabuse story, *The Thousand Eyes of Dr Mabuse* (1961) – his last film.

Although Lang continued to work on a number of ideas, his failing eyesight made further films impossible: 'How can I work if I can't *see*? I *have* to look at everything, control every visual detail.' Despite being unable to work in film Lang remained lucid and full of his rather feisty spirit to the end. He died in his sleep in Beverly Hills in 1976.   DAVID OVERBEY

M

It is astonishing that Fritz Lang's first sound film, *M*, should already have so completely mastered the new medium that it could not have been made with the same effect as a silent film. In the opening, a large shadow falls across a poster warning the public about the murderer, just as a little girl tosses her ball against it. We only hear a voice saying, 'What a nice ball you have. What is your name?'; and we feel the implied threat all the more for not actually seeing the man.

The scene switches to the girl's mother who is making lunch for her. She anxiously puts the absent child's meal back into the oven to keep it warm. In the next shot we see the unknown man for the first time, but only from behind, as he buys Elsie a balloon from a blind pedlar. He begins to whistle, off-key, a few bars of Grieg's *In the Hall of the Mountain King*. The whistled tune becomes a gruesome leitmotif indicating that the murderer is on the prowl.

Frau Beckmann, worried about her daughter, leans over the bannister of the stair-well and cries, 'Elsie!' The cry resounds through the block of flats and an empty loft. The murder is not shown. Instead Lang supplies a series of images – Frau Beckmann's cries echoing over shots of the empty building, Elsie's vacant place at table, Elsie's ball rolling from beneath a bush and her new balloon caught in telegraph wires – and leaves the audience to imagine the crime itself. The final shot of the sequence is of a paperseller who shouts out the latest headlines: a new murder!

Panic grows in the menaced town, and the police make random raids on the underworld. Gangsters cannot pursue their 'work' quietly, so they resolve to find the murderer. Two conferences about the murders are then paralleled; that of the police authorities and that of the gangsters. Here Lang uses a startlingly new sound technique: the overlapping of sentences from one scene to the next. This emphasizes the parallel action while tightening and accelerating the drama. He does not neglect visual effect, but bathes the gangsters in shadows.

In contrast to the plodding investigations of the police, the gangsters organize the network of beggars to watch for the murderer. Ironically he is detected by the blind balloon seller who recognizes the whistling. The blind man tells a boy to follow the murderer, who has a little girl with him.

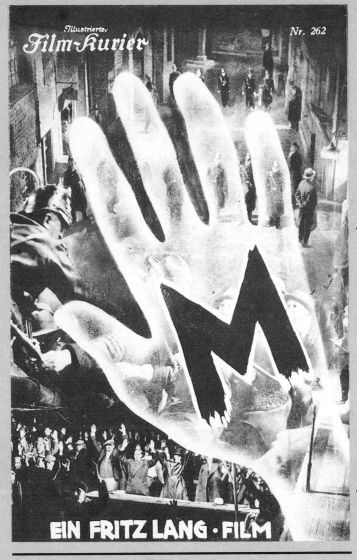

Illustrierter Film-Kurier Nr. 262

EIN FRITZ LANG · FILM

Directed by Fritz Lang, 1931
Prod co: Nero Film, A. G. Ver. Star Film GmbH. **prod:** Seymour Nebenzal. **sc:** Fritz Lang, Thea von Harbou, from an article by Egon Jacobson. **dial:** Thea von Harbou. **photo:** Fritz Arno Wagner, Gustav Rathje, Karl Vash. **sd ed:** Paul Falkenberg. **art dir:** Carl Vollbrecht, Emil Hasler. **backdrop photos:** Horst von Harbou. **mus:** excerpts from *Peer Gynt* by Edvard Grieg ('murderer's theme' whistled by Fritz Lang). **sd:** Adolf Jansen, **r/t:** 120 minutes. Berlin premiere, 11 May 1931.
Cast: Peter Lorre (*the murderer*), Otto Wernicke (*Inspector Karl Lohmann*), Gustav Gründgens (*Schraenker*), Theo Lingen (*Baurenfaenger*), Theodor Loos (*Commissioner Groeber*), Georg John (*peddler*), Ellen Widman (*Frau Beckmann*), Inge Landgut (*Elsie Beckmann*), Ernst Stahl-Nachbaur (*Chief of Police*), Paul Kemp (*pickpocket*), Franz Stein (*minister*), Rudolf Blümner (*defence lawyer*), Karl Platen (*watchman*), Gerhard Bienert (*police secretary*), Rosa Veletti (*owner of the Crocodile Club*), Hertha von Walter (*prostitute*), Fritz Odemar (*safe-breaker*), Fritz Gnass (*burglar*).

The murderer buys the child some oranges and pulls out his flick-knife – but only to peel one. Alarmed, the watching boy chalks an 'M' (for murderer) on his hand, jostles the murderer and manages to mark the man's back with a sign.

Realizing he has been spotted, the murderer panics and runs into the nearby courtyard of an office block. Two fire engines rush past ringing their bells, and by the time they have gone, the murderer has disappeared. The gangsters, alerted by the beggars, break into the building. Again, sound betrays the murderer: accidentally locked in an attic, he tries to hammer a nail into

a makeshift key. The sound is heard by the hunters, who break in and seize him. Wrapped in a carpet, he is caried off for 'trial'.

Before a jury largely made up of criminals and prostitutes, the murderer screams out his confession:

'Who are you . . . all of you? . . . Criminals! Perhaps you're even proud of being able to break safes, to climb into buildings or cheat at cards . . . Things you could just as well keep your fingers off . . . But I . . . I can't help myself! I haven't any control over this evil thing that's inside me – the fire, the voices, the torment . . . I want to escape . . . but it's impossible.'

The police, meanwhile, have been told of the gangsters' activities and break into the 'courtroom' just as the mob is howling for the murderer's death. No silent film could have created the emotional climax of the murderer's confession with titles alone.

Although Lang's use of the underworld was influenced by Berthold Brecht's famous satirical play *Die Dreigroschenoper* (*The Threepenny Opera*), he based much of the screenplay on contemporary press reports. Lang also investigated police methods of detection and spoke to gangsters (even giving them parts in the film). He asked his set designer, Emil Hasler, for 'everyday' sketches for decor, and his cameraman, Fritz Arno Wagner, to adopt newsreel techniques when shooting.

This well-documented approach is typical of Lang's films, but does not obscure his genuine human concern. In an interview with Gero Gandert, Lang recalled:

'In *M*, I was not only interested in finding out why someone was driven to a crime as horrible as child murder, but also to discuss the pros and cons of capital punishment. But the film's message is *not* the conviction of the murderer but the warning to all mothers, "You should keep better watch over your children". This human message was felt particularly strongly by my wife at the time, Thea von Harbou.'
LOTTE H. EISNER

2

3

A shadow looms over Elsie Beckmann (1). Her name will soon figure on the list of the murderer's victims. As the townsfolk panic, an innocent man is seized by a mob (2). Unaware that every beggar in the city is on the watch for him, the murderer eyes yet another victim (3). He catches sight of the tell-tale 'M' chalked on his back by a boy who suspects him (4) and panics (5). He hides in an attic full of bric-a-brac (6), but is eventually caught by a vigilante force of gangsters and taken to an abandoned factory to be 'tried' by criminals (7). The gang boss confronts him with a picture of Elsie (8), and a blind balloon-seller also gives evidence against him (9). Finally he makes his confession (10).

5

6

7

8

9

10

Marlene
Dietrich

'One sees what one wants to see',
said Josef von Sternberg, 'and I gave her nothing
that she did not already have.'

The Blue Angel

Josef von Sternberg described his first film with Dietrich as 'a celluloid monument to her'. It certainly made her a star.

The Blue Angel is the story of an elderly, respected school professor who becomes obsessed with a cabaret singer at the Blue Angel nightclub. Sacked from the school after being seduced by Lola-Lola, he marries her and becomes a clown in her travelling troupe. When it visits his old town he is painfully humiliated and, looking for solace, finds instead Lola with her new lover. Cast out, the pathetic figure wanders to his former classroom and dies there alone.

In Sternberg's cruellest study of sexual desire, Dietrich was teasingly provocative as the heartless Lola, stealing most of the scenes as she huskily sings 'Falling in Love Again' and 'I'm Naughty Little Lola', and bares her legs to Emil Jannings' professor. Heinrich Mann, author of the original novel, told Jannings during production that 'the success of this film will be found in the naked thighs of Miss Dietrich!'

'She makes reason totter on her throne' wrote the critic James Agate. Marlene Dietrich, who for so many years defied time, has also denied history. For more than two decades she included in her remarkable stage act some fragments of purely mythical autobiography that obliterated all that she had achieved before Josef von Sternberg made her an international star with *Der Blaue Engel*.

Dietrich has claimed that she was an unknown drama student when Sternberg 'discovered' her. She was, in fact, a veteran of 7 years and 17 films, not counting walk-on parts that date from as early as 1919.

Never the most modest of men, even Sternberg grew irritated with her insistence that he was her 'Svengali':

'She has never ceased to proclaim that I taught her everything. Among the many things I did not teach her was to be garrulous about me . . . I did not endow her with a personality that was not her own; one sees what one wants to see, and I gave her nothing that she did not already have. What I did was to dramatize her attributes and make them visible for all to see; though, as there were perhaps too many, I concealed some.'

The new angel

Maria Magdalene Dietrich was born in 1901, the daughter of an officer in the Royal Prussian Police. Abandoning a musical training in favour of the stage, she telescoped her names into 'Marlene' and in January 1922 had her first break with a small part in *Der Grosse Bariton* (The Great Baritone).

Her first credited film role is as a maidservant, helping her mistress to escape, in the comic costume romance *So Sind die Männer* (1922, Men Are Like This). In Joe May's

Right: the myth takes shape in the silent Three Loves. *Left: a scene from* Shanghai Express *and an early incarnation of the myth.*

Tragödie der Liebe (1923, *Tragedy of Love*), a rambling four-part murder serial starring Emil Jannings, she plays the girlfriend of a lawyer.

She moved into supporting roles in films which included *Manon Lescaut* (1926), and *Cafe Electric* (1927), and was leading lady to the 'adventure king' Harry Piel in *Sein Grösster Bluff* (1927, His Greatest Bluff). Alexander Korda cast her as a coquette, enraged by the shopgirl heroine who borrows her gown in *Eine Dubarry von Heute* (1926, A Modern Dubarry). in *Ich Küsse Ihre Hand, Madame* (1929, *I Kiss Your Hand, Madame*) she has an unrewarding lead part in an operetta tale of thwarted love and mistaken identity. In Maurice Tourneur's *Das Schiff der Verlorenen Menschen* (1929, The Ship of Lost Souls), she is again in the lead, playing an aeronaut pursued by the woman-hungry crew of the ship that rescues her from a crash.

Fatal attractions

Die Frau, nach der Man Sich Sehnt (1929, *Three Loves*), directed by Kurt Bernhardt, showed a clear understanding of Dietrich's *femme fatale* quality and strange sexual aura.

She bewitches a young man on his honeymoon – travelling on the same train – and begs him to rescue her from her sinister companion, later revealed to be her lover. He abandons his bride to pursue this lovely creature, but she seems unable, or unwilling, to break from Karoff, her jealous lover who, it seems, has murdered her husband with her knowledge. She eventually dies at Karoff's hands. The decorative manner of this film remarkably anticipates the visual style of Sternberg: in a party scene, balloons and streamers fill the air to confuse and torment the characters; lighting is used to model the star's face; and in one memorable shot a shaft of light from an opening door gradually creeps up Dietrich's silk-clad legs, with startlingly sensuous effect.

It is apparent that somebody already recognized the mythical possibilities of Dietrich. The tempting conclusion is that it was the star herself, for it was she who approached the writers Walter Wassermann and Walter Schlee to give her a 'similar script' for her next film. They obliged with *Gefahren der Brautzeit* (1929, Dangers of the Engagement), in which a baron meets an unknown beauty (Dietrich) on

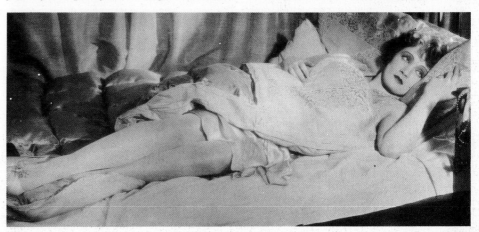

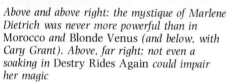

Above and above right: the mystique of Marlene Dietrich was never more powerful than in Morocco *and* Blonde Venus *(and below, with Cary Grant). Above, far right: not even a soaking in* Destry Rides Again *could impair her magic*

a train; the first glimpse of her, framed in a frosted carriage window, might well be from a Sternberg film. The train breaks down and the couple spend a night of love in a hotel. The next morning the lady has disappeared. Arriving at his destination the Baron meets his best friend, who introduces his fiancée – the unknown beauty. She later comes to the Baron's room to tell him their meeting must be forgotten; but they are surprised by her betrothed who shoots his friend in a fit of jealousy. The Baron pretends the injury is nothing and succeeds in reconciling the couple; he then dies alone, using his last strength to feign suicide. The film is almost a carbon copy of its predecessor, with the significant difference that here it is the man, not the *femme fatale*, who dies.

And along came Jo

Then Josef von Sternberg entered her life. According to him, he chose Dietrich for the part of Lola-Lola after seeing her on stage in *Zwei Krawatten* (Two Neckties). Only later did he see her screen-work which he described as:

'. . . an ordeal. If I had first seen her films . . . my reaction would have been the same as everyone else's. In them she was an awkward, unattractive woman, left to her own devices, and presented in an embarrassing exhibition of drivel.'

This is patently untrue, though perhaps Sternberg saw the wrong films. In *Die Frau, nach der Man Sich Sehnt* and *Gefahren der Brautzeit* the form of the mythical Marlene is evident, though still rough-hewn. Sternberg's role was to perfect it, and provide a wonderful visual framework for the image: 'What I did was to dramatize her attributes and make them visible for all to see'.

This extraordinary man was born Jonas Sternberg in Vienna in 1894. His early life seems to have been a struggle for survival and self-education, which permanently marked a sensitive but defiantly arrogant personality.

Emigrating to the United States as a child, he found his way into the cinema, worked his way up in various technical jobs, and in 1925 directed a low-budget, independently produced feature, *The Salvation Hunters*. It brought him work in Hollywood on successful silents like the gangster story, *Underworld* (1927), and *The Last Command* (1928), which earned Emil Jannings the first Best Actor Oscar.

As a result Jannings, having now returned to Germany, requested Sternberg as the director of his first all-talkie film – *Der Blaue Engel* (*The Blue Angel*). The film was a triumph and so was its leading lady – Dietrich.

The road to Morocco

Summoned by Paramount, she departed immediately after the film's premiere. She was preceded by Sternberg, who had persuaded the studio to sign her and was the obvious choice to direct her first American film.

Again Dietrich seems to have taken the initiative in selecting her vehicle. She is said to have given Sternberg a copy of the novel *Amy Jolly* to read on the boat. Later she cabled him that it was, after all, 'weak lemonade' but Sternberg proceeded to make *Morocco* (1930) from it. The story centres on a woman (Dietrich plays another cabaret artist) whose feelings are divided between loyalty to a wealthy socialite (Adolphe Menjou) and passion for a legionnaire (Gary Cooper) whom she eventually follows into the desert. Even today the sexual suggestions and ambivalences in Marlene's cabaret act can still raise eyebrows. In any event, *Morocco* consolidated the legend and securely launched her American career.

Paramount partners

In the next five years Dietrich and Sternberg worked together on five more films that, ultimately, were to elevate her into a screen goddess. In *Dishonored* (1931) she is a beautiful spy in the Mata Hari mould, dying with *sang-froid* in front of the firing squad. In *Shanghai Express* (1932) she is spellbindingly erotic as Shanghai Lily, the woman with a past, sacrificing herself to a Chinese rebel to save the man she loves. This is perhaps Sternberg's most perfect film; visual spectacle and narrative are totally integrated. In *Blonde Venus* (1932) she

is a woman who turns singer (and perhaps worse) to pay for the operations needed to save her husband's life. Perhaps the most startling sequence of *Blonde Venus* is the 'Hot Voodoo' number in the nightclub with its chorus of spear-carrying girls. In the midst of them Dietrich emerges, like a butterfly out of a chrysalis, from a huge and hairy gorilla suit, which she proceeds to remove before singing the song. In *The Scarlet Empress* (1934), a witty interpretation of history, she is a sensuous Catherine the Great. In *The Devil Is a Woman* (1935) she becomes a Spanish siren who enslaves a young political refugee and an older grandee. Here Sternberg's ability to decorate the *femme fatale* myth reached a peak, but the film's commercial failure (the Spanish government demanded its withdrawal) was the excuse for Paramount, alarmed by his extravagance and dogged independence, to end his contract. In any case, he had announced during filming that it would benefit neither Dietrich nor himself to stay together.

The parting of the ways

'I didn't leave Sternberg. *He left me!*' Dietrich told the *Sunday Times* nearly 30 years later. 'That's very important. In my life, he was the man I wanted to please most. He decided not to work with me any more and I was very unhappy about that.'

Dietrich's dependence and attachment to Sternberg were intense. Sternberg's wife had earlier sued her for alienation of affection and libel. Dietrich won the case but it sparked off a great deal of controversy and speculation about the exact nature of the union between the director and his protégée, and may have been a major cause of their separation.

Only once between *Der Blaue Engel* and *The Devil Is a Woman* had Dietrich worked under another director – Rouben Mamoulian in *Song of Songs* (1933). It was apparently an uneasy collaboration for director and star. Dietrich is said to have been in the habit of murmuring into the microphone before a take 'Where are you, Jo?' In later years she herself elaborated this story; her actual words, she told director Peter Bogdanovich (*Esquire*, January 1973) were 'Oh Jo – why hast thou forsaken me?'

For both director and star, the cycle of pictures they made together represented the summit of their achievement in the cinema. Sternberg had proved himself one of Hollywood's supreme artists, with Dietrich at the centre of the decadent, dreamlike world created by his lush, exotic style. He worked on only 9 more features in the remaining 18 years of his career, and of these, Korda's *I, Claudius* (1937) was abandoned and 3 were reworked by other directors. Only *The Shanghai Gesture* (1941) and *The Saga of Anatahan* (1953) can stand alongside the great Sternberg pictures of the Thirties.

Dietrich's career also suffered a decline. She made the kitschy *The Garden of Allah* (1936) with Richard Boleslavsky; a couple of frothy comedies, Frank Borzage's *Desire* (1936) and Ernst Lubitsch's *Angel* (1937); and in Britain, Jacques Feyder's beautiful but dull *Knight Without Armour* (1937). By this time she was ungallantly labelled 'box-office poison' and ranked at number 126 in the list of money-making stars. Shortly afterwards Paramount announced: 'Marlene Dietrich will be permitted to work elsewhere'.

Dietrich rides again

Her career revived dramatically in 1939 with George Marshall's tongue-in-cheek Western, *Destry Rides Again*, in which she plays Frenchy, a saloon singer in love with the mild-mannered sheriff (James Stewart). None of the many films that followed framed and deified her as carefully as the Sternberg pictures had done: but by this time it hardly seemed to matter. The myth was already complete, unchangeable and impregnable, and – whatever Sternberg may have contributed – it was clear that its conservation was mostly due to Dietrich herself.

We have the evidence of nearly everybody who worked with her that nothing she did was accidental or unconscious. Lee Garmes, Sternberg's cameraman, said, 'She had a great mechanical mind and knew the camera. She would always stop in the exact position that was right for her . . .' Harry Stradling, who filmed *The Garden of Allah*, confirmed:

'While each shot was being lined up she had a full-length mirror set up beside the camera and was able to see just how she would look on the screen. If she thought the light on her arms was too strong, or her shoulders were catching too much from a certain arc, she never hesitated to say so; and she was always right.'

Perhaps the surest proof of her great professionalism lay in the dramatic roles she played in her last pictures: the wife giving treacherous evidence in Billy Wilder's *Witness for the Prosecution* (1957); the tough madame in Orson Welles's *Touch of Evil* (1958); and the widow of a Nazi general in Stanley Kramer's *Judgement at Nuremberg* (1961). To be a star and a myth, she revealed, did not preclude intelligent and concentrated dramatic interpretation. Then in 1979, after a 16-year absence, she returned to the screen, playing another madame in David Hemmings's *Just A Gigolo*. Her career in motion pictures now spans over 60 years.

The eternal superstar

Yet the masterpiece of the myth was perhaps the Dietrich who emerged as a solo concert performer during and after World War II.

In 1953 she began the series of tours that were to take her around the world. Dietrich never disappointed her audiences. And every night the myth was brought to life on stage. In private she could be a loving mother and wife (Dietrich married Rudolf Sieber, one of Joe May's production assistants, in 1924), an industrious housekeeper, a practical and willing nurse, a determined trouper and a sensible traveller. On stage, however, the glamour of that solitary figure, sheathed in sequins and furs, never flickered; it defied all the inroads of time. And her performance was not just a magnificent illusion. When she sang 'Where Have All the Flowers Gone' and 'Lili Marlene', or touched the past with 'Falling in Love Again', she became a tragic actress – as well as a mythical figure encompassing a lifetime of all our history.
DAVID ROBINSON

Quotations from: Fun in a Chinese Laundry *by Josef von Sternberg;* Marlene Dietrich *by Sheridan Morley; All My Yesterdays by Edward G. Robinson.*

Filmography
1922 So Sind die Männer/Napoleons Kleiner Brüder/Der Kleine Napoleon. '23 Tragödie der Liebe (USA/GB: Tragedy of Love); Der Mensch am Wege. '24 Der Sprung ins Leben/Die Roman eine Zirkuskindes. '25 Die Freudlose Gasse (USA: Streets of Sorrow, reissued with post-synchronized sound in 1937 as The Street of Sorrow; GB: The Joyless Street). '26 Manon Lescaut; Eine Dubarry von Heute; Kopf Hoch, Charly!; Madame Wünscht Keine Kinder; Der Juxbaron. '27 Sein Grösster Bluff/Er Oder Dich; Cafe Electric/Wenn ein Weib den Weg Verliert (A: Die Liebesbörse). '28 Prinzessin Olala; Die Glückliche Mutter (short: edited version of home movies made by her husband in mid-1920s, reputedly shown publicly). '29 Ich Küsse Ihre Hand, Madame (USA: I Kiss Your Hand, Madame); Die Frau, nach der Man Sich Sehnt (USA/GB: Three Loves); Das Schiff der Verlorenen Menschen; Gefahren der Brautzeit/Liebesnächte. '30 Der Blaue Engel (English-language version: The Blue Angel, USA/GB, 1931). *All remaining films USA unless specified:* '30 Morocco. '31 Dishonored. '32 Shanghai Express; Blonde Venus. '33 The Song of Songs. '34 The Scarlet Empress. '35 The Devil Is a Woman. '36 Desire; I Loved a Soldier (unfinished; refilmed without her as Hotel Imperial in 1939); The Garden of Allah. '37 Knight Without Armour (GB); Angel. '39 Destry Rides Again. '40 Seven Sinners; The Flame of New Orleans; Manpower. '42 The Lady Is Willing; The Spoilers; Pittsburgh. '43 Stage Door Canteen (publicity sketch not used in actual film). '44 Follow the Boys (guest); Kismet. '46 Martin Roumagnac (FR) (USA: The Room Upstairs). '47 Golden Earrings. '48 A Foreign Affair. '49 Jigsaw (guest); Stage Fright (GB). '51 No Highway (GB) (USA: No Highway in the Sky). '52 Rancho Notorious. '56 Around the World in 80 Days (guest); The Monte Carlo Story. '57 Witness for the Prosecution. '58 Touch of Evil (guest). '61 Judgement at Nuremberg. '62 The Black Fox (narr. only). '63 Paris When It Sizzles (guest). '79 Schöner Gigolo – Armer Gigolo (GER) (GB: Just a Gigolo).

Below: Dietrich as the madame in Just a Gigolo; *half a century after* The Blue Angel *and the allure of Lola-Lola lingers on*

37

Kings of the Underworld

The Twenties spawned gangsters in the gutters and ghettos of America's cities; the Thirties immortalized them on the screen

Gangster movies are about professional criminals for whom crime is a way of life. Films about gangsters were being made in the USA before World War I, and two fine examples – Josef von Sternberg's *Underworld* (1927) and Lewis Milestone's *The Racket* (1928) – were produced during a gangster cycle that preceded the talkies. But the golden age of the gangster movie is the Thirties, and its heyday lasted only three or four years, from shortly after the coming of sound until 1933.

In his autobiography, *Child of the Century*, screenwriter Ben Hecht (a former Chicago newspaperman, as many other screenwriters were) explained the thinking behind his *Underworld* screenplay, which set the pattern for many subsequent talking gangster films:

'The thing to do was to skip the heroes and heroines, to write a movie containing only villains and bawds. I would not have to tell any lies then. As a newspaperman I had learned that nice people – the audience – loved criminals, doted on reading about their love problems as well as their sadism. My movie, grounded on this simple truth, was produced with the title *Underworld*. It was the first

> I'm going to run the whole works. There's only one law – do it first, do it yourself and keep doing it.
> **Tony Camonte, Scarface**

gangster movie to bedazzle the movie fans and there were no lies in it – except for a half-dozen sentimental touches introduced by its director Joe von Sternberg.'

All that was needed to enhance this cynical recipe was to capture the noises of gangland on a soundtrack: the background jazz music of night-clubs and speakeasies; the mobsters' abrasive speech; the chatter of machine-guns and pistols; the ominous wail of police sirens; the roar of engines and the screech of tyres.

The gangster films of the years 1929–34 charted a world of nightclubs, flophouses, deserted streets, clandestine drinking-places, flashy apartments, crowded tenements, below-street cafés, gambling dens and police stations – a world that was both realistic and oddly abstract. Virtually all these films were shot on

Hollywood studio sets, and while Chicago or New York might be specified as the locale, the action seemed to be placed in a universal city rather than in any particular one.

From the 250 to 300 gangster films made in those years, only 3 have enduring reputations – Mervyn LeRoy's *Little Caesar* (1930), William Wellman's *The Public Enemy* (1931) and Howard Hawks's *Scarface* (1932). They were immediately recognized by contemporary critics as superior works, though each one was greeted by reviewers professing their weariness of gangster pictures. These films stood out not because they were new but for the definitive way they handled familiar material.

With chilly detachment these three films show the rise and fall of professional crooks from Catholic immigrant backgrounds. In each the main character was modelled on Al Capone, and all three turned a well-known stage actor into a movie star. Edward G. Robinson's Caesar Enrico Bandello (*Little Caesar*) and Paul Muni's Tony Camonte (*Scarface*) are Italians; James Cagney's Tom Powers (*The Public Enemy*) is Irish. All are short, strutting, violent men, driven by burning ambition,

hungry for power and social acceptance. They shoot their way to the top of the criminal heap and are then destroyed – partly because conventional morality demands such an ending, but mainly through pride and a talent for self-destruction. Like all the gangsters of this era, they are denied domestic comforts. They desert loving mothers and are then torn between the blonde 'molls' they despise and the high-class, chaste brunettes they aspire to marry. They die alone, miserably and memorably – bullet-riddled Little Caesar asking 'Mother of Mercy – is this the end of Rico?', Tom Powers being delivered home dead and wrapped in a blanket, and Tony Camonte gunned down beneath a neon sign which ironically proclaims, 'The World Is Yours'.

Although the forewords and afterwords to these films point up a moral to the action – Little Caesar ends with the title 'Rico's career had been a skyrocket, starting in the gutter and ending there', Scarface was compelled by the authorities to carry the sub-title 'Shame of a Nation' – these movies are not moralizing tracts. We are not invited to see their central characters as psychopaths. Killings are frequent, but not dwelt upon sadistically. When Tom Powers bumps off his treacherous former mentor Putty Nose, for example, and then immediately starts thinking about a date with his mistress Gwen, we are confronted with an association of killing and sex that might well be interpreted as psychotic. However the scene's overall message is that murder is just a particularly ruthless way of conducting business – Powers is just 'settling debts'.

The gangster was a product of metropolitan alienation at a time when the USA was changing from being a rural agrarian society to becoming a predominantly urban, industrial one. For the audiences of the early Depression years, the gangster represented a number of things, both fearful and reassuring. His career was a parody of the American Dream, reflecting the way the Rockefellers, Goulds, Fisks and other so-called robber barons had made their fortunes. The gangster was also a social bandit driven into crime as the only way to advance in a society that denied him proper channels of expression. His life challenged and exposed a corrupt system.

The careers of these ethnic gangsters closely resemble those of the immigrant movie

Below: Underworld, *a silent picture, fired the public's imagination and anticipated the talkie gangster films of the Thirties*

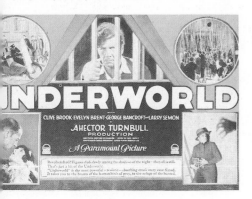

pioneers, men such as Jack Warner, Louis B. Mayer, Adolph Zukor and Harry Cohn. The movie moguls also fought their way up from the ghetto and were briefly outlaws themselves when resisting the viciously repressive Motion Picture Patents Company: it tried to put them out of business before World War I by the imposition of levies on cameras and projectors, and sanctions on their use. The studio bosses had spent the Twenties building commercial empires using methods only a little more honest (though much less violent) than the beer barons of Prohibition. The movie tycoons enjoyed the company of gangsters and mixed with them freely while pursuing their passion for gambling and horse-racing. The West Coast head of the Syndicate and creator of modern Las Vegas, Bugsy Siegel, was well known to many Hollywood personalities, and set up house in Beverly Hills, where, in 1947,

he was murdered. Among his Hollywood admirers were the writer-producer Mark Hellinger, responsible for The Roaring Twenties (1939), Brute Force (1947) and The Naked City (1948), who liked to dress like a gangster, and the actor George Raft, who in Scarface created the famous coin-tossing gesture that reflected so accurately the uncertainty of a gangster's life. Raft knew Capone and numerous hoods, and in the Sixties was denied entry to Britain by the Home Office on the grounds that he was a front man for Mafia gambling interests. More seriously the movie tsar Will H. Hays brought in hoodlums to settle strikes, and for a time in the Thirties and Forties, the Chicago branch of

Below: Tom Powers (James Cagney) watches helplessly as his boyhood pal and partner in crime Matt Doyle (Edward Woods) is gunned down by a rival gang in The Public Enemy

JAMES CAGNEY · PRISCILLA LANE
"THE ROARING TWENTIES"

Left: Mark Hellinger, author of The Roaring Twenties, *described this tale of Prohibition as 'a memory of the past'. By 1939 the gangster had become a romantic anachronism*

the Syndicate controlled the principal Hollywood union for non-specialist studio employees (IATSE – the International Alliance of Theatrical Stage Employees), including cameramen, sound recordists and projectionists.

While Hollywood churned out gangster pictures in the early Thirties, a new wave of crime was sweeping the middle-west of the USA resulting in an orgy of robberies, bank holdups and kidnappings. The perpetrators were not big-time urban crooks from the newly-arrived immigrant groups. They were disorganized criminals from the hills and farms of the mid-west and south-west, from Indiana, Missouri, and Texas – white Anglo-Saxon Protestant boys and girls with names like John Dillinger, Bonnie Parker and Clyde Barrows. They loved the movies and were much impressed by them. Dillinger, for instance, would vault bank counters in imitation of his hero Douglas Fairbanks, and was shot down outside

Below: in G-Men *Cagney is a young lawyer who joins the FBI to avenge the murder of his best friend. Below right: Duke Mantee (Humphrey Bogart) threatens his hostages (including Bette Davis and Leslie Howard) in* The Petrified Forest

Chicago's Biograph cinema in 1934 after seeing Clark Gable and William Powell in the gangster film *Manhattan Melodrama* (1934).

When he heard of Dillinger's death, Will H. Hays sent a telegram to his chief adjutant and enforcer of the Hays Office Code, Joe Breen, which read in part:

'No picture on the life or exploits of John Dillinger will be produced or exhibited by any member [of the Motion Picture Producers and Distributors Association of America] . . . This decision is based on the belief that the production, distribution or exhibition of such a picture could be detrimental to the best public interest. Advise all studio heads accordingly.'

The FBI, however, found posturing psychopaths like Dillinger and Baby Face Nelson easier to capture than big city criminals. J. Edgar Hoover made capital out of them to boost the Bureau's public image. He also enlisted the help of Hollywood, and the result was a series of films glorifying the FBI. The first was *G-Men* (dir. William Keighley, 1935); for this James Cagney crossed over from public enemy to public defender, playing a young lawyer recruited by the FBI. The basic scenario was similar, as was the quantity of violence. The glorification of investigators rather than

criminals tended to make audiences condone unorthodox methods of law enforcement and turn current discontent not against society but against petty criminals.

William Keighley followed *G-Men* with a second trend-setting film, *Bullets or Ballots* (1936). This rehabilitated another gangland hero Edward G. Robinson by putting him on the right side of the law as an incorruptible New York cop. The film is important for two reasons. Firstly, in having Robinson infiltrate Barton MacLane's New York mob, it introduced the key figures of the undercover agent who was to play such a prominent part in crime pictures of the next two decades. Secondly, it laid particular stress on the real power behind the rackets being in the hands of conservatively dressed businessmen, who meet in tastefully appointed boardrooms and leave the messy job of killing people to underworld minions. This, too, was to become part of the pattern of American crime in both the movies and real-life.

G-Men was a conscious part of Hollywood's effort to change its image in the face of outside pressures from such organizations as the newly-formed Catholic Legion of Decency (to which Capone is said to have contributed) that demanded the cleaning up of the motion picture industry. In 1934 the Production Code, designed to protect public morals, became mandatory, and the essentially amoral character of the early gangster pictures could not be maintained. Equally, the coming of Roosevelt's New Deal policy, with its belief in the possibility of progress through social organization and reform, induced in Hollywood's producers and film-makers a greater sense of responsibility and optimism than they had shown in the earlier years of the decade.

Three important Broadway plays of 1935, helped the genre to diversify after its classic period. In Robert E. Sherwood's *The Petrified Forest*, Duke Mantee (played on stage and in Archie Mayo's 1936 film by Humphrey Bogart) is a Dillinger-type hoodlum who represents the final dying gasp of the 'free-enterprise' criminal system. In Maxwell Anderson's verse drama *Winterset* (filmed by Alfred Santell in 1936) the gangster Trock Estrella (Eduardo Ciannelli), a life-hating figure dying of cancer, is the link between the underworld and a crooked judiciary in a story concerning the

Above: Bogart and Robinson shoot it out to the death in Bullets or Ballots, *one of the first films to show organized crime as a threat to the whole of American society. Above right: Wallace Beery as the leader of desperate convicts in* The Big House

Below: Bogart in High Sierra, *where he played Mad Dog Earle, a gangster with a soft heart, hoping to pull one last big job. Bottom: The Dead End Kids, watched by Father Connolly, are stunned by news of Rocky's cowardice in* Angels with Dirty Faces

exposure of a frame-up. In Sidney Kingsley's *Dead End* (filmed in 1937 by William Wyler) the doomed criminal 'Baby Face' Martin, played by Humphrey Bogart, returns to the Manhattan slum that spawned him.

These three plays came to Hollywood wreathed in theatrical glory and cloaked in cultural respectability, for all three dramatists had recently won the Pulitzer Prize. They gave new impetus to the gangster movie during the next four years before it gave way to the private-eye picture, the war movie and the *film noir*. Tame as they may appear today, these earnest, carefully constructed works seemed hard-hitting, progressive pieces to most audiences at the time.

The old-style lone-wolf gangster was beginning to look something of an anachronism in an age of confident bureaucrats and burgeoning corporations. Edward G. Robinson played, somewhat prematurely, *The Last Gangster* (dir. Edward Ludwig, 1937), who after 10 years in jail finds himself bewildered by the new world of the late Thirties, and anxious to give up his former way of life. The opportunity is denied him. In *Brother Orchid* (dir. Lloyd Bacon, 1940) Robinson guys his old Warner Brothers roles in a rather sombre comedy as a hoodlum who seeks refuge in a monastery from would-be assassins. There he finds the 'class' that had eluded him outside. He helps his fellow monks reorganize their flower-growing business on profitable lines, and briefly slips out to fix the treacherous gangster, played by Humphrey Bogart, who double-crossed him.

The whole Thirties cycle came to an end the following year with Raoul Walsh's *High Sierra*. Adapted from a novel by W.R. Burnett, author of *Little Caesar*, the picture is tinged throughout with nostalgia – the crooked Big Mac (Donald MacBride) who springs Roy Earle (Humphrey Bogart) from jail for one last job observes sadly that 'All the A-1 guys are gone – dead or in Alcatraz'; a mob doctor looks back dreamily to the golden days when he removed bullets from fugitive gangsters in the Mid-west.

High Sierra was produced by Mark Hellinger, who had anticipated the enduring nostalgia for the Twenties with the original story for *The Roaring Twenties* (dir. Raoul Walsh, 1939), wherein the careers of three World War I friends were traced from the trenches of the Western Front to their post-war lives during the Prohibition: Bogart as a former saloon-keeper turned bootlegger, Cagney as a taxi-driver brought by economic circumstances into the underworld, and Jeffrey Lynn as a struggling lawyer who joins a crime-busting squad. The movie is a kind of superficial social history, an affectionate re-creation of a free-wheeling decade, a digest of familiar gangster plots and imagery, and a slick study of the effect of environment on character.

This last theme was much affected by current ideas of social reform that saw slums as the high-schools of crime and prisons as its universities. *The Big House* (dir. George Hill,

1930) led to a series of films depicting prison life. *The Big House*, was an MGM picture, but it was at Warner Brothers that virtually every one of the studio's contract players 'did time' in such films. *20,000 Years in Sing Sing* (dir. Michael Curtiz, 1933) has Spencer Tracy behind bars; in *San Quentin* (dir. Lloyd Bacon, 1937), Bogart is locked up, Barton MacLane plays a sadistic turnkey, and Pat O'Brien is the reformist warden seconded from the army; and in *Each Dawn I Die* (dir. William Keighley, 1939) a crusading journalist, who has been framed for manslaughter, joins forces with 'honest' gangster George Raft against the corrupt politicos on the outside.

In the late Thirties, under the influence of the New Deal and in response to pressure from Federal agencies, films took on an increasingly sanguine tone about the possibility of steering potential criminals into constructive activities and rehabilitating the sinners. *Invisible Stripes* (dir. Lloyd Bacon, 1939), based on a novel by a former prison warden, is one of numerous pictures pleading for ex-convicts to be given the opportunity to 'go straight'. In this case George Raft and Humphrey Bogart are two newly released prisoners who return to crime, the former involuntarily, the latter by choice.

Left: Bonnie and Clyde try to escape a hail of bullets. Below: Eddie Bartlett (James Cagney) dies in the arms of Panama Smith (Gladys George) in The Roaring Twenties

The most optimistic string of movies involve the cinema's first gang of juvenile delinquents, The Dead End Kids, who came out of the play and film *Dead End*. In *Angels with Dirty Faces* (dir. Michael Curtiz, 1938) they were won away from an allegiance to hoodlum Rocky Sullivan (James Cagney) by Rocky's old school friend Father Connolly (Pat O'Brien). Sullivan, perhaps because of Father Connolly's persuasiveness, or maybe because he truly is 'yellow', goes screaming to the electric chair, so destroying his heroic image among the slum kids. In *Crime School* (dir. Lewis Seiler, 1938) they are reformed by a liberal Commissioner of Correction (Humphrey Bogart) after an insensitive reformatory superintendent's brutal methods had only served to confirm them in a life of crime. In *They Made Me a Criminal* (dir. Busby Berkeley, 1939), the Kids learn to walk the straight and narrow on an Arizona farm under the influence of an underworld fugitive from New York. They finally took their place on the side of law and order in the 1941 serial *Junior G-Men*.

The gangster film did not vanish with the war and the end of the Depression. It appeared sporadically throughout the Forties and Fifties until *Bonnie and Clyde* (dir. Arthur Penn, 1967), *The St Valentine's Day Massacre* (dir. Roger Corman, 1967) and *The Godfather* (dir. Francis Coppola, 1972) revived the genre for another generation of film-goers.

PHILIP FRENCH

The angel with a dirty face

James Cagney is remembered as the toughest and wildest gangster hero of the screen. Yet his forceful personality has many sides. Born on July 17, 1899, in the Lower East Side of New York, Cagney began his show business career as a song and dance man on the vaudeville stage. It was his solid popular and critical reputation as a singer and dancer that resulted in a contract with Warner Brothers in 1930.

The arrival of sound was a crucial factor in Cagney's rapid rise to stardom. Although he was a trained dancer, which endowed his movements with particular grace and style, much of his success depended upon his distinctive, staccato, and thoroughly 'modern' voice and delivery.

Cagney himself suggests that he was simply one of hundreds of Broadway actors and actresses snapped up by the studios in the scramble to find new stars capable of adapting quickly and easily to talking pictures:

'Sound was coming in and they were using all the Broadway people they could get. They just shipped them out by the car load.'

Hoodlums from headlines

Cagney soon found himself on the road to Hollywood. Al Jolson spotted him in a stage musical, *Penny Arcade*, bought the film rights to the play and sold it to Warner Brothers. On Jolson's recommendation the studio hired Cagney to play the lead part in the film version, *Sinner's Holiday* (1930).

Above: Cagney said of his favourite film role, 'Once a song and dance man, always a song and dance man. In that brief statement you have my life . . .' Below: Cagney decked out as a Regency buck in Ladykiller, *where he plays a criminal who becomes a star actor*

Not only did he arrive at the right time, but at the right studio. Had it been MGM or Paramount he might not have stayed very long. His energy, his intensity, his sense of high-octane fun, and his thoroughly contemporary 'off the streets' delivery of dialogue exactly suited the films then being made under the supervision of Darryl F. Zanuck at Warners. Cagney recalled:

'When we were doing those hoodlum pictures at Warners we were making pictures of headlines . . . They would appear in the Los Angeles *Examiner* or any paper, [for instance] the story of Jake Lingel – a newspaper man who was not exactly honest [who] had done a little bit of work here and there with the boys, the hoods, and . . . some other things they *didn't* like. Well, Jake Lingel's body was found in a subway . . . immediately [the studio produced] a story about a crooked newspaperman and they had it in work within two weeks and maybe finished it in four.'

The very style of Warners – fast-paced tales usually lasting just over an hour, with functional and unpretentious direction and quick editing to push the story forward – paralleled the actor's own verve and energy. He recalls with affection both the tight studio schedules and the men working to meet them:

'Well now, this *Sinner's Holiday*, if I remember rightly, the schedule for that was 21 days . . . We did pictures naturally on things like that – 15 days, 18 days, . . . We had one director, Lloyd Bacon, who was a good man, a good technician, and Lloyd actually shot rehearsals . . . Well, we were kind of quick.'

A tough at the top

Although Cagney had already done four features at Warners in 1930–31, which were well received, *The Public Enemy* (1931) made him a star and linked his name with gangster roles. He had first been chosen to play the second lead. William Wellman, who directed the film, gives his version of what happened:

'We hire a guy named Eddie Woods to play the lead. We get a relatively unknown guy named Jimmy Cagney who has a tough little way, and he is playing the second part. I didn't see the rushes for three days because I was working late and said, "Aw, to hell with them. I'll see them over the weekend." When I looked at the rushes I said to Zanuck, "Look, there is a

horrible mistake. We have the wrong guy in there. Cagney should be the lead'' . . . We changed them, and Cagney became a big star.'

Seen today, *The Public Enemy*, not unlike a number of Cagney's early Warners' films, is effective only in fits and starts – most of it looks and sounds dated, except for Cagney himself. Darryl F. Zanuck, who was later to claim as 'personal discoveries' Cagney, Bette Davis and Joan Blondell, all of whom signed with Warners on successive days, admitted years later that, 'What makes the movie a classic is Cagney and the character of Tom, and they are inseparable.' The strength of Cagney's performance stems entirely from his vitality which turns Tom into a life-affirming force – despite his killing of two men and a horse – in contrast to the priggery, timidity and self-righteousness of almost everyone around him in the film. Cagney claims that his ability to give life to hoodlums and heavies by finding exactly the right gestures and manner for each one, and that this skill came from his careful observation of actors and vaudevillians early in his career:

'A heavy can be made an interesting and

Above: the frequent teaming of Cagney's dynamism with O'Brien's sensitivity reached its peak in this classic gangster film. Below: in The Irish in Us *O'Brien played a cop and Cagney his tearaway brother. Below right: The Strawberry Blonde was a romance, in which a dentist (Cagney) remembers his first love*

likeable fellow . . . all through the years in playing heavies [I took] any opportunity that presented itself [for] dropping the little goodies in . . . I think it makes for a better impression.'

The gangster loves to dance

The link between Cagney and gangster parts is, of course, a strong one, but rather misleading in terms of his entire 31-year career. It was, however, reaffirmed by Cagney returning to such roles, often when his popularity had begun to slip at the box-office. Still, he never repeated himself. Cagney's gangsters were always different characters, motivated by vastly different emotions and forces. In *White Heat* (1949) he played Cody Jarrett, a psychopath whose repressed sexuality erupts into violence. So assured was Cagney in his understanding of the part that he took risks which might have made other actors look ridiculous, such as crawling into his mother's lap to be comforted. His instincts and craftsmanship were almost always correct, and such risks rounded out what might otherwise have been an incomplete characterization. In an even later return to a gangster role, *Love Me or Leave Me* (1955), Cagney begins with a thoroughly unsympathetic and nasty character and proceeds to turn him into a tortured and understandable human being caught between his own cruel and bitter vision of the world and his romantic obsession with the woman (played by Doris Day) that he has made into a singing star. In Cagney's hands such characters may

remain monsters but they are thoroughly believable monsters.

Warners did not confine Cagney's huge talent to gangsters and heavies, nor to any particular type of film, although he was obviously more at home with contemporary 'street' characters and stories. He was cast in Westerns, biographies, war stories, domestic melodramas, comedies and even Shakespeare, playing the part of Bottom in *A Midsummer Night's Dream* (1935) with great gusto. Cagney also brought his drive and carefully observed creation to his first love – musicals. He claimed his early musical experience in vaudeville was central to everything he did:

'It was tremendously important . . . to the point, when my sister graduated from college and decided to go into the theatre, . . . I said "the first thing you have to do is get into a school, a dancing school, and work at it until you get some body facility . . .".'

The gloves come off

Although never typecast as a heavy by the studio, Cagney was not completely happy within the contract system at Warners. Like Bette Davis and Olivia de Havilland, his dissatisfaction took various forms. There was first the question of salary. His films were usually cheaply made and highly profitable at the box-office, but no matter what the studio's profit,

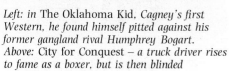

Left: in The Oklahoma Kid, *Cagney's first Western, he found himself pitted against his former gangland rival Humphrey Bogart. Above:* City for Conquest – *a truck driver rises to fame as a boxer, but is then blinded*

Above: Cagney as a Pepsi-Cola salesman in One, Two, Three *in 1961. His next role as the New York police commissioner in* Ragtime *was not until 1981*

he took home the same $1400 a week. He said:

'A player should be in a position to demand what he is worth so long as he is worth it. When his box-office value drops, his earnings should be lopped off accordingly.'

A dispute ensued: he left Hollywood and threatened to give up acting, sacrificing several parts which made other actors into stars – in particular the Paul Muni role in *I Am a Fugitive From a Chain Gang* (1932). Warners finally gave him a new contract beginning at $3000 with stated increases up to $4500 a week. Then there was the question of studio dictated material and the number of films he was required to make each year. He fought and won a court action which freed him to work anywhere he liked. For Grand National, an independent company, he made two films – *Great Guy* (1936) and *Something to Sing About* (1937) – neither of which had budgets that would allow for first-rate directors nor the production values Warners could provide. Nonetheless, *Great Guy* was popular enough and Cagney returned exclusively to Warners only when a new five-year contract was drawn up providing him with $150,000 and 10 per cent of the gross on each picture he chose to make. Under that contract were made two of his most popular films: *Angels With Dirty Faces* (1938), in which he plays a charming hoodlum whose influence over the local slum kids is stronger than that of a dull but very worthy priest, and *Yankee Doodle Dandy* (1942), the musical biography of George M. Cohan for which Cagney won an Oscar and which he still considers his favourite film.

In 1942, at the end of his Warners contract, Cagney began to freelance, setting up his own production company with his brother William so that he could produce his own films for release through a major studio, or finance films in collaboration with a larger company. This remained the pattern throughout the rest of his career, although he would often sign for a film simply as an actor with a high salary and a percentage of the profits. He never cut his strong ties with Warners but was now able to choose his material, directors and co-stars. He also had original material developed for him, for example, the life of Admiral Halsey, entitled *The Gallant Hours* (1960), which he produced with Robert Montgomery who also directed.

Out like a lion

His next film was Billy Wilder's *One, Two, Three* (1961), in which he plays a highly volatile, blustering, soft-drink executive who tries to sell his beverage and 'the American way of life' to East Berlin. In many ways it marked a return to the old Warners period (although not produced there). This comedy rattles along at breakneck speed as if it had been shot and edited at his old studio in the Thirties. That pace suited Cagney's particular talents as he raced through dialogue, often shouting it at the top of his voice. His performance has so much furious energy that one is somehow whisked along by him even in those places where Wilder's comic invention seems to flag.

Since then Cagney has rarely acted again. He was almost tempted to play Alfred Doolittle in Warners' *My Fair Lady* (1964) but only returned to the screen in Miloš Forman's *Ragtime* (1981). Nonetheless he has been content to divide his time mostly between his farm on Martha's Vineyard in Massachusetts, and his houses in Beverly Hills, Switzerland and New York.

'In this business you need enthusiasm. I don't have the enthusiasm for acting any more. Acting is not the beginning and the end of everything.'   DAVID OVERBEY

Quotations from: The Films of James Cagney *by Homer Dickens, Citadel Press, 1972;* Don't Say Yes Until I Finish Talking *by Mel Gussow, Pocket Books; NFT John Player interview, London, 23 November 1958.*

Filmography
1930 Sinner's Holiday; The Doorway to Hell (GB: A Handful of Clouds); Steel Highway/Other Men's Women; Intimate Interview (short). **'31** The Public Enemy (GB: Enemies of the Public); The Millionaire; Smart Money; Practice Shots (short); Blonde Crazy (GB: Larceny Lane). **'32** Taxi!; The Crowd Roars; Winner Takes All. **'33** Hard to Handle; Picture Snatcher; The Mayor of Hell; Footlight Parade; Lady Killer; Hollywood on Parade No 8 (short). **'34** Jimmy the Gent; He Was Her Man; Here Comes the Navy; The Hollywood Gad-About (short); The St Louis Kid (GB: A Perfect Weekend). **'35** A Trip Thru a Hollywood Studio (short); Devil Dogs of the Air; G-Men; The Irish in Us; A Midsummer Night's Dream; Frisco Kid; Ceiling Zero. **'36** Great Guy (GB: Pluck of the Irish). **'37** Something to Sing About. **'38** Boy Meets Girl; Angels with Dirty Faces; For Auld Lang Syne (short). **'39** The Oklahoma Kid; Each Dawn I Die; The Roaring Twenties. **'40** The Fighting 69th; Torrid Zone. **'41** City for Conquest; The Strawberry Blonde; The Bride Came C.O.D. **'42** Captains of the Clouds; Yankee Doodle Dandy. **'43** You. John Jones (short); Johnny Come Lately (GB: Johnny Vagabond); Show Business at War (short). **'44** Battle Stations (short). **'45** Blood on the Sun. **'46** 13 Rue Madeleine. **'48** The Time of Your Life. **'49** White Heat. **'50** The West Point Story (GB: Fine and Dandy); Kiss Tomorrow Goodbye. **'51** Come Fill the Cup; Starlift (guest). **'52** What Price Glory. **'53** A Lion Is in the Streets. **'55** Run for Cover; Love Me or Leave Me; Mister Roberts; The Seven Little Foys (guest). **'56** Tribute to a Bad Man; These Wilder Years. **'57** Man of a Thousand Faces; Short Cut to Hell (dir; +guest). **'59** Never Steal Anything Small; Shake Hands with the Devil (GB). **'60** The Gallant Hours. **'61** One, Two, Three. **'62** The Road to the Wall (narr. only). **'66** Ballad of Smokey Bear (cartoon; voice only). **'67** Arizona Bushwhackers (narr. only). **'81** Ragtime.

GRAND HOTEL

HOLLYWOOD'S FIRST ALL-STAR SPECTACULAR

Herman Shumlin, an experienced Broadway producer. He stipulated that the film should not be shown until the play closed or until 15 months after its opening in November 1930. This left MGM plenty of time to work out a script, assign the artists and build up publicity for the film.

Fejos did not direct *Grand Hotel*. Thalberg tested him for it by assigning him to *The Great Lover* (1931) but then withdrew him – and that was the end of Fejos's more-than-promising Hollywood career. Thalberg next considered using Lewis Milestone, fresh from his success with *All Quiet on the Western Front* (1930), but eventually decided on Edmund Goulding, an English-born director and former writer who had made several films for MGM. The $700,000 budget was well above average but not unprecedented: what made the film an unusual production was its galaxy of stars.

Fans camped outside the Palace Theatre the night before *Grand Hotel* opened in London and contemporary critics were delighted with the film. Mordaunt Hall, writing in the *New York Times*, said, 'It is a production thoroughly worthy of all the talk it has created.' C.A. Lejeune wrote in *The Observer*:

'To see Garbo in a fine new freedom of mood – even her poses have broken down their old contours – balanced by a Barrymore who has forgotten his mannerisms; to see Wallace Beery in full control of his vast ebullience, and Crawford turning her slick youth to grim and logical purpose; to see Lionel Barrymore suddenly towering . . . over the rest of the cast – to be given all this in one film, is good measure for any audience, but a measure that reserves its special bouquet for the movie connoisseur.'

Garbo's performance – it is here she sobs 'I want to be alone' – was judged flawless by most contemporary critics: '. . . the essence of a fragrant and exquisite disappointment' (*Arts Weekly*, 1932). We now know she can do better, and it has been suggested since that Joan Crawford steals the film from her. Both are more effective than their male co-stars: John Barrymore's account of his role now seems particularly specious; Lew Stone and Jean Hersholt, two stalwart MGM character actors cast in minor roles, provide more than adequate support for the stars, however.

The fates of the characters devised by Miss Baum and MGM's scenarists are perhaps less important than the film's atmosphere – which was largely created by Cedric Gibbons's art deco interiors. Above all, Goulding and MGM sought to convey a 'German' feel – though it is only with difficulty today that we can imagine ourselves in Berlin. The brittle, detached quality borrowed from the German cinema, which once seemed a virtue when most films were sentimental, sits oddly on this wholly American product, and *Grand Hotel* now appears rather dusty.

DAVID SHIPMAN

Few all-star specials had emerged from Hollywood before MGM's *Grand Hotel* brought together Greta Garbo, Joan Crawford, Wallace Beery and the Barrymore brothers to portray characters whose lives are dramatically interwoven as they pass through a stylish Berlin hotel. The film popularized the multi-stranded, star-laden movie – it was immediately followed by the Studio's *Dinner at Eight* (1933) which, in its souvenir programme, claimed *twelve* stars.

Menschen im Hotel (People in a Hotel), the novel on which *Grand Hotel* was based, was published in 1929. It followed a number of cross-section studies of Berlin low-life, by

painters, cartoonists, novelists and film-makers, that were very popular in Germany in the Twenties. Vicki Baum, author of *Menschen im Hotel*, had worked as a parlour-maid for six weeks in a Berlin hotel in order to get authentic material for her book.

The novel was an instant success and a dramatization appeared on the Berlin stage in 1930. This was *not* a success, but MGM's property-finder, Kate Corbaley, read a short newspaper article about the play and sent for a copy. Paul Fejos, a newly-contracted director, was the first to read it and had the studio

pursue the stage and screen rights, only to find they had been sold by Miss Baum to an agent, Dr Edmund Pawker, for $4500. He had recently arrived in New York and was to co-produce the play with Harry Moses, a manufacturer of ladies' underwear. Mr Moses had seen the play performed in Berlin and considered it an ideal property for launching his wife on a theatrical career. MGM secured the film rights for a $15,000 contribution to the New York production, with an equal amount from Moses.

After one rehearsal Mrs Moses dropped out. MGM then brought in

---

Directed by Edmund Goulding, 1932
Prod co: MGM. **dir:** Edmund Goulding. **sc:** William A. Drake, and Frances Marion (uncredited), adapted from novel *Menschen im Hotel* by Vicki Baum. **photo:** William Daniels. **ed:** Blanche Sewell. **art dir:** Cedric Gibbons. **cost:** Adrian. **mus:** Herbert Stothart. **rec eng:** Douglas Shearer. **ass dir:** Charles Dorian. **r/t:** 112 min. New York premiere, 12 April 1932.
Cast: Greta Garbo (*Grusinskaya*), John Barrymore (*Baron Felix von Gaigern*), Joan Crawford (*Flaemmchen*), Wallace Beery (*Preysing*), Lionel Barrymore (*Otto Kringelein*), Lewis Stone (*Dr Otternschlag*), Jean Hersholt (*Senf*), Robert McWade (*Meierheim*), Purnell D. Pratt (*Zinnowitz*), Ferdinand Gottschalk (*Pimenov*), Rafaela Ottiano (*Suzette*), Tully Marshall (*Gerstenkorn*), Morgan Wallace (*Schweinke, the chauffeur*), Frank Conroy (*Rohna*), Murray Kinnell (*Schweimann*), Edwin Maxwell (*Dr Waitz*), Mary Carlisle (*honeymooner*), John Davidson (*hotel manager*), Sam McDaniel (*bartender*), Rolfe Sedan, Herbert Evans (*clerks*), Lee Phelps (*extra*).

1

2

3

Grusinskaya, a ballerina whose popularity has waned, books in at the hotel (1) and is soon seen languishing in her room. She will not wear her pearls, believing that they have brought her bad luck (2), and the impoverished Baron von Gaigern sets out to steal them.

Meanwhile, Preysing, who has checked in to settle a business deal upon which his survival depends, attracts Flaemmchen, one of the hotel's stenographers. She has decided there are quicker ways to a mink coat than taking shorthand.

Grusinskaya, still in her tutu after another unhappy performance (3), interrupts the Baron who has had to hide quickly in her room after taking the pearls. Seeing that she is seriously contemplating suicide he hastily comes out of hiding. He explains his presence by claiming to be an admirer but soon realizes he is in love with her (4).

He returns the pearls, she falls in love with him and they plan to go away to start a new life.

The dying Kringelein, Preysing's former clerk, has befriended the Baron but the latter steals from him – once again returning his prize, this time from remorse.

Desperate for money, the Baron then attempts to rob Preysing who catches him in the act and kills him with the telephone (5). Flaemmchen, who has been with Preysing (6), tells Kringelein and he takes revenge on his former employer, calling the police to arrest Preysing (7). Kringelein and Flaemmchen, now thrown together, discuss their future and decide to leave for Paris.

Grusinskaya leaves the hotel happily, still expecting to meet the Baron. The hotel doctor checks in at the desk that morning but there is no news for him and he complains that nothing ever happens at the hotel.

4

5

6

7

Hollywood's Boy Wonder
Irving Thalberg

Irving Thalberg and Sam Marx met at Universal's studios in New York when Thalberg was 19 and Marx 16. They remained friends until Thalberg's death. In 1930 Sam Marx was working as a Broadway reporter when Thalberg, vice-president in charge of film production at MGM, invited him to the studio where he became story editor. Marx, who went on to produce many Hollywood films and is still working as a scriptwriter, talks here about the man he knew as a colleague and friend.

By the time Irving Grant Thalberg reached the age of 20 he was already known in Hollywood as 'the Boy Wonder'. This frail, soft-spoken youth, born in Brooklyn in 1899, was an executive producer in the film industry before that title was even invented. He was better at the job than all who followed, and it is doubtful if he will ever be equalled.

Thalberg suffered throughout his short life from a rheumatic heart condition. As a child he spent long weeks in bed, reading incessantly and developing an appreciation of good writing. This was to have its rewards; he became a master in the art of recognizing film potential in properties suggested for the screen. Sometimes a single sentence from a book or play was all that Thalberg needed to see before deciding whether or not it would be suitable for a full-length feature.

Above: Thalberg married Norma Shearer in 1927. When they first met the star thought MGM's 'boy wonder' was the office junior

He was 19 when Carl Laemmle, president of Universal, promoted him from his personal secretary to executive in charge of production. Thalberg gained his early 'Boy Wonder' reputation through the quality of the films he produced. He also earned considerable respect for his action in challenging the imperious director Erich von Stroheim.

It was at Universal that he first encountered Stroheim, firing him from *Merry-Go-Round* (1923) for his extravagance. But a few years later at MGM Thalberg refused to allow Louis B. Mayer to fire Stroheim from *The Merry Widow* (1925) – and the film was a success.

Youth at the helm

Thalberg left Universal in 1922 when Laemmle's daughter displayed unwelcome matrimonial intentions. He also felt that his job was not challenging enough and his salary too low. He went to work for the independent Louis B. Mayer, an ambitious and ruthless administrator who, realizing his own shortcomings as a producer, offered a vice-presidency to Thalberg. Then began a tandem sovereignship over MGM (formed in 1924 when Mayer merged his concern with Loew's Metro and the Goldwyn companies to become Metro-Goldwyn-Mayer) which eventually placed that studio in front of all its Hollywood rivals. Mayer was chief studio executive; Thalberg, his second-in-command, supervised film production at the Culver City lot.

Until differences arose between him and Mayer, Thalberg applied a tough and carefully reasoned policy:

Above left: the success of The Merry Widow *justified Thalberg's belief in the talent of Erich von Stroheim. Left: Thalberg's doubts about shooting parts of* Ben Hur *in Italy were ignored and the film proved a costly triumph*

Above: the great producer put everything into making Romeo and Juliet *(1936) – including his 32-year-old wife as the 14-year-old heroine*

'In a business in which few men had the courage of their convictions, I decided that if I made them do things my way they would never know if their way would have been better.'

He avoided using anyone who opposed his authority, though talented craftsmen in all aspects of picture-making received unfailing loyalty if they conformed to his methods.

Thalberg also avoided using directors who wanted to write their own scripts and have total control over their films, insisting that only scriptwriters did the scriptwriting. He never wrote a word himself and, unless invited, never went on the set of a film.

Thalberg was never averse to the profit motive of film-making, but he firmly believed higher profits followed higher quality. He strove to improve every picture with which he was involved. He would emerge from well-received previews still determined on revisions and retakes. MGM even became known as 'Mayer's Valley of Retakes' in Thalberg's time – but it should be noted that his instinct for improvement was markedly superior to that of his contemporaries at his own and rival studios in Hollywood.

The star-maker

The great young producer used the star system – which had evolved before he came to Hollywood – with outstanding success. He fostered the careers of Greta Garbo, Clark Gable, Joan Crawford, Jean Harlow, Spencer Tracy, Robert Taylor, Norma Shearer (whom he married in 1927 and helped to the top of the film star popularity polls) and others. Many were relatively unknown before he lifted them to stardom. To maintain their success he insisted on careful story selection, appropriate co-stars and top directors. Thalberg believed it the duty of motion pictures to entertain

('Entertainment is Thalberg's god', said the writer Charles MacArthur) and enthrall the money-paying public – and he therefore showcased his stars in pictures characterized by polish, glamour and style. To this end he provided the finest available experts in makeup, wardrobe, cinematography and art direction. Not all of his films were star-laden prestige vehicles, however; he produced the first all-negro feature, *Hallelujah* (1929), and ventured into the unglamorous world of circus sideshows with *Freaks* (1932).

'The public makes the stars', said Thalberg, and he claimed to sense the star potential in minor players by judging audience reactions to them. He was also convinced that there were no has-beens among actors. 'Once a champion, always a champion', he insisted, and proved it by regaining stardom for Marie Dressler, Wallace Beery and William Powell, who had all suffered from waning popularity. Thalberg was not infallible: he failed to resurrect the career of silent star John Gilbert which had declined with the coming of sound.

Down but not out

Thalberg's position at MGM changed early in 1933 shortly after he suffered a serious heart attack. He and Mayer had already fallen out. Mayer was jealous of Thalberg's control over film production and Thalberg resented Mayer's more substantial share of the profits. Although Thalberg remained a major producer, he was forced to share his responsibilities with others – notably David O. Selznick who was given equal status as an inducement to join the studio. Other producers came to MGM and Thalberg no longer supervised the complete programme. Among the many great films he had made as production supervisor were *The Big Parade*, *Ben Hur* (both 1925); *The Broadway Melody* (1929); *Min and Bill* (1930); *The Champ*, *Trader Horn* (both 1931); *Grand Hotel*, *Red-Headed Woman*, *Tarzan the Ape Man*, and *Rasputin and the Empress* (all 1932).

He returned from a long holiday in Europe after his heart attack to resume work at MGM but now only controlled one production unit. During his absence, MGM's roster of stars was utilized in films produced by men under Mayer's control. Thalberg was unable to cast in his films many of those whose careers he had hitherto guided. His first year back was frustrating and most of his productions fell below his earlier standards. But as the stars became available to him again, his fortunes improved. He made a new series of box-office hits including *The Barretts of Wimpole Street*

Above: MGM was sued for its version of the murder of Rasputin – Thalberg was not afraid of controversial subjects. Below: with A Night at the Opera *he revived the Marx Brothers*

(1934) with Shearer and Laughton; *Mutiny on the Bounty* (1935) with Gable and Laughton; *Camille* (1936) with Garbo and Taylor; and *The Good Earth* (1937) with Luise Rainer and Paul Muni. He also revived the faltering Marx Brothers in their greatest hit *A Night at the Opera* (1935). But Thalberg's triumphs were cut short by illness again.

The prince of producers

By then, MGM's producers – Thalberg excepted – were identifying themselves on the credit titles of their films. The shy, modest Thalberg had shunned personal publicity throughout his career (even though his marriage to Shearer meant that fan adulation greeted every public appearance) and none of his 600 films bears his name. 'Credit you give yourself isn't worth having', he maintained. But he received credit from most people he worked with. 'As long as Irving lives we're all great men', said one who had enjoyed the benefits of Thalberg's supervision. But in September 1936 Thalberg died. He was just 37.

A year later the Academy of Motion Picture Arts and Sciences decided on the annual presentation of an Irving G. Thalberg Memorial Award: 'To be given to a creative producer whose work reflects a consistently high quality of motion picture production comparable to that of the man whose name it bears.' But since inaugurating the award the Academy has often had to struggle to find producers whose achievements match Thalberg's triumphs, and on as many as 17 occasions has failed to find anyone worthy of the honour.
SAMUEL MARX

Children of the Night

'Listen to them…children of the night…what music they make.' Count Dracula on the baying wolves that prowl outside his castle grounds could equally well refer to the directors and stars who composed those incomparable masterpieces of the American cinema – the horror films of the Thirties

Horror movies are almost as old as the cinema itself. Primitive, heavily abridged versions of *Dr Jekyll and Mr Hyde* and *Frankenstein* were made in America in 1908 and 1910 respectively. Vampires appeared – in *The Vampire* – in 1911, and three years later Edgar Allan Poe's short stories, *The Tell-Tale Heart* and *The Pit and the Pendulum*, provided inspiration for D.W. Griffith's grisly *The Avenging Conscience*. But the first mature horror films came from the pre-war German cinema which, reviving the dark romantic spirit of E.T.A. Hoffmann's stories of the supernatural and demonic, laid the groundwork for its later Expressionist triumphs with early versions of *Der Student von Prag* (1913, The Student of Prague) and *Der Golem* (1914, The Golem).

Beauties, beasts and boffins
Then, in 1919, in Germany, Robert Wiene's *Das Kabinett des Dr Caligari* (The Cabinet of Dr Caligari) drew up what was to become virtually a blueprint for a specifically cinematic horror genre. Cesare, the somnambulist invoked by the evil Dr Caligari to murder those who sneer at his work, is sent to kill the pretty heroine in her bedroom. Instead, hesitating before her beauty, the black-garbed sleepwalker steals away with her over the rooftops into the night – trailing white draperies in a sequence of weird grace. All this takes place against a painted backdrop of tortured angles and shadows.

These three characters – the mad doctor, the monster he has created, and the girl they terrorize – were to become the key figures in Hollywood horror. The ghost-ridden *angst* of defeated, depressed Germany after World War I was, however, a far cry from the euphoria of America in the Twenties. *The Cabinet of Dr Caligari* and the other great German Expressionist fantasies came to Hollywood's attention just as Broadway, the source of so much of its raw material, was revelling in a profitable vogue for spoof horrors.

Horror films made during the last years of the American silent cinema were condemned to play for laughs (Rex Ingram's *The Magician* of 1926, and Tod Browning's *The Unknown* of 1927 were rare exceptions). At the same time, the Expressionist lesson had clearly been learned: dramatic use of effects of light and shadows could be used to enhance tormented gestures and graceful movements, and a sense of the beauty in horror began to filter through the work of directors like Tod Browning, Roland West, Benjamin Christensen, and especially Paul Leni.

Leni had been an important director and art director in the early German cinema. The first Hollywood film he directed, *The Cat and the Canary* (1927), opens superbly with a hand brushing cobwebs from the screen to reveal the credit titles. Although the plot of this haunted-house movie tends to creak, the supernatural, as conjured up by Leni's camera, became a distinct, alarming possibility. After making only three more, equally atmospheric films, Leni died from blood poisoning in 1929.

The wages of fear
Universal earned its reputation as Hollywood's legendary home of horror with 3 films it made at the beginning of the Thirties. Tod Browning's *Dracula*, released on St Valentine's Day 1931, with Bela Lugosi repeating the role of the bloodsucking Transylvanian Count he had created on Broadway in 1927, soon emerged as the studio's leading contender for money-maker of the year; the gamble that sound would add a new dimension to terror had paid off handsomely. Then came *Frankenstein*, which was originally scheduled to be directed by Robert Florey, but was finally made by James Whale and starred Boris Karloff after Lugosi had refused to appear in a non-speaking

role as the Monster. Released in November 1931, it grossed twice as much at the box-office as *Dracula*. Lugosi and Florey emerged with their consolation prize for missing out on *Frankenstein* when they made *Murders in the Rue Morgue* (1932). It was another major success for Universal though less profitable.

Like *The Cabinet of Dr Caligari*, all three films featured white-robed maidens assailed by mad geniuses and monsters (even if *Dracula* combined the two latter roles into one). And all three had the same atmosphere of dark, fairy-tale magic. Although this special quality was later tapped by other film-makers – Cocteau, for example, in his superlative version of *La*

Above: Bela Lugosi's Hungarian background made him an ideal choice for the Transylvanian Count Dracula. Left: Fredric March as Mr Hyde, the only monster to win an Oscar. Right: Elsa Lanchester played Mary Shelley as well as Karloff's intended in The Bride of Frankenstein.

Belle et la Bête (1945, *Beauty and the Beast*) – it disappeared when Hammer Films decorated its horror revival of the Fifties and Sixties with a splash of blood and amputated limbs. Ironically, the enduring charm and fantasy of the Universal tradition was thereby ensured.

The beautiful and the damned

Soon mad geniuses were everywhere: busily hypnotizing heroines in *Svengali* (1931), fashioning murderous hands from synthetic flesh in *Doctor X* (1932), modelling human waxworks in *The Mystery of the Wax Museum* (1933), creating man-beasts in *Island of Lost Souls* (1933), and animating fiendish manikins

in *The Devil Doll* (1936). Meanwhile a bizarre assortment of beasts, from Frankenstein's Monster to King Kong himself, were impelled to pursue Beauty in a forlorn, foredoomed hope that they might turn out to be the long-awaited prince.

In addition to this fairy-tale element, another factor that contributed to the mythical status of horror films was their underlying appeal to post-Depression dissatisfaction with authority. Many of these films implied a desire to rise up against the authoritarian regimes that callously curtailed man's inalienable freedom to pursue happiness. Enclosed by a prologue and an epilogue in which the Doctor is shown to be

Above left: the complex plot of The Black Cat *had virtually nothing to do with Poe's short story. Above: Lugosi on the prowl in* Dracula, *which at least paid lip-service to Bram Stoker's original novel*

the sinisterly benevolent director of a lunatic asylum and all the other characters to be inmates, *The Cabinet of Dr Caligari* was the product of a similar mood of oppression in post-war Germany. It is governed, as the film's scriptwriters Carl Mayer and Hans Janowitz have observed, by Mayer's brushes with an army psychiatrist who diagnosed his rebellious attitude to authority as mental instability, and

by Janowitz's obsessive conviction that undetected and unrepentant murderers were roaming the streets by their thousand.

The legacy of all this as far as the horror genre is concerned, is that the films present, in microcosm, a world of dictatorial authority in which any straying from the norm is regarded as monstrous, intolerable behaviour to be rejected in disgust and ruthlessly exterminated. In *Frankenstein*, newly born from electrodes harnessing the elemental power of an electrical storm, Dr Frankenstein's creature ecstatically raises his face and hands to the warmth of the sun; it is only after encountering the implacable hostility and incomprehension of his fellow-beings in authority over him that he becomes a monster. In *King Kong* (1933), daring to aspire to love and beauty, Kong is hunted down and killed by outraged society. The monster in the great horror movies is the classic hero: Byronic, misbegotten, misjudged.

The quest for sanity

The few classic horror films that escape the madman-monster-maiden format also drew their power from this vision of the world as a lunatic asylum in which a tiny oasis of sanity and innocence must be fought for and preserved. It takes only a very small stretch of the imagination to see Count Zaroff (Leslie Banks), a hunter and disciple of De Sade who likes to titillate his jaded palate by pursuing human prey in *The Most Dangerous Game* (1932, also known as *The Hounds of Zaroff*), as a prototype Führer. In *Island of Lost Souls*, adapted from an H.G. Wells story, Dr Moreau (Charles Laughton) – like Zaroff, another megalomaniac figure – finally gets his comeuppance from the mutants he has sadistically crossbred; they rise against him in a peasant's revolt. *The Black Cat* (1934), set in a marble mansion built over the fort where thousands of men were betrayed and killed in World War I, concerns two men left morally dead by their experiences of war.

The Men Behind the Monsters

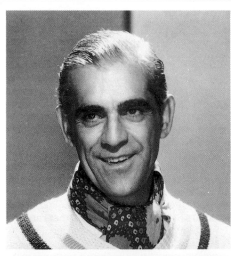

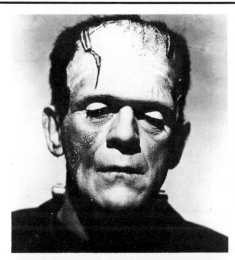

Lon Chaney was originally chosen for the lead role in *Dracula* (1931). When he died in August 1930, less than two months after the release of his first and only sound film, *The Unholy Three*, Bela Lugosi inherited the part – but not Chaney's mantle as the undisputed king of horror. That honour went to the Englishman Boris Karloff (1887–1969), an actor of intelligence, elegance, and a much greater range.

Lugosi (1882–1956), though very proud of his stage background in his native Hungary where he played in Shakespeare, Shaw, Wilde and Ibsen, was basically a ham, best remembered for the impressive, but somewhat absurd, oratory of his first two lines in *Dracula*: 'I am Dracula! I bid you welcome', and, referring to the wolves howling outside, 'Listen to them . . . children of the night . . . what music they make'. In *Frankenstein* (1931), Karloff hardly seems to be acting at all, but his eyes, huge pools of pain, and his dangling hands, uncertain whether to plead or to strangle, speak volumes. In contrast, Lugosi's only attempt at the Monster, in *Frankenstein Meets the Wolf Man* (1943), is risibly overplayed. But cast opposite Karloff for the first time in Edgar Ulmer's *The Black Cat* (1934), and for once in a sympathetic role, Lugosi gives what is probably his best performance. He is forced into restraint by Karloff and matches the master's subtleties.

Peter Lorre's chief assets for acting in horror films were his sinister baby face and whiningly caressing voice. He arrived in Hollywood a little late to partake in the first great days of horror, though he was memorable as Dr Gogol in *Mad Love* (1935). Lorre (1904–64) worked only occasionally at Universal and never with Whale or Browning. Condemned for most of the Thirties to appear in a series of routine thrillers and horrors, invariably providing their brightest moments, he came into his own in the Forties, perfecting the idiosyncratic brand of menace he had displayed earlier with Lang in Germany and Hitchcock in England.

Top: Boris Karloff – Frankenstein's Monster
Centre: Bela Lugosi – Count Dracula
Bottom: Peter Lorre – Dr Gogol

Now given over to devil worship, betrayer (Boris Karloff), and a surviving victim (Bela Lugosi), are locked in a duel over an innocent girl – ended when the arsenal concealed in the fort explodes. Weaving an almost abstract web of anguish out of its sense of all-pervasive evil, *The Black Cat* is surely one of the bleakest indictments of war and its spiritual aftermath to have emerged from any studio.

Tales from other crypts

Universal's success was not allowed to go unchallenged. *Svengali*, for instance, was a Warner Brothers film, the first of two in which John Barrymore confirmed the gift for outlandish characterization he had revealed in his *Dr Jekyll and Mr Hyde* of 1920. But Warners lacked directors like Whale and Browning who had a real flair for horror. Michael Curtiz, who directed the second Barrymore vehicle, *The Mad Genius* (1931), went on to make *Doctor X* and *The Mystery of the Wax Museum*; these films are workmanlike rather than inspired by the breath of dark poetry and Warners' challenge to Universal's supremacy faded away.

Other studios contributed occasional films. Paramount made *Island of Lost Souls* and Rouben Mamoulian's superb *Dr Jekyll and Mr Hyde* (1931), the only version to have really investigated the underlying sexuality in Stevenson's story. MGM terrified itself with its own daring in using real circus freaks – midgets, pinheads, a living torso, a half-man, a frog-man, an armless woman – in Tod Browning's widely banned *Freaks* (1932), but the studio did let Browning loose again, on *The*

Devil Doll. MGM finally retreated into respectability with a staid *Dr Jekyll and Mr Hyde* (1941) which, despite the implications of a dream sequence that has Spencer Tracy whipping Ingrid Bergman and Lana Turner harnessed to a chariot, was sexually whitewashed compared with the Mamoulian film. RKO, later to usurp Universal's leadership with Val

Above: in Frankenstein, *the poignant meeting of the Monster and the little girl is followed by the discovery of her death at his hands – and implications of far worse*

Lewton's excellent series of low-budget features celebrating the horrors that are sensed rather than seen, produced *The Most Dangerous Game* (1932) and the immortal *King Kong* (1933). But RKO also drowned their remake of *The Hunchback of Notre Dame* (1939) and star Charles Laughton (in the role which had made a star of Lon Chaney in Universal's marvellous 1923 original) in a deluge of spectacle.

Universal decline

Apart from Mr Hyde, Quasimodo was the only monster who did not belong to Universal in the Thirties. But although the studio retained the services of Dracula, Frankenstein's Monster, the Invisible Man, the Wolf Man, the Mummy, and the Phantom of the Opera, it never really discovered new directors to match Whale and Browning. Karl Freund, a great cameraman of the German Expressionist cinema, had been given a chance to direct, but *The Mummy* (1932) is excruciatingly dull – apart from the one eerie moment when Boris Karloff comes back to life. *Mad Love* (1935, MGM), the only other film Freund directed, is memorable chiefly for Peter Lorre's macabre performance as the mad, bald-headed, glassy-eyed Dr Gogol who gives Orlac new hands – those of a knife-murderer. Subsequently, with rare exceptions like Rowland V. Lee's stylishly architectural *Son of Frankenstein* (1939) and Robert Siodmak's spooky *Son of Dracula* (1943), Universal came to rely on studio workhorses and top cameramen who produced often enjoyable but pallid imitations of the characters and images created by Whale and Browning.

There was also the problem of scripts. In his autobiography, playwright and scriptwriter R.C. Sherriff recalls how he was hired to write the script of *The Invisible Man* (1933) for Whale. He asked Universal for a copy of H.G. Wells's novel but was instead given a stack of scripts which had been developed and rejected in turn – and in which the original character had been

James Whale

Born in Dudley in 1889, Whale was an Englishman whose career as a stage actor and producer brought him to New York in the late Twenties. He became a film director after directing dialogue on *Hell's Angels* (1930). Although he made only four horror films, they remain Universal's unmatched masterpieces. *Frankenstein* (1931), the first and best known, is also, for all its sombre visual beauty and archetypal quality, the least successful. Whale was most at home with comedy of manners in which he could express his yearning for gracious living and at the same time puncture it with malicious wit. It is possible that Whale, a working-class boy who made good, was compensating for his dubious upper-crust position in society. In his horror films the results are irresistible: the waspishly effeminate Horace Femm in *The Old Dark House* (1932), serenely observing the social niceties in a household that includes a mute, drunken giant of a butler, a killer with a knife, and a pyromaniac; the unseen hero of *The Invisible Man* (1933), gloating over his new-found power but lamenting that an invisible man must be hungry, naked, and spotlessly clean; the frizz-wigged, adder-tongued woman created for the Monster in *The Bride of Frankenstein* (1935), glancing at her intended mate and hissing with dismay. Without ever jeopardizing the grave beauty he found in horror, Whale was able to laugh long before the audience began.

Right: Claude Rains in The Invisible Man

Filmography
1929 The Love Doctor (dial.dir.only). **'30** Hell's Angels (dial.dir.only); Journey's End (USA/GB). **'31** Waterloo Bridge; Frankenstein. **'32** The Impatient Maiden; The Old Dark House. **'33** The Invisible Man; The Kiss Before the Mirror; By Candlelight. **'34** One More River (GB: Over the River). **'35** The Bride of Frankenstein; Remember Last Night? **'36** Show Boat. **'37** The Road Back; The Great Garrick. **'38** Sinners in Paradise; Port of Seven Seas; Wives Under Suspicion. **'39** The Man in the Iron Mask; Green Hell. **'41** They Dare Not Love. **'49** *ep* Hello Out There (rest of film released as Face to Face, 1952).

Above: Universal's tortured lycanthrope was largely the creation of Lon Chaney Jr and had little to do with Endore's original werewolf

subjected to increasingly imaginative inflations so that he ended up as an invader from Mars. Sherriff quietly returned to the novel for a script from which Whale made a masterpiece. The inflations, needless to say, began to turn up in sequels. It is small wonder that, by the Forties, Universal's monsters had flitted to Poverty Row studios, became foils for comedy teams like the Bowery Boys or Abbott and Costello, or were packed in three or four to a film, hopefully to provide the requisite thrills. *House of Frankenstein* (1944), for example, brought together the Monster, Dracula and the Wolf Man.

Shadows of the originals
Both the lasting power and the severe limitations of the Universal tradition are perhaps most keenly indicated by the failure of that studio and its imitators to translate the major source novels of the horror film with any measure of adequacy. Mary Shelley's *Frankenstein*, for example, has an astonishing epic sweep, ending in a kind of frozen eternity with the Monster being endlessly pursued across icy arctic wastes by its despairing creator: an image that no one has ever faithfully committed to film. Bram Stoker's *Dracula* is invariably adulterated so badly that the character of Renfield, the Count's acolyte, and his education in bloodlust as he progresses from eating flies and spiders to birds, is always rendered meaningless. And Guy Endore's superb novel, *The Werewolf of Paris*, has never been filmed with any fidelity whatsoever. All the Wolf Man films ignore the novel's historical and religious account of the evolution of the werewolf, as well as Endore's ironic vision of how a werewolf's savagery pales into insignificance when compared to the barbarisms committed by man upon man during times of stress (here during the siege of Paris in 1870). Doubtless for copyright reasons, Universal created its own distinctly inferior Wolf Man myth – *The Werewolf of London* (1935), *The Wolf Man* (1941) – which has been slavishly followed ever since.

Nothing is more indicative of the way Universal and the horror movie ran out of creative steam than the emergence of Lon Chaney Jr as the all-purpose replacement for Boris Karloff in the early Forties. Even in his worst films, Karloff was an actor of rare quality: Chaney Jr was not – but by then the films, endlessly churning over old ground, did not ask him to be.

TOM MILNE

Tod Browning

More solemn than James Whale, Browning was interested in the freakish psychopathic nature of his characters rather than in their picturesque possibilities. Born in Louisville, Kentucky, in 1880, he ran away from school to become a circus performer and then entered films as an actor in 1913. He had already started to direct his own films when he assisted D.W. Griffith in *Intolerance* (1916).

Browning's best work was done during the Twenties in a string of films with Lon Chaney, who always tried to provide his monsters with a basis of psychological realism. The climax of their association was *The Unknown* (1927), in which Chaney, hiding out in a circus disguised as an armless knife-thrower, decides to have his arms amputated to remove the thumb-prints which would convict him of murder. Having thus escaped justice, he also happily congratulates himself that as the disturbed girl whom he desires (played by Joan Crawford) cannot bear to be held by a man, she will now be able to love him.

A horrifying and utterly convincing exercise in sado-masochism, *The Unknown* was surpassed in intensity only by *Freaks* (1932). This film is a nightmarish collision between normality and abnormality. Olga Baclanova plays a trapeze artiste who marries a dwarf for his money, planning to poison him with the aid of her strong-man lover. As a result she is subjected to hideous mutilation by the vengeful circus freaks – they turn her into a chicken. Browning presents the closed world of the freaks with immense sympathy and clearly shows the human emotions beneath their inhuman forms so that these misshapen men and women seem more 'normal' than the 'normal' characters. After disastrous premieres *Freaks* was banned in some States and eventually 'lost' in MGM's vaults. It was not seen in Britain for over 30 years.

Below: Browning surrounded by the circus freaks who starred in his and MGM's most controversial film.

In the rest of his sound films Browning was stylish but patchy. Magnificent moments, like Lugosi's first appearance on the steps of his castle in *Dracula* (1931), the concentrated eeriness in the misty churchyard at the beginning of *Mark of the Vampire* (1935), and the Lilliputian assassin in *The Devil Doll* (1936) methodically scaling a giant dressing table in search of a hat pin as her murder weapon, are followed by disastrous drops in temperature. Especially after *Freaks*, Browning was prevented by cinema conventions from probing the psychological motivations and scars he found interesting. He retired early and though his death was announced in 1944, he did not in fact die until 1962.

Filmography (films as director)
1915 The Lucky Transfer; The Slave Girl; An Image of the Past; The Highbinders; The Story of a Story; The Spell of the Poppy; The Electric Alarm; The Living Death; The Burned Hand; The Woman From Warren's; Little Marie. **'16** Puppets; Everybody's Doing It!; The Deadly Glass of Beer/The Fatal Glass of Beer. **'17** Jim Bludso (co-dir; +co-sc); A Love Sublime (co-dir); Hands Up! (co-dir); Peggy, the Will o' the Wisp; The Jury of Fate. **'18** The Eyes of Mystery; The Legion of Death; Revenge; Which Woman; The Deciding Kiss; The Brazen Beauty; Set Free (+sc). **'19** The Wicked Darling; The Exquisite Thief; The Unpainted Woman; A Petal on the Current; Bonnie, Bonnie Lassie (+co-sc). **'20** The Virgin of Stamboul (+co-sc). **'21** Outside the Law (+prod; +co-sc); No Woman Knows (+co-sc). **'22** The Wise Kid; The Man Under Cover; Under Two Flags (+co-adap). **'23** Drifting (+co-sc); The Day of Faith; White Tiger (+co-sc). **'24** The Dangerous Flirt (GB: A Dangerous Flirtation); Silk Stocking Sal. **'25** The Unholy Three (+prod); The Mystic; Dollar Down. **'26** The Black Bird; The Road to Mandalay. **'27** The Show (+prod); The Unknown; London After Midnight (+prod) (GB: The Hypnotist). **'28** The Big City (+prod); West of Zanzibar. **'29** Where East is East (+prod); The Thirteenth Chair (+prod). **'30** Outside the Law (+co-sc). **'31** Dracula; The Iron Man (+prod). **'32** Freaks (+prod). **'33** Fast Workers (+prod). **'35** Mark of the Vampire. **'36** The Devil Doll. **'39** Miracles for Sale.

LOOKING FOR A SILVER LINING

Poverty and unemployment were the realities of the Depression, but dreams could be bought – if you could spare a dime for a cinema ticket

At the beginning of the Thirties the Hollywood tycoons did not have to look too hard for a formula to match the mood of their audience. Faith in American capitalism had been badly dented by the Wall Street Crash: millions of citizens were victims of the Depression and of the accompanying unemployment. It was the era of 'Buddy can you spare a dime?' What people needed was a means of escaping, if only temporarily, from the harsh realities of life.

Every kind of film gained a new dimension with the introduction of sound; but one genre, the musical film, appeared to evolve specifically for the purpose of escapism – and that was what Hollywood was in business to provide.

This magical world of the musical was opened up by some of Hollywood's finest directors. Thanks to Mamoulian and Lubitsch, the camera was liberated from its early sound-proof boxes. Lubitsch's *Monte Carlo* (1930) had Jeanette MacDonald in a railway compartment singing 'Beyond the Blue Horizon' while what seemed to be all the peasantry of Europe waved back at her as she passed; in Mamoulian's *Love Me Tonight* (1932) the opening sequence had a footloose camera swooping and swerving over early morning Paris.

To the freedom regained by the cameras and the microphones could now be re-united something at which Hollywood had always excelled – spectacle. The man responsible for the biggest production numbers in the history of the musical was Busby Berkeley. In his peacock displays of female pulchritude nothing was too lavish or extravagant.

From his early films like *42nd Street* and *Footlight Parade* (both 1933) through to the surrealistic *The Gang's All Here* (1943), his choreographic style accurately reflected the shifting moods of the movie-going public.

Perhaps the most significant Berkeley musical of the era was *Gold Diggers of 1933* which was the story of a backstage show foreclosed by the bank. In the space of one number entitled 'Remember My Forgotten Man' Berkeley has his singers and dancers describe the progress of young American men from the trenches of World War I to the dole queues of the early Thirties.

At RKO the musical was not so much an ensemble spectacle as a vehicle for the brilliant duo of Fred Astaire and Ginger Rogers. The titles of their films formed a sort of litany of escapism: *Flying down to Rio* (1933), *The Gay Divorcee* (1934), *Top Hat* (1935), *Shall We Dance?* (1937), and *Carefree* (1938). The perfection of their dancing, the pellucid black and white photography, the excellence of the music and dialogue made every one of their films a must for filmgoers.

There were other avenues of escape available to moviegoers. One of these was the cathartic process of enjoying a good fright. Even in the silent days horror films had something of a vogue, but the addition of sound increased the impact immensely – owls hooted, stairs creaked and heroines screamed. Universal studios led the way with a cycle of horror

talkies in the early Thirties. In their doomed pursuits of beauty and happiness, the movie monsters – *Dracula* (1931), *Frankenstein* (1931) and *The Mummy* (1932) reflected something of the despair of the Depression years.

From this great wave of horror films MGM's *Freaks*, directed by Tod Browning in 1932, earned the distinction of being one of the most censored films in the history of the cinema, on account of its portrayal of malformed human exhibits in a travelling circus show. Highly unusual for its time, *Freaks* suggests a community that, though physically abnormal, is in fact ideal and constitutes a challenge to the 'civilized' normal world of the early Thirties. If any one horror movie undermined that world, however, it was *King Kong*. In a thrilling narrative composed of potent images of destruction, the theme of nature reclaiming 'civilization' emerges as a powerful reaction to the bankruptcy of twentieth-century life. The film enlists our sym-

Top and above: crowds queued on the streets of America's cities for a piece of escapism (here, The Great Ziegfeld, *1936) and for a bite to eat (news photo of a New York bread line from the compilation film* Brother, Can You Spare a Dime? *(1975), Left: even Laurel and Hardy sing for their supper in* Way Out West *(1937), though by this time the economy was on the mend*

pathy for the ape by underscoring the corruption of modern urban man – the hunters, reporters, photographers and the showmen are all targets of abuse.

Laughter, on the other hand, was an equally potent antidote to the Depression blues, and the Thirties was one of the richest decades for film comedies. Laurel and Hardy, originally teamed together in the silent era, had no hesitation in adapting to sound films. Their voices were perfect, especially Hardy's veneer of refinement which he built up from the underlying softness of a Southern accent. No other screen comedians, not even Chaplin, made such subtle and brilliant use of sound. From 50-odd two-reel shorts, they extended their art into features such as *Fra Diavolo* (1933), *Bonnie Scotland* (1935), *Our Relations* (1936), *Way Out West* (1937), *Swiss Miss* (1938) and *A Chump at Oxford* (1940); of these their comic dance routine from *Way Out West* has become a classic scene as has their rendering of 'The Trail of the Lonesome Pine' song.

Their formula was simple. Setting out to be helpful or to do a good job they managed with the best will in the world to reduce all around them to chaos and confusion. They performed each piece of mayhem with a slapstick style that often achieved a dreamlike quality. Such scenes removed the audience so far from the harsh realities of life that they felt able to participate in the orgies of destruction.

The same was also true of W.C. Fields, another comedian who found fulfilment in the sound film.

His destructive sprees – in *If I Had a Million* (1932) where he and Alison Skipworth spend a day ramming and bashing innumerable automobiles – together with his innate hostility towards authority and propriety, made him a hero of the downtrodden despite his screen persona as a misanthrope.

At their best the Marx Brothers' films carried the same anarchic charge and lifted their audiences into a dreamland of wish-fulfilment. Who would not have enjoyed a chance to treat the imperishable Margaret Dumont the way Groucho did? Or to bicycle speedily with Harpo across moonlit glades in pursuit of girls? The brothers took a world weary of Depression and stood it on its head.

Beyond the escapist tendencies of the familiar movie genres and the implicit escapism of the exotic Dietrich and Garbo films, Hollywood made a few bold, if compromised, attempts to deal with the rigours of the Depression.

Warner Brothers took the lead in this sensitive field and the work of two directors, Mervyn LeRoy and William Wellman, gave the studio a reputation for honest, no-punches-pulled film making. Whether the films made at Warners in the early Thirties represented Hollywood's social conscience or appeared as mere sensationalism is a question explored in the next chapter. It is important here, however, to indicate that films like *I am a Fugitive From a Chain Gang* (1932), *Heroes for Sale* (1933) and *Wild Boys of the Road* (1933) attributed the plight of their 'heroes' to the Depression.

Significantly LeRoy's *I Am a Fugitive from a Chain Gang* and Wellman's *Heroes for Sale* both portray war veterans returning to encounter unemployment and falling 'innocently' into crime. *Chain Gang* amounts to an indictment not only of the penal system but of the society that forces its hero, played by Paul Muni, outside the law. *Heroes for Sale* is less clear about its targets, and is therefore a more confused kind of protest film. Richard Barthelmess plays Tom Holmes, a victim of the post-war years who is at root an (American) individualist, frustrated by the contemporary hard times. A muddled, desperate film that is by turns anti-capitalist and anti-communist, *Heroes for Sale* nevertheless provides some memorable images of the dole queue and the bread line. In the final analysis, however, the film affirms its faith in capitalism as a system, singling out crooked capitalists as the villains.

Wellman's next film *Wild Boys of the Road* is reputed to have been inspired by screenings of Nikolai Ekk's *The Road to Life* (1931), a Russian film about roving gangs of youths rendered homeless by the Civil War. *Wild Boys* takes up the same theme, billing it as 'the story of half a million young Americans, neglected, maltreated and marching to hell', pitting innocent youths against seasoned hobos and freight car guards, as the unemployed rode the trains in search of work. When the boys make their home in 'Sewer City' they are raided by police and fight back with stones, an anti-authoritarian gesture that made the film trade jittery. Again, despite the genuine concern with injustice, the film stops short of attacking the social ills and posing new solutions, but it does at least broach the dangerous issues of the day.

By late 1933 the bank scare was over, Franklin D. Roosevelt was elected and the New Deal was being drafted. The movie industry was beginning to recover and to see the box-office value of the new spirit of optimism that had brought FDR to the White House. In future chapters we return to the question of realism and Hollywood's view of the man on the street. For the time being Hollywood had laughed, sung and danced its way through the Depression, with the occasional glance over its shoulder at reality.   BASIL WRIGHT

Above: the epitome of Hollywood's response to the Depression. Below: W.C. Fields and Alison Skipworth prepare to do battle in If I Had a Million. *Bottom: a somewhat rare image from Hollywood films of the early Thirties – unemployed men in* Heroes for Sale

Fay Wray: King Kong's girl

The Screen's favourite screaming lady talks about the part she played in the making of a cinema legend

'When Merian C. Cooper . . . told me I was going to have the tallest, darkest leading man that had ever been in Hollywood, I thought he meant Cary Grant . . . But then he began to describe the idea of *King Kong*.'

It was not difficult, Fay Wray recalls, to establish a relationship with the huge ape even though he was played either by a tiny model or by disembodied, animated limbs:

'It just demanded imagination. It was not difficult if, when you were in the hand, you imagined what's above it – the head and the eyes and the appalling size of it all.'

She emphatically denies that the girl in any way responded to Kong's admiration:

'She had no regard for him – only apprehension. In the last scene, where she's on the ledge of the Empire State Building, all she's concerned about is whether she'll eventually get off it.

'Last year I saw what is called the "uncensored version"; and I was very distressed by the

Two contrasting views of Fay Wray – as the beautiful and terrified Ann Darrow, helpless in Kong's enormous grasp (above right), and (below) looking composed and sophisticated in a studio publicity shot

scene where the monkey is . . . pulling at the girl's clothes . . .

'Originally she was supposed to have fainted; and Kong held her in his hand, turned his head from side to side, looked at her and pulled at her like a little child might pull at a flower petal. There was nothing sensual about it at all. But in this other version, the camera looks down on her as if from his viewpoint, and she is struggling a great deal and it seems as if a rectangular patch of cloth has been superimposed, so that the monkey can pull it away . . . Now everyone I talk to about *King Kong* says, "Oh, the scene where he tries to undress you – that's back in". But no such scene was ever designed.

'*Kong* . . . represents a kind of mythology . . . I like to think of things in a metaphysical sense, and choose to find *that* [in the film] rather than the sensual things that people are now hoping to find in it. There is something extraordinary just in the way that animal looked at the human creature, and it made him a thinking, sensitive, soulful entity that is beautiful.'

Fay Wray's film career began when she was 16. At 21 she played the role of Mitzi in von Stroheim's *The Wedding March* (1928). She remained in films for 15 years after *King Kong*. Her directors included William Wellman, Mauritz Stiller and Josef von Sternberg. Among her leading men were Gary Cooper, Emil Jannings and John Gilbert. Yet her role as Ann Darrow in *King Kong* eclipses all else in her career:

'It has felt strange to become part of a legend . . . but it's better not to try turning away from it, but to realize that there was something lovely about it.'

Filmography
1923 Gasoline Love (short). '25 What Price Goofy (short); No Father to Guide Him (short); The Coast Patrol; A Cinch for the Gander. '26 Lazy Lightning; The Man in the Saddle; The Wild Horse Stampede; Loco Luck; A One Man Game. '27 Spurs and Saddles. '28 The Wedding March; The Legion of the Condemned; The Street of Sin; The First Kiss. '29 The Four Feathers; Painted Heels; Thunderbolt. '30 Behind the Makeup; The Border Legion; Captain Thunder; Paramount on Parade; The Sea God; The Texan (GB: The Big Race). '31 The Finger Points; The Conquering Horde; Not Exactly Gentlemen (GB: The Three Rogues); Dirigible; The Lawyer's Secret; The Unholy Garden. '32 Stowaway; Doctor X; The Most Dangerous Game (GB: The Hounds of Zaroff). '33 The Vampire Bat; Mystery of the Wax Museum; King Kong; Below the Sea; Ann Carver's Profession; The Woman I Stole; The Big Brain (GB: Enemies of Society); One Sunday Afternoon; Shanghai Madness; The Bowery; Master of Men. '34 Madame Spy; Once to Every Woman; The Countess of Monte Cristo; Viva Villa!; The Affairs of Cellini; Black Moon; The Richest Girl in the World; Cheating Cheaters; Woman in the Dark; White Lies. '35 Bulldog Jack (GB); Come out of the Pantry (GB); Mills of the Gods (GB); The Clairvoyant (GB). '36 Roaming Lady; When Knights Were Bold (GB); They Met in a Taxi. '37 It Happened in Hollywood (GB: Once a Hero); Murder in Greenwich Village. '38 The Jury's Secret; Smashing the Spy Ring. '39 Navy Secrets. '40 Wildcat Bus. '41 Adam Had Four Sons; Melody for Three. '42 Not a Ladies' Man. '53 Treasure of the Golden Condor; Small Town Girl. '55 The Cobweb; Queen Bee; Hell on Frisco Bay. '57 Rock Pretty Baby; Crime of Passion; Tammy and the Bachelor (GB: Tammy). '58 Summer Love. '59 Dragstrip Riot (GB: The Reckless Age).

KING KONG

King Kong is the most potent myth that the cinema has given to the 20th century. It is the archetypal legend of Beauty and the Beast: after Kong's death, a policeman triumphantly tells Denham, 'Well, the planes got him'. 'No', Denham replies sadly, 'it wasn't the airplanes. It was Beauty killed the Beast.' The giant ape is an authentic figure of tragedy, cruel as Timon, strong as Samson, jealous as Othello, cursed as Orestes and as vulnerable as them all.

Appropriately for a legend, the authorship of *Kong* is not entirely clear. The idea seems to have begun with Merian C. Cooper, who had become fascinated, while on safari, with the habits of the gorilla, and wished to make a film in which a great ape would terrorize New York.

Cooper and Ernest B. Schoedsack, co-producer and director of the film, had previously made two travel documentaries together, *Grass* (1926) and *Chang* (1927), and two narrative films one of which, *The Four Feathers* (1929), starred Fay Wray, Kong's leading lady. In 1932 David O. Selznick brought Cooper to RKO, where there was a project for a film using Willis J. O'Brien, who had done the animation work on the 1925 version of *The Lost World*. Cooper and O'Brien made some test sequences for *King Kong*, which encouraged RKO to embark on a project which, at $650,000, was very costly for those times. Edgar Wallace, under contract to the studio, was commissioned to write the screenplay, but died before the film was properly under way, and it is still uncertain how much the famous English thriller writer contributed to the finished film. His daughter, in a letter to *The Times* in 1978, suggested that the whole conception was his; but Fay Wray recalls:

'I looked up Wallace's own version of the story recently, and it has different characters, different names, different scenes from the ones I knew in the film.' Cooper and Schoedsack in later interviews confirmed Miss Wray's opinion. The writers actually credited on the film are James Creelman and Ruth Rose (Mrs Schoedsack).

In any event, though the film is a masterpiece of narrative structure, the writing is less important than its plastic qualities. Once under way *King Kong* often looks like a silent film: the action is essentially visual, and complemented by Max Steiner's highly dramatic musical score. Its pictorial qualities too are notable: Skull Island might have come from some nightmare etching by Gustave Doré.

Above all, credit is due to Willis O'Brien's animation. Kong and the other fantastic creatures, like the pterodactyl he fights, were three-dimensional models, not more than 16 inches high, which were filmed using stop-action photography. Between every frame of film, the camera was stopped and the eyes and the limbs of the figures reposed, barely perceptibly, to give an impression of lively, realistic movement when the finished film was projected. Generally the animated figures were combined with shots of the actors in subsequent process work; but for some close-ups – for example where Fay Wray has to lie in the monster's paw – huge working models of parts of the body were made.

Technical qualities alone cannot explain the instant hold that *King Kong* took on the imagination of the world, and which it continues to exert. (Kong himself was publicized at the time as the 'Eighth Wonder of the World'.) It is myth and it is dream: the apparition of Kong in the jungle, or the great eye peering through a Manhattan window, are elemental nightmares. The film enshrines the essential eroticism of the Beauty and the Beast myth.

Moreover the film appeared at the height of the Depression: Ann Darrow is first discovered starving near a bread queue and stealing an apple. It may be significant that the 1977 remake came at a comparable moment of economic uncertainty. Was there some deeper satisfaction to audiences in watching Kong's triumphant destruction of that urban jungle of steel and glass which had brought betrayal?

DAVID ROBINSON

Directed by Ernest B. Schoedsack, Merian C. Cooper, 1933
Prod co: RKO-Radio Pictures. **prod**: Ernest B. Schoedsack, Merian C. Cooper. **sc**: James Creelman, Ruth Rose, from a story by Merian C. Cooper, Edgar Wallace. **photo**: Edward Lindon, Vernon Walker, J.O. Taylor. **sp eff**: Willis O'Brien. **ed**: Ted Cheesman. **art dir**: Carroll Clark, Alfred Herman, Mario Larrinaga, Byron L. Crabbe. **mus**: Max Steiner. **sd**: E.A. Woolcott. **sd eff**: Murray Spivak. **prod ass**: Archie S. Marshek, Walter Daniels. **r/t**: 99 minutes. New York premiere 2 March 1933.
Cast: Fay Wray (*Ann Darrow*), Robert Armstrong (*Carl Denham*), Frank Reicher (*Englehorn*), Bruce Cabot (*Driscoll*), Sam Hardy (*Weston*), Noble Johnson (*native chief*), James Flavin (*lieutenant*), Victor Wong (*Lumpy*), Steve Clemento (*witchdoctor*).

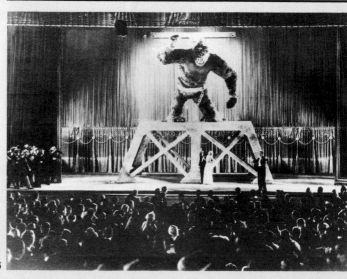

1

2

3

5

4

7

Carl Denham, a film producer, selects an unknown and impoverished girl, Ann Darrow, to play in a mysterious film to be made on a remote tropical location with the forbidding name of Skull Island. Soon after their arrival (1), Ann is seized by natives (2), who need a beautiful girl to placate their god, Kong. Helpless, Ann is bound to two great pillars (3).

At last Kong, a monstrous ape, appears (4). He picks up Ann in his huge hand and carries her off into the jungle, pursued by Denham and the crew. Most of the crew are killed when Kong hurls them off a log bridge, but Denham and his assistant Driscoll rescue Ann while Kong is distracted by a fight with a pterodactyl (5).

Subdued by a gas bomb, Kong is taken to New York to be exhibited (6). He escapes, however, and wreaks terrible havoc. Snatching Ann from the window of a skyscraper, he carries her to the top of the Empire State Building (7). There the great beast is attacked by fighter planes (8) and dies riddled with machine gun bullets.

8

ALFRED HITCHCOCK

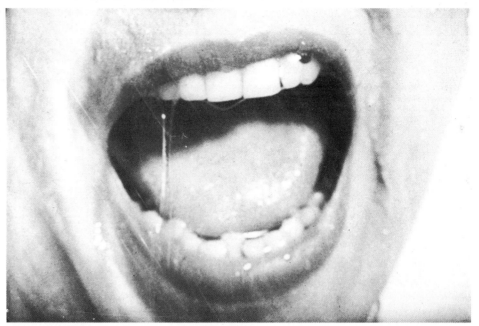

MOMENTS OF FEAR

A first glimpse of the Master's world of terror

Hitchcock's creative genius expresses itself through a series of visual or aural effects – startling conjuring tricks calculated to make audiences gasp or giggle. In the course of his long career – he was born in 1899 and started working in films in 1919 – Hitchcock has created hundreds of these moments of virtuosity. He employs trick photography, bizarre settings, striking film and soundtrack editing, and telling single shots or whole sequences that have a fantastic or nightmarish reality of their own. Some of these devices are present in his earliest films, but their full impact was first visible in *The Lodger* (1926).

This silent film is built largely upon a succession of effects. A quick, impressionistic montage at the beginning shows London terrorized by an unknown Jack the Ripper-like murderer. The opening is followed by a series of 'virtuoso' set-piece scenes which made audiences, at that time not usually aware of the director's hand, realize that here was someone of importance behind the camera. *The Lodger*'s most famous device shows the anxiety of an ordinary suburban family disturbed by the endless pacing of their mysterious lodger upstairs. Hitchcock built a glass floor and filmed from below as the man paced across it – an effect that greatly impressed critics and public in 1926.

His next substantial success, *Blackmail* (1929), was begun as a silent movie, but by this time cinema audiences were eager to see talking films, so the producers decided to insert a few lines of dialogue into the last reel. This did not satisfy Hitchcock who secretly shot

additional scenes for the film in sound.

His gamble paid off: the producers were so encouraged by what he showed them that they allowed *Blackmail* to be reshot with sound. It was Britain's first all-talking film. Despite the addition of sound and dialogue, Hitchcock retained the silent film's freedom of movement and avoided the danger of making 'photographs of people talking'. It, too, had a show-piece scene which attracted particular attention. The heroine has, half-accidentally, stabbed a would-be seducer to death and returned home just in time to cover her absence. At breakfast the next morning a neighbour chatters about the murder – now reported in the papers: 'What a terrible way to kill a man. With a *knife* in his back. A *knife* is a terrible thing. A *knife* is so messy and dreadful . . .' The words run together so as to be almost indistinguishable, except for the word 'knife' stabbing out of its context again and again, as though audibly striking the guilt-ridden girl.

The effect is there to be noticed, and noticeable it is, perhaps at the expense of the rest of the film, since it is rather showy and self-conscious. Nevertheless, at the time it demonstrated to producers, the public and especially the unwilling critics – who looked askance at the new talkie medium – that sound, and even dialogue, could be used creatively. The talkie did not have to be merely a photographed stage play but had other, more exciting possibilities. *Blackmail* confirmed Hitchcock as the most important and talented British film-maker of his day.

In 1934, he began the great series of six suspense thrillers, made in four years, which carried his reputation round the world and finally took him to Hollywood in 1939. The first of them, *The Man Who Knew Too Much*, established his penchant for the brilliantly conceived effect as the basis of film-making. A family on holiday in St Moritz witness the murder of a secret agent who, before he dies, tells them of a plan to assassinate a foreign diplomat in London. Realizing this, the enemy spies kidnap the couple's daughter to ensure their silence. The couple have to thwart the villains' plans without police help.

Whereas in *The Lodger* and *Blackmail* the tricks had tended to stand out from the overall texture, *The Man Who Knew Too Much* was virtually a succession of memorable scenes and incidents which kept the audience totally at the director's mercy. This became Hitchcock's hallmark during the Thirties and still remains an important part of his style.

Not everyone approved – Graham Greene,

Right and far right: tennis star Guy Haines (Farley Granger) and suave, beguiling Bruno (Robert Walker) meet as Strangers on a Train. *Bruno tells Guy his plan for the perfect murder – two people exchange victims and so the crimes appear motiveless. A shocked Guy learns later that his wife has been murdered by Bruno – who wants his father murdered in return . . . at a society party, Bruno playfully demonstrates strangling to a guest. Barbara (Patricia Hitchcock), looking on, does not share his macabre sense of fun . . .*

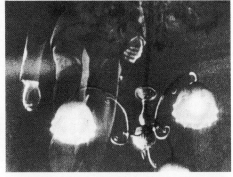

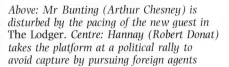

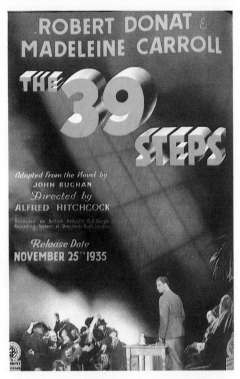

Above: Mr Bunting (Arthur Chesney) is disturbed by the pacing of the new guest in The Lodger. *Centre: Hannay (Robert Donat) takes the platform at a political rally to avoid capture by pursuing foreign agents*

Above: the Suspicion *that her charming husband Johnny (Cary Grant) is a murderer haunts Lina (Joan Fontaine). She is paralyzed with fear when he brings her a bedtime glass of milk. Is it poisoned? Does he want to kill her too . . .?*

then influential film critic of the *Spectator*, wrote of *The Secret Agent* (1936):

'His films consist of a series of small "amusing" melodramatic situations: the murderer's button dropped on the baccarat board; the strangled organist's hands prolonging the notes in the empty church; the fugitives hiding in the bell-tower when the bell begins to swing. Very perfunctorily he builds up to these tricky situations (paying no attention on the way to inconsistencies, loose ends, psychological absurdities) and then drops them: they mean nothing: they lead to nothing.'

It is curious that Greene, of all people, should have been quite so unsympathetic to what Hitchcock was doing in these films, since it was so close to those stories of his own that he labelled 'entertainments'. Hitchcock was always first and foremost a popular entertainer, with no overt pretensions, leaving

others to find deeper meanings in his work. His way of involving his audience was to deploy his unique technical skills and extraordinary inventive faculties in the elaboration of telling incident through specific effect. There are many single shots in the British thrillers which everyone who has seen them remembers. There is, for instance, the famous shot near the end of *Young and Innocent* (1937) in which the camera travels slowly across a crowded ballroom during a *thé dansant*, moving closer and closer to the black-face band, then concentrating on the drummer and finally pausing in an arresting close-up of his eye twitching – the crucial identifying mark of the murderer.

But memorable though such isolated moments are, and though Hitchcock enjoyed devising them and making them work, the dramatic effects in his films are usually more far-reaching. There are whole sequences that use or exploit well-known conventions of suspense. Take, for example, the idea of there being 'safety in numbers'. In *The Thirty-Nine Steps* (1935), the hero, Hannay, hotly pursued by foreign agents, stumbles into a political meeting. Realizing that his only hope of escape

is to get up and speak, he delivers an absurd, off-the-cuff speech and makes himself so conspicuous that the villains are unable to do anything to him for fear of giving themselves away. Hitchcock liked this idea so well that he later used variations of it in the two American films which had similar chase formulas to *The Thirty-Nine Steps*, *Saboteur* (1942) and *North by Northwest* (1959).

Yet crowds and public places are not always havens from danger – they can also conceal it. The climactic scene of *The Man Who Knew Too Much* occurs at the Royal Albert Hall during the performance of a cantata; the sound of the assassin's bullet is planned to coincide with the clash of cymbals at the end of the piece. In *The Thirty-Nine Steps*, Mr Memory is murdered on stage in full view of the music-hall audience, while, in a superb sequence in *Foreign*

Above: in The Man Who Knew Too Much, *Dr McKenna (James Stewart) and his wife, Jo (Doris Day), witness the murder of a French agent. With his dying breath he tells McKenna of an assassination plot. The doctor soon discovers that he knows too much for his own – and his family's – good . . .*

Correspondent (1940), a diplomat, surrounded by umbrella-carrying crowds, is murdered during a downpour. His assassin, posing as a reporter, shoots him with a gun hidden in his camera.

Hitchcock arrived in Hollywood in 1939. He still continued to work primarily within the thriller genre, telling his stories in the same strongly graphic style and taking the same infinite pains to set up particular effects. Indeed, there were many critics who complained in the Forties that he became even more self-conscious in his use of gimmicks in order to disguise a lack of inspiration. However, some of his devices did transcend gimmickry even during this comparatively slack period: the idea of shooting, completely against the Hollywood convention of the time, all the exteriors of *Shadow of a Doubt* (1943) in the real-life town of Santa Rosa, instead of on a studio back-lot, paid handsome dividends in terms of authenticity and vivid local colour. Other devices, like employing Salvador Dali to devise the dream sequence in *Spellbound* (1945), were at least interesting failures.

Hitchcock's most powerful film of this period is *Notorious* (1946). This has one-shot effects in plenty, such as the alleged longest kiss in screen history, between Cary Grant and Ingrid Bergman, and the climactic shot in which the camera takes in a smart party from the top of the stairs and then gradually swoops down into extreme close-up of a vital key secretly held in Ingrid Bergman's hand as she stands at the door greeting guests; it also has a powerfully constructed screenplay by Ben Hecht from a story by Hitchcock himself. Devlin, played by Cary Grant, is an American agent given the task of discovering Nazi secrets in Rio de Janeiro. He offers Alicia Hubermann (Ingrid Bergman), whose father has earlier been sentenced for treason against the USA, a job as an undercover agent. This she accepts, hoping to expiate her father's crimes. The prime suspect is Alexander Sebastian (Claude Rains), who soon falls under Alicia's spell and desires to

marry her. She agrees, despite her feelings for Devlin, in order to find out more information. The organization's secrets are discovered, but Sebastian realizes Alicia's identity and plans to poison her. She is almost on the point of death when she is rescued by Devlin, who has grown to trust and love her. Sebastian is left to explain this situation to his irate confederates.

Despite the success of *Notorious*, Hitchcock's tendency to allow style to dominate content in his films was still criticized, and not until his second great period, which runs from *Strangers on a Train* (1951) to *Marnie* (1964) did he satisfy the most determined doubters.

Though these films still have surprising effects, such as the fairground strangling of *Strangers on a Train* portrayed solely as a series of reflections in the victim's glasses which have fallen on the grass, these are normally integrated into the structure of the film. A whole film may be dominated by a single effect, such as *Rear Window* (1954) with its studied observation of everything outside from the point of

Below and bottom: in North by Northwest *a bad case of mistaken identity finds Roger Thornhill (Cary Grant) cornered in an auction room by would-be killers. His plan of escape is to create such an uproar that he has to be escorted out . . . Tracking down the villainous foreign agents to their hideout on Mt Rushmore, he is captured, but escapes at night with a beautiful double-agent, Eve (Eve Marie Saint). The climax is truly cliff-hanging . . .*

Left: As Melanie (Tippi Hedren) is collecting Cathy (Veronica Cartwright) from school, the children are attacked by The Birds. *She gets Cathy into her car but the birds swoop down, crashing against the windscreen . . .*

Above: in Family Plot, *George (Bruce Dern) and Blanche (Barbara Harris) are stranded on a lonely mountain road. Though Blanche is a medium, she fails to foresee peril when a car appears in pursuit of them . . .*

view of the temporarily crippled hero. But most of the later films have a new depth, a new disturbing charge of emotion. The feelings may sometimes be bizarre, as in *Vertigo* (1958) in which the hero morbidly tries to remake a girl he picks up into the image of his (as he supposes) dead love, or *Marnie*, where the hero perversely determines to rape a pathological liar and thief into normality; but there is no doubt about their strength and consistency. *North by Northwest* (1959) and *Psycho* (1960) are perhaps the best of these later films. The former is a sort of nostalgic harking-back to the world of the British thrillers, while *Psycho* is the most beamingly brutal, blackest of black comedies, a technical and dramatic *tour de force* which Hitchcock has never surpassed. Almost every scene is a set piece, until one ends by accepting its baroque texture as some kind of crazy standard. However often the spine-chilling murder in the shower is seen, it is impossible to be completely prepared, completely impervious to its terrors.

Hitchcock began his career with a young man's fascination with innovation. His sheer delight in putting all his goods in the shop window was in itself infectious. But from *Strangers on a Train* onwards Hitchcock proved himself a master of his medium, able to integrate his effects into the structure and content of the film instead of being carried away by them.

He wryly observed in *Film Review* in 1946:
'In the old days of melodrama they used to bring the sawmill in out of the blue – no excuse for it, it was just there when the heroine's neck needed cutting.

'We are more realistic now. It is an age of enlightenment and taste. We make the heroine the daughter of a lumberjack.'

JOHN RUSSELL TAYLOR

Filmography

1922 Number Thirteen (unfinished). '23 Always Tell Your Husband (short) (uncredited dir). '25 The Pleasure Garden. '26 The Mountain Eagle (USA: Fear o' God); The Lodger (+co-sc) (USA: The Case of Jonathan Drew). '27 Downhill (USA: When Boys Leave Home); Easy Virtue; The Ring (+co-sc). '28 The Farmer's Wife (+co-sc); Champagne (+co-sc); The Manxman. '29 Blackmail (silent and sound versions) (+co-sc). '30 Juno and the Paycock (+co-sc) (USA: The Shame of Mary Boyle); Elstree Calling (co-dir); Murder (+co-sc); An Elastic Affair (short); Mary/Sir John Grieft Ein! (GB-GER) (German version of Murder). '31 The Skin Game (+co-sc). '32 Rich and Strange (+co-sc) (USA: East of Shanghai); Number Seventeen (+co-sc); Lord Camber's Ladies (prod. only). '33 Waltzes from Vienna (USA: Strauss's Great Waltz). '34 The Man Who Knew Too Much. '35 The Thirty-Nine Steps. '36 The Secret Agent; Sabotage (USA: The Woman Alone/Hidden Power (reissue)). '37 Young and Innocent (USA: The Girl Was Young). '38 The Lady Vanishes. '39 Jamaica Inn. *All remaining films USA unless specified:* '40 Rebecca; Foreign Correspondent. '41 Mr and Mrs Smith; Suspicion. '42 Saboteur. '43 Shadow of a Doubt. '44 Lifeboat; Bon Voyage (GB) (short for war effort); Aventure Malagache (GB) (short for war effort). '45 Concentration (doc. unfinished); Spellbound. '46 Notorious. '47 The Paradine Case. '48 Rope (+prod). '49 Under Capricorn (+prod) (GB); Stage Fright (+prod) (GB). '51 Strangers on a Train (+prod). '52 I Confess (+prod). '54 Dial M for Murder (+prod); Rear Window (+prod). '55 To Catch a Thief (+prod). '56 The Trouble with Harry (+prod); The Man Who Knew Too Much (+prod). '57 The Wrong Man (+prod). '58 Vertigo (+prod). '59 North by Northwest (+prod). '60 Psycho (+prod). '63 The Birds (+prod). '64 Marnie (+prod). '66 Torn Curtain (+prod). '69 Topaz (+prod). '72 Frenzy (+prod) (GB). '76 Family Plot (+prod).

Charles Laughton

Charles Laughton brought an immensity of performance to the screen that has seldom been equalled. His Henry VIII, Javert and Captain Bligh are among the most powerful screen portrayals of all time

Charles Laughton occupies a unique position in cinema history. Other character actors of the Thirties became stars but Laughton alone vied for public popularity with the screen heart-throbs like Cooper, Colman and Gable.

Laughton was born in Scarborough in 1899. From his early childhood he had always wanted to act. He persuaded his family to send him to study at RADA (Royal Academy of Dramatic Art). Before long he had become a popular and respected actor on the screen in a series of 'arty' short comedies, the star of which was a young actress called Elsa Lanchester whom he married in 1929. The same year he played his first feature-film role, as an unpleasant night-club diner in *Piccadilly* which was directed by E.A. Dupont.

Laughton's next three British films were unremarkable. He went to New York in the play *Payment Deferred*, and his Broadway success in this and *Alibi* inevitably brought him offers from Hollywood. He signed with Paramount, who cast him as a submarine commander in a triangular drama of love and hate in *The Devil and the Deep* (1932). It was the kind

of authoritarian figure that Laughton was to play many times in his career.

While waiting for *The Devil and the Deep* to begin shooting, Paramount loaned Laughton to Universal for *The Old Dark House* (1932), based on the novel *Benighted* by J.B. Priestley. Here he plays an industrialist from Manchester with a strong Northern accent, a giant inferiority complex and an obsession with his dead wife.

Emperors and kings

It was *The Sign of the Cross* (1932) which made him a star. De Mille thought he did not take the part of Nero seriously enough; and he is said to have based his vain, petulant, childish and vicious Emperor on Mussolini. The character might have been short on development, but audiences loved its extravagance. Laughton later told critic Patrick Murphy:

'Cecil De Mille, the director, saw Nero as a robust, domineering personality. I visualized a type exactly the opposite – a man whose preciousness would heighten the horror of the orgies staged for his pleasure.'

Monarchs have long provided a field-day for actors of literal or metaphoric size; Emil Jannings, for instance, had played Nero in an Italian *Quo Vadis?* (1923), and Henry VIII in Lubitsch's *Anna Boleyn* (1920). Laughton played Henry in Korda's *The Private Life of Henry VIII* (1933) and his portrayal earned him an Oscar. No screen Henry before or since has so caught the imagination of the public, and to all but historians the king became a bawdy, hearty and much-married bigot, chomping on his chicken bones and roaring: 'Refinement's a thing of the past . . . manners are dead'. It is a performance beaming with size and self-confidence. Yet it appears that when Laughton played his third ruler, the emperor in Josef von Sternberg's abandoned *I, Claudius* (1937), he was tortured by insecurity and doubt. These fears and anxieties were to be with him for most of his career, but at this time they were acute.

Punishing roles

Laughton was always self-conscious about his physical appearance – his stoutness and sagging features – yet they contributed to his very distinctive qualities as a villain. Hollywood's other 'bad' men were lean – Basil Rathbone, Joseph Schildkraut, Henry Daniell, Raymond Massey. Laughton turned his weight to expert use, transforming it into *dramatic* weight in portrayals of ugly martinets and cruel tyrants like the testy, morose, forbidding Mr Barrett in *The Barretts of Wimpole Street* (1934). This was for a generation the definitive portrait of a stern Victorian father. Yet John Gielgud's later

Above: Charles Laughton and his wife Elsa Lanchester arrive in Hollywood in 1929

performance (1957) is more convincing. He saw Barrett as dessicated and entirely self-absorbed; Laughton is merely a bully.

Laughton dominated such films and did not disguise his relish in his own performances. Lewis Milestone, who remade *Les Miserables* in 1952, with an unusually restrained Robert Newton as Javert, disapproved of Laughton's

Below: Laughton, who had long held the ambition to play the artist, gave a sensitive and restrained performance in Rembrandt

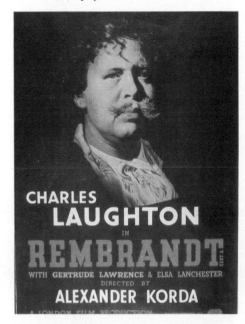

Below: 'Nero was nuts. I play him straight', Laughton said after making The Sign of the Cross; *after* Mutiny on the Bounty *(bottom) he cryptically remarked 'Everything I know about screen acting I learned from Clark Gable'*

Above: in The Hunchback of Notre Dame
Laughton's Quasimodo was a tortured gargoyle
consumed by loneliness and moved by beauty

Above: in The Barretts of Wimpole Street
Laughton was co-starred with Norma Shearer,
an actress he greatly admired

Filmography

1928 Daydreams (short); Bluebottles (short); The Tonic (short). '29 Piccadilly. '30 Comets (USA: Frankie and Johnny, shortened version); Wolves (USA: Wanted Men, shortened version). '31 Down River. *All remaining films USA unless specified:* '32 The Old Dark House; The Devil and the Deep; Payment Deferred; The Sign of the Cross; If I Had a Million. '33 Island of Lost Souls; The Private Life of Henry VIII (GB); White Woman. '34 The Barretts of Wimpole Street. '35 Ruggles of Red Gap; Les Miserables; Mutiny on the Bounty. '36 Rembrandt (GB). '37 I, Claudius (unfinished) (GB). '39 Vessel of Wrath (GB) (USA: The Beachcomber); St Martin's Lane (GB) (USA: Sidewalks of London); Jamaica Inn (GB); The Hunchback of Notre Dame. '40 They Knew What They Wanted. '41 It Started with Eve. '42 The Tuttles of Tahiti; Tales of Manhattan; Stand By for Action (GB: Cargo of Innocents). '43 Forever and a Day; This Land Is Mine; The Man from Down Under. '44 The Canterville Ghost; The Suspect. '45 Captain Kidd. '46 Because of Him. '47 The Paradine Case. '48 A Miracle Can Happen (retitled On Our Merry Way); The Big Clock; Arch of Triumph; The Girl from Manhattan. '49 The Bribe; The Man on the Eiffel Tower. '51 The Blue Veil; The Strange Door. '52 O. Henry's Full House *ep* The Cop and the Anthem (GB: Full House); Abbott and Costello Meet Captain Kidd. '53 Salome; Young Bess. '54 Hobson's Choice (GB). '55 Night of the Hunter (dir. only). '57 Witness for the Prosecution. '60 Sotto Dieci Bandiere (IT-USA) (USA/GB: Under Ten Flags); Spartacus. '62 Advise and Consent.

performance in Richard Boleslavsky's 1935 version: 'Laughton's performance has become history, beyond criticism, but I think it's terrible. He hammed it all over the place.' Later in his career Laughton *was* inclined to overdo his acting: usually, to be fair to him, it was to brighten up poor material. It is not the case, however, with his obsessive, icy Javert.

Laughton's third notable study of a disciplinarian was Captain Bligh in *Mutiny on the Bounty* (1935). Trevor Howard, in the 1962 remake, may be more of a roaring bull pitting himself against the inevitable – both Blighs are piggish to their men, despising them, and pompous and blinkered – but Laughton's Bligh is a sulky, lonely man with a habit of holding his head as if ashamed or selfconscious; but he can also be uncharacteristically jocular with those he rates as equals.

Larger than life

Bligh joined Laughton's Henry and Mr Barrett in the public imagination and, long after his death, impersonators are still offering their versions of his querulous staccato lines . . . 'Mr Christian, Mr Christian!' At the peak of his Hollywood career, he returned to Britain to play roles of his own choice, including his warm-hearted *Rembrandt* for Korda in 1936. With that sober, under-stated performance should be bracketed his earlier appearance as *Ruggles of Red Gap*. In this film, made for Paramount back in Hollywood in 1935, he played the English gentleman's gentleman who takes with such aplomb to the Wild West. These were good years for Laughton though he was rarely satisfied with his acting.

He finished the Thirties with the cunning beachcomber in *Vessel of Wrath*, the bemused busker in *St Martin's Lane* (both 1939), and the wicked squire in Hitchcock's *Jamaica Inn* (1939), all of which he co-produced with Erich Pommer for their company Mayflower Pictures. Back again in the USA he was larger than life as the sad Quasimodo in *The Hunchback of Notre Dame* (1939). He played the impish grandfather in *It Started with Eve* (1941), the mild schoolteacher in *This Land Is*

Mine (1943), the patient, henpecked husband in *The Suspect* (1944), the lonely widower in *The Blue Veil* (1951), the drunken Salford bootmaker in *Hobson's Choice* (1954) (his last English film), and, at the end, the old-hand Southern senator in *Advise and Consent* (1962). By this time he had declined into playing lead supporting parts – though these were to be preferred to leading roles in nonsense like *Captain Kidd* (1945), or, even worse, *Abbott and Costello Meet Captain Kidd* (1952). If there is one performance in his later films that ranks alongside his Bligh and Barrett, it is that of the

Below: Laughton on the set of his last film,
Advise and Consent, *shortly before his death in 1962; Otto Preminger, who directed him, later said it was one of his greatest experiences to become Laughton's friend*

publishing tycoon in *The Big Clock* (1948) – petulant and bad-mannered, wilful in his absolutism and, ultimately, pathetic. It is this inner vulnerability that makes Laughton's villains so effective: audiences loathed them – but there are always hints that the man loathes himself. Charles Laughton was gifted with the insight to explore human weakness in the best and worst of men. His villains, too, afford glimpses of the same humanity with which Ruggles and Rembrandt are more richly endowed.   DAVID SHIPMAN

Coloured Souvenir of
The PRIVATE LIFE of HENRY VIII
INSIDE

The MARCH
ROYAL 6ᴰ
PICTORIAL

The Private Life of Henry VIII

Directed by Alexander Korda, 1933

Prod co: London Film Productions. **prod:** Alexander Korda. **dir:** Alexander Korda. **sc:** Arthur Wimperis. **story/dial:** Lajos Biro and Arthur Wimperis. **photo:** Georges Périnal. **ed:** Harold Young, Stephen Harrison. **des:** Vincent Korda. **cost:** John Armstrong. **mus:** Kurt Schroeder. **song:** 'What Shall I Do for Love' by King Henry VIII, sung by Binnie Barnes. **sd:** A.W. Watkins. **r/t:** 96 minutes. London premiere, 17 August 1933.

Cast: Charles Laughton (*Henry VIII*), Robert Donat (*Culpeper*), Lady Tree (*Henry's Old Nurse*), Binnie Barnes (*Catherine Howard*), Elsa Lanchester (*Anne of Cleves*), Merle Oberon (*Anne Boleyn*), Wendy Barrie (*Jane Seymour*), Everley Gregg (*Catherine Parr*), Franklyn Dyall (*Cromwell*), Miles Mander (*Wriothesly*), Claude Allister (*Cornell*), John Loder (*Thomas Peynell*), Lawrence Hanray (*Cranmer*), William Austin (*Duke of Cleves*), John Turnbull (*Holbein*), Frederick Culley (*Duke of Norfolk*), Gibb McLaughlin (*French executioner*), Sam Livesey (*English executioner*), Judy Kelly (*Lady Rochford*).

The Hungarian Alexander Korda had a favourite story about how he got the idea for *The Private Life of Henry VIII*. Shortly after his arrival in England, he was travelling in a London Taxi when he heard the driver singing, 'I'm Henery the Eighth, I Am'. Misunderstanding the old song about a widow's eight marriages – all to men called Henry ('And every one was an Henery, she wouldn't have a Willie or a Sam') – Korda reflected that Henry VIII must be a figure of wide popular appeal.

However, studio after studio failed to share his enthusiasm and rejected his idea. Korda finally obtained enough backing from the United Artists Company to start filming. Such was the belief in the project, that many of the crew and cast agreed to wait until its completion before being fully paid. Eventually enough money was found to finish the film. It had been shot in five weeks for the modest sum of £60,000. Korda's faith in the film was soon justified. The script had a daring which might not have been possible under an English director – and was the first ever to be published in book form. The cast displayed an assurance still not common in the British cinema. Georges Périnal was the cameraman and the visual images were beautiful: the outdoor scenes clear and brilliant, the interiors rich with velvety darkness. Above all the film had an irreverence new to the cinema. Surprised critics hailed it as a cinematic event – the best production, they said, to come out of a British studio.

Of course there were dissonant voices. One pedantic authority on armour and costume complained that Henry wore his spurs 'like a cowboy', with the buckles on the inside of his feet instead of the outside. In 1936 James Agate was saying that Charles Laughton had 'permitted himself to label a bundle of buffooneries "Henry VIII"'. Despite criticism, however, the piece captured not only the British but also the American public. For the first time a British-made film was a very big commercial success in the USA.

The attitude of disrespect no doubt made the film a sensation. A beautiful woman (Anne Boleyn, played by Merle Oberon), who is also a queen, is to be beheaded: the victim is bravely resigned, and executioner whets his axe – and a spectator in the crowd grumbles that she can't see the block. Another woman is crowned, then another: for a while no more heads are cut off. But in the royal kitchens servants can still make a joke of the previous lethal 'preliminaries' to a wedding: 'chop and change', is one

fellow's waggish comment.

Yet the light, flippant handling of the story is not allowed to obscure the drama. Jealousy and passion are there. The King is besotted with Catherine Howard and he genuinely suffers when his ministers convince him that she has been unfaithful to him. And behind the scenes torture lurks; the threat of it induces Catherine's waiting-women to betray her. But the treatment remains ironic: the King, for all his authority is mocked; Anne of Cleves makes a fool of him; Catherine Parr bullies him in his old age.

Sometimes the abrupt changes of mood have a tastelessness for which the virtues of the film – its wit, its entertaining emphasis on royal follies and frailties – fail to compensate. That the piece nevertheless achieves a kind of unity is largely owing to the performance of Charles Laughton. He was already a distinguished actor when he took the role (which brought him an Oscar). But although he went on to a score of successes, it is still his portrait of Henry VIII – arrogant, lecherous, vengeful, finally absurd – which comes first to mind. Especially memorable is the bedroom scene between him and Anne of Cleves (played by his real-life wife, Elsa Lanchester), who on their wedding night evades the King's unwelcome physical attentions by engaging and beating him in a game of cards.

The film's popularity in the USA was perhaps something of a fluke – the outcome of a chance combination of a favourite leading player, an impudent handling of British history, a strain of vulgarity pleasing to spectators who liked to think an English king had no table-manners. Time has softened the vulgarities, turning them into the mildest of sick jokes. The irreverence persists: Henry wrangling with his barber, Henry challenged by his own guard as he creeps upstairs on an amorous nocturnal expedition. And irreverence it was which, in 1933, endeared the film to a public ready to enjoy a joke at the expense of royalty: especially British royalty.

DILYS POWELL

Below: Korda supervises the shooting of the famous banquet scene with Laughton at the table

1

2

3

4

5

6

The King (1) has divorced Catherine of Aragon, and, as the film begins, is ridding himself of his second wife, Anne Boleyn. Nervously, but with dignity, she prepares for execution (2); the waiting crowds treat the occasion as an enjoyable outing.

Meanwhile Jane Seymour waits excitedly to become Henry's third wife. Her success is brief. Out hunting, the King learns that he has a son (3); but the Queen dies. He is reluctant to marry again, but popular sentiment persuades him to consider Anne of Cleves as his fourth wife (4). Anne, however, decides to make herself unattractive to the King. The marriage night is spent playing cards (5); she wins the game and her release from wedlock. Henry is next introduced to Catherine Howard by Thomas Culpeper (6) and falls hopelessly in love (7). Ambitious to be Queen, Catherine marries Henry, but in secret she and Culpeper are lovers. Her adultery is discovered, and again crowds gather to see a queen beheaded. Finally a sixth wife, Catherine Parr, bullies the King, supervising his food and drink. When we last see him he is a henpecked, shambling old man, guzzling behind his wife's back (8).

7

8

Alexander Korda
Director, producer and maker of stars

Korda was born Sándor Kellner on September 16, 1893, near Túrkeve, Hungary. He worked as a journalist and editor of a film magazine before directing his first film in 1914. Two younger brothers, Zoltán and Vincent, were later to work with him as director and art director respectively.

Korda's turbulent 25 years in Britain tend to overshadow his previous 17 years as a director in his native Hungary and later in Vienna, Berlin, Hollywood and Paris. Although he and Michael Curtiz dominated the early Hungarian film industry between 1917 and 1919, Korda was scarcely known outside his own country during that period.

When the communist regime of Béla Kun fell in 1919, Korda fled the country. He emigrated with his actress wife, Maria Corda, to Vienna where he directed four films. The first, an adaptation of Mark Twain's novel *The Prince and the Pauper*, was successfully released in America. The praise for its evocative recreation of British pageantry convinced Korda that foreign directors could effectively handle national subjects outside their own experience. In Berlin, from 1922–26, with films like *Das Unbekannte Morgen* (1923, *The Unknown Tomorrow*) he accommodated his own preference for light romantic subjects, adopting the Expressionist preoccupations with destiny and mysticism then fashionable in German cinema. Determined to make films that would attract Hollywood, Korda directed the lavish and sophisticated *Eine Dubarry von Heute* (*A Modern Dubarry*) in 1926. It earned him a contract with First National in Hollywood which he took up early in 1927.

During his four years in Hollywood (1927–30), however, Korda was typecast as a director of female stars or of films with Hungarian settings. The only notable film he made there, *The Private Life of Helen of Troy*

Alexander Korda remains one of the most remarkable and controversial figures in British film history. His charismatic personality combined ambition and great charm with a flair for showmanship that delighted his admirers as much as it infuriated his critics

(1927), was an impressively photographed version of the Greek legend, reshaped into a marital comedy, with the characters given contemporary speech and attitudes. This humanizing approach to history, though anticipated by Lubitsch's German costume pictures, became the model for Korda's later films.

Korda returned to Europe in 1930. At Paramount's French subsidiary at Joinville he made *Marius* (1931), the first of the trilogy of film adaptations from Marcel Pagnol's plays about Marseilles life.

In the autumn of 1931 Alexander Korda came to Britain to direct 'quota' pictures for Paramount's British subsidiary, but within a few months he had decided to form his own company, London Film Productions. The company's sixth production, *The Private Life of Henry VIII* (1933), achieved Korda's goal of successful competition in world markets. It captured the American box-office and earned ten times its cost in its first world run. Historical costume films were considered passé at the time, but Korda 'humanized' a well-known historical subject, turning it into a sex romp which owed much to the vitality of Charles Laughton's performance.

For the next seven years, Korda sought to build on *Henry*'s success, first with other 'private life' films (*The Rise of Catherine the Great* and *The Private Life of Don Juan* in 1934, both box-office failures) and then with a series of over 30 prestige films for which Korda mixed and matched the nationalities and talents he had collected to achieve an international production. Although none of the subsequent films equalled *Henry*'s profitability (as they all cost much more to make, they could hardly be expected to recoup proportionally as much), even a selective list shows how much the British film industry owed to this emigré Hungarian: *The Scarlet Pimpernel* (1934), *Things To Come* and *Rembrandt* (both 1936), *Fire Over England* and *Knight Without Armour* (both 1937), *The Drum* (1938), *The Four Feathers* (1939) and *The Thief of Bagdad* (1940).

All these films exhibited the Korda stamp in varying degrees, according to the amount of control he exerted as head of production. This stamp is best defined by a brief analysis of his strengths and weaknesses as a film director.

Although associated with all the 100 films which London Films produced between 1932 and 1956, he directed only 8 of them. The subjects he chose tended to fall into two categories: the satirical, high-society comedies: *Wedding Rehearsal* (1933), *The Girl from Maxim's* (1933) and *An Ideal Husband* (1947); and the 'private life' films (*The Private Life of Henry VIII*, *The Private Life of Don Juan*, *Rembrandt* and *That Hamilton Woman!* (1941).

The most outstanding quality common to all these films is their visual polish, which owes much to French cameraman Georges Périnal and to Korda's brother Vincent, London Films' head of art direction. These two men created impressive films that rivalled anything produced in Hollywood, both in grandeur of scope and sumptuousness of detail. Established actors and actresses were chosen for the lead parts, while Korda cast the supporting roles from his stable of young contract starlets. There is an urgency and vitality in the acting of the experienced players, but Korda sometimes seems unsure in the direction of his untrained actors (the new stars he loved to create), contenting himself with glamorizing them or treating them as part of the decor. Even though Korda considered the script stage the most important in the making of a film (he worked uncredited on many of the scripts of his and others' movies), the basic structure of his films is often too flimsy to support their load of over-elaborate detail. There is a tendency towards repetition of scenes and dialogue, and the dialogue itself is unconvincing and often depends heavily on rather childish metaphors. The films he directed and those he produced mostly share a nostalgic view of Britain and

Left: Alexander Korda. Top left: nymphs and satyrs sport together in The Private Life of Helen of Troy. *Top right and right:* The Four Feathers *and* The Drum *were action-packed 'British Empire' films directed by Zoltan Korda. Below:* Things to Come *was a bold attempt to forecast 100 years of Man's future*

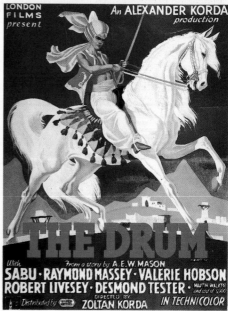

proudly champion her past glories.

What Korda lacked as a film-maker, however, he made up for as a film impresario, combining a fertile imagination, always open to new ideas, with a journalist's understanding of publicity and promotion. But his special gift was his ability to manipulate finance and financiers, and it was this which was to be most exercised during the late Thirties.

The business of making internationally marketable films was an expensive one, and London Films required immense financial investment. This came from two sources: the American United Artists Company (in which Korda became a full partner in 1935) and the City of London's Prudential Assurance Company. The United Artists tie-up was a mixed blessing as UA owned no cinema chains itself and could not guarantee American distribution for Korda's films. Heavy investment by the Prudential became Korda's mainstay in the Thirties and led to the building of Denham studios. Opened in 1936, Denham was the most up-to-date studio in Europe, yet it was too large for a single producer and, by the time it was fully operational, the investment boom in the film industry, caused by the success of *Henry VIII*, had given way to a slump. Korda was forced to add cheaper features to his production schedules and to accept independent producers as tenants to fill Denham's empty stages. Korda found himself losing control of Denham to the financiers (eventually to J. Arthur Rank). He was finally forced to become a tenant producer in the studio he had built just a few years before.

Having gone to Hollywood in 1940 to supervise the completion of *The Thief of Bagdad*, Korda stayed there to direct *That Hamilton Woman!* in which Nelson's efforts against the French became an open metaphor for Britain's current war with Germany. This film earned him a subpoena from isolationist American senators who charged him with making the American branch of his company a centre for pro-British propaganda. Although criticized by many in Britain for having 'deserted' to Hollywood, Korda did in fact make several transatlantic crossings during the war and it now seems clear that he was acting as a courier for Winston Churchill. In 1942 he was knighted by King George VI, the first film personality to be so honoured.

In the summer of 1943, Sir Alexander

Korda returned to London and spent two frustrating years trying to set up the merged MGM-British/London Film Productions company from which he then resigned in late 1945 having completed only one film, *Perfect Strangers* (1945). Throughout 1946 he was busy resurrecting London Films as a separate company. Korda, tired of directing, was now the executive producer – an administrator and businessman. After 1947, his name ceased to appear on the film credits, and as the name disappeared, so did the old Korda style. His major triumph during his last years was in drawing a large number of independent British film-makers to his company and allowing them freedom to work without interference. Directors like Michael Powell and Emeric Pressburger, Carol Reed, David Lean, Anthony Asquith, Frank Launder and Sidney Gilliat and Laurence Olivier made some of their best films while working under the aegis of Korda's umbrella organization.

To obtain adequate distribution for these films, Korda gained control of British Lion in 1946, and rebuilt and refitted Shepperton Studios which became London Film's production base. During the 1948 financial crisis in the film industry, Korda's British Lion secured the first government loan to the film business through the newly created National Film Finance Corporation. By 1954 the NFFC loan, amounting to £3 million, had still not been repaid, and with the appointment of an official receiver for British Lion, the second Korda film empire collapsed. Even after this debacle, Korda was able to form new financial alliances which enabled him to continue producing films until his death in 1956.

Top left: Merle Oberon, the star Korda created and married. Top right: That Hamilton Woman!, *Winston Churchill's favourite film, caused a political storm in the USA. Below: Laurence Olivier in* Richard III, *one of the last and most prestigious films backed by Korda*

Korda was almost as famous for the films he did not make as for the ones he did – indeed, he received the honour of having an entire television documentary devoted to footage from a film, *I Claudius* (directed by Josef von Sternberg), which was abandoned after a month's shooting. He was more successful as a producer than as a director and his reputation for extravagance now seems deserved. Yet he demonstrated to the world 'that in spectacle and lavishness of production the British industry could legitimately hope to match the best that America could produce'.

KAROL KULIK

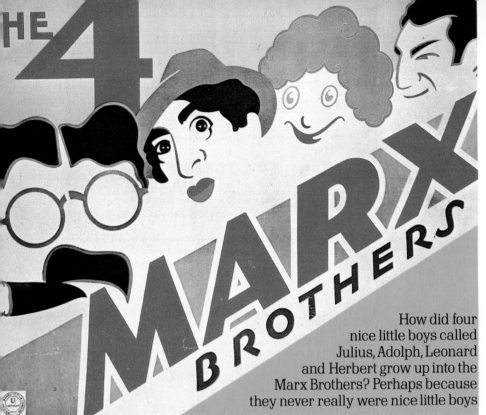

THE 4 MARX BROTHERS

How did four nice little boys called Julius, Adolph, Leonard and Herbert grow up into the Marx Brothers? Perhaps because they never really were nice little boys

gether into a singing act called first *The Three Nightingales*, then *The Six Mascots*. She was their agent, and sometimes joined the act with her sister, Hannah. Sam Marx (known as 'Frenchie'), the father of the Marx Brothers, stayed at home with the cooking and housework, as well as a threadbare tailoring business. Apparently this pioneering role-sharing worked out perfectly: Sam was a superb cook while, in Groucho's words: 'Minnie couldn't make anything except my father.' But as an agent she was unsurpassed: 'Without her, we wouldn't have been anything,' Groucho often said. 'She was the most important woman in my life.'

As a singing act the Marx Brothers were condemned to second-rate or even third-rate vaudeville, and it was only by accident that they discovered how funny they could be. Groucho described the moment:

'We were playing a small town in Texas, a

Above: stowaways Harpo, Zeppo, Chico and Groucho about to create havoc aboard ship in Monkey Business. *Below: in* Room Service *it is a hotel that suffers their onslaught*

Groucho Marx seldom ventured any comment on his own comic style. He felt that humour, like romance and sex, loses its magic if examined too closely: 'If you talk about those things, they go away.' When asked why he thought he was funny, he would answer simply, 'I'm a funny-looking jerk'. He did believe, however, that all great comedy is based on character.

People who had known the Marx Brothers before they became famous (when they were still Julius, Adolph, Leonard, Milton and Herbert), even before they entered show business, all agreed that the five brothers never had to create the characters they played so convincingly on stage, screen, and television – they already *were* those characters. A neighbour of the Marx family in New York City during the early 1900s remarked:

'They were wild youngsters with a talent for having fun. The place would be a shambles, especially if Mrs Marx left them alone. They would tear down the draperies. There was a woman across the way, a doctor's wife, who used to send over notes saying that she was going to call the police, which probably made them do it even more.'

The poor Marx Brothers

The Marx family was poor but, as Groucho said of his childhood:

'We didn't know it, so we were happy. At Christmas we didn't have a tree, just a branch, and we each hung up one of our black socks and got a half an orange each for Christmas. All our neighbours even had better garbage than we did. Harpo used to skate in Central Park with one ice skate he tied on. When my Aunt Hannah cooked the clam chowder, she used the same pot she used for the laundry, and there was plenty of starch in both.'

Although the Marx Brothers' theatrical characters were based on real people and actual experiences, their mannerisms and costumes were developed through trial and error during their years in vaudeville. For Groucho

this all began in 1905 when he joined a travelling troupe as a boy soprano. He got the job out of economic necessity:

'I became an actor because I had an uncle in show business who was making $200 a week, and I wasn't making anything, not even an occasional girl.'

Although the job didn't last long, and three times he found himself stranded on the road without money, Groucho persisted. Eventually he landed work with the Gus Edwards school act – his first professional encounter with stage comedy.

Donkey business

Three years later Minnie Marx gathered her sons (Groucho, Gummo, and later Harpo) to-

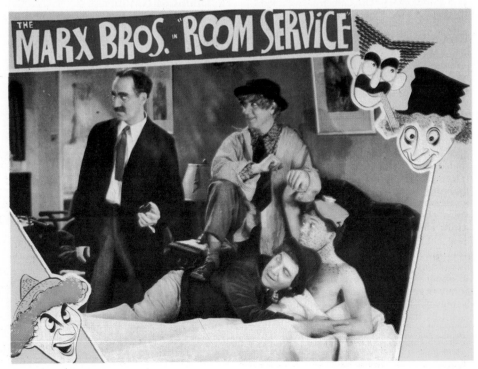

farming town. The farmers came in and tied up their horses beside the Pantages Theatre. We were doing a singing act, a mule runs away, and the whole audience left to catch the mule. Then they came back. By this time we were so angry we started making sarcastic remarks. Like, ''Nacogdoches is full of roaches'' and ''The jackass is the finest flower of Texass.'' Instead of getting mad, the audience laughs. This is the first time we ever did comedy like that.'

This incident happened in 1912 during a tour through Louisiana, Texas and Oklahoma.

School Marx

After their unexpected triumph they attempted comedy whenever it seemed appropriate, and in Denison, Texas, *The Six Mascots* were received so enthusiastically that they were invited to stay over, this time with a guarantee. Wishing to please an audience of teachers who were there for a conference, Groucho wrote a comedy sketch based on the Gus Edwards school act. Groucho became Herr Teacher, Harpo played the stupid boy, and the other members of the troupe, who included Gummo, became the standard school act characters of that day. This act was called *Fun in Hi Skule*, and much of what the Marx Brothers did afterwards was influenced by it. Most notable of all, Harpo donned his famous red wig (later to become blond for the films) and became himself; Groucho assumed a stern countenance and an air of unqualified authority; and Gummo played the juvenile straight-man role that Zeppo later inherited. Then Chico joined the act as the confidently ignorant 'Eye-talian'.

All of the Marx Brothers shows that followed *Fun in Hi Skule*, including the films and even Groucho's TV programme, owed a great deal to it. *You Bet Your Life* was the same routine but in modern dress, with Groucho still playing Herr Teacher. *Horse Feathers* is *Fun in Hi Skule* graduated to college and Hollywood. As the great white hunter in *Animal Crackers*, the prime minister in *Duck Soup*, or the bogus doctor in *A Day at the Races*, Groucho is still in many respects Herr Teacher, and his brothers play almost exactly the same roles as in *Fun in Hi Skule*.

Harpo loses his voice

It was their uncle (Minnie's brother), Al Shean – himself a big star in American vaudeville – who had helped to crystallize further each brother's stage personality. Groucho was allowed to talk incessantly, while Harpo became mute, and Chico played comic straight-man to both. According to Groucho, Al Shean felt that Harpo's voice did not match his whimsical appearance. Harpo was disappointed, but accepted Uncle Al's dictum. Thereafter Harpo talked professionally only once again during his entire career. A quarter of a century later, he spoke at the end of the stage tryouts for *Go West*. The brothers decided that this speech, whilst comically effective, departed from the innocent Harpo character, and it was omitted from the movie. In later life, after his retirement from films, Harpo would not accept any speaking engagements, and requested that his family never allow a recording of his voice to be played. He felt that to allow his voice to be heard by the public would be unfaithful and destructive to the character he had created. Groucho said the question he was most often asked was, 'Can Harpo talk?' His answer was

Above: A Day at the Races *marked a crucial point in the Marx Brothers' career as a team*

always, 'Of course not.'

By 1914, *Mr Green's Reception*, as *Fun in Hi Skule* was now called, had established the Marx Brothers as rising vaudeville stars. They were not yet, however, known by their famous 'O' names. This happened while they were touring Illinois in 1914. Another performer on the bill with them had a penchant for giving nicknames to his friends. Julius became Groucho because of his serious demeanour. Adolph became Harpo for the obvious reason. Leonard became Chico because of his passion for the chicks, as girls were then called. (Thus the correct pronunciation of his name is 'Chicko') Milton became Gummo because, as he later explained: 'I always had holes in my shoes, so I'd wear rubbers, or gumshoes, over them even when it wasn't raining, and I got called Gummo.' Herbert was only 13 and at home in Chicago when his brothers were being renamed, but he became Zeppo later. No one, especially Zeppo, is certain why. They continued to use their real names until 1924, but the 'new' names eventually took over.

He stoops to conquer

Harpo's devotion to the harp was not accidental. His grandmother had played, in the family's travelling magic show in Germany, on a wondrous instrument without strings. As a child Harpo would also 'play' on this harp which was stored in a closet in their New York apartment, and when he finally got a harp with real strings he taught himself to play, but

Below: Chico and Harpo lose their clothing, but not their ability to win out, in Horse Feathers. *Right: in the same film Harpo has already proved that he is a law unto himself*

in an unorthodox style that in later years amazed professional harpists.

Before they were established as stars, however, the Marx Brothers ran through a number of what were then called musical tabloids: several thinly plotted scenes, as sumptuously mounted as a tight budget and difficult physical conditions would allow, were held together by song, dance and comedy. In each of these shows the brothers enriched their comic characters and developed routines that would serve them – with variations – for decades. The sloping, stooping Groucho walk, for instance, happened by accident. 'I was just kidding around one day, and I started to walk funny. The audience liked it so I kept it in.'

After one failure, the Marx Brothers appeared in the successful *On the Mezzanine Floor*, which, along with *Home Again*, toured Great Britain in 1922. They opened at the Coliseum in London. At first, the audience did not understand the Marx Brothers' humour and responded by throwing pennies onto the stage. 'In those days,' Groucho recalled, 'it was the custom when the audiences didn't like an act – a pretty dangerous custom, too, since the English penny was as large as a silver dollar.' Groucho waded into the shower of coins and addressed the audience: 'We came all the way from America to entertain you, so you might at least throw some shillings.' His ad lib won over the audience, and their entire British tour was enormously successful.

A night in New York

Back in the United States in 1923 they had serious difficulties with the United Booking Office, which controlled virtually all of vaudeville. Unable to get work they were forced to put on their own show. They were helped by a Pennsylvanian industrialist who owned a theatre in Philadelphia and the sets and props from several theatrical flops, and were thus able to put together *I'll Say She Is*, their most ambitious musical tabloid to date. Although Groucho always referred to this show as 'a real turkey,' it was a huge success in Philadelphia. After a tepid road trip, they came to Broadway. Fortunately, on the night they opened in 1924 a more important show postponed its premiere, and the most influential New York drama critics went to *I'll Say She Is* instead. Their rave reviews established the Marx Brothers as permanent superstars.

Two even bigger Broadway hits followed: *The Cocoanuts* in 1925 and *Animal Crackers* in 1928; both were later filmed in New York – in 1929 and 1930 respectively – almost exactly as they were presented on the stage.

After filming *Animal Crackers*, the Marx Brothers left for California, where they remained. Their first three Hollywood pictures were produced for Paramount by Herman J. Mankiewicz, writer of *Citizen Kane* (1940) and one of Hollywood's great non-conformists. (Assigned to write a Rin-Tin-Tin picture, he had the courageous police dog carry the baby *into* a burning building instead of out of it. He was never assigned to a Rin-Tin-Tin film again.) The Marx Brothers' pictures of this period – *Monkey Business* (1931), *Horse Feathers* (1932), and *Duck Soup* (1933) – all bear the imprint of their iconoclastic producer.

Under Thalberg's wing

The next two films, *A Night at the Opera* (1935) and *A Day at the Races* (1937), were produced by Irving Thalberg at MGM. Groucho credited Thalberg with saving their careers after *Duck Soup* had done poorly at the box office. Thalberg felt that the Marx Brothers were appealing only to a minority, and that they

Above: Chico and Harpo in the scene from At the Circus *where they attempt to rob the strong man's room, and (above right) in* Animal Crackers *the Marxes were let loose on high society*

were missing especially the female audience that so often decided which film the family attended. He found the Marx Brothers characters of the Paramount films 'unsympathetic' because they were not helping anyone. To remedy this, he reinforced the plots so that they could stand alone as romantic comedies, recast the Marx Brothers as helpful avuncular types rather than totally uninhibited anarchists, and added the kind of lavish production numbers that a major studio like MGM could afford. He also allowed the Marx Brothers to try out material for their next picture in front of audiences on a road tour; this was especially helpful, as the Marx Brothers had always depended heavily on the reaction of live audiences to their ad libs. Thalberg returned to the original successful formula of George S. Kaufman who, with Morrie Ryskind, had conceived and written *The Cocoanuts* and *Animal Crackers*; and at Groucho's behest, Kaufman and Ryskind were imported from the East Coast to write *A Night at the Opera*.

After *Duck Soup* Zeppo had quit the act and

Filmography
Groucho, Harpo, Chico and Zeppo: **1926** Humorisk (unreleased and no cast list); **'29** The Cocoanuts. **'30** Animal Crackers. **'31** Monkey Business. **'32** Horse Feathers. **'33** Duck Soup.
Groucho, Harpo and Chico: **'35** A Night at the Opera. **'37** A Day at the Races. **'38** Room Service. **'39** At the Circus. **'40** Go West. **'41** The Big Store. **'46** A Night in Casablanca. **'49** Love Happy. **'57** The Story of Mankind (separate appearances). *Harpo only*: **'25** Too Many Kisses. **'36** La Fiesta de Santa Barbara (short). **'43** Stage Door Canteen. **'44** Hollywood Canteen. **'45** All-Star Bond Rally. *Groucho only*: **'37** The King and the Chorus Girl (co-sc. only). **'47** Copacabana. **'50** Mr Music. **'51** Double Dynamite. **'52** A Girl in Every Port.

started a talent agency. Zeppo had never been happy with his role as a straight-man. 'I always wanted to be a comedian, but I came along too late, and three comedians in the act was already enough.' Gummo, who had been out of show business since his discharge from the army in 1919 and never appeared in the films, joined Zeppo, and the two built their agency into one of the biggest in Hollywood. One of Zeppo's first deals for the Marx Brothers was buying the rights to the Broadway hit *Room Service* for their next picture in 1938.

Thalberg's premature death during the filming of *A Day at the Races* marked a crucial point in the Marx Brothers' career as a team. No longer did they have their champion at the biggest studio in Hollywood. Their next three pictures, *At the Circus* (1939), *Go West* (1940), and *The Big Store* (1941), were made for MGM on a production-line basis, and by 1942 they were ready to retire as a team, each brother going his own way professionally.

The laughter maker

Groucho, who had published *Beds* in 1930, continued to write, eventually writing five books. He had always aspired to being a writer, even before wanting to become an actor, and he was as proud of his literary output as of anything else he ever did. He was also proud of being able to make people laugh. 'It's a lot easier to make people cry than it is to make them laugh,' he said. Groucho also tried radio but was unsuccessful until *You Bet Your Life* in 1948. Although he was known as one of the screen's great talkers, the visual aspects of his comic style were important, too. 'The way he moved greatly enhanced his character,' Lee Strasberg noted. Studying the famous dialogues between Groucho and Chico, one immediately becomes aware of Groucho's sense of movement, even in a static scene. He is always in motion, yet what he does is so appropriate to what is being said that it heightens it while not being obtrusive. Director King Vidor noted that Groucho's reactions were always perfect, and that reacting is the most difficult aspect of film acting.

Final Marx

During their first 'retirement' Harpo and Chico continued to make personal appearances on stage, in concert, or at nightclubs, sometimes alone, sometimes together. Occasionally Chico would join Groucho on a radio broadcast, but by 1945 Chico, who was an inveterate gambler, was broke. To help Chico, the other brothers agreed to come out of retirement and made *A Night in Casablanca* in 1946. This film, which satirized *Casablanca* (1942), was successful but the team disbanded again immediately afterwards. However, a later reunion, *Love Happy* (1949), was not successful, and the team made only one more professional appearance, in a television special called *The Incredible Jewel Robbery* (1960). In neither of these last two productions does Groucho make more than a cameo appearance. At the time his own career was soaring with starring roles in major motion pictures and with his own successful TV quiz show, *You Bet Your Life*.

Chico died in 1961 (aged 74), Harpo in 1964 (aged 75), Gummo in 1977 (aged 80) and Groucho in 1977 just before his 87th birthday. Zeppo, who was born in 1901, lives in Palm Springs. He has not been associated with show business for years.

Others have tried this same kind of irreverent comedy, but none with the *élan* or style of the Marx Brothers. Groucho, Harpo, Chico, and Zeppo really *were* those zany characters they played on stage and screen.

As children, the Marx Brothers slept four in a bed, two at each end, and early developed the respect for each other's privacy and the close friendship that lasted throughout their lives. Groucho once said:

'We played every town in America and I think we were the only group that never fought. No act in vaudeville got along better than we did. There never was anyone like my brothers and me.' He was right.

CHARLOTTE CHANDLER

Margaret Dumont

Margaret Dumont was a versatile actress who played a wide range of roles during her 60-year theatrical career, but she will always be remembered as the naive social climber who so confidently entrusted her rise in society to Groucho in seven Marx Brothers films.

Born Daisy Baker in 1889 in Atlanta, Georgia, she was brought up in the home of her godfather, Joel Chandler Harris, creator of Uncle Remus, Brer Rabbit, and Brer Fox. While still in her teens she became an actress, choosing as her stage name Daisy Dumont. She trained first for the opera, and then served her theatrical apprenticeship for two years as a show girl in the music halls of England and France, making her debut at the Casino de Paris. Reviewers commented on the 'tall, statuesque and beautiful' Daisy Dumont. She was playing in a musical, *The Summer Widowers*, when she met John Moller Jr, son of a wealthy businessman and a member of New York's socially prominent '400' families. They were married in 1910.

When her husband died, Margaret Dumont resumed her theatrical career; 'My husband's family didn't entirely approve of my return to the stage,' she used to say, and it was while she was acting the part of a social climber in *The Four Flusher* that Sam Harris, who was producing *The Cocoanuts* on stage, cast her as Mrs Potter which was to be the first of her many comic trysts with Groucho.

Morrie Ryskind, co-author of *The Cocoanuts* (1929), *Animal Crackers* (1930) and *A Night at the Opera* (1935), recalled that Margaret Dumont really was the character she played so successfully on stage and screen:

'She'd been a social lady, and her husband died, so she needed a job. Groucho would explain to her that something was funny, and she would walk out to the audience and ask them what was going on.'

Groucho described his favourite leading lady in the same way:

'I enjoyed all my romantic scenes with Margaret Dumont. She was a wonderful woman. She was the same offstage as she was on it – always the stuffy, dignified matron. She took everything seriously. She would say to me: "Julie, why are they laughing?"'

Actress Margaret O'Sullivan said that Margaret Dumont actually believed that *A Day at the Races* (1937) was a serious film:

'I used to get a lot of fun out of Margaret Dumont. She had no idea why *A Day at the Races* was funny or even that it was funny. When we started, she told me: "It's not going to be one of *those* things, I'm having a very *serious* part this time".'

But in fact Margaret Dumont herself was far from naive about her contribution to *A Day at the Races*, for which she won the Screen Actors Guild award in 1937:

'I'm a straight lady, the best in Hollywood. There is an art to playing the straight role. You must build up your man but never top him, never steal the laughs.'

She once expressed her own conception of her famous dignity:

'It isn't the gown or its fine material that makes a woman stylish or otherwise nowadays, but her carriage and the amount of clothing she has on beneath the gown.'

Besides the 7 Marx Brothers films, Margaret Dumont appeared in 36 others, including memorable performances in *Never Give a Sucker an Even Break* (1941) with W.C. Fields and *The Horn Blows at Midnight* (1945) with Jack Benny. In her last film, *What a Way to Go* (1964), she played Shirley MacLaine's shrewish mother so convincingly that few recognized her as the *grande dame* of the Marx Brothers comedies. She herself was happily resigned to being type-cast.

She died of a heart attack on March 6, 1965, at the age of 76. That inimitable quality which set her apart from all other actresses was perhaps best described by George Cukor, who directed her in *The Women*: 'Her elegance was so perfectly bogus.'

CHARLOTTE CHANDLER

Below: Captain Spaulding woos Mrs Rittenhouse in Animal Crackers

Filmography

1917 A Tale of Two Cities. '29 The Cocoanuts. '30 Animal Crackers. '31 The Girl Habit. '33 Duck Soup. '34 Fifteen Wives (GB: The Man With the Electric Voice); Kentucky Kernels (GB: Triple Trouble); Gridiron Flash (GB: Luck of the Game). '35 A Night at the Opera; Orchids to You; Rendezvous. '36 Song and Dance Man; Anything Goes. '37 A Day at the Races; Life of the Party; Youth on Parole; High Flyers; Wise Girl. '38 Dramatic School. '39 The Women; At the Circus. '41 The Big Store; For Beauty's Sake; Never Give a Sucker an Even Break (GB: What a Man). '42 Born to Sing; Sing Your Worries Away; About Face; Rhythm Parade; Dancing Masters. '44 Up in Arms; Seven Days Ashore; Bathing Beauty. '45 The Horn Blows at Midnight; Sunset in Eldorado; Diamond Horseshoe. '46 Little Giant (GB: On the Carpet); Susie Steps Out. '52 Three for Bedroom C. '53 Stop, You're Killing Me. '56 Shake, Rattle and Rock. '59 Auntie Mame (uncredited). '62 Zotz! '64 What a Way to Go!

Busby Berkeley:
the man who matched girls like pearls

If Ziegfeld had not used the film title *Glorifying the American Girl* in 1929, it would make an ideal description for the work of Busby Berkeley. Berkeley knew a very great deal about girls, even though at first he did not know much about dance. However, dance directors in the Twenties had a rather different job from those of today. Then, the dance director was more a stage manager who had picked up the rudiments of moving people around on stage, and less a trained dancer or experienced choreographer.

Although Busby Berkeley's background was appropriate for this kind of occupation – he was born in 1895 of an actress mother and a stage-director father – his parents determinedly turned him away from a stage career. But in the army during World War I, he discovered a talent for devising trick drills to display the skill and precision of as many as 1200 men. After the war he sought work in the theatre.

Before long he found himself playing comic leads in touring musicals, while earning a bit of extra money by turning his skill in patterned drilling to the fairly elementary demands of stage choreography at the time. His first Broadway show was called *Holka Polka*, performed in 1926; his first big hit was Rodgers and Hart's *A Connecticut Yankee* in 1927, followed by another Rodgers and Hart musical *Present Arms*. With no special musical or dance training, he was already getting favourable notices for his use of intricate jazz rhythms in his routines, which he improvised in rehearsal with the girls on stage in front of him.

His arrival in Hollywood seems to have been equally unpremeditated. Early in 1930, Sam Goldwyn persuaded him to make the journey westward to direct the dance numbers of *Whoopee!*, starring Eddie Cantor. It was still early days in the talkies, and musicals had not yet outgrown their first flush of popularity. As a musical specialist on Broadway, Berkeley was an obvious choice to direct film musicals.

Probably no one expected him to do anything more than recreate on film the kind of routine he had done on stage. But that was not his way. His first action (after insisting that he direct the camera as well as the dancers) was to dismiss three of the four cameras normally placed around the set, and use a single camera-eye which he treated as a dynamic participant in the action.

Berkeley seems to have appreciated instinctively that film space is completely fictional and may be rearranged at will from shot to shot without any necessity for literal continuity. Nevertheless, literal-minded critics objected to his filmed routines at first, saying that his scenes shot from immediately above the centre of a pattern of girls did not correspond to any natural human viewpoint. Later, when many of his biggest sequences were ostensibly set on a theatre stage, they objected that no real theatre could possibly accommodate them – and in any case no theatre audience could possibly see enough from a real auditorium to make sense of them.

All of which seems to have worried him not a jot. Berkeley firmly avoided theorization. And though it is unlikely that he would have wished to claim any kinship between his

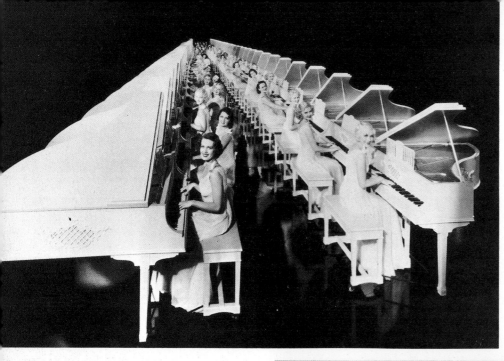

Above: the piano number from Gold Diggers of 1935. *Above right: slave girls in the 'No More Love' number from* Roman Scandals, *the first Hollywood musical to feature nude girls. Right: human harps in* Fashions of 1934

musical numbers and European avant-garde art, it is still tempting to see connections with the so-called 'Cubist' experiments of Léger, Man Ray and others during the Twenties. They sought to film people and objects in a manner that would transform them into abstract patterns. Berkeley's is also an abstract world, in which the pictures seldom tell a story but instead evoke a vague, diffused eroticism.

Berkeley's remarkable approach to the musical routine was first fully realized in *42nd Street*, made for Warner Brothers in 1933. By this time, the early talkie craze for musicals had passed and for a couple of years they had been regarded as box-office poison. Berkeley, almost single-handedly, re-established them with his unparalleled gift for spectacle. The title number of *42nd Street* was outstanding, as was the 'Shuffle Off to Buffalo' routine which showed a whole train of sleeping cars dividing and reconnecting on stage.

The style revealed in *42nd Street* was then ever more extravagantly exploited in *Gold Diggers of 1933*, *Footlight Parade* (both 1933), *Dames* (1934) and in many more Warner Brothers films throughout the Thirties – his great period. He directed several complete musicals and a handful of dramatic films, including *They Made Me a Criminal* (1939), but only in the conceiving and filming of dance numbers was his touch truly original.

In 1939 he moved to MGM and repeated the formula with decreasing success for another decade. The arrival of the integrated dramatic musical, following the success of *On the Town* (1949, dir. Gene Kelly, Stanley Donen), made his 'plums-in-the-pudding' approach to musical routines look old-fashioned, though he continued to work on the occasional speciality piece in other directors' films up to 1962.

Since his death in 1976 his reputation has rested on these 'plums'. It is difficult to describe Berkeley's art because many of his best sequences have no plot or narrative structure. However, there are some set pieces which do tell a story of sorts, like 'Lullaby of Broadway'

in *Gold Diggers of 1935* (1935), a hectic account of a 'Broadway baby's' dance-mad night and tragic dawn. It includes some of his most extraordinary effects. The opening shows the singer's face in close-up against a black background; the face revolves in camera and then, upside down, dissolves into an aerial view of Manhattan. The 'conventional' tap sequence in the middle is rendered fantastic by its sheer size (over 100 male and female dancers do a tightly choreographed routine in unison). Berkeley conveys the frenzy of it all by inventive use of camera angles.

'Pettin' in the Park', from *Gold Diggers of 1933* and 'Honeymoon Hotel' from *Footlight Parade* are examples of Berkeley's lighter side. Both show his (pre-Hays Code) gift for sexual double entendre and innuendo. 'Pettin' in the Park' is an illustration of eager boys and coquettishly uncooperative girls having some fun in a park until interrupted by a rainstorm. The girls strip off their wet clothes in provocative silhouette behind screens and emerge apparently more accessible. In fact they are actually armoured in tinfoil bras, and in the

final shot Billy Barty – Berkeley's favourite midget, playing as usual a sly, precocious child – offers Dick Powell a tin-opener. 'Honeymoon Hotel' mixes the pleasures and embarrassments of a honeymoon with suggestions that our hero and heroine are the only couple in the hotel who are actually married; again, Billy Barty intrudes in several of the tableaux as the youngest and most voyeuristic member of the newlyweds' accompanying family.

Though a case could be made out for some kind of serious political message on Berkeley's part in 'Remember My Forgotten Man', also from *Gold Diggers of 1933*, it is doubtful if he did more than stage (with imaginative play of marching shadows and a boldly expressionistic setting) another of the then fashionable Depression songs. His own deepest involvement seems to have been with the abstract researches of numbers like 'By a Waterfall' in *Footlight Parade*, 'I Only Have Eyes for You' in *Dames*, or 'The Words Are in My Heart' in *Gold Diggers of 1935*. 'By a Waterfall' virtually beggars description: the notion behind it is a sort of midsummer night's dream, suggested

Filmography

1930 Whoopee! (chor. only); '31 Kiki (chor. only); Palmy Days (chor+actor only); Flying High* (GB: Happy Landing). '32 Night World*; Bird of Paradise*; The Kid From Spain (chor. only). '33 42nd Street (chor. only); Gold Diggers of 1933 (chor+actor); She Had to Say Yes (co-dir. with George Amy); Footlight Parade (chor. only); Roman Scandals (chor. only). '34 Fashions of 1934 (GB: Fashion Follies of 1934) (chor. only); Wonder Bar (chor. only); Twenty Million Sweethearts*; Dames (chor. only). '35 A Trip Thru a Hollywood Studio (short) (actor only); Gold Diggers of 1935 (+chor); Go Into Your Dance* (GB: Casino de Paree); In Caliente (chor. only); Bright Lights (GB: Funny Face); I Live for Love (GB: I Live for You); Stars over Broadway (co-chor. only). '36 Stage Struck; Gold Diggers of 1937 (chor. only). '37 The Go Getter; The Singing Marine (chor. only); Varsity Show (chor. only); Hollywood Hotel. '38 Gold Diggers in Paris (GB: The Gay Imposters) (chor. only); Men Are Such Fools; Garden of the Moon; Comet Over Broadway. '39 They Made Me a Criminal; Broadway Serenade (GB: Serenade) (chor. only); Babes in Arms; Fast and Furious. '40 Forty Little Mothers; Strike Up the Band. '41 Blonde Inspiration; Ziegfeld Girl (chor. only); Lady Be Good (chor. only); Babes on Broadway. '42 Born to Sing (chor. only); Calling All Girls (short) (chor. only); For Me and My Gal (GB: For Me and My Girl). '43 Three Cheers for the Girls (short) (chor. only); Girl Crazy (chor. only); The Gang's All Here (GB: The Girls He Left Behind). '45 All Star Musical Revue (short) (co-dir. with Leroy Prinz). '46 Cinderella Jones. '48 Romance on the High Seas* (GB: It's Magic). '49 Take Me Out to the Ball Game (GB: Everybody's Cheering). '50 Two Weeks with Love (chor. only). '51 Call Me Mister (chor. only); Two Tickets to Broadway (chor. only). '52 Million Dollar Mermaid (GB: The One-Piece Bathing Suit) (chor. only). '53 Small Town Girl (chor. only); Easy to Love (chor. only). '54 Rose Marie (chor. only). '62 Jumbo/Billy Rose's Jumbo (2nd unit dir. only). '70 The Phynx (guest actor only).
* Choreography attributed to Berkeley, but no screen credit given.

Above: the Berkeley girls form a gigantic jigsaw of Ruby Keeler's face in the dream number 'I Only Have Eyes for You' from Dames. *Right: a tableau from the water ballet in* Footlight Parade

by the image of falling water, with hundreds of gorgeous girls in and around it. With dream-like speed and arbitrariness the action moves from a moderately realistic stage setting to a succession of cascades thick with water nymphs, giant swimming pools in which the girls swim into intricate geometrical patterns (viewed from directly above), and a staggering finale with girls piled on a revolving fountain.

'I Only Have Eyes for You' is the ultimate hymn to the charms of Ruby Keeler, star of so many of Berkeley's films in the early Thirties. Again it is – explicitly this time – in the form of a dream, dreamed by Dick Powell on a subway train. A host of dancing girls, wearing Ruby Keeler masks and dressed to look like her, finally tilt, displaying a portrait of Ruby Keeler formed piecemeal by boards attached to their backs. 'The Words Are in My Heart' routine has 56 girls in white, each one sitting at a white grand piano while the whole ensemble gyrates smoothly in waltz time to make up a series of intricate patterns. It has always prompted spectators to ask 'How *did* he do it?' Here, the answer is simple: little men in black, unnoticeable (unless they are pointed out) were placed under each piano against the black reflecting floor, and it is their movements which dictate the movements of the pianos.

Not all of Berkeley's solutions were so simple. Often what we see has been run backwards in the camera, so that what appears to be a pattern forming with incredible speed is actually a pattern that is dissolving. But though there is often extreme technical ingenuity in his routines, in the way of camera movement and trickery, it is usually the inventiveness of the basic idea that is their most impressive feature. It is not surprising that a contemporary lobby display for the film *Fashions of 1934* (1934) gave enormous prominence to the statement: 'Pageant of Ostrich Plumes – Hall of Human Harps – Web of Dreams – Venus and Her Galley Slaves – and Other Spectacle Creations by . . . Busby Berkeley'. His inventive genius is still apparent in his later, simpler creations like 'I Gotta Hear That Beat' in *Small Town Girl* (1953), in which Ann Miller (who was not, needless to say, the small town girl in question) taps her way all over a fantastic set in which all we can see of a full orchestra is arms coming out of floor and walls holding and playing instruments. Berkeley's concepts are inconceivable in any medium other than film. He remains one of the cinema's great originals.   JOHN RUSSELL TAYLOR

Screenwriters

The hacks, wordsmiths and literary giants who invaded the new sound stages of Hollywood

Until the arrival of the talkies, scenario writers conceived camera shots that depicted action whereas dialogue appeared in brief titles. These were usually terse one-liners enclosed in quotation marks: 'I love you' or 'I hate you' predominated. Titles describing time and place, many along the lines of 'Came the dawn . . .' or 'Meanwhile back at the ranch . . .' became clichés after uncontrolled repetition. This tended to be the general quality of screen-writing until fate and Warner Brothers combined to bring talking pictures into the land of make-believe. Before the Thirties were two years old, title-writing had died out.

Of all the frantic changes to be made with the coming of sound, dialogue-writing was the most demanding and most difficult. Tech-nicians could wrestle with recording the voice, and actors, directors and producers could test their abilities in their chosen fields and succeed or be replaced. But dialogue-writing appeared to be a mysterious and evasive gift bestowed on very few. It also called for producers who recognized good dialogue when they saw it.

The studios scouted for authors writing for the theatre (there was some importation of novelists too, as their skills were believed to be close to those of their theatre-wise counter-parts). Playwrights knew what to do with the spoken word, but no-one expected them to know what to do with the camera. To over-come deficiencies, studios teamed new arrivals with old timers.

Scripts for comedies were concocted in a highly specialized way and the gag man became an integral part of the writers' colony. He rarely wrote a complete screenplay but instead was called in when another writer had completed its construction – it was then his job to insert a special touch of humour. Highly prized and paid, gag men flitted from studio to studio, an irreverent group made up from graduates of vaudeville, burlesque, night club revues, newspaper comic strips, and a few survivors of title-writing. Best known were Al Boasberg, Robert 'Hoppy' Hopkins, Ralph Spence, Lew Lipton, Billy K. Wells, Edgar Allen Woolf and Joe Farnham.

Behind the scenes

Pert, diminutive Anita Loos, author of the novel *Gentleman Prefer Blondes*, was one who made the transition from early-day silent films to latter-day talkies. She was much in demand, working for the highest pay that studios could afford. Married to playwright John Emerson, and for a time teamed with him on material ranging from Fairbanks comedies to Garbo tragedies, Miss Loos did the writing while her husband basked in the glory. She was one of the most talented scenarists in Hollywood.

Around the same time Frances Marion arrived in Hollywood. She wrote brilliant

Above: Anita Loos, who started writing screenplays in her teens and became one of Hollywood's most prolific authors, with husband John Emerson. Left: Clark Gable in San Francisco *(1936), scripted by Loos and produced by Emerson*

Above: Frances Marion, centre, with stars Binnie Hale and Ann Harding during the making of Love From a Stranger *(1937). Below: another British picture Marion worked on was* Knight Without Armour *(1937) with Robert Donat and Marlene Dietrich*

adaptations of other authors' works but was also adept at creating original screen material. Once established, she used her writing and her influence at the studio to help needy friends and strangers alike. She effected the comeback of Marie Dressler after the stout comedienne fell on hard times, and softened the last days of her terminally-ill collaborator, Lorna Moon, with a skilful adaptation of the latter's book, *Dark Star*. Miss Marion turned the dour romance of the Scottish moors into the hilarious and touching *Min and Bill* (1930), an Academy Award triumph. It was on that occasion that Marie Dressler, who won the Best Actress Oscar, said, 'You can have the finest producer and director, but it won't mean a thing if you don't have the story'.

Other notable women writers who made the transition from silent films to talkies, were June Mathis, Jane Murfin, Lenore Coffee, and Bess Meredyth.

Married teams, besides Loos and Emerson, included Dorothy Parker and Alan Campbell; Sarah Y. Mason and Victor Heerman; Albert and Frances Hackett, who blazed a trail into sophisticated detective movies with their Thin Man series; and Sam and Bella Spewack, who distilled the hit stage comedy, *Boy Meets Girl*, from their Hollywood experiences.

There were other important writing teams. Ben Hecht and Charles MacArthur, one-time Chicago newspapermen turned Broadway playwrights, scripted such varied successes as *Rasputin and the Empress* (1932) and *Wuthering Heights* (1939). Kubec Glasmon and John Bright concentrated on scripting hard-hitting gangster films at Warner Brothers.

A varied catalogue of excellent screenplays was supplied by Allen Rivkin and P.J. Wolfson, who handled assignments ranging from musicals to melodramas. Billy Wilder brought his experience of Austrian society and European film-making to bear in his partnership with Charles Brackett, an erudite gentleman from the staff of the *New Yorker* magazine. Together they comprised a polished duo at Paramount, delivering superb comedy classics, such as *Midnight* and *Ninotchka* (both 1939).

Horses for courses

The pattern of Hollywood film-making has, to a large extent, always reflected the tastes of its studio heads and this often dictated the casting of staff writers. The studios also tried to select men and women capable of fashioning screenplays suitable for their stars. As a result many writers became identified with a particular type of material and, in their own way, became a part of the studio system themselves.

At Paramount, for example, the staple diet was glossy, sophisticated comedy. To find writers for these, executive-producer Walter Wanger and journalist-turned-playwright Herman J. Mankiewicz continually scoured the literary circles of the more cultured East. Among those they brought to Hollywood were poet and press agent Samuel Hoffenstein; playwright Zoe Akins; Preston Sturges, who wrote and later directed sharp, sometimes black comedies; and Benjamin Glazer, who functioned as a writer-producer.

The system of teaming writers with directors at Paramount was initiated with teams such as Brackett and Wilder; Samson Raphaelson and Ernst Lubitsch, and Claude Binyon, who worked with directors Leo McCarey and Gregory La Cava before becoming a producer.

Above: writers Ben Hecht, left, and Charles MacArthur on the set of Crime Without Passion *(1934), which they also directed. Right: their later adaptation of* Wuthering Heights *(1939) was both ruthless and successful. Below right: Billy Wilder and Charles Brackett brought their abrasive humour to films like* Ninotchka *(bottom)*

Paramount had grown out of the Famous Players-Lasky company, and its biggest films under both trade marks were the creations of Cecil B. DeMille. A pioneer writer-director, he had a marked preference for biblical epics and wielded a sure touch with this type of spectacle. He worked closely with scenarists Jeanie Macpherson and Gladys Unger, but the writing always showed evidence of his contributions.

Samuel Goldwyn, the independent producer, made a bid for literary quality with his Eminent Authors feature series. He imported great talent from Europe to add to his American writers. Many, including the distinguished Belgian writer Maurice Maeterlinck, were unable to grasp the intricacies of screenwriting. The average newcomer proved unadaptable to the needs of the cinema, and

Above: Robert Riskin, who scripted nine of Frank Capra's pictures between 1931 and 1941. They included It Happened One Night – *which won him an Oscar – and* Mr Deeds Goes to Town *(right), starring Gary Cooper*

Goldwyn's lofty hopes of establishing literary folk as film personalities collapsed. Much of this occurred in the silent era; its failure seemed to indicate to Hollywood that literary writing was not necessarily a guarantee of good movie-making.

As Warner Brothers became one of the major studios in the Thirties it began to diversify its output and, with the addition of Errol Flynn to its star roster, turned to swash-buckling adventure films. Writing craftsmen like Seton I. Miller, who co-wrote *The Adventures of Robin Hood* (1938) and *The Sea Hawk* (1940), and Casey Robinson, whose first screenplay for the studio was *Captain Blood* (1935), became the foundation of the Warners' writing staff. Robinson later moved on to scripting powerful tearjerkers for Bette Davis, including *Dark Victory*, *The Old Maid* (both 1939) and *Now, Voyager* (1942).

Waiting for Thalberg

At MGM all films pivoted around the taste and talent of Irving Thalberg. Amused and exasperated by Thalberg's endless demands for script changes, his friend Charles MacArthur complained: 'Irving has a theory writers never write the stories they intended to write!' Thalberg's methods were motivated by an unceasing search for excellence; his insistence on re-writing worked well at MGM where the output in the early talking era rated as the best in Hollywood. His daily life was a series of story conferences – writers spent long hours in his outer office, waiting for his suggestions, okays or, to their regret, abandonment. They constantly complained they were wasting their lives working for Thalberg, but, aware of his high regard for them and their calling, left meetings feeling the delays were worth it, full of praise for his picture-making instincts.

And, if their art was stifled by wasting time, their feelings were often assuaged by the weekly pay check. The wages averaged out to nearly $2000 a week each, but many writers were employed on long-term contracts that carried them well above this figure. There were more than 30 writers at MGM at the start of the

Above: Sidney Buchman, whose script for Capra's Mr Smith Goes to Washington *contained 186 speaking parts and an impassioned filibuster for James Stewart (below), cast as a senator fighting corruption*

decade and that number had doubled by 1934. Frances Marion, Anita Loos, Bess Meredyth, John Meehan, Charles MacArthur, Gene Markey, Donald Ogden Stewart often received more than $3000 a week; writers with four-pictures-a-year deals, such as Ernest Vajda, received $100,000 annually, and single picture deals with George S. Kaufman, Frederick Lonsdale, Willard Mack, Bayard Veiller and others ran to similar amounts. To balance this were junior writers receiving only $50 a week.

David O. Selznick, Thalberg's closest rival at MGM, was more concerned with achieving authentic resemblance to the classic books and plays he brought to the screen as producer. Despite the noble efforts of Hugh Walpole and Howard Estabrook on *David Copperfield* and S.N. Behrman and W.P. Lipscomb on *A Tale of Two Cities* (both 1935), Selznick often lamented that Charles Dickens himself was not on hand to help adapt his work to film. But when Selznick first brought Walpole to Hollywood to script *Vanessa, Her Love Story* (1935) from his book *Vanessa*, it suffered from the lack of necessary dramatization.

Free-lance writers, who were accustomed to moving out of a studio when their assignment was complete, expected to be called back for others. But those who worked for Harry Cohn at Columbia usually considered an assignment there a one-way ticket. This made for a large turnover of staff at what was a comparatively small studio. There was, by contrast, one major attraction: writers vied for the chance to work with Columbia's ace director, Frank Capra. Except for an occasional adaptation of a book (*Lost Horizon* 1937), or a short story (*It Happened One Night*, 1934). Capra preferred to develop original ideas like *Mr Deeds Goes to Town* (1936) and *Mr Smith Goes to Washington* (1939). In his long period of employment at Columbia through the Thirties Capra mostly worked with four, highly accomplished authors: Dorothy Howell, Jo Swerling, Robert Riskin, and Sidney Buchman. To invest his characters with his own brand of idealism, the director also worked with his close friend, Myles Connolly.

Hard lines for the literati

There has never been a workable way to make a bad writer perform well, nor can good writers be forced to write badly. But it is not always easy to make a playwright or novelist change his style to meet the demands of screenwriting, or for him to understand its particular techniques and skills.

Hollywood's most celebrated case in the Thirties was F. Scott Fitzgerald, a great writer of books, but a legendary failure in Hollywood. Nothing he worked on there survived untouched, and his material for *The Women* and *Gone With the Wind* (both 1939) was not used. He received just one credit – for *Three Comrades* (1938). P.G. Wodehouse hardly fared any better: when he left MGM after a year's contract, he told the press, 'I have been paid $24,000 to do nothing'. Thalberg contended that Wodehouse's efforts were hilarious on the written page but failed to transfer to the screen. While writers, in general, are inclined to place the blame on others for their failure (and in some cases this was true), the medium has always been more complicated than some writers anticipated. Edna Ferber, who sold her stories to film companies but refused to adapt them, said: 'When I write a book, the only heart I break is my own.'

Novelist William Faulkner might have been another great writer to fail in Hollywood if he had not been rescued by Howard Hawks; the director took him under his wing and eventually worked closely with him on such films as *To Have and Have Not* (1944) and *The Big Sleep* (1946). When British playwright Frederick Lonsdale was brought to Hollywood by Thalberg, he confessed his ignorance of creating screenplays. Thalberg advised him to write in play form – but without confining himself to the limitations of the stage. In this way a character could walk out of a parlour and reappear in a street on the other side of the world. Having learned this, Lonsdale delivered accordingly – among his scenarios were *The*

Below and below right: F. Scott Fitzgerald and P.G. Wodehouse, who both failed as screenwriters. Below, far right: William Faulkner fared much better in Hollywood; his script credits include Howard Hawks' The Big Sleep *and* To Have and Have Not

Above: Donald Ogden Stewart, the distinguished playwright and scenarist of witty romances and stylish costume pictures like Marie Antoinette *(1938), co-written with Claudine West and Ernest Vajda for MGM*

Devil to Pay (1930) and *Lovers Courageous* (1932) – but like fellow British writers Ivor Novello, John Van Druten and Wodehouse, he soon departed Hollywood for England.

Protecting the pen

After an incredible effort by the studios to save money at the expense of their employees, screenwriting became unionized. In the lean years of the Thirties, however, writers and other staff members were asked to accept cuts in their salaries and many studios threatened reprisals against those who refused.

Outrage at these demands brought about the formation of acting, directing and writing guilds. Hollywood's screenwriting fraternity split into two groups, motivated by strong political leanings. The battle for supremacy between the Screen Playwrights, led by James Kevin McGuinness and Howard Emmett Rogers, and the Screen Writers' Guild (now called Writers' Guild of America) led by John Howard Lawson, Samuel Ornitz and Ernest Pascal, was long and bitter. The Writers' Guild emerged the winner, but the enmities between

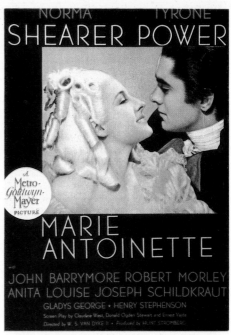

the factions only died with the participants.

Hollywood itself has often been castigated by those who failed there, but some talented writers have also heaped scorn on Hollywood's system of movie-writing. Ben Hecht was one who bombarded producers and studios with a non-stop barrage of mockery. Among those who came under his fire were his own employers, David O. Selznick and Howard Hughes. Selznick had engaged Hecht for *Viva Villa* (1934), and Hughes for *Scarface* (1932). Hecht was paid $1000 a day (in cash, at his request) for these scripts.

In the main, however, sincere writers toiled in the studio mills throughout the Thirties. Some were incensed by attitudes they considered ungrateful. Witty, urbane S.N. Behrman, dialogue writer for many of Garbo's best films, including *Queen Christina* (1933), hit back at those who ridiculed the Hollywood scene: 'So conditions are lousy,' he said. 'The people you work for are lousy. The movies are lousy. And what do you get for it? A lousy fortune!'
SAMUEL MARX

JEAN HARLOW

Jean Harlow, the 'Platinum Blonde', was one of Hollywood's flashiest sex symbols. She always portrayed seductive sirens. These had an innocent, animal quality in her early roles and an air of tart sophistication in her later ones. Because she died when she was 26, she appears an ageless incarnation of sex to modern moviegoers. In real life, regardless of what certain unscrupulous biographers may have written, she was trusting and naive, with an instinctive talent for comedy.

The girl from Missouri

She was born in Kansas City, Missouri, and christened Harlean. Her father, Dr Montclair Carpenter and her mother, whose name was originally Jean Harlow, split up before their daughter reached her teens. Harlean had a twangy voice, unblemished skin and a beautifully rounded body. Adopting her mother's maiden name, she began work as an extra in silent films; her film debut occurred in Chicago in 1926 when she was 15. That year she eloped with Charles McGrew for a brief, passionless marriage that failed to survive parental displeasure.

By that time, Jean's mother had married a florid dandy with loud ways named Marino Bello. Although he claimed to be a successful business man, he was most successful at meddling in Jean's life. Her dislike for him was matched by her love for her mother and these conflicting emotions created constant discord in the Bello home.

In the late Twenties, the family moved to California. Hollywood was a Mecca for the world's most beautiful girls. Even against that competition, Jean's attractiveness was spectacular, but though she worked regularly in films, proper recognition eluded her until Howard Hughes gave her the lead in his talking version of *Hell's Angels* (1930). This flying epic lifted her to instant stardom.

The impact she made in *Hell's Angels* was short-lived. Although audiences appreciated her flip personality and platinum blonde locks, her acting was less well received. She drew loud guffaws everywhere when, attired in a thin, revealing dress, she asked the hero, 'Would you be shocked if I slip into something more comfortable?' But it was her sexy appearance that wrought the damage, enraging puritans, women's clubs and censor boards. To escape their wrath, producers chose other actresses for roles ideally suited to Harlow.

Red-haired dynamite

Howard Hughes held her to a contract but neglected her when casting subsequent films. She was sent plummeting from instant stardom to near-instant oblivion. She engaged in a series of disastrous personal appearances in the American Midwest and along the Atlantic seaboard, until MGM producer Paul Bern persuaded his boss, Irving Thalberg, that she would be an asset to their cinematic constellation. Her contract was bought from Hughes and she soared to new prominence when, dark-wigged, she starred in Bern's production of *Red-Headed Woman* (1932) – a film that not only incurred the wrath of her existing critics but created new ones. Defying them, MGM

Right: Jean Harlow, flagrantly clad in furs and skin-clinging gown, was a head-turning status symbol every Thirties American male dreamed of possessing

THE BLONDE BOMBSHELL

continued Harlow's rejuvenated career.

Harlow took all this in her stride. She was likeable, happy-go-lucky, and now suddenly successful. Her frank, outgoing personality contrasted with the mild, intellectual Bern. But more than a mutual interest in film-making drew them together and they were soon married. Then, two months after the wedding, Bern shot himself.

Harlow was never involved in the controversy that followed. Although touched by his death, she threw herself into film after film, starring in a dozen MGM movies in less than four years. Some, like *Red Dust* (1932), *Bombshell*, *Dinner at Eight* (both 1933), *China Seas* (1935) and *Libeled Lady* (1936), reveal a comedienne who rates with the screen's best.

She married cinematographer Hal Rosson a year after Bern's suicide. Like her late husband, Rosson was short, quiet, intellectual and devoted to her and her career. But her third marriage was also short-lived, ending in divorce after only six months.

Beautiful losers I

During 1934, Harlow completed a semi-erotic novel called *Today Is Tonight*. MGM, always watchdogging the image of its stars, purchased every available copy and the film rights. The embarrassing work was quickly filed away and forgotten.

Harlow's last love was William Powell, urbane on and off screen and her co-star in *Reckless* (1935) and *Libeled Lady*. He was the former husband of Carole Lombard, who was popular, like Jean, as a sexy comedienne. The Harlow/Powell affair was hectic and quarrelsome. When it broke up, Jean became ill, contracting a dangerous kidney disease. Severely depressed, she seemed not to care what happened to her. Her mother, a devoted Christian Scientist, tried to effect a cure without recourse to medicine but failed, and Jean died of uremic poisoning.

In life and death, Jean Harlow, Carole Lombard and Marilyn Monroe were counterparts. All three were blonde and beautiful, and all three were fated to die young and needlessly.

SAMUEL MARX

Filmography
1928 Moran of the Marines; Double Whoopee (short); The Unkissed Man (short). **'29** Close Harmony; New York Nights; The Love Parade; The Saturday Night Kid; Weak but Willing. **'30** Hell's Angels. **'31** The Secret Six; The Iron Man; The Public Enemy (GB: Enemies of the Public); City Lights; Goldie; Platinum Blonde. **'32** Three Wise Girls; The Beast of the City; Red-Headed Woman; Red Dust. **'33** Hold Your Man; Bombshell (GB: Blonde Bombshell); Dinner at Eight. **'34** The Girl From Missouri (GB: 100 Per Cent Pure). **'35** Reckless; China Seas. **'36** Riffraff; Wife vs Secretary; Suzy; Libeled Lady. **'37** Personal Property (GB: The Man in Possession); Saratoga (died during filming; a double replaced her in some scenes).

Harlow's leading men ranged from the debonair William Powell in Reckless *(top far left) to the wild James Cagney in* The Public Enemy *(bottom left), and included Spencer Tracy in* Riffraff *(top left), Wallace Beery in* Dinner at Eight *(centre left) and Ben Lyon in* Hell's Angels *(centre far left). Clark Gable, here in* Red Dust *(bottom far left), was her most frequent partner*

MOVIES AND MORALS

Scandals on and off screen brought Will Hays to the Hollywood censor's throne; in Britain films were censored by gentlemen's agreement

America perceived the moral threat of the movies from the start – an Edison film of 1896, *The Kiss*, outraged the high-minded, although it was not until 1908 that a National Board of Censorship of Motion Pictures was set up, changing its name in 1916 to the National Board of Review (a title it still holds). The Board's role was essentially advisory. The first moves towards effective regulation of the cinema were provoked by disapproval not so much of the films but rather of the people who made them. A speaker in Congress in 1922 fumed:

'At Hollywood is a colony of these people where debauchery, riotous living, drunkenness, ribaldry, dissipation, free love seem to be conspicuous. Many of these "stars" . . . do not know what to do with their wealth, except to spend it in riotous living, dissipation and "high rolling". From these sources our young people gain much of their views of life, inspiration and education. Rather a poor source, is it not? It looks as if censorship is needed does it not?'

The early Twenties saw a rash of sensational scandals in the movie colony. In 1921, in the course of a day-and-night drinking party in a San Francisco hotel, a hopeful actress called Virginia Rappe became critically ill and soon afterwards died. Roscoe (Fatty) Arbuckle, a well-loved screen comic, was charged with manslaughter. The public delightedly created its own fantasies of Beauty and the Fat Beast; and even after the prosecution case collapsed, and Arbuckle was cleared, they condemned him by disapproval and boycott. His films were withdrawn but he did some work as an actor after the case.

While the Arbuckle trial was still going on, an English-born director of dubious background, William Desmond Taylor, whose own films included *Morals* and *Sacred and Profane Love* (both 1921), was murdered in Hollywood. Mary Miles Minter, then a rival to Mary Pickford, was discovered to have been in love with him, and Mabel Normand, the brilliant commedienne, was the last person to have seen him alive. Smears, entirely unjustified, ended Minter's career and permanently harmed that of Normand. Then in January 1923 Wallace Reid, who was the ideal of the handsome, clean-living, all-American hero, died as a result of narcotic addiction. These were only the more notorious scandals of the time.

In an attempt to put their own house in order – and forestall those others who were all too eager to do it for them – the film industry formed the Motion Picture Producers and Distributors of America (the MPPDA):

'To foster the common interests of those engaged in the motion picture industry in the United States, by establishing and maintaining the highest possible moral and artistic standards in motion picture production, by developing the educational as well as the entertainment value and the general usefulness of the motion picture, by diffusing accurate and reliable information with reference to the industry.'

The MPPDA invited William Harrison Hays, who

had been Postmaster General under President Harding, to head the industry at a salary of $100,000. Hays demonstrated his political skill by devising a network of agreements and contracts that ensured his permanence in office and his commanding role in an industry given to suspicion, deceit and impermanence.

Hays made it clear that the citizens of Hollywood had to become more circumspect in their private behaviour: 'Acquittal from a charge of larceny' he said laconically, 'is no guarantee of acting ability.' At the same time he launched a publicity campaign to persuade America's would-be censors that self-regulation within the industry was infinitely to be preferred to State or Federal censorship.

In 1924 the Hays Office introduced a 'formula' which was to bind all members to endeavour:

'. . . to establish and maintain the highest possible moral and artistic standards of motion picture production . . . to exercise every possible care that only books or plays which are *of the right type* are

---

Noel Coward's wartime film *In Which We Serve* was found to contain ten 'damns', two 'hells', two 'Gods' and one 'lousy'

used for screen presentation; to avoid the picturization of books or plays which leave the producer subject to a charge of deception; to avoid using titles which are indicative of a kind of picture which should not be produced, or by their suggestiveness seek to obtain attendance by deception, a thing equally reprehensible; and to prevent misleading, salacious or dishonest advertising.'

It is interesting that the elaboration of this broad formula into a more specific code coincided with the arrival of sound films. Dialogue pictures encouraged more sophisticated psychological themes and also introduced the moviegoing public to the racy idioms of gangsterdom and the backstage world. In June 1927, following an investigation and report by the Hays Office's Colonel William Joy, the MPPDA issued a famous series of 'Don'ts' and 'Be Carefuls'. Yet with no sanctions to enforce them, the new guide-lines still did not satisfy the critics. The Depression had made things worse: faced with tougher competition to win audiences, producers were inclined to make the easiest appeal to the moviegoing public.

At this point Hays sought the help of Martin Quigley, the Catholic publisher of *The Motion Picture Herald*, and Father Daniel J. Lord SJ, a Jesuit priest with an interest both in ethics and cinema. Between them they drew up a Production Code – based, they explained, on the Ten Commandments – which became industry law, providing a right of appeal from the Hays Office to a Hollywood Jury of three producers, and thereafter to the Board of the MPPDA itself. The Hays code explicitly defended the

Stars whose careers were wrecked by scandals. From top: Mary Miles Minter, Fatty Arbuckle, Mabel Normand and Wallace Reid

Top: suffering for Christ: nude actress in The Sign of the Cross *directed with a remarkable mixture of erotic fantasy and religious fervour by Cecil B. DeMille, possibly the only film-maker in Hollywood who, because of his standing with the clergy and high moral reputation, could get away with scenes like this.*
Above: The May Irwin-John C. Rice Kiss, known familiarly as The Kiss, *lasted for only one minute but opened the door for film censorship. 'It was', wrote historian T. Ramsaye, 'a high-vacuum kiss, attended at its conclusions by sounds reminiscent of a steer pulling a foot out of the gumbo at the edge of a water hole'*

establishment; its general principles were:

No picture shall be produced which will lower the moral standards of those who see it. Hence the sympathy of the audience shall never be thrown to the side of crime, wrong-doing, evil or sin.
Correct standards of life, subject only to the requirements of drama and entertainment, shall be presented.
Law, natural or human, shall not be ridiculed, nor shall sympathy be created for its violation.
The police must not be presented as incompetent, corrupt, cruel or ridiculous, in such a way as to belittle law-enforcing officers as a class.
The use of the Flag shall be consistently respectful.

Races and religions were to be respected. Crime was never to be shown in an alluring light; and criminals were to be seen paying the penalties of their acts. Rulings on sex included:

Miscegnation (sex relationships between the white and black races) is forbidden.
Sex hygiene and venereal diseases are not proper subjects for motion pictures.
Children's sex organs are never to be exposed.

Pointed profanity, declared the Code (including the words God, Lord, Jesus, Christ, hell, son-of-a-bitch, damn and Gawd), was forbidden. This rule was to make a notable cause out of Noel Coward's *In Which We Serve* (1942) when it arrived in the USA in 1945, and was found to contain ten 'damns', two 'hells', two 'Gods', two 'bastards', and one 'lousy'. On appeal, the Hays Office yielded a damn or two but immediately regretted it. 'Four appeals on

American pictures followed', wrote Raymond Moley in *The Hays Office* (1945). 'If "those words" could be allowed in Coward's picture, why not in ours? In the first two of these pictures the appeal was granted. In the next two it was denied. Then the Board, seeing the danger of exceptions, solemnly resolved that no more exceptions would be granted.'

Moley, who enthusiastically defended the Hays Office in his book, described the acute problems of cleaning up *Anna Karenina* for the screen:

'It was agreed . . . that all mention of the illegitimate child which appears in Tolstoy's original story would be eliminated . . . that at several points in the picture "the matrimonial bond" would be "positively defended" . . . that the sin of Anna and her lover Vronsky would not be presented as attractive or alluring . . . The producers agreed to do their best never to leave the audience in doubt throughout the picture, about right or wrong.'

Other films which gave the Hays Office qualms in the Thirties included *A Star Is Born, The Good Earth* (both 1937) and *These Three* (1936).

'It's hard to be funny when you have to be clean' Mae West

Artists like Mae West and W.C. Fields continued to be a thorn in the side of the censors. Even if they changed the title of *It Ain't No Sin* to *Belle of the Nineties* (1934) and cut out all the best lines, Mae West could still suggest, with a curl of the lip or the intonation of the most inoffensive word, a wealth of wicked sexuality. Fields turned the uncensorable phrase 'Godfrey Daniels' into an oath of dreadful profanity. When objections were made to his 'vulgar and suggestive scenes and dialogue' and innumerable jocular references to drinking and liquor, Fields retaliated with typical wit:

'I have been in the entertainment business some 43 years and I have never said anything . . . that might be construed as belittling any race or religion. I would be a sucker to do so because you can't insult the customers . . .

'Regarding the wiggle of the girl's backside – this crept in the script "unbeknownst" to me and there will be no wiggle as was permitted in *My Little Chickadee* . . .

'How anyone could read any vulgarity or obnoxiousness into castor oil and Snoop's following line about exercise is beyond me. I think if you'll have your office read this again they will get a proper understanding of the joke. "Take two of these in a glass of castor oil two nights running, then skip one night", followed by Snoop's remark "I thought you told me not to take any exercise." However to keep peace in the family I'll have it read cod liver oil . . .

'With reference to the name of the cafe, The Black Pussy, Mr Leon Errol, the renowned comedian, runs a cafe on Santa Monica Boulevard called The Black Pussy. It can be changed, but why? . . .
A hearty handclasp from Bill Fields'

Despite the efforts of such rare souls, the Hays Code was all-powerful, particularly after 1934 when Joseph Breen took over its administration. At more or less the same time the Catholic Legion of Decency was formed; its members boycotted and demonstrated against films of which they disapproved and Charles Chaplin was to be one of the more notable victims of their witch-hunting. Many other serious film-makers found their ideas blocked by the Hollywood censors for a crucial period of two decades.

THE NEW BABY . . . . . . By Hungerford

TEN DAYS
THAT **SHooK** THE **WoRLD**
(OCTOBER)

EISENSTEIN'S EPIC FILM
OF THE RUSSIAN
REVOLUTION

BRITISH PREMIERES
FRI · SAT · O^{CT} 18 & 19
CONWAY HALL
RED LION SQ WC1

Top: Will Hays, the 'Czar of Hollywood' and guardian of America's morals. Centre: a cartoonist's view of Hays. Above: poster for Eisenstein's October, *a film that was a victim of political censorship in Britain and had to be shown under club conditions.*
Top right: in 1897 a fire started by a careless cinematograph projectionist resulted in the destruction of the annual Paris Charity Bazaar. The fatalities included a cross-section of the French aristocracy and led to world-wide demands for official control of film exhibition

Censorship entered the British cinema by way of the fire escape. In nineteenth-century Europe theatre-going had become a very hazardous entertainment. Inflammable buildings and gas lighting had resulted in a terrible record of fatal fires. The new-fangled cinematograph, it seemed, was likely to be particularly lethal, owing to the highly inflammable nature of nitrate film.

In Britain local authorities diligently devised fire safety regulations to control cinematograph shows. In 1909 the Cinematograph Act, still in the cause of the physical safety of premises, imposed a duty on local authorities to *license* all cinema premises. The authorities interpreted their powers widely; conditions imposed in the granting of licenses came more and more to control the content or type of films shown. Matters came to a head in 1910 when a number of councils ordered bioscope operators not to exhibit films of the Johnson–Jeffries prize fight; the special offence in this celebrated sporting event lay in the fact of a black boxer defeating a white opponent.

Censorship entered the British cinema by way of the fire escape

The film trade, alarmed at the prospects of hundreds of local censors and unpredictable rulings, realized that one central censorship was a preferable evil. The Home Office declined to appoint a censor, so the trade created its own self-censoring body, the British Board of Film Censors (the BBFC) which commenced operation on January 1, 1913. The Board depended for its effectiveness upon the cooperation both of the film business (in submitting its films) and the local authorities (in recognizing and acting upon its classification). Though not too cooperative at first, local councils in Britain gradually accepted the authority of the BBFC.

Herbert Morrison, himself President of the BBFC from 1960 to 1965, said of the Board when he was Home Secretary in 1942: 'I freely admit that it is a curious arrangement, but the British have a great habit of making curious arrangements work very well – and this works.'

Unlike its Hollywood counterpart, the BBFC has never had a formal code, but in evidence to the Cinema Commission of Inquiry in 1916, T.P. O'Connor the Board's President, an MP and journalist, helpfully laid out 43 rules which he said, 'cover pretty well all the grounds you can think of'.

Predictably, O'Connor's rules range over every area of cruelty, vulgarity, indecorum, nudity, drugs, prostitution, venereal disease, excessive violence, and so on. The fact that Britain was at war at the time also prompted forms of political censorship. The Board's rules prohibited:

Relations of Capital and Labour
Scenes tending to disparage public characters and institutions
Incidents having a tendency to disparage our allies
Scenes holding up the King's uniform to contempt or ridicule
Subjects dealing with India, in which British officers are seen in an odious light, and otherwise attempting to suggest the disloyalty of native states, or bringing into disrepute British prestige in the Empire

As had happened in America, the Jazz Age brought new perils and new prohibitions. The British Board of Film Censors became concerned with such subjects as:

Advocacy of the doctrine of free love
Infidelity on the part of husband justifying adultery on the part of wife
Provocative and sensuous exposure of girls' legs
Abdominal contortions in dancing
Girls and women in a state of intoxication

And the 1926 annual report indicated new areas of political susceptibility:

American law officers making arrests in this country
Inflammatory sub-titles and Bolshevist propaganda

The last proscription led the Board energetically to ban a whole group of films destined to become classics – among them Eisenstein's *The Battleship Potemkin* (1925) and *October* (1927), Pudovkin's *Mother* (1926) and *The End of St Petersburg* (1927). All had originally been shown in London by the Film Society, which as a private organization was technically exempt from the regular licensing and censorship laws – a condition that survives today.

From the advent of the talkies in 1929 until 1947 the BBFC had one man in the key position of Secretary. His name was J. Brooke Wilkinson; he died in office when he was 78 years old and almost blind, a condition which has never seemed any grave deterrent to film censors.   DAVID ROBINSON

BIG BAD MAE

'Virtue has its own reward but no sale at the box office'

About two-thirds of the way through a quite unremarkable gangland drama, a new character suddenly enters, swaying easily and provocatively into a swank speakeasy. She leaves her coat, and as she removes it there is a glint of diamonds. The checkroom girl, impressed, remarks: 'Goodness, what beautiful diamonds.' 'Goodness had nothing to do with it, dearie,' replies Mae West, and sways on up the stairs into screen history. The film is *Night After Night*, the date 1932.

Even at this time she was no newcomer to show business. She was, according to her own estimate, pushing 40 (others put the year of her birth back from 1893 to 1886), and had been on stage in various ways since the age of six. She had played all the 'littles' (Little Lord Fauntleroy, Little Eva) in repertory, been billed as the 'Baby Vamp', originated the 'shimmy', been a top star in vaudeville, and since 1926 had been a phenomenon of the legitimate stage in a series of plays written by herself. These included the luridly titled *Sex, Diamond Lil, Pleasure Man,* and *The Constant Sinner*. The contents had been scarcely less alarming: one of her plays, *The Drag*, about a group of homosexuals, never reached New York for fear of puritan wrath, and *Pleasure Man* was the subject of a famous court hearing on the grounds of obscenity – which, let it be said, Mae West won.

She was good at winning out in such situations. And rightly so. She made sex a joke, which, though it may not be the only reasonable way of looking at it, was at least a lot better than pretending it did not exist unless it was disguised as 'romance', which was, of course, sacred to every shopgirl and never involved anything nasty unless it was immediately paid for in the worst possible way. But Mae kept everyone guessing. Her stream of snappy and outrageous innuendoes could never quite be pinned down or brought to book by public moralists. Even in New York theatre in the Twenties, she stood almost alone in her defence of sex against the repressive forces of puritanism. A rush of prosecutions in 1928 led to the introduction of an official code of morals for drama which set back freedom of speech in the theatre by several decades. This new era of restriction was, perhaps, a measure of America's increasing self-consciousness about where it stood in the modern cultivated world once it had left bold, bawdy pioneering days behind.

'It's not the men in my life that counts – it's the life in my men'

If so, Hollywood, with much less conscious yearning after culture, still lagged behind. The movement to clean up the movies was still hanging fire, and the freedom of speech and action allowed in the early talkies was surprising. Mae West was the perfect person to exploit it – and she did so with entirely fetching verve and good humour. To begin with, she was herself a parody of sex. If there was ever an era in her early career when she could have passed muster as a serious sex siren, the surviving

Left: Mae, shortly after arriving in Hollywood in 1932, in a publicity shot for Night After Night

The lady is a vamp – Mae around 1910 (left); the heavily censored Belle of the Nineties *(below left);* I'm No Angel *(above); Mae's screen debut,* Night After Night *(right)*

photographs do not show much evidence of it. By the time she made her first film she was already middle-aged and her always generous curves had filled out to a more than Junoesque amplitude; her rather pudgy features were made up in what was already an anachronistic fashion with a Cupid's-bow mouth and much eye-shadow and mascara. This was emphatically *not* the dutiful wife and mother image, nor was it a frontier woman – unless by the artificial light of a Western saloon. The effect was enhanced by her avoidance of modern dress: whenever possible she was decked out in the feathers and flounces of the Gay Nineties, and even when it was not possible she still somehow managed to leave that impression. Not only did goodness have nothing to do with it, nature had precious little to do with it either.

'I used to be Snow White – but I drifted'

And yet the overall tone of her films – the scripts of which she always wrote, largely or wholly, herself – was of a breezy realism, at least about the basic facts of life. She was funny too. A natural clown, deflating pomposity and self-importance, making fun of herself and what she seemed to represent in terms of outrageous sexual promise, she dominated every film she made and emerged as one of the cinema's great originals. Even Mae's belated appearance in *Night After Night* took over the film completely. She was already writing her own dialogue and ordering the director around; she felt she knew what was best for herself – and the world agreed with her. As a result of the sensation she caused with this film she was given a free hand with the next, and produced one of the most important and successful pictures of the decade. *She Done Him Wrong* (1933) financially saved the ailing Paramount studios, to whom she was under contract, from having to sell out to MGM. The

film was an adaptation of her play *Diamond Lil*, which suffered a title change because of its theatrical notoriety but was otherwise left alone – a cheerfully amoral tale of a lady of easy virtue, the men in her life, and the way that everything obstructing her is shunted aside to leave her completely on top and without a shade of guilt.

'Any time you got nothing to do – and lots of time to do it, come on up'

From here, with the public screaming for more, she went straight into perhaps her most extravagant role, as a nightclub singer who is also a glamorous lady lion-tamer, in *I'm No Angel* (1933). The picture was based on a script by Lowell Brentano, entirely reworked, as usual, by Mae West to conform with her characterization and its requirements. For like all the screen's great comedians, she essentially played the same role in all her films. And if, at first, it was not herself she was playing, it rapidly became a pretty good approximation. Even so it is noticeable that there has always been a clear separation between Mae West the person and Mae West the product: she tends to talk, in regard to her films, of how 'Mae West would not do this, might do that' rather than in the first person. And as she was the creator of this personage, so she was really the *auteur* of her films – on those occasions when she was not, they fell below past standards.

'Is that a gun in your pocket, or are you just glad to see me?'

Evidently she hit it off very well with Lowell Sherman, director of *She Done Him Wrong*, and Wesley Ruggles, director of *I'm No Angel*, but much less so, it seems, with Leo McCarey, who directed her third vehicle, *Belle of the Nineties*

In She Done Him Wrong *Mae resists Owen Moore (above) but later tells Cary Grant to 'Come up sometime, see me'. Klondike Annie (top) was brutally cut after complaints by women's groups. My Little Chickadee (top right), which was not a great box-office success, was the only film to co-star Mae and W.C. Fields, whose heavy drinking she frowned upon*

(1934). McCarey had his own ideas about how to put together a film comedy, and these frequently did not coincide with Mae's. This may well be one of the reasons for the film's relative feebleness compared with the previous two. Also it is another, lesser version of *Diamond Lil* (to be followed in 1936 by another, the even lesser *Klondike Annie*). But most damaging, no doubt, was the tightening up in 1934 of the Hays Office regulations regarding morality in films; everything touching on sex in movies became subject to scrutiny under this organization's notorious code with its petty, finely graduated rules and restrictions. *Belle of the Nineties* was the first of Mae's films

to be seriously interfered with in production. Both plot and dialogue were censored, and the title had to be changed from the more challenging *It Ain't No Sin*. It was still a big success with the public, but the golden era of Mae West in movies was past. Her next film, *Goin' to Town* (1935), had moments of memorable lunacy – in the craziest plot of all her films she is a cattle rustler's widow who breaks into high society and sings an aria from *Samson and Delilah* along the way – but from then on it was downhill. Even a screen encounter with W.C. Fields, in *My Little Chickadee* (1940), fell rather flat.

The reasons for this decline seem to be intimately bound up with censorship. A lot of her humour is very direct and, in a way, naive. It depends on statement and absolutely unavoidable inference. What could, and did, provoke a belly laugh becomes (when forced to go undercover and be slyly circumspect) either totally colourless and innocuous or else smutty. The necessity to be devious took away Mae West's most effective weapon, and she

was never happy without the power to say what she meant – and leave no doubts.

MAE: I like sophisticated men
    to take me out
MAN: I'm not
    really sophisticated
MAE: You're not
    really out yet either

Strangely, this decline did little or nothing to reduce Mae West's status as a legend. Of course, she continued working in other media – radio in the mid-Thirties, the theatre again in the late Forties with *Catherine Was Great* and revivals of *Diamond Lil*, and cabaret in Las Vegas in the Fifties. *The Heat's On* (1943), her next film, was neither here nor there, though she did look extraordinary in it. Her 'comeback' in *Myra Breckinridge* (1970) was hardly more than a guest appearance. And her latest film, *Sextette* (1978), is bizarre beyond belief, with this lady of 85 (or maybe 92) as the centre of amorous intrigue, lusted after by half a dozen men young enough, in a couple of cases, to be her great-grandsons. And yet somehow it does not matter. She is still Mae West, and the Mae West of today is only marginally more of a fantasy than the Mae West of 50 years ago. She was and is her own creation, and as such gave something unique to the cinema – herself. If the censors ruined her screen career, they also helped her towards immortality.

JOHN RUSSELL TAYLOR

Filmography
1932 Night After Night. '33 She Done Him Wrong; I'm No Angel (+sc). '34 Belle of the Nineties (+sc). '35 Goin' to Town (+sc). '36 Klondike Annie (+sc); Go West, Young Man (+sc). '38 Every Day's a Holiday (+sc). '40 My Little Chickadee (+co-sc). '43 The Heat's On (GB: Tropicana). '70 Myra Breckinridge. '78 Sextette.

Fresh Fields

The flowery gestures, the exaggerated drawl, the bulbous nose, the absurd pseudonyms, the love of gin, and the general hatred of mankind – these were the unlikely characteristics that made W.C. Fields one of the most popular screen comics of all time

Mean, moody and magnificent, W.C. Fields died on Christmas Day, 1946, the day he despised above all others. Perhaps the thought of all that good cheer, Christian charity, brotherly love and odious bonhomie finally did to Fields what 10,000 bottles of gin could not. Among his other pet hates were children, dogs, old ladies, Hollywood producers, water ('it rusts pipes') and Philadelphia (his birthplace). Fields was the man who gave misanthropy a good name. He hid his money away in several hundred separate bank accounts scattered across the world. Many still lie undiscovered, accruing dust and compound interest. He was fond of dressing his mistresses up as Chinamen and referred to Death as the old man in the nightgown. His epic battles with his occasional co-star, Baby LeRoy, are the stuff of legend: he once spiked the baby's milk with gin and was afterwards heard to shout, 'Walk the lush around – that boy's no trouper!'

For years he wore a hideous clip-on false moustache simply because everyone else loathed it. He was fond of picnics, booze, John Barrymore and extracting money from Hollywood producers. Though his films were never great box-office moneymakers, he none the less managed to secure a high salary for himself. This he did by insisting that he was the greatest, and that the studios were getting his services for a cheap price.

The names Fields invented for his characters, Egbert Sousé and Cuthbert J. Twillie, show a man creating his own world and insisting that if you entered it you accepted it on *his* terms. The pseudonyms he chose for himself when he was writing, like Mahatma Kane Jeeves and Otis Criblecoblis, were equally unlikely. His 'scriptwriting' usually consisted of an outline scribbled on the back of an envelope. It was just another way of making the producers pay him more money.

Fields expected the worst from the world and this is what he always got – right from the start, with his brutally wretched childhood, until his lonely, alcoholic end as the greatest American comedian of his time. He was born William Claude Dukenfield in 1879. He left home at the age of 11 after nearly braining his father (so he claimed), and slept rough – earning his living as a pool-room hustler. He painfully taught himself juggling and became one of the greatest tramp-jugglers in vaudeville. Soon he was making a running commentary of jokes during the course of his act.

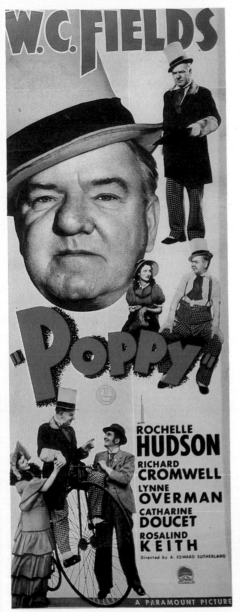

As the jokes grew, the juggling decreased and the comedian W.C. Fields was born. He was a comedian, not a clown. There is something inherently sentimental about the word 'clown'. Fields had no sentiment, no pathos, no self-pity. His view of life was baleful. As it showered disasters on his thoroughly deserving head, he became more treacherous and cowardly, unaware, it seemed, of the supremely comic figure he cut, and trying at all times to retain an impossible dignity and respectability. The flowery gestures, the slow, slurred speech of a drunken Jeeves, proclaimed a fraud: here was a man you could never trust. Everyone who does a W.C. Fields impersonation always misses out, lacking the characteristic pain and bitterness threaded through the distinctive speech patterns. And what of the famous bulbous nose with the blood showing through the pitted skin tissue? Who remembers

Left: adapted from his biggest stage success, Poppy *starred Fields as Professor Eustace McGargle, an itinerant quack. Below: in* The Old Fashioned Way *he is the Great McGonigle, an equally itinerant showman. Baby LeRoy was cast as Albert Wendelschaffer. Bottom: as golf champion S.B. Bellows, just before he flies off in his scooter-airplane*

that his nose got to look like that through repeated childhood beatings and not because of drink?

By 1900 Fields had become a top name in vaudeville and the following year embarked on a series of tours that were to take him all over the world. From 1915 until 1921 he was a major star of the Ziegfeld Follies – in which he performed his pool-room and golfing sketches – and in the Twenties made a number of silent

'If at first you don't succeed, try again. Then quit. No use being a damn fool about it'

films. These were variable in quality but all suffused with a typically sleazy bar-room tang which is his trade mark. Two of them, *Sally of the Sawdust* and *That Royle Girl* (both 1925), were directed by D.W. Griffith – not the best director for Fields: he always seemed to cut away at precisely the wrong moment.

It was not until the coming of sound, when his nasal, gin-soaked voice was finally heard, that Fields' persona flowered like some gorgeous, tropical, flesh-eating plant. His sound films can be divided into two kinds: 'wormy' and 'demonic'. In his 'wormy' films, like *It's a Gift* (1934) and *The Man on the Flying Trapeze* (1935), he is the hen-pecked husband who never raises rebellion to more than a constant mutter. They contain classic moments but they lack the invigoratingly destructive energy of his 'demonic' films in which he plays the bombastic huckster, ham and fraud. These include *The Old Fashioned Way* (1934), *You Can't Cheat an Honest Man* (1939) – Fields' favourite title, for like every successful con man, he believed there are no honest men – and *Never Give a Sucker an Even Break* (1941). The two modes, 'wormy' and 'demonic', co-exist in the masterly *The Bank Dick* (1940). The film is every middle-class male's Walter Mitty fantasy: any lazy, incompetent bank employee with an obnoxious wife and children can be a hero, financial genius, great writer, Hollywood director, *bon vivant* and general all-round good fellow. All you need is a little luck.

But generally in his films, Fields is alone in the midst of chaos – a chaos he himself has inspired by his interfering maladroitness – receiving no support from his appalling families who despise him for the worthless, lying layabout he undoubtedly is. So this extraordinary failure, this living embodiment of

'Anyone who hates small dogs and children can't be all bad'

every vice the bourgeoisie were taught to hate, trudges sourly from one certain catastrophe to the next. Anyone who takes such a low view of humanity is usually funny, and among screen comics only Will Hay takes a lower view.

In many ways like a low-life Dickensian character himself, Fields played Micawber in Cukor's *David Copperfield* (1935). It remains his best-known role but it is not representative – certainly far from his best. Fields in an 'art

Filmography
1915 Pool Sharks. '24 Janice Meredith (GB: The Beautiful Rebel). '25 Sally of the Sawdust; That Royle Girl. '26 It's the Old Army Game; So's Your Old Man. '27 The Potters; Running Wild; Two Flaming Youths. '28 Tillie's Punctured Romance; Fools for Luck. '30 The Golf Specialist (short). '31 Her Majesty Love. '32 Million Dollar Legs; If I Had a Million; The Dentist (+sc) (short). '33 The Fatal Glass of Beer (+sc) (short); The Pharmacist (+sc) (short); The Barber Shop (+sc) (short); International House; Tillie and Gus; Alice in Wonderland. '34 Six of a Kind; You're Telling Me; The Old Fashioned Way; Mrs Wiggs of the Cabbage Patch; It's a Gift. '35 David Copperfield; Mississippi; The Man on the Flying Trapeze (GB: The Memory Expert). '36 Poppy. '38 The Big Broadcast of 1938. '39 You Can't Cheat an Honest Man. '40 My Little Chickadee (+co-sc); The Bank Dick (+sc) (GB: The Bank Detective). '41 Never Give a Sucker an Even Break (GB: What a Man). '42 Tales of Manhattan (ep cut before film was released). '44 Follow the Boys; Song of the Open Road. '45 Sensations of 1945 (as himself).
All screenplay credits under aliases.

Above: Fields as Larson E. Whipsnade, the moneyless circus boss in You Can't Cheat an Honest Man. *Above right: as Micawber in* David Copperfield, *with Freddie Bartholomew. Right: as O'Hair the barber who is prone to cutting off his customers' ears in* The Barber Shop. *Far right: as Egbert Sousé in* The Bank Dick, *so agitated that he has stuck a pen in his head. Below right: as, simply, 'The Great Man', a story-writer at 'Esoteric Studios'*

movie' like *David Copperfield* was almost like Fields playing Hamlet – stricken with a touch of the 'cultures', restricted and strait-jacketed by a script. The supreme improvisor and inventor of comic business was not even allowed to juggle. The film really needed an actor like Laughton but it got Fields instead.

The one and only teaming of Fields and Mae West, in *My Little Chickadee* (1940), did not

'I exercise extreme self control. I never drink anything stronger than gin before breakfast'

work. Their egos and slow, drawling styles were too similar. But those who wish to take Fields neat – as undiluted as he took his own gin – must go to the shorts he made for Mack Sennett: *The Pharmacist, The Barber Shop* and, best of all, *The Fatal Glass of Beer* (all 1933). This great tale of the wild Yukon has Fields telling the story of how his son was brought low by the demon drink. Fields plays the zither in mittens, milks a herd of elks, and repeatedly opens the door of his log cabin to be hit by a handful of paper snow and mutter, 'It ain't a fit night for man nor beast'.

Why is this brandy-bottle figure funny? There is no simple answer, except that Fields was his own man. His humour came from his own worm's eye view of the world, from a vision made up from his own unique days of living. The laughs didn't come easily – he earned them hard. And that wisdom, that pain, was turned into liberating laughter.

PETER BARNES

REAL LIFE ON THE SCREEN

During the Thirties in the great movie industries of America, Russia and Western Europe, film-makers sought their new subjects and styles in the 'real world' beyond the studios

The other side of the coin from escapism was a new gritty realism in films of the Thirties. The collapse of traditional American values, that began with the introduction of Prohibition in 1919 and culminated in the Wall Street Crash of 1929, provided Hollywood with 'realistic' material that ranged from the sensational, newspaper-headline stuff of the gangster movies to the more earnest, socially aware films reflecting the spirit of Franklin D. Roosevelt's New Deal.

It would indeed have been extraordinary if Hollywood had not sought to exploit the breakdown of law and order as potential film themes. Among the gangster films *The Public Enemy* (1931) aroused official opinion against the genre on account of its unprecedented violence. *Scarface* (1932) pushed official antagonism further and had the effect of sharpening Hollywood censorship, owing to the close parallels the film made with the real-life story of Al Capone. Never had murder been shown so casually and lightheartedly as in the machine-gunning of the restaurant; never had massacre been so nonchalantly filmed as in the famous St Valentine's Day Massacre sequence; never before had Hollywood got close to depicting incest as in the relations between Scarface (brilliantly played by Paul Muni) and his sister. But the gangster always got his comeuppance. Justice was meted out and injustice was rooted out; such was the moral code of the Warners 'social-conscience' movies.

Mervyn LeRoy, who had made *Little Caesar* in 1930, consolidated his reputation for tough, uncompromising films with *I Am a Fugitive From a Chain Gang* (1932). Once again Paul Muni gave a wonderful performance, this time as a man unjustly accused, condemned, tortured and finally turned into a hunted escapee.

LeRoy delved further behind the headlines in *Five Star Final* (1931), exposing the gutter press, and in *Hard to Handle* (1933), a satire on the money-grubbing race of con men. It was LeRoy, too, who in 1937 made an anti-lynching film, *They Won't Forget*, which on balance improved upon Fritz Lang's *Fury* of the same year, if only because it avoided Lang's implicit excuse that lynchers are 'only human'. In *They Won't Forget* LeRoy makes no such excuses; he excludes forgiveness. Claude Rains plays the shifty local governor who gets his way by dubious and questionable means. LeRoy employs some stunningly effective high-angle shots (of an interrogation; of a girl's body crumpled at the bottom of a lift shaft), and builds to a sickening climax when the hanging of the innocent schoolmaster is shown through the image of a high-speed train snatching a mailbag off its post.

Boldness was very much the keynote of the series of screen biographies that William Dieterle made for Warners in the Thirties. Although they were far removed from the 'real life' of their subjects, *The Story of Louis Pasteur* (1935), *The Life of Emile Zola* (1937) and *Juarez* (1939) dealt with progressive historical figures who pioneered medical science (*Pasteur*) or fought for liberty (*Zola* and *Juarez*).

In a parallel development the documentary movement began to make its presence felt on filmgoers. The work of the American 'father' of documentary, Robert Flaherty, and the influence of John Grierson's British documentary group had not gone unnoticed in the United States. Various young filmmakers became interested in this new approach to cinema in terms of realism and public education.

One of these directors was Pare Lorentz, a former film critic, who made *The Plow That Broke the Plains* (1936), an imaginative documentary on the dust-bowl. The same subject was given a fictional treatment a few years later by John Ford in *The Grapes of Wrath* (1940) – a dramatization of one family's heroic attempts to escape the misery of agricultural poverty.

Lorentz returned to the dust-bowl phenomenon – and the specific problems of the Mississippi basin – in his next film *The River* (1938). Both *The Plow* and *The River* had declamatory narrations, and powerful musical scores by the distinguished composer Virgil Thomson. These films attracted the attention of President Roosevelt, who set up a government film agency whose purpose was to assist the

production of this kind of film.

Lorentz planned two more films: one, on unemployment, never came to fruition; the other, *The Fight for Life* (1940), about Chicago's maternity services, was impressive enough to be banned in Chicago and highly praised elsewhere.

Some of the ideas about the portrayal of reality and the 'truthfulness' of the documentary image surfaced in the *March of Time* series in the mid to late Thirties. An offshoot of the magazines *Time* and *Life*, this dramatized account of world events set out to be provocative. Departing from the principle of documentary film, the series mixed actualities with

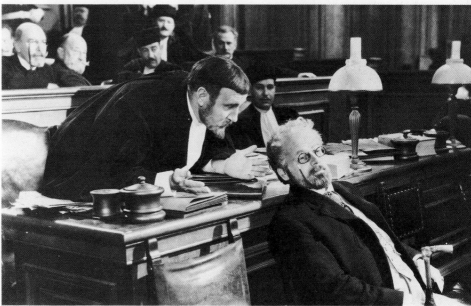

Top: still a polished Hollywood product, but a new raw quality was apparent in the look and sound of The Public Enemy, *starring James Cagney. Above: Paul Muni as Zola, interrogated over his defence of civil liberties in* The Life of Emile Zola, *the story of the 19th-century novelist who pioneered realist fiction*

Top: I Am a Fugitive From a Chain Gang. *Top right:* The River *and (centre)* The Plow That Broke the Plains *by Pare Lorentz. Above: how the* March of Time *saw its role*

completely reconstructed scenes using actors and look-alikes.

From its inception in 1935 the *March of Time* was an instant success. (When it opened a British branch Grierson protégés Edgar Anstey and Harry Watt directed films for it.) On issues like the Spanish Civil War it was characteristically outspoken and filmgoers seemed not to care about the nature of the realism – 'fakery in allegiance to the truth' as *Time* magazine's boss Henry Luce described it.

Certainly the series created an easier climate of opinion for genuine documentaries like *The City* (1939), a critique of slum conditions directed by Ralph Steiner and Willard van Dyke. In the same period Frontier Films made *China Strikes Back* (1937), a film that dared to suggest that Mao Tse-tung, rather than Chiang Kai Shek, might prove to be the saviour of that country.

In Britain, however, documentary film-making was founded on John Grierson's genius for attracting governmental and industrial sponsorship. A new concept of non-theatrical distribution was established that bypassed public cinemas and took films to people in other social situations, like clubs and town and village halls.

This was a period of great collaboration between film-makers and artists from other disciplines. The poet W.H. Auden and the composer Benjamin

Britten joined forces under Grierson's banner with film-makers like Basil Wright, Paul Rotha, Harry Watt, Arthur Elton and Edgar Anstey. Among the most acclaimed documentaries of this period are *Song of Ceylon* (dir. Basil Wright, 1934), *Shipyard* (dir. Paul Rotha, 1935), and *North Sea* (dir. Harry Watt, 1938). Towards the end of the decade there were signs that the documentary idea was having some influence on feature films in Britain, notably in King Vidor's *The Citadel* (1938) and Carol Reed's *The Stars Look Down* (1939) – two fictional films set against the harsh world of mining communities.

In the Soviet Union cinematic realism underwent several major changes during the Thirties. The revolutionary experimentation of film-makers like Eisenstein and Vertov gave way rather abruptly to a state-imposed style introduced under Stalin as 'socialist realism'. Vertov's *Enthusiasm* (1931) and *Three Songs of Lenin* (1934) were perhaps the last examples of radical approaches to film realism before Stalin appointed Shumyatsky to take a firm grip on film-making policy and ensure that only socialist realist films were produced. Films should henceforth deal with the construction of a new socialist state and with 'positive' Soviet heroes.

Most of Russia's innovative directors met censorship problems under the new regime. Alexander Dovzhenko's *Earth* (1930) and *Aerograd* (1935) suffered from official cutting and the director described the terror with which he used to answer midnight summonses to the Kremlin to see Stalin and his chief of police, Beria. For Eisenstein, too, the Thirties involved massive frustrations and compromises. He returned from the USA having failed to complete *Que Viva Mexico* (1931) and his next production, *Bezhin Meadow*, fared no better.

At the Kino Conference in Moscow in 1935 a new film, *Chapayev*, by Sergei and Georgi Vassiliev was extolled as a model of socialist realist film-making; Eisenstein, however, was severely criticized for his lack of creative effort and his unconventional attitudes. He thus began *Bezhin Meadow* under the growing displeasure of the authorities. Work was interrupted when Eisenstein fell ill with smallpox, and eventually production was halted on the orders of Shumyatsky, who proceeded to attack Eisenstein both in print and during a three-day discussion of the film. All that remains of *Bezhin Meadow* is a collection of stills which were incorporated into a short film two decades after Eisenstein's death.

Within the straitjacket of socialist realism a number of fine films did emerge as classics, notably

the *Maxim* trilogy (1935–39) by Kozintsev and Trauberg and the *Gorky* trilogy (1938–40) by Mark Donskoy, two of the finest filmic achievements in the entire decade.

In German sound cinema the tradition of representing scenes from real life took new impetus from Ruttmann's *Die Melodie der Welt* (1929, Melody of the World). By the early Thirties G.W. Pabst had established a reputation for realist fiction allied to a social cause: pacifism in *Westfront 1918* (1930) and cooperation between workers of different nations in *Kameradschaft* (1931, Comradeship), though Pabst's simplistic handling of *Die Dreigroschenoper* (1931, *The Threepenny Opera*) caused the celebrated lawsuit.

Documentary became an art form and also found its way into the look of fiction films. But 'realism' didn't mean the same thing in Russia as it did to the Hollywood moguls

---

A much more radical approach to the conditions of the man in the street, through its violent editing and superimpositions of shots, was *Kühle Wampe* (1931, *Whither Germany?*), the story of a society fighting for its life in a dangerous political arena. By the time the Nazis had come to power, however, fiction film was more or less all escapism and the documentary film had to follow a prescribed format – a skill supremely handled by Leni Riefenstahl.

For *Triumph des Willens* (1934, *Triumph of the Will*) the entire Nuremberg Rally was turned over to her so that she could do as she pleased. The result was sensational: Hitler arrived by air, like God coming down from heaven, and the vast crowd scenes were choreographed to fit powerful compositions. Unfortunately the film degenerated into a series of propaganda speeches, unlike her later Nazi epic *Olympia* (1936, *Berlin Olympiad*) which had the events of the Games themselves to hold the interest.

Elsewhere in Europe documentary was very much the province of a handful of individuals. In 1934 the Dutchman Joris Ivens completed *Nieuwe Gronden* (*New Earth*), a beautifully shot and edited film about the reclamation of the Zuiderzee. As a dedicated communist, Ivens went to the Spanish Civil War front and directed *Spanish Earth* (1937) for which Ernest Hemingway wrote the narration.

The following year Ivens was in China, accompanied by his compatriot John Ferno who was already well known for his film on *Easter Island* (1934). Between them they filmed *The 400 Million* (1939) which incurred some censorship problems in China, though the material itself was splendid. To the completed film was added a narration written by Dudley Nichols and spoken by Fredric March; it had a satisfactorily controversial reception.

Ivens' other great collaborator was the Belgian documentarist Henri Storck, famous for his films of social criticism. Together they made *Borinage* (1933), an unusually committed film that exposed the appalling working conditions among Belgian coal-miners and revealed their brutal treatment at the hands of the police during a strike. As might be expected the film was made in some secrecy and though it was shown in cine-clubs and film societies, it was officially banned.

Storck met further official disapproval over *Les Maisons de la Misère* (1937), an exposure of shocking slum conditions in some towns in Belgium that amounted to a vigorous plea for housing reform. During the Thirties both Ivens and Storck maintained regular contact with the British documen-

tarists and in 1937 I went to Brussels to collaborate with Storck on the making of an anti-fascist film.

Another form of realism began to emerge in France principally through the work of the great Jean Renoir. In *Toni* (1934) – a film that deserves more recognition than it has hitherto received – Renoir did not hesitate to expose the exploitation of poor immigrant workers in the south of France. Filming in a harshly realistic style and in pitiless sunlight, Renoir brought an impression of authenticity to his images that contributed to a style later known as 'poetic realism'. In the light of his subsequent work, however, Renoir's unique style becomes impossible to sum up in a handy formula. Writing about *La Bête Humaine* (1938) some 20 years later one French critic described it as 'at once a naturalistic drama, a lyrical work and a documentary essay'. Renoir's outstanding films of the Thirties are treated in depth in later chapters but it is important to note here that the commitment of *La Grande Illusion* (1937), *La Marseillaise* (1937) and *La Règle du Jeu* (1939) ensured that Renoir's approach to film-making always had a sharp political edge.

During the decade that witnessed the Wall Street Crash, the Depression, the rise of Fascist Parties in Italy and Germany, and the emergence of Stalin's autocratic rule in the Soviet Union, one film-maker made three comedies that helped filmgoers laugh at the ways of the world. Chaplin's *City Lights* (1931), *Modern Times* (1936) and *The Great Dictator* (1940) all contained overtones and undertones of social and political comment and reflected grave world events through the mirror of comedy.

BASIL WRIGHT

Top: Robert Donat led Welsh miners to better working conditions in King Vidor's The Citadel. *Centre: Belgian miners scratched a living from the coal they dug in Storck and Ivens'* Borinage. *Above: Basil Wright directing* Song of Ceylon

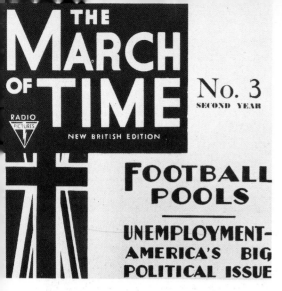

THE MARCH OF TIME

No. 3
SECOND YEAR
NEW BRITISH EDITION

RADIO PICTURES

FOOTBALL POOLS

UNEMPLOYMENT – AMERICA'S BIG POLITICAL ISSUE

Edgar Anstey, British documentary director, became Foreign Editor with the *March of Time* newsreel in New York in 1936. Here he recalls its aggressive style of presentation

After being trained by John Grierson, I believed that the only other person in films who had anything to teach me was Louis de Rochemont, the creator of the *March of Time*. This was a crusading American 'newsreel' series that assembled on the screen not only the facts but the ideas that linked them. When de Rochemont invited me to join his organization in 1936 – on the recommendation of Grierson himself – it seemed a heaven-sent opportunity. Louis's brother Richard was about to set up a London-based production unit for *March of Time*.

I had just finished making *Enough to Eat?* a social documentary which revealed the extent of malnutrition in Britain. For my first subject at *March of Time*, I was asked to make another film on malnutrition and the difference in the approaches of the two films serves to illustrate the distinction between documentary (in Grierson's original sense) and Louis de

Above: March of Time's *typical mixture – foreign news and national sport. Below: how the series was promoted to exhibitors*

Rochemont's treatment of such issues.

Enough to Eat? had attacked malnutrition as a social evil to be scientifically analyzed, but for the *March of Time*, the theme was designed to alarm its worldwide audiences by illustrating the effect of British malnutrition on the physical stamina of any army Britain might be required to recruit against Hitler and Mussolini.

This was my first experience of how the *March of Time* would slant whatever story they wanted to make towards a topical issue, preferably one involving emotional confrontation, while avoiding those documentary techniques such as animated diagrams and 'talking heads' which they believed the cinema exhibitors regarded as anathema.

When the film I had written and directed came back from *March of Time* HQ in New York with the title *Britain's Food Defences*, I was astonished at how the narrative substituted bold assertion for the analysis of evidence. Yet what it said was true, and whereas *Enough to Eat?* had got a very great deal of attention in the press – including a first leader in *The Times* – only a handful of cinemas showed such documentaries. Against that, RKO were distributing each issue of *March of Time* to somewhere in the region of 1200 British cinemas.

In spite of the flat pictorial composition and staccato editing which characterized *March of Time* yet seemed foreign to my documentary training, I quickly detected an alternative skill of an equally high order. It lay in the precision of the relationship between image, word and musical phrase. When – after making nine subjects – I arrived in New York for a spell as Foreign Editor at the heart of the organization, I was not surprised to find that every *March of Time* film was personally shaped by Louis.

It was in the cutting room, under the close scrutiny and sometimes tyrannical supervision of Louis de Rochemont, that the power of each episode was generated. But the planning and shooting of the material was no less intensive. My English film unit could schedule to cover in one day three different locations with synchronous sound (long before the ease of magnetic tape) and light the settings sufficiently for the insensitive film stock of the time. We hoped that when Louis saw the 'rushes' he would be persuaded to adhere to

Top: a shot from Edgar Anstey's footage obtained, at personal risk, during a miners' strike. Centre: the interchange of USA and British news via the March of Time *consolidated the two countries' alliance*

the line I had scripted and not substitute stock shots or re-enactment to enhance the drama (as was often the practice at *March of Time*). Yet when Louis did so, I never remember wanting to challenge the correctness of his decision. So-called facts must, in any case, be distorted by the interpretative characteristics of the camera and the microphone themselves; the 'honesty' of a film could only be finally judged in terms of the pattern of ideas left with its audience – and this was the instinctive test Louis de Rochemont applied.

In seeking material for Louis to accept or reject, one became involved in an often hazardous adventure where enterprise provided no guarantee of success. The anti-Nazi film which brought me into the dock at Bow Street was censored in Britain and never shown there for being unfriendly to Germany which was officially a friendly power at that time.

Louis de Rochemont and John Grierson always seemed a bit offhand about each other and absent-minded as to whether they ever met. Yet both men did their finest work in awakening the societies they served to an understanding of the link between fascism and social privilege and, over the years, developed a guarded admiration for each other.

EDGAR ANSTEY

Mervyn LeRoy is today best remembered for his hard-edged social-problem films of the early Thirties, but he also earned a reputation as a competent, dependable director of nearly every type of entertainment movie. In many ways LeRoy was the epitome of the Hollywood studio-contract director

LeRoy was born in San Francisco in 1900. As a young man he worked on the vaudeville stage and began his career in films as an actor in the early Twenties. Later in the decade he directed programme fillers for First National Pictures, where his colleagues included Archie Mayo, Roy del Ruth and Lloyd Bacon.

Along with hundreds of technicians, actors, writers and directors, LeRoy was 'inherited' by Warner Brothers when that then fledgling company acquired First National in 1928. From then on he continued to turn out one film after another, staying well within studio re-quirements, limitations and style. Between 1930 and 1939 LeRoy directed no less than 33 films, running the entire studio gamut from low-budget 'quickies' to important A productions, and touching every possible genre (except the Western) along the way: comedies, melodramas, gangster movies, historical romances, social-problem films and musicals. His own reputation ran parallel, and grew, with that of Warners.

Moving to Metro

In 1938, after proving that he could handle major prestige productions with big budgets and bring in a handsome profit, as with *Anthony Adverse* (1936), LeRoy moved to MGM – where the budgets were consistently higher – as a producer and director. (He had worked for MGM twice before when Warners loaned him to them to direct *Gentleman's Fate* in 1931 and *Tugboat Annie* in 1933.) His new salary was $300,000 a year – so huge for its day that it was announced as $150,000 so that none of the other MGM producers would ask for a rise.

At MGM the films LeRoy directed were mostly sentimental melodramas based on best-selling novels and plays that could be turned

Above: LeRoy with Paul Muni, star of I Am a Fugitive From a Chain Gang *which the director considered his most important film. Below: first in line on the chain-gang, Muni as the wrongly imprisoned Jim Allen*

The Real LeRoy

Above: the costume romance Anthony Adverse *starred Fredric March as a globe-trotting adventurer. Right:* Random Harvest *provided blissful wartime escapism*

into vehicles for his favourite leading ladies, Greer Garson and Lana Turner. It was LeRoy who discovered Turner, directing her in her debut, *They Won't Forget*, for Warners in 1937, and then taking her with him to MGM where her career as a major star of the Forties was launched. In the Fifties, with the studio system dying, LeRoy set up his own production company, co-producing with and releasing through first MGM and later Warner Brothers. By the end of the decade he was producing and directing no more than one film a year, a pattern he followed through the first half of the Sixties.

The social question

It is difficult and dangerous to assign personal responsibility to studio-contract directors like LeRoy for the content, theme, or style of their films. LeRoy's reputation at Warners in the

Below: Clinton Rosemond as the terrified negro janitor in They Won't Forget, *LeRoy's indictment of mob rule and lynch law*

Thirties rests, it is true, on a handful of contemporary social-problem films: *Little Caesar* (1930), *Two Seconds, I Am a Fugitive From a Chain Gang* (both 1932), and *They Won't Forget*. But the fact that these pictures are often revived while others he made – such as *The World Changes* (1933), *Hi, Nellie!* (1934), or *Page Miss Glory* (1935) – are seldom seen, tends to emphasize the socially aware aspect of his career at the expense of other aspects. And although LeRoy later enjoyed more freedom at MGM, it is noticeable that social-problem pictures did not figure highly in his choice of films. Even *Blossoms in the Dust* (1941) – about illegitimate children – and *Homecoming* (1948) – about soldiers returning from the war – are essentially forays into sentiment, dealing with emotional and romantic personal problems

Above: Quo Vadis?, *LeRoy's epic, with Finlay Currie, Deborah Kerr and Robert Taylor. Below: Margaret O'Brien and 17-year-old Elizabeth Taylor in* Little Women

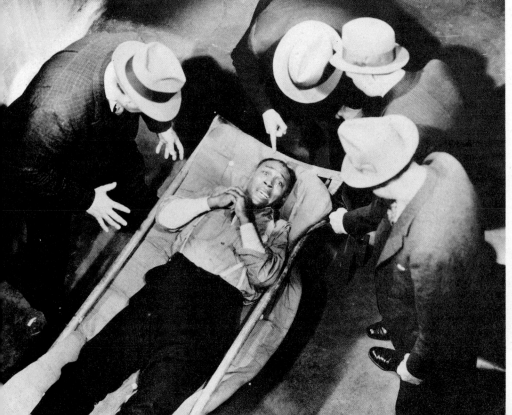

rather than social issues.

Moreover, if LeRoy's socially conscious films are compared with similar films of the period, they seem less original and less unique in style or content; an example is *Little Caesar*, which has dated far more than its two contemporary 'companions'. *The Public Enemy* (1931) and *Scarface* (1932). Whether certain sorts of 'punch-pulling' can now be thought of as LeRoy 'touches', or simply a matter of studio policy, is debatable. *I Am a Fugitive From a Chain Gang* had a tremendous impact at the time of its release (although the amount of actual prison reform that resulted from it has been greatly exaggerated) and is still effective enough to outrage audiences. Nevertheless, the film's rather obsessive insistence on the innocence of the protagonist (Paul Muni), almost to the point of making him seem a fool, now tends to blunt its supposed purpose. It is as if society's fault was in sentencing an innocent man to a chain-gang rather than in allowing injustice and deplorable conditions in prisons.

Again, one would be hard pressed to identify anything in either *Little Caesar* or *I Am a Fugitive From a Chain Gang* that makes them uniquely LeRoy films. There is little doubt that LeRoy was as effective a craftsman as any other studio-contract director, and indeed rather more effective than most, but it was Warner Brothers that finally dictated the look, the pace, even the lighting of their pictures.

Sentimental values

At times during his MGM career, LeRoy was arguably a better producer than director; he guided *The Wizard of Oz* (1939) to box-office success and to the level of a classic, bravely scrapping everything shot by Richard Thorpe and beginning again with Victor Fleming. As a

Above: Natalie Wood doing a chaste striptease in Gypsy, *LeRoy's film about Gypsy Rose Lee.*
Below: James Stewart (kneeling) in The FBI Story, *a tribute to the Hoover organization.*
Below right: Jean Seberg and Sean Garrison in the melodrama Moment to Moment

director LeRoy was certainly uneven. His Greer Garson vehicles – *Blossoms in the Dust*, *Random Harvest* (1942), and *Madame Curie* (1944) – are striking sentimental soap operas, but neither better nor worse than William Wyler's *Mrs Miniver* (1942) with the same star and formula. Indeed, as the Forties wore on, LeRoy's direction became slower in pace, heavier, more pretentious and literary. By the time of *Little Women* (1949), *Quo Vadis?* (1951) and *Rose Marie* (1954), the name Mervyn LeRoy had become synonymous with expensive production values.

Although his methods had not much changed, LeRoy did far better commercially in the late Fifties and early Sixties by buying 'presold' hit plays and books for transposition to the screen: *The Bad Seed* (1956), *No Time for Sergeants* (1958), *The FBI Story* (1959), *Gypsy* (1962), and *Mary, Mary* (1963).

Oddly, his reputation had long since ceased to rest on his ability to turn out fast-moving,

hard-hitting social problem films, but on his huge budgets, his 'respect' for 'literature' and the commercial importance of his subjects. Oddly too, his earlier enforced anonymity at Warners as a competent studio director had finally become an anonymity that stemmed from the fact that his films were directed primarily by their budgets.   DAVID OVERBEY

Filmography
1920 Double Speed (actor only). '**22** The Ghost Breaker (actor only). '**23** Little Johnny Jones (actor only); Going Up (actor only); The Call of the Canyon (actor only). '**24** Broadway After Dark (actor only); The Chorus Lady (actor only). '**27** No Place to Go/Her Primitive Mate. '**28** Flying Romeos; Harold Teen; Oh, Kay! '**29** Naughty Baby (GB: Reckless Rosie); Hot Stuff (+co-ed) (both sound and silent versions); Broadway Babies (GB: Broadway Daddies); Little Johnny Jones. '**30** Playing Around; Showgirl in Hollywood; Numbered Men; Top Speed; Little Caesar. '**31** Gentleman's Fate; Too Young to Marry/Broken Dishes; Broadminded; Five Star Final; Local Boy Makes Good; Tonight or Never. '**32** High Pressure; Heart of New York; Two Seconds; Big City Blues; Three on a Match; I Am a Fugitive From a Chain Gang. '**33** Hard to Handle; Tugboat Annie; Elmer the Great; Gold Diggers of 1933; The World Changes. '**34** Heat Lightning; Hi, Nellie!; Happiness Ahead. '**35** Page Miss Glory; I Found Stella Parish; Sweet Adeline. '**36** Anthony Adverse; Three Men on a Horse. '**37** The King and the Chorus Girl (+prod); They Won't Forget (+prod); The Great Garrick (prod. only). '**38** Fools for Scandal (+prod); Stand Up and Fight (prod. only); Dramatic School (prod. only). '**39** At the Circus (prod. only); The Wizard of Oz (prod. only). '**40** Waterloo Bridge; Escape (+prod) (reissued as When the Door Opened). '**41** Blossoms in the Dust (+prod); Unholy Partners; Johnny Eager. '**42** Random Harvest. '**44** Madame Curie; Thirty Seconds Over Tokyo. '**45** The House I Live In (co-prod. only) (short). '**46** Without Reservations. '**48** Homecoming. '**49** Little Women (+prod); Any Number Can Play. '**50** East Side, West Side. '**51** Quo Vadis? '**52** Lovely to Look At; Million Dollar Mermaid (GB: The One Piece Bathing Suit). '**53** Latin Lovers. '**54** Rose Marie (+prod). '**55** Strange Lady in Town (+prod); Mister Roberts (co-dir. only). '**56** The Bad Seed (+prod); Toward the Unknown (+prod) (GB: Brink of Hell). '**58** No Time for Sergeants (+prod); Home Before Dark (+prod). '**59** The FBI Story (+prod). '**60** Wake Me When It's Over (+prod). '**61** The Devil at 4 O'Clock (+prod); A Majority of One (+prod). '**62** Gypsy (+prod). '**63** Mary, Mary (+prod). '**65** Moment to Moment (+prod).
LeRoy also worked as a gag writer on 10 films between 1924 and 1927.

Meet the people
The birth of the British documentary movement

John Grierson coined the word 'documentary' in 1926 to describe Robert Flaherty's *Moana*, a romantic picture of life in the South Sea Islands, but many films made long before this date could well have been called documentaries. Notable among these were a three-reeler about Peek Frean and Company's biscuit works made in 1906; the film records of Scott and Shackleton's Antarctic expeditions of 1910–13 and 1914–17 (the latter film, brilliantly photographed by Frank Hurley, showed in spectacular long panning shots the death-throes of Shackleton's ship the *Endurance*); and Mary Field and Percy Smith's *Secrets of Nature* series which was being produced by British Instructional Films all through the Twenties.

What, then, was so different or new about the movement Grierson founded in 1929? The answer, at least at the beginning, is only partly to be found in the films themselves. The most distinguished of those made in the early years were Grierson's own *Drifters* (1929), photographed by a professional cameraman Basil Emmott, and *Industrial Britain* (1933), which Grierson and others edited together from material shot by the brilliant Robert Flaherty. Neither makes a very strong impression today.

What *was* fundamentally different was the kind of sponsorship that Grierson obtained, and the publicity line he adopted in order to attract that sponsorship. The money for *Drifters* – and for setting up a new film unit – came from a government department, the Empire Marketing Board, so the operation had to seem prestigious. Grierson, through his writing, quickly created such an image for it. His propaganda – rather than the films – enabled his unit to survive the EMB's dissolution in 1933. It was taken over by the General Post Office, where it began to flower.

Grierson's young recruits, Basil Wright, John Taylor, Arthur Elton, Edgar Anstey, Stuart Legg and Harry Watt, had unprecedented opportunities for all kinds of experiment, even personal expression – a rare set-up at any time. Even so, the freedom had definite political limits. Despite the movement's left-wing sympathies, Grierson's films could never be instruments of the working-class in the sense we understand the phrase today. His sponsors were always either government departments or private industry, and the British establishment, then as now, does not pay for working-class propaganda. The message had to be indirect. Consequently, most of the documentaries reflected another strong British tradition, that of compromise.

The working man tended to be idealized.

Above: the relationship between the pit machinery and the indomitable mine-worker is underlined in Coal Face. *Below: Man dwarfed by the vastness of the Antarctic –* Endurance

Edgar Anstey recalls:

'The ordinary man was seen as a heroic symbol . . . If he's not heroic, he can't be a working man, almost.'

Another director, Harry Watt, comments:

'We were trying to give an image of the working man, away from the Edwardian, Victorian, capitalist attitudes . . .'

None of this had very much to do with the desperate plight of large numbers of working-class people during the Depression years of the Thirties. Even at the time it was made, the famous *Drifters* was attacked for failing to include any mention of the price the fishermen got (and paid) for their large haul. But some of the later films were a good deal bolder. It took genius to see that the gas industry could be persuaded to pay for such direct indictments of bad living conditions as *Housing Problems* (1935) and *Enough to Eat?* (1936).

Housing Problems, officially directed by Elton and Anstey, owes its success to interviews with slum tenants in their homes; the first instance of something that has become commonplace on television, but has never been done better, despite vast improvements in modern technical equipment. The Thirties' documentaries, in fact, consistently demonstrate that technical facilities matter a good deal less than talent and a passionate sense of purpose. Grierson's sister, Ruby, credited as assistant on *Housing Problems*, is remembered for her ability to win people's confidence, and there seems little doubt that the sincerity of the interviews is due to her and to John Taylor, who was cameraman. At the end of his life, Grierson praised the film above all the others:

'You could recognise right away that this was a new relationship entirely between the film-makers and the films, that they were making films with the people and that they were, well, very close to the people indeed.'

In this context also, the work of Paul Rotha, a maverick independent whose early association with the Grierson unit was brief, but who has chronicled their activities ever since, must

Drifters (above) emphasized the corporate spirit and 'joy in work' of the trawlermen. Certain later films like Enough to Eat? *(right) and* Housing Problems *(below) used statistics and interviews to show the misery of those trapped by social conditions*

be mentioned. His grim shots of industrial England in *The Face of Britain* (1935), the tragic picture of unemployed miners in the Rhondda valley in *Today We Live* (produced by Rotha with Ruby Grierson and Ralph Bond as directors in 1937) showed a profound social concern that pointed the way to Rotha's later and better known *World of Plenty* (1943), *Land of Promise* (1945) and *The World is Rich* (1947). Rotha, more than any of the others, increasingly asked penetrating questions, and there is an idealism in his work that seems doubly disturbing in the light of subsequent history.

Grierson began to lose interest in the aesthetic side of film-making during the Thirties; his reputation still rests on the experimental work that he made possible (both in Britain and in Canada) and on the talent he had the inspiration to employ; in Britain, after Flaherty, the list of names includes Richard Massingham and Lotte Reiniger, Norman McLaren and Len Lye. However the single individual crucial to the consolidation of

Grierson's original ambitions for his unit was Alberto Cavalcanti.

Cavalcanti, was a professional film director who had worked with the industry and the *avant-garde* in France. He joined Grierson in 1934. The unit had just acquired its own sound recording equipment, and Cavalcanti was vitally interested in experimenting with sound. Under his leadership, the whole unit involved itself in a crazy parody of middle-class suburbia called *Pett and Pott*, for which they recorded the sound first and added the picture afterwards. Humphrey Jennings, the unit's newest recruit and a favourite of Cavalcanti's, designed the sets. The film now seems somewhat classbound in the same way as the feature films of the period, but from an imaginative point of view it was years ahead of its time.

Cavalcanti proceeded to salvage a good deal of material which had been shot without sound. The outstanding case of this was *Coal Face* (1935), which consisted of coal mining shots that had been lying around for several years,

padded out with additional material shot by almost everyone in the unit. All this Cavalcanti edited together with an inspired soundtrack based on a poem by W.H. Auden and with music by Benjamin Britten, both unknown names at the time. Auden was a personal friend of Basil Wright whose contribution to the success of a collaboration that continued into *Night Mail* (1936) is as incalculable as that of Cavalcanti himself.

Before *Night Mail*, Wright had completed his beautiful *Song of Ceylon* (1934). This film too depended very much on its sound track, which Wright worked on with the composer Walter Leigh. According to Cavalcanti, 'Basil Wright knew very well what he wanted, and I gave him a few ideas . . . But the whole construction of the sound of *Song of Ceylon* is Basil's and Walter Leigh's, of course . . .' Wright himself has praised Grierson's influence on the final editing of *Song of Ceylon*.

Of all the films of the Thirties, *Night Mail* was probably most responsible for putting the British documentary on the map. It made drama, poetry and first-class entertainment out of the overnight journey of the mail train from London to Glasgow. A paean of praise for an existing institution, the idea behind *Night Mail* can only be regarded as conservative, but nobody who cares about the cinema would surely dream of approaching such a work from an exclusively political point of view.

Night Mail is also perhaps the most authentic example of creative teamwork, as opposed to being the inspiration of any single *auteur*. Certainly Basil Wright, Harry Watt, Cavalcanti and Grierson himself all made valid contributions, and it seems fitting that this is the film by which the movement as a whole is most usually remembered.

Almost immediately after *Night Mail* the movement split up. In June 1937 Grierson resigned from the GPO film unit in order to set up Film Centre, which had some kind of formal link with Shell. At the same time his interest in developing non-theatrical distribution became

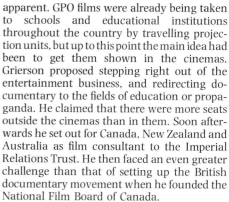

Above: Children at School *contrasted romantic notions of childhood with the realities of State education.* Left: *a potent image of man-made beauty from* Shipyard. *Bottom: sailors battle with the elements in* North Sea

apparent. GPO films were already being taken to schools and educational institutions throughout the country by travelling projection units, but up to this point the main idea had been to get them shown in the cinemas. Grierson proposed stepping right out of the entertainment business, and redirecting documentary to the fields of education or propaganda. He claimed that there were more seats outside the cinemas than in them. Soon afterwards he set out for Canada, New Zealand and Australia as film consultant to the Imperial Relations Trust. He then faced an even greater challenge than that of setting up the British documentary movement when he founded the National Film Board of Canada.

Basil Wright, Arthur Elton, Stuart Legg and John Taylor were among those who followed the new pattern set by Grierson. From then on, they had little time for developing their personal style, and in the main became producers dedicated to the idea of extending the field of documentary. The effect on Basil Wright was almost immediate. In his estimable film record of conditions in British schools, *Children at School* (1937), it is hard to recognize the same hand that made *Song of Ceylon*.

Meanwhile Harry Watt, Humphrey Jennings and Pat Jackson – who later directed the distinguished feature documentary *Western Approaches* (1944) – and others remained with Cavalcanti at the GPO. Watt made the excellent dramatized documentary about ship-to-shore radio, *North Sea* (1938), Jennings made *Spare Time* (1939), a film about the leisure activities of ordinary people, while Anstey became Director of Productions of the *March of Time* series. The group Grierson left behind him lifted British documentary to its second peak of achievement during World War II, but afterwards the movement foundered owing to lack of leadership and an inflated sense of its own importance, left over from the golden years when a handful of films miraculously succeeded in living up to the expectations aroused for them by Grierson's persuasive prose.

ELIZABETH SUSSEX

John Grierson founder of film documentary

John Grierson has a special place in the history of the cinema – though less as a film-maker than as an organizer of the medium. He shared Lenin's vision of the way in which the aesthetic power of the arts could serve society.

Having been a prominent student at Glasgow University in the early Twenties (and a fiery lay-preacher), it was not until Grierson went to the USA on a Rockefeller scholarship, and started to write about modern art and the (still silent) movies, that he began to examine and debate the social role of the communications media.

Returning to Britain in 1927, Grierson found common ground in an unexpected quarter that was to provide an international role for the documentary movement he had already envisaged. Grierson met Stephen Tallents, the Secretary of the Empire Marketing Board – a Government Department which had been set up to promote the interests of the British Empire. The Board had already been persuaded to sponsor a film and was committed to a romantic piece of pageantry, entitled *One Family* (1930), in which elegantly robed ladies symbolizing far-flung and exotic colonies would be seen contributing the fruits of Empire to King George V's Christmas pudding. This prospect so shocked Grierson that he persuaded Tallents – with whom he had by now embarked upon a life-long alliance – to set about the filmic re-education of the Board in the virtues of realism. They were shown the pioneering work of Eisenstein and his Soviet colleagues, who were beginning to compose in images instead of following the contemporary practice of finding pictures to support what were basically literary ideas. They also viewed the camera 'symphonies' of city life which had been filmed by Walter Ruttmann in Berlin and by Alberto Cavalcanti in Paris. More temptingly Grierson offered them the romantic nostalgia for primitive life to be found in Robert Flaherty's *Nanook of the North* (1922) and *Moana* (1924).

Grierson's ultimate definition for the documentary form was 'the creative interpretation of actuality'. This was to combine such disparate styles as Russian montage, Flaherty's poetically intuitive camerawork and, later, Cavalcanti's eloquent orchestrating of factual images with natural sounds and music, using words as little as possible.

So the EMB embarked, in some bewilderment, on the financing of a second film – *Drifters* (1929) – an account of the British herring-fishing industry. It was to be Grierson's only 'personal' film. It stole Eisenstein's thunder at a famous London Film Society premiere shared with *The Battleship Potemkin* (1925), and it was to enable Grierson to found an international school of film-making.

In an age that still promoted aggressive individualism, Grierson, himself aggressive by nature, was seeking perhaps to expiate the sins of the selfish and to refute the individualistic arguments of his schoolteacher father. Certainly by film (always for him the work of a team) he sought to reveal and celebrate the neglected excitements of man as a collective creator and the builder of a prouder and more affectionate civilization. There is some irony in that the first international role of documentary was in World War II when Grierson created his most permanent monument, the National Film Board of Canada. Yet in Britain and Canada Grierson inspired many documentaries which equated anti-fascism, not only with the preservation of democracy, but with the political development of a new superstructure of public enterprise and social service to replace the private hierarchies of the world before 1939.

Grierson's eventual sphere of influence was

Above: John Grierson, who engineered a new and vital role for film in Britain

to stretch from Canada through New Zealand and Australia to Malaysia and India; and from Venezuela through Britain to Denmark, with smaller, intermittent offshoots in Africa and the Caribbean. Many basic cinematic techniques can be traced back to the Thirties. Documentaries which use their images poetically – the rarest of factual films to survive today – are in line of descent from *Song of Ceylon* (1934). Films demonstrating that beauty can reside in such unexpected places as a precise scientific account of Man's invention of the gear-wheel, are in debt to *Transfer of Power* (1939). Films that warm the heart with their insight into the human pattern of the daily round owe something to *Night Mail* (1936). Then again, *Housing Problems* (1935) has been credited as the beginning of *cinéma-vérité*; and *Enough to Eat?* (1936) was the first film to present sociology as a science and to screen animated diagrams of shocking statistics alongside the personal accounts of the victims of deprivation – thereby preparing the way for much of television's 'investigative journalism'. All these films of the Thirties – still preserved and studied – were either produced under Grierson's supervision or made by people he had trained, and who had been exposed therefore to Grierson's extraordinary creative intuitions.

His influence has not died. Remarkable confirmation of that fact may be found by analyzing the Hollywood Academy's honours lists of films nominated for Oscars in the Shorts and Documentary classes each year since 1941 (when the Academy first officially recognized the Documentary category). The production credits show that 64 of them (including 13 Oscar winners) were made by film-makers trained by Grierson or by production units for which Grierson was originally responsible. In 1977 such films – with John Grierson already dead five years – won five nominations and two Oscars. Not a bad outcome from *Drifters* and its first celebration nearly 50 years before of the world at its everyday work!

EDGAR ANSTEY

Below: Grierson filming Drifters; *his 'epic' film of herring-fishing in the North Sea attracted sponsorship and helped launch the British documentary movement*

1

2

CHAPAYEV

What Eisenstein's *The Battleship Potemkin* was in 1925 to Soviet silent cinema, *Chapayev* became 10 years later to the young Soviet talkie. *Potemkin* only required its titles to be translated to make a universal impact; *Chapayev's* great quality is its characterization, but as this is necessarily heightened by dialogue, the film is a favourite chiefly in its own country.

Like *Potemkin*, *Chapayev* is based upon real events which are altered in detail but remain in essence. Its subject is the character and fate of a civil war hero, Chapayev, who successfully led partisans of the Red Army against Kolchak's White Army in Siberia for a period in 1918 and 1919, before falling in battle. Its main theme is the conflict between the personalities of the peasant Chapayev and the communist commissar assigned from headquarters to advise and help him. The film traces the growth of trust and affection between the two men after their initial clash.

The commissar himself, Dmitry Furmanov, who was transferred from the detachment before its final battle, wrote of his adventures in a popular novel, altering the names of most of the participants. The book was popular and in 1932 Furmanov's widow suggested it as a film. The Lenfilm studio liked the idea and turned the project over to two young novice directors, Sergei and Georgi Vasiliev.

The Vasilievs plunged into *Chapayev* with enthusiasm. The result was an extraordinary success – a film packed with wit, humour, and earthy dialogue. The clash of personalities is as tense and gripping as the clash of armies; the battles are spectacular, but depicted with clarity.

The impression given throughout is one of freshness and spon-

taneity. Yet it had been achieved only with infinite pains. More than two years were taken on scripting and shooting. Scenes were written, rewritten, and rewritten again.

Chapayev was chosen for the Revolution anniversary show in November 1934; it was the star again for the fifteenth anniversary of the 'official' birth of Soviet cinema in January 1935, and again one month later at an international film festival in Moscow. 'Public, industry and film-makers joined in its praise,' says Jay Leyda in his book *Kino*: 'it was known that the heads of Government and Army had endorsed it at earlier screenings in the Kremlin.' Why did everybody like it so much? Certainly not just because of the official approval.

Leyda calls it 'an easy film to love'. The characters are recognizable and believable. The heroes show fear as well as courage, weakness as well as strength, folly as well as wisdom; love and gaiety is mixed with sacrifice and suffering. And deep down, the kernel of the story is something that everyone knew was true and important – the need for trust between two good men.

Some wiseacres have seen in *Chapayev* an initial victory for the school of socialist realism over the experimental work of Eisenstein, the theorists of montage, and other innovators. But the facts of the case do not fit.

When *Chapayev* first appeared, Soviet artists were on the eve of a great and long-lasting ideological debate. At the first All-Union Congress of Soviet Writers in the summer of 1934, Maxim Gorky had formulated the idea of 'socialist realism'. He contrasted it with the 'critical realism' of nineteenth-century literature, which, he said, only exposed society's imperfections.

'Socialist realism' he lauded as creative: its chief characteristic was the development of people, to help them achieve wealth and love and life and turn the earth in its entirety into 'the magnificent dwelling-place of mankind united in one big family'.

In other words it is identified by its social and political function. It is not narrow, not a style. Tragedy is acceptable and even the fairy-tale may fit so long as the general tenor is true to human nature and society, and is not pessimistic but helps strengthen confidence and hope for the future. Eisenstein's experiment-laden *Battleship Potemkin* (1925) or *Alexander Nevsky* (1938) suit the definition just as well as the more 'realistic' *Chapayev*.

In later years the confrontation became bitter and the opposed terms 'socialist realism' and 'formalism' were used as weapons. 'Socialist realism' was an accolade without argument, 'formalism' was the ultimate in sin. Actually, of course, 'realism' is no synonym for 'naturalism', and 'formalism' does

not mean 'experiment in form' – a sense in which it was often far too casually employed – but 'distortion of reality for the sake of formal experiment'. Whether in art, literature or music such phrases have been the ammunition of controversy in every period and clime – convenient for pundits to veil personal prejudices or whims of taste, for administrators to hide a motive or join a stream.

Chapayev, as I have said, fits into the principle of 'socialist realism'. But there never was any conflict between the theoretical school and those who liked *Chapayev*. The Vasilievs were actually favoured pupils of Einsenstein, who went out of his way to praise the film, greeting it as heralding 'a "third period" in Soviet film history, synthesizing the mass film of the first period with the individual, naturalist stage of the second (or sound) period'.

IVOR MONTAGU

Quotations from: Kino, A History of the Russian and Soviet Film by Jay Leyda.

3

4

In the Russian Civil War of 1918–19 Chapayev (1) is leading a detachment of partisans against Kolchak's White Army. A workers' detachment arrives to augment his forces. At first the relationship between Chapayev and Furmanov, the new commissar sent with the reinforcements, is uneasy (2). Chapayev fears that his authority is being undermined. Furmanov does not ease the situation by arresting Chapayev's lieutenant for allowing looting, but Chapayev is reconciled when he finds peasant support is won over by the return of their livestock.

After explaining his tactics to his officers with the help of potatoes (3), he quells a mutiny, and then makes his final plans for the next encounter with the enemy.

The day of the battle arrives. Chapayev watches from a hilltop as the White Army officers' detachment advances in parade order, banners flying, drums beating, in a terrifying display. The partisans hold their fire, according to orders, but with morale shaken (4). When the battle is joined (5) the Whites are defeated.

Quiet days follow. Chapayev's machine-gunner Petka, and his sweetheart Anna, the worker

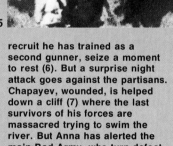

5

recruit he has trained as a second gunner, seize a moment to rest (6). But a surprise night attack goes against the partisans. Chapayev, wounded, is helped down a cliff (7) where the last survivors of his forces are massacred trying to swim the river. But Anna has alerted the main Red Army, who turn defeat into victory.

6

7

Directed by Sergei Vasiliev and Georgi Vasiliev, 1934
Prod co: Lenfilm (USSR). **sc:** Sergei Vasiliev and Georgi Vasiliev, based on a book by Dmitry Furmanov and the writings of Anna Furmanova. **photo:** Alexander Sigayev and A. Ksenofontov. **art dir:** Isaak Makhlis. **mus:** Gavril Popov, Moscow premiere, 7 November 1934.
Cast: Boris Babochkin (*Chapayev*), Boris Blinov (*Furmanov*), Varvara Myasnikova (*Anna*), Leonid Kmit (*Petka*), Illarian Pevtsov (*Colonel Borozdin*), Vyacheslav Volkov (*Yelan*), Nikolai Simonov (*Zhikharev*), Stepan Shkurat (*cossack*), Boris Chirkov (*peasant*).

Spencer Tracy
the face of integrity

Chester Erskine, director of the Broadway play that projected Tracy to stardom, provides a penetrating insight into his old friend's work and character

---

'The best movie actor in the world', wrote an effusive journalist – just after Spencer Tracy had been nominated for an Academy Award for *Father of the Bride* in 1950. A lot of people, including most of his fellow actors, would agree to this. The notable exception was Spence himself.

'Now how can anybody declare me to be the best in the world? It's kind of silly. Like this Academy Award business, I'm damned pleased to be nominated and included amongst the other nominees, worthy actors all of them. That's enough of an honour for me. But if I should win, would that make me better than them? Of course not. A good performance depends on the role, and what the actor brings of himself to it. And him alone. I bring Spencer Tracy to it. Nobody else can bring Spencer Tracy to it because they're not me. I'm the best Spencer Tracy in the world. If they want to give me an award for that. I've truly earned it.'

This is a true insight into his own work – Spencer did not act roles, the roles acted Spencer. His performances were part of him. They *were* him.

He came upon this special approach during rehearsals of *The Last Mile* in 1930, a landmark play of the time in which society's right to take the life of even a murderer was questioned. It was directed by me in a new style of realism – one that I had successfully introduced into several previous productions, a true realism born out of a world in economic depression, a world impatient with euphemism. The play is about a convicted murderer awaiting execution in the death house of an American prison who chooses to die in violent protest rather than by passive compliance.

Spencer had previously appeared in a potpourri of plays in repertory and in New York. He was a promising actor who occasionally showed flashes of true talent. I had seen a few of his performances, and was not overly impressed by him as a candidate for the lead in *The Last Mile*. I was just about to dismiss him, when something about our too brief casting interview stayed with me. Since it was getting on to dinner-time I invited him to join me at a theatrical haunt. There, in a less strained atmosphere, I was suddenly made aware as we were talking that beneath the surface, here was a man of passion, violence, sensitivity and desperation; no ordinary man, and just the man for the part.

On the play's opening night, I stationed myself at the back of the auditorium. I suddenly saw him, after a hesitant start, realize his power as he felt the audience drawn into the experience of the play and respond to the measure of his skill and the power of his personality. I knew that he had found himself as an actor, and I knew that he knew it. The play – and his performance – projected Tracy to permanent stardom.

It was inevitable, of course, that the new realism of the theatre would pass to films, then in the transitional period from silent pictures to dialogue pictures.

The film director John Ford came to New York and saw *The Last Mile*. He was fascinated by Tracy and invited him to make a picture. It turned out to be *Up the River* (1930), a slapstick prison comedy of no quality. It was an unfortunate start for Spencer. Fox, the company to which he was under contract, typecast him in similar roles and inferior material, though his performances rose far above the banal level of the films. Eventually a respite (inspired by film critics who complained of this misuse of his talent) came in the form of several interesting pictures. In particular there was *The Power and the Glory* (1933), a brilliant study by Preston

Opposite page: a mysterious, one-armed stranger (Tracy) arrives in a sleepy little town in Bad Day at Black Rock. *Above: Tracy as 'Bugs' Raymond, a truckdriver turned racketeer in* Quick Millions. *Right:* Woman of the Year, *Tracy and Hepburn's first film together. Below: Manuel (Tracy) sings Harvey (Freddie Bartholomew) a shanty in* Captains Courageous. *Below right: in* Mannequin *a failed businessman (Tracy) keeps the love of his wife (Joan Crawford). Bottom: Tracy as Father Flanagan in* Men of Boys' Town

"I want you to kiss me — for luck!"

Sturges of an industrialist's rise to power, in which Spencer came to maturity as a film actor in a role worthy of him.

This honeymoon period was short-lived, however, and Tracy found himself again assigned to pot-boiler fare. But he had endured enough by now and rebelled. Following his angry protests – and some bad behaviour – Fox released him from his contract. Shortly afterwards he signed for MGM. The second and crucial phase of his career had begun.

Louis B. Mayer, head of MGM, was not convinced that Spencer had sex appeal, so he was cast as a second lead to Clark Gable. Anyone acquainted with Spencer's private life could have reassured Mayer on this point, as Irving Thalberg, head of production, finally did. He freed Tracy from bondage to Gable and cast him opposite some of Hollywood's loveliest ladies, all of whom he was permitted to win by the script, and several of whom he won off-screen, regardless of script or permit.

MGM was soon aware that it had gained a genuine star worthy of 'first top billing over the title', as it is officially denoted. He did not stereotype himself into a single character or role to be repeated in various stories as other stars did. What is striking in a random selection of his film roles is their variety: the harried victim of Fritz Lang's *Fury* (1936); the loveable Portuguese fisherman of Kipling's *Captain's Courageous* (1937); the gentle Father Flanagan of *Boys' Town* (1938); the redoubtable Stanley in *Stanley and Livingstone* (1939); Pilon, a Mexican peasant not above a little petty larceny, in Steinbeck's *Tortilla Flat* (1942); Joe the pilot in *A Guy Named Joe* (1943).

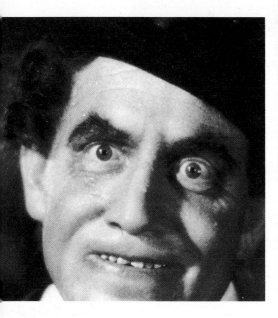

Above: Tracy dressed to kill as the evil Hyde in Dr Jekyll and Mr Hyde. *Above right: Tracy and Hepburn as rival – but married – lawyers in* Adam's Rib. *Right: a stormy family meal in* Guess Who's Coming to Dinner?

Tracy finished his contract at MGM with a masterful performance in *Bad Day at Black Rock* (1955) as the one-armed war veteran who uncovers a town's guilty secret; for this he received his fifth Oscar nomination. He next appeared in several distinguished films for Stanley Kramer with social themes close to Spencer's personal convictions. *Inherit the Wind* (1960) was a fictional account of the Dayton 'monkey' trial in Ohio during the Twenties, in which he played a lawyer, based on Clarence Darrow, who defends a teacher arraigned for teaching the Darwinian theory of evolution. In *Judgement at Nuremberg* (1961) he was the troubled judge at a Nazi war criminal trial. And *Guess Who's Coming to Dinner?* (1967), Tracy's last appearance, was a courageous story for the time, in which a couple, played by Tracy and Katharine Hepburn, come to accept the fact of a black husband for their daughter.

Spencer's famous partnership with Katharine Hepburn began in 1942 with *Woman of the Year*. It was an historic occasion, both professionally and personally. For the next 25 years they appeared together in a variety of films. Perhaps the best were two sophisticated comedies, *Adam's Rib* (1949) and *Pat and Mike* (1952).

When working, Spencer was very strict with himself. He examined the script carefully, defining his place in the story. He learned lines quickly, and asked for few if any changes. He relied on his ability to meet the requirements of the dialogue, no matter what. He did not go in for improvisation of any kind. He was a good listener in rehearsal and tried to do what was asked of him. Directors loved to work with him.

As a star, Tracy avoided publicity and interviews, which did not make him a favourite with the PR boys: 'I don't have to do those things,' he would say, 'Everybody knows me. They see me in pictures. That's who I am.'

But behind Spencer's strong, confident, craggy visage, there was an angry man disposed to self-destruction. When the strain became too intense he drank – drank fiercely to oblivion. He was not the only actor so afflicted. There were others – too many others. We talked about this, and I suggested it might be because acting imposed on the actor the burden of being his own instrument so that he was in danger of becoming a split personality.

He smiled. 'Jekyll and Hyde? I played that part. Maybe. And maybe it's just that acting is no proper job for a grown man. I've never really felt comfortable about it.'

'But', he added, 'I wouldn't do anything else for the whole world!'   CHESTER ERSKINE

Filmography

1930 Taxi Talks (short); The Tough Guy/The Hard Guy (short); Up the River. **'31** Quick Millions; Six Cylinder Love; Goldie. **'32** She Wanted a Millionaire; Sky Devils; Disorderly Conduct; Young America (GB: We Humans); Society Girl; Painted Woman; Me and My Gal (GB: Pier 13). **'33** 20,000 Years in Sing Sing; Face in the Sky; Shanghai Madness; The Power and the Glory (GB: Power and Glory); The Mad Game; A Man's Castle. **'34** Looking for Trouble; The Show-off; Bottoms Up; Now I'll Tell (GB: When New York Sleeps); Marie Galante. **'35** It's a Small World; Murder Man; Dante's Inferno; Whipsaw. **'36** Riffraff; Fury; San Francisco; Libeled Lady. **'37** They Gave Him a Gun; Captains Courageous; Big City. **'38** Mannequin; Test Pilot; Boys' Town. **'39** Stanley and Livingstone. **'40** I Take This Woman; Northwest Passage; Edison, the Man; Boom Town. **'41** Men of Boys' Town; Jekyll and Mr Hyde. **'42** Woman of the Year; Tortilla Flat; Keeper of the Flame; Ring of Steel (short; narr. only). **'43** A Guy Named Joe. **'44** The Seventh Cross; Thirty Seconds Over Tokyo. **'45** Without Love. **'46** untitled trailer for American Cancer Society (guest only). **'47** The Sea of Grass; Cass Timberlane. **'48** The State of the Union (GB: The World and His Wife). **'49** Edward, My Son (GB); Adam's Rib. **'50** Malaya (GB: East of the Rising Sun); Father of the Bride. **'51** Father's Little Dividend; The People Against O'Hara. **'52** Pat and Mike; Plymouth Adventure. **'53** The Actress. **'54** Broken Lance. **'55** Bad Day at Black Rock. **'56** The Mountain. **'57** Desk Set (GB: His Other Woman). **'58** The Old Man and the Sea; The Last Hurrah. **'60** Inherit the Wind. **'61** The Devil at 4 O'Clock; Judgement at Nuremburg. **'63** It's a Mad, Mad, Mad, Mad World; How the West Was Won (narr. only). **'67** Guess Who's Coming to Dinner?

FILM AND FASCISM

With the Nazi Party in power in Germany and the Fascist Party in control of Italy, light comedies, musicals and historical epics became vehicles of propaganda. Newsreels, too, took on a new slant

In the aftermath of World War I, Western governments sought to contain the two opposing forces of National Socialism (or fascism) and International Socialism (or communism). The democracies of Britain, the USA, France and the Scandinavian countries survived, to a greater or lesser extent, through to the outbreak of World War II. Elsewhere in Europe the forces of fascism triumphed: in Italy Benito Mussolini had assumed totalitarian control with the aid of the Fascist Grand Council and was to survive as 'Il Duce' until the progress of World War II went against him; in Germany Adolf Hitler's Nazi Party became the majority power in 1933 and the following year Hitler was proclaimed 'Führer of the German Reich'.

The instability of the pre-fascist period and the growth of totalitarian rule is reflected in the interwar cinema of Italy and Germany.

After a 'Golden Age' of epic splendour, the Italian cinema of the Twenties represented something of a decline. Starved of foreign capital and of indigenous talent many film-makers, actors and technicians had emigrated to the USA, France and Germany. When Mussolini came on the scene, however, he took a keen personal interest in the cinema, as befitted his nationalistic vanity. In 1926 he approved a ten per cent quota (later increased to 25 per cent) of Italian films in all cinemas. He also implemented a recommendation to turn the privately owned L'Unione Cinematografia Educativa (LUCE) into a state-controlled institution under his direct supervision. LUCE was instructed to make and distribute films:

'. . . of an essentially scientific, historical and patriotic nature . . . to correct public taste which has been corrupted by films, whose moral and aesthetic qualities have all too often left much to be desired.'

LUCE quickly became a vehicle for state propaganda, disseminating official news via its newsreel, *Luce Gazette*. It also put out idealized documentaries such as *Il Duce* (a three-part saga of Mussolini and his blackshirts) and *Path of the Heroes*, an account of the Italian invasion of Abyssinia in 1935–36.

Screening of LUCE titles was compulsory in Italian cinemas and the exhibition of these films abroad was assisted by massive state subsidies.

State control of the feature film industry was not so easy to impose. In 1929 Mussolini banned the screening of foreign language films and entrusted Stefano Pittaluga, a veteran from the early days of Italian cinema, with the task of converting the native film industry to sound. Initially his efforts were concentrated on dubbing the persistently popular French and American films, but he gradually gained a monopoly of the Italian-speaking film production. When Pittaluga died, the writer and art critic Emilio Cecchi took over the re-equipped Cines studios and pursued a vigorous cosmopolitan policy. Walter Ruttmann was hired from Germany in 1933 to film a Pirandello novella *Acciaio* (1933, *Steel*) – the first example of cross-fertilization between the Italian and German fascist cinemas.

The Cines studios proved incapable of leading a forceful revival of Italian film production, and during one of its periods of bankruptcy Mussolini set up a General Office for the Discipline and Guidance

Top: trade mark of Italy's Cines studio, destroyed by fire in 1935. Above: a typically heroic shot from Blasetti's propaganda epic La Vecchia Guardia. *Left: Mussolini inspects the building of the Cinecittà studios in 1937. A new 'film factory' was vital to the fascist propaganda machine, and Il Duce took a personal interest in its progress*

Above: an idealized picture of Italian youth in the service of the mother country. Top: echoing Mussolini's conquest of Abyssinia, fascist-style salutes acclaim a Roman hero on his return from Africa in Carmine Gallone's Scipione L'Africano. *Top right: a French poster for the same film showing how images of the Roman Empire were invoked by the fascist ideology. Right: in Germany Arnold Fanck's 'mountain films' raised physical endeavour to the level of a cult and foreshadowed the Nazi stress on strength and purity. His* The White Hell of Pitz Palu *was co-directed with G.W. Pabst*

of Film Production. In this way he was able to intervene more directly, controlling films at the script and exhibition stages, while not subjecting film-makers to the kind of rigorous regime imposed by Goebbels in Germany.

Military successes in Africa encouraged Mussolini to invest further in a cinema worthy of its country's imperial past and present. In 1935 he approved the founding of the Centro Sperimentale di Cinematografia to train film technicians. In the same year building began on what was to become the great studio of Cinecittà. By the time this monument to Mussolini's cinema was completed in April 1937, the Italian feature film industry had been put back on its feet. The quality of its productions, however, was as thin as the façade of Mussolini's own brand of fascism, especially when compared to the viciousness of German Nazism.

Underlying the blandness of most of the films of this period was the 'realist' style that recurs throughout the history of the Italian Cinema. The work of Alessandro Blasetti is typical here. In his first film *Sole* (1928, *Sun*) he tackled the government's land reclamation policies with a realism that recalled the 'verismo' style of Italian films prior to World War I. The heroes of the film are the peasant workers in the Pontine marshes, captured and framed on film as in a still life. Blasetti is better remembered, however, for his 1933 epic *1860* which deals with an episode in Garibaldi's campaign for the liberation of Sicily – a most appropriate subject for a fascist regime to endorse. In his 1934 film *La Vecchia Guardia* (*The Old Guard*) Blasetti paid tribute to the Fascists who had marched on Rome in 1922, but his subsequent films were less overtly propagandist and his historical fantasy *Corona di Ferro* (1935, *The Iron Crown*) looks, with hindsight, a worthy predecessor to the Italian costume epics of the Sixties.

Blasetti had an inspired vision of creating a recognizably Italian cinema; his own career went some way towards realizing that ambition.

By contrast the other outstanding Italian director of the Thirties, Mario Camerini, retreated to comedy instead of to history as a means of avoiding official censorship. He achieved international success in 1932 with his comedy *Gli Uomini, Che Mascalzoni* (*What Rascals Men Are!*) which starred Vittorio de Sica in the first of his many roles as the weak but charming lover. Like any other contemporary

director, however, Camerini was obliged to make a piece of fascist propaganda and his *Il Grande Appello* (1936, *The Great Roll-Call*) was one of a spate of 'Africa' films which followed in the wake of Mussolini's conquest of Abyssinia.

Camerini's light comedies were often an inspiration to many lesser Italian directors who otherwise churned out a depressingly large number of anodyne 'bianco telefono' films, which took their nickname from the white telephones over which so many of the heroines languished. That these films were so distant from the realities of life under Il Duce was a constant source of embarrassment to all subsequent schools of Italian film-making. They also reveal the way in which the fascist ideology can be made to masquerade as escapist entertainment.

Recent analyses of the films of the Third Reich have revealed a similar process at work in the German cinema of the Thirties, instead of the traditional view of a marked distinction between overt propaganda and mere escapist cinema.

In Germany the forceful realism of *Neue Sachlichkeit* ('new objectivity'), the strong avant-garde movement in the arts, and the implicit threat posed by Expressionist art and cinema, all conspired to make the Nazi ideologists anxious to control film. In retaliating they not only commissioned their own Party films but also mounted a campaign of

attack on subversive trends within German cinema, staging 'spontaneous' demonstrations against several films of the early Thirties that showed an awareness of social and political trends.

Pabst's World War I epic *Westfront 1918* (1930) was a victim of these attacks. Banned seven months after its premiere, it was severely cut and rescreened in late 1931 before being completely banned in the spring of 1933. A similar fate befell the same director's *Kameradschaft* (1931, Comradeship) which was an appeal to international solidarity among working men.

The psychological themes that characterized the German Expressionist films persisted into the early sound period. Leontine Sagan's *Mädchen in Uniform* (1931, *Girls in Uniform*) is, in fact, more striking as a study in female psychology than as a plea for a humane system of education. Again with the films of Fritz Lang, especially the story of the manic Dr Mabuse (in *Das Testament des Dr Mabuse*) attempting to take over the world from his base in the

lunatic asylum, we can see the survival of the same undercurrent of psychological anxiety that made the German films of the Twenties so disturbing.

By 1936 systematic purges of the German film industry – prohibition of Jews, abolition of film criticism and the operation of a ruthless censorship – ensured that virtually all the native German film talent had emigrated, most of it to the USA. Hollywood had benefited from the influx of talent represented by directors and actors like Fritz Lang, William Dieterle, Robert Siodmak, Edgar G. Ulmer, Douglas Sirk, Marlene Dietrich, Conrad Veidt, Billy Wilder, Peter Lorre and Fred Zinnemann.

The combined effect of Goebbels' control of the bureaucracy of film-making (under the aegis of the *Reichsfilmkammer* or Chamber of Film) and Alfred Hugenberg's financial control of Ufa (the country's major production company) was to bring about the gradual nationalization of the German film industry.

By 1933 *Reichsfilmkammer* members were the only people allowed to make films. They enjoyed exclusive filming rights in Germany free from foreign competition. As it grew in strength the *Reichsfilmkammer* introduced a series of prizes and approved a system of grading films as culturally and politically valuable. By 1935 they took control of all exports of German films and newsreels: all cinematic images of Germany seen abroad now stemmed from the *Reichsfilmkammer*.

Ufa had been responsible for financing the peculiarly German genre of 'mountain films', such as Arnold Fanck's *Die Weisse Hölle von Piz Palü* (1929, *The White Hell of Pitz Palu*) and Luis Trenker's *Der Rebell* (1932, *The Rebel*). The appeal of these films seemed to lie in the 'racial purity' of the glaciers and rocks and the selfless idealism of the Aryan heroes. From these films it was only a short step to the overtly Nazi films like *Hitlerjunge Quex* (1933).

Tobis, Ufa's only real rival in film production, conformed equally to the edicts issued by the *Reichsfilmkammer*. Both companies issued regular newsreels – *Deutsche Tonwoche* (Tobis) and *Deutsche Wochenschau* (Ufa) – which were blatantly used by Goebbels as mouthpieces for National Socialist policies and activities.

Outstanding among Third Reich films were Leni Riefenstahl's documentaries which stand analysis both as propaganda and as art. In 1934 it was her own company that made *Triumph des Willens*

Left: Mädchen in Uniform. *Above left: Goebbels attends a film premiere. Top: Emil Jannings as Emperor Frederick in* The Old and the Young King. *Centre: poster for* Triumph of the Will. *Above: Goebbels addresses the 1935 Film Congress*

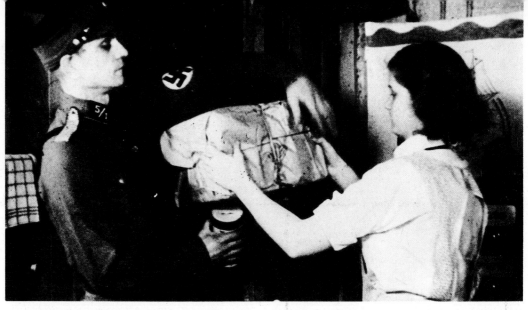

Above: Neville Chamberlain's
return from the 1938 Munich
summit was captured for history
on newsreel: the document signed
by Hitler fluttered in the wind –
an image that became an omen of
the impending conflict. Right:
March of Time's famous exposé
Inside Nazi Germany. Below: the
familiar trade mark of the Pathé
newsreel. Bottom: the 'objective'
eye of the newsreel camera was
questioned in Before Hindsight
(1977), a film that explored the
documentation of history on film
and the role of newsreels in
reporting the events of the Thirties

(*Triumph of the Will*), but by 1936 she had rather lost favour with Hitler and was obliged to make *Olympia* (1936, *Berlin Olympiad*) under Goebbels' close scrutiny.

The overtly propagandist feature films of the Nazi period follow certain themes and archetypes. They encourage the cult of the leader and the Fatherland; they celebrate discipline and comradeship; they advocate euthanasia and anti-semitism and they promote an image of 'Perfidious Albion' as a means of attacking British imperialism. At the same time it was always Goebbels' intention that propaganda should work, to use his own words:

'. . . invisibly to penetrate the whole of life without the public having any knowledge at all of the propagandist initiative.'

It is this covert ideology that makes the otherwise trite German comedies and musicals of the Thirties quite fascinating.

Newsreels were considered as entertainment – audiences wanted 'action' sequences. But somewhere between the streets and the screen the truth was being lost

Since newsreel audiences seldom questioned the truthfulness of the images presented to them on the screen, viewers outside Germany and Italy were not aware that all film coming from these countries had been shot by accredited members of the *Reichsfilmkammer*, nor that the vast amount of footage of goose-stepping Italian troops had been shot by LUCE cameramen. No-one, except a tiny minority of left-wing film-makers, expected the newsreels to provide anything but additional entertainment alongside the weekly feature film. All the major American, British and French newsreel outfits (Fox Movietone, Hearst Metrotone, Pathé, Paramount, Gaumont British, Pathé Frères and Gaumont) did, in fact, swap footage with Ufa and LUCE film crews.

Politicians were among the first to exploit the value of sound news, making themselves available for carefully vetted 'interviews' which usually gave the politician a golden opportunity to state a policy without any fear of it being criticized. When Germany walked out of the League of Nations in 1933, Goebbels did not even condescend to speak into Movietone's microphone – he merely sat at a desk while his interviewer stated Germany's reasons for quitting the League. Equally, when an interviewee chose to say something out of line with government policy, the American parent com-

panies could be relied upon to ban the offending passages at the request of the relevant European ambassador. A 'quiet word', for example, ensured that no film of the Duke of Windsor's wedding appeared on British screens.

Throughout the Thirties American and non-fascist European newsreels were anxious 'not to rock the boat'. Strikes and demonstrations by the millions of unemployed were largely ignored. Official censure, local government banning or private lawsuits would ensue whenever anything politically or morally controversial was shown. None of this excuses, however, the newsreel companies' failure to report what was happening to the Jews in Nazi Germany.

Newsreels were happiest covering 'action'; and when Mussolini invaded Abyssinia they adopted an almost festive air. The mood changed to one of more responsible journalism as civil war wrought havoc in Spain, although the 'Reds' came in for more biased criticism than the Nationalist forces. Actuality footage of disasters was still what the average newsreel cameraman craved and occasionally got: moments like the assassination of King Alexander I of Yugoslavia in 1934, the explosion of the zeppelin *Hindenburg* in May 1937 and the bombing of the US gunboat *Panay* by Japanese aircraft in December 1937.

The regular output of American and British newsreels in the Thirties was criticized by many including the maliciously superior Dr Goebbels for being trivial, ephemeral and often frivolous in content and commentary. The American *March of Time* series took a deliberately provocative stance and considered two or three hard news topics in depth. Later each edition was devoted to a single topic. Unfortunately it did little to influence the fare of contemporary newsreels and was, of course, subject to censorship. But the *March of Time* was able to avoid Nazi controls on location shooting by shamelessly reconstructing or faking the events under discussion.

Inside Nazi Germany (1939), the most famous of *March of Time*'s reports of this period, contained vivid shots of people in prison and of Jewish scientists being shut out from their laboratories, with no indication on the commentary that these 'authentic' scenes had been filmed in American studios.

On both sides of the impending struggle, film could be used as open propaganda and as a subtle means of influencing public opinion. But the problem was also one for the moviegoer – of how to know when a film was telling the truth.

VICKI WEGG-PROSSER

Leni Riefenstahl

The career of the director whose brilliant documentaries for Hitler demonstrated to the world the awesome power of Nazi Germany

In Germany in 1933 the new Nazi government embarked on wide-scale reorganization and a policy of assimilating all political, economic and cultural activities into the National Socialist state. Within the 'co-ordination' of the film industry, the new rulers paid particular attention to the documentary film. Entertainment films would continue to exert *indirect* political influence. But it was through documentary that film – a medium which Hitler and Goebbels considered most important – could be used to increase the impact of the Nazis' mass rallies and demonstrations of power. Direct and straightforward propaganda became the province of newsreels, shorts and full-length documentary films. In the latter category a peak of effectiveness was achieved by the work of one particular film artist: Leni Riefenstahl.

The mountain road

Riefenstahl was born in 1902. She came from a respectable middle-class Berlin family in which the fine arts were highly regarded. In her youth she was interested in the theatre, and was a student at the Academy of Art in Berlin; later she went to ballet school and attained some success as a dancer before an injury forced her to give up this career.

She was 23 when she entered films. Her first work was for Dr Arnold Fanck – the outstanding director of 'mountain films'. This curious genre, popular from the mid-Twenties on-

wards, incorporated wild mountain scenery into the action in such a way that it almost became the major protagonist. Fanck perfected his unique contribution to cinema in pictures like *Der Berg des Schicksals* (1924, The Mountain of Fortune) and *Der Heilige Berg* (1926, *The Holy Mountain*) and it was in the latter that the young Riefenstahl made her film debut playing the lead female role. She went on to make several more films for Fanck but was not content with her successes in front of the camera – she wanted to succeed as a director as well.

Light of experience

The 'mountain films', with their emphasis on natural laws, found favour with the Nazi politicians and could be used to promote National Socialist ideals. In 1931 Riefenstahl realized her ambition to direct when she made *Das Blaue Licht* (1932, *The Blue Light*), a 'mountain film' on which she was assisted by Fanck's experienced cameraman, Hans Schneeberger, and the Marxist film theoretician Béla Belász (whose contribution as scriptwriter was later conveniently forgotten by the Nazis). It was this film that attracted Hitler's attention and greatly impressed him. *The Blue Light* is the dramatization of a mountain legend: the light in question shines out from a crystal grotto in the mountains and only the wild and secretive Junta knows the way to it. But it is discovered by a painter who shares the secret with the superstitious villagers – and brings about the girl's death from a fall. As well as directing the film, Riefenstahl produced it and also took the star part of Junta.

Riefenstahl was pleased with the outcome of her first film as director. It was, as she had hoped, successful in creating an atmosphere – through montage and effects – that made the audience susceptible to the power of myth.

Above and above left: early acting performances by Leni Riefenstahl in The White Hell of Pitz Palu *and in her directorial debut* The Blue Light. *Top: filming* Triumph of the Will *and (left) at Nüremberg with Hitler*

She met Hitler shortly afterwards in 1932 and was personally commissioned by him to make a documentary film of the Nazi Party Rally at Nuremberg. There was little time to prepare the picture, *Der Sieg des Glaubens* (1933, Victory of Faith), which emerged as a kind of test-run for her next, and major, work – *Triumph des Willens* (1934, *Triumph of the Will*). The following year Walter Ruttmann, the highly respected documentary film-maker, worked briefly on a plan for a film of the 1934 Nuremberg Rally, but his intention to incorporate a history of the Nazi Party into the film did not fit in with the political climate that followed the purging of the SA (the Nazi storm troops) under Röhm in June 1934. Riefenstahl took on the project afresh. The result was *Triumph of the Will*, a documentary of perfect film craftsmanship and propaganda.

Triumph of technique

The first principle that the film follows is that its overall arrangement does not seek to impose any intellectual meaning on the political event as a whole. The film-maker herself seems silent in the face of things and refrains from any words of commentary. The images and sounds on the film appear to speak for themselves – though Riefenstahl's montage technique constantly suggests to the spectator an emotional commentary on the action. The film begins, however, with a title sequence (said to be the work of Walter Ruttmann) which expresses an unequivocally positive attitude towards the Nazi regime. The Party Rally, held 18 months after the rebirth of Germany, is Hitler's review of the faithful.

The second principle concerns the emphasis on atmosphere. Here, it is a matter of evoking atmosphere by means of the rhythm of the film, and Leni Riefenstahl has always made it clear that the word 'effect' is important to her work. She has arranged the film in such a way that it forcibly presents a series of highly charged images interspersed with quieter sequences. These highlights include the arrival of Hitler at the rally by aircraft, and his addresses to the SA, and SS (Hitler's bodyguard), the Hitler Youth and the Labour Service. The quieter sequences are typified by shots of early morning and life under canvas in the huge tent city, the pageant of national costume, and parts of the parades.

The key to the atmosphere and impact achieved in the film is the montage. Riefenstahl consistently intercuts the great and the small. Close-ups of the spectators, long shots of the event as a whole, and shots from the point of view of the Party leaders are constantly mixed together by the rapid editing.

Thus the illusion is created of the all-embracing presence of both the camera and the film audience. Through the film, therefore, the Party Rally can be experienced in a much stronger, more intense, but also more emotionally manipulative, manner than would have been possible at the event itself.

In conclusion, Leni Riefenstahl's ideal was visual harmony (enhanced by music). The result was the suggestion of unity of leader, army, Hitler Youth, SA, SS, and the people – an encouraging and uplifting ideal indeed for the Party still inwardly shaken by the murder of Ernst Röhm. Riefenstahl used the occasion of the Party Rally for a study in harmony; the Party used Riefenstahl for a filmically brilliant and politically effective lesson for the German cinemagoer. To argue that the camera merely photographs what is at hand is naive and denies the film artist's creative power. *Triumph of the Will* was a success artistically and commercially and covered its production costs twice over.

Spirit of the Olympics

The second high point of Leni Riefenstahl's directorial career came in 1936 when she made *Olympia*, the much-praised film of the Olympic Games in Berlin. The film is in two parts: *Fest der Völker* (Festival of the People) and *Fest der Schönheit* (Festival of Beauty). The Olympic idea, its origin in classical Greece and its resurrection in modern times, offered the sportswoman and aesthete Riefenstahl a richly attractive source of material. She utilized this material in a film that is far more than mere reportage of a sporting event and reveals her own cinematic ideals more directly than *Triumph of the Will*. In the prologue the director draws heavily on cinematic special effects,

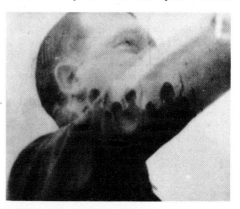

beginning with shots of classical statues which dissolve into shots of athletes in similar poses. From the outset Riefenstahl formulates her ideal visually: in men strength and competitiveness should be dominant, in women grace, charm and liveliness.

Fest der Völker concentrates on events in the Berlin Olympic Stadium, but quite differently from the way television covers sporting events today: the film is in no sense a detailed and comprehensive documentary analysis of a sports meeting, but rather, like *Triumph of the Will*, a dramatization of highlights. Here, how-

Left and above left: the ominous pomp, pageantry and power of the Nazis at the Nuremberg Rally as displayed in Triumph of the Will. *Above: a portentous superimposition of Hitler's salute over shots of Germany's soldiers on the march*

ever, there is no slackening of tempo.

Fest der Schönheit disregards the stresses and strains of the athletic feats and concentrates instead on emphasizing bodily aesthetics, on the grace of athletically trained bodies in motion, and, in the final analysis, pays homage to the same anti-intellectual cult as *Triumph of the Will* . The beauties of nature and the relaxed atmosphere of the Olympic village are also brought into play. Riefenstahl again achieves a sense of harmony and underlines it with an intense musical accompaniment. The piling on of aesthetic elements finally becomes tiresome, though the film does possess a certain charm.

Olympia was a great international success for Leni Riefenstahl. Compared with other documentary films of the time its craftsmanship was highly developed. It stood far above conventional newsreel reportage. The press,

national and foreign, generally received it positively. But the fame it brought Riefenstahl may have exceeded personal success in career terms. By the time the later footage was in preparation she was encountering opposition from the Propaganda Ministry under Goebbels who had never forgiven her for being appointed, without his authority, by Hitler. The film's coverage of the Negro athlete Jesse Owens outstripping the 'master race' on the track was too much for the authorities. It would have been better for Riefenstahl's career as a propagandist if she had left such 'embarrassing' scenes out of the film.

Out of favour

From that time she had no further opportunity to make her mark in the German cinema. As it was, her film company was responsible for a few short films (some of them

compiled from surplus material from the Olympic film) and was active during the war on unimportant documentaries. In 1940 Riefenstahl herself resumed work on her abandoned feature film *Tiefland* and this occupied her throughout the war. Based on the opera by Eugene d'Albert and starring Riefenstahl as a gypsy, it was not completed until 1953, and even then some of the footage was missing.

After the war Riefenstahl was blacklisted by the Allies for her propaganda work. She was arrested and spent time in prison camps before eventually clearing her name. Her critical reputation has always been overshadowed by her ostensible celebration of Nazism and as a result, this great film artist has directed no more pictures. She has, however, made a name for herself as one of the world's leading photographers and lives today as a respected citizen in Munich.
GUNTER KNORR

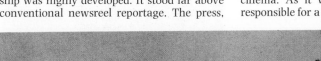

Filmography
1926 Der Heilige Berg (actress only). (GB: The Holy Mountain). **'27** Der Grosse Sprung (actress only). **'29** Die Weisse Hölle vom Piz Palü (actress only) (USA/GB: The White Hell of Pitz Palu). **'30** Stürme über dem Montblanc (actress only) (USA: Storm Over Mont Blanc; GB: Avalanche). **'31** Der Weisse Rausch. **'32** Das Blaue Licht (+prod; +act) (GB: The Blue Light). **'33** SOS Eisberg (actress only); Der Sieg des Glaubens (doc). **'34** Triumph des Willens (doc) (USA/GB: Triumph of the Will). **'35** Tag der Freiheit – Unsere Wehrmacht (doc). **'36** Olympia (Pt 1: Fest der Völker; Pt 2: Fest der Schönheit) (doc) (+sc) (USA: The Olympic Games; GB: Berlin Olympiad). **'53** Tiefland (+sc;+act) (unfinished). **'56** Schwarze Fracht (doc. unfinished).

Above and left: the concept of the beauty, grace and strength of the ideal Aryan form was extolled by Riefenstahl through her images of gymnasts and athletes in Olympia, *her documentary of the 1936 Olympic Games*

NAZI CINEMA

Hans Schwarz's *Liebling der Götter* (1930, *Darling of the Gods*) tells the story of a tenor, played by Emil Jannings, who takes an engagement in South America and lands in the unscrupulous hands of Jewish businessmen, who dominate not only commerce but the world of culture as well. After a brief illness, however, he returns to his beloved Tyrol where he is nursed back to life by his devoted wife. As he returns to the stage his operatic career is re-launched with a triumphant performance of 'Lohengrin'. Thus, schematically, the films plays off the seamy side of life abroad against the fresh air of the Aryan homeland. Anti-semitism was seen to emerge gradually but the discrimination was clearly intended.

As for as Goebbels was concerned *Das Flötenkonzert von Sanssouci* (1930, *The Flute Concert at Sanssouci*) and *Yorck* (1931, both directed by Gustav Ucicky), were exemplary films. *Das Flötenkonzert* showed the Prussian army ready for battle, with the actor Otto Gebühr playing Frederick II as a Führer.

Left: military parades against a backdrop of the famous Brandenburg Gate in Ucicky's Yorck *provide potent images of a nation, unified and regimented. Below and bottom: the actor-director Luis Trenker cast himself as the archetypal German rebel*

The Rise to Power

Even before Hitler became Chancellor, films in Germany reflected a fascist spirit

The battle for Germany, waged in the Twenties and early Thirties by the Nazis, was also a struggle for the control of German cinema. In the early days it was conducted through the press, since none of the party propaganda chiefs had any experience of working with the film medium.

When Dr Josef Goebbels arrived in the political arena, however, the situation changed abruptly. Like Hitler, Goebbels was a passionate cinéaste and he understood the importance of film as an influence, having carefully studied the effect of the Soviet revolutionary films on the Russian people.

On his initiative a National Film Agency (*Reichsfilmstelle*) was set up and placed directly under the Propaganda Ministry. This agency independently supervised the various stages of film production, distribution and exhibition. A system of control was established whereby stories and shooting scripts had to be submitted to the agency; even then all finished films had to be seen and approved.

As early as the 1932 election campaign which confirmed the pre-eminence of the National Socialist Workers' Party (or Nazis), documentary and recruiting films made by the Party were used at meetings and rallies. Time and money were lacking for specifically Nazi feature films and the better alternative seemed to attempt to influence the existing German studios indirectly.

The first ideological confrontation with German cinema appeared in the Nazi press: the German character, nationalism and the army were subjects to be popularized with the moviegoing public. At the same time, the 'Jewish film industry' was attacked on the grounds that it was sapping the vital power of the nation and leading the truly German industry to the brink of ruin.

Some film producers came to terms with the Nazi ideology and furthered it in their work. Compromise was attractive: World War I had been lost, the economic and cultural power of Germany was at a low ebb; on top of this, talk of nationalization of the film business made the situation more difficult.

Once Alfred Hugenberg, an ultra-right politician and chairman of Ufa, allowed his company to fall within the Nazis' control, the rest of the film industry gradually succumbed.

The timely arrival of sound had provided the propaganda machine with an infinitely more subtle and effective medium. Ufa led the field in fascist-inspired films with *Die Letzte Kompagnie* (1930, *The Last Company*), a story of German soldiers in a Napoleonic campaign. Outnumbered by the French, the Germans occupy a mill and fight desperately to cut off a vital road. They win the battle and save the lives of their comrades, but at the cost of their own. Appeals to extreme patriotism were now acceptable on film.

Another early example of the new spirit in Germany was manifested in *Ein Burschenlied aus Heidelberg* (1930, *A Youth's Song From Heidelberg*), starring Willy Forst and Betty Bird. The future elite of the nation came across as a unified crowd of students, dressed alike and sporting duelling scars on their cheeks – young people meeting the future with song and sword.

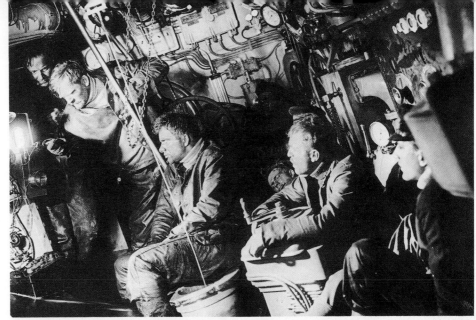

Goebbels arranged for the movie to be a success. He organized a claque and a speaking chorus that accompanied screenings and, on his orders, enthusiastic reviews appeared in the newspapers. In working-class districts, communists, social democrats and workers without any political axe to grind condemned the film as 'warmongering' and tried to have it banned. Police and SA troops were often out in force at screenings and fights were provoked, but despite this, the film was rated third in the year's box-office successes. At the same time it achieved the status of a model film for numerous directors under the Nazis.

By the time *Morgenrot* (1933, *Dawn*) appeared early in 1933, Nazi ideology was well established in German films. This story of a German U-boat in action during World War I had two naval officers committing suicide in order that their comrades could escape the striken sub using the last eight diving suits. The plot line is meagre but the heroism is unmistakable. *Morgenrot* idealized the supreme sacrifice and discriminated against the English, thus appealing to the German national consciousness. In World War II new prints of the film were made and it was shown to the troops to stimulate their fighting spirit. The film's theme song 'Germany Lives Even if We Die' was ominously typical.

A more curious manifestation of the Nazi spirit occurred in the 'mountain film' genre. Two films by Luis Trenker, *Berge in Flammen* (1931, Mountains in Flame) and *Der Rebell* (1932), were set in the German and Austrian mountains. *Der Rebell* was particularly significant for the way in which the story suppresses the Tyrolean struggle for independence and transforms the war against France into the private war of an individual.

Although the influence of the Nazi propaganda machine on the film studios was quite evident in the foregoing films, it was under the guise of entertainment cinema that the Nazi ideology was seen to be working most effectively as the decade progressed.

HERBERT HOLBA

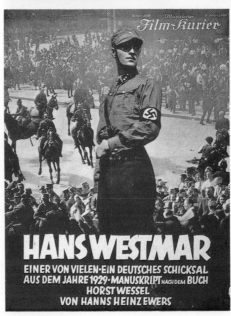

Left: heroic tales of paramilitary recruits like Hans Westmar *were less effective as propaganda than gripping war films such as* Morgenrot *(top) in which a U-boat crew prepares to die for the Fatherland. Above: the same honour is reserved for the Prussian troops in* Die Letzte Compagnie, *seen here making their last stand in a flour mill*

Propaganda for War

For seven years before the outbreak of war, German films extolled the virtues of Hitler's Third Reich

The Nazi takeover in 1933 was followed, within months, by the production of three straightforward propaganda features: *SA-Mann Brand*, a fictional story about a heroic 'brownshirt', *Hans Westmar*, a heavily fictionalized biography of Horst Wessel, and *Hitlerjunge Quex*, a drama based on the life of a member of the Hitler Youth, murdered by the Communists in 1932. All three films extolled devotion to the party and to the Führer, and all three were box-office failures. As a result, Propaganda Minister Dr Goebbels decided definitively to restrict the bulk of the overt propaganda to the newsreels, which were eventually extended in length to 45 minutes.

Believing that the place for the SA was on the streets and not on the screen, Goebbels preferred to use films to inculcate in his audience – the German cinemagoers – the virtues and attributes that the Nazis could best exploit to maintain and extend their power. For this reason he was opposed to the making of *Triumph des Willens* (1934, *Triumph of the Will*), Leni Riefenstahl's feature-length documentary which could not be construed as anything other than direct propaganda. But since it was Hitler's personal project, filming went ahead, though not without Goebbels trying to hamper its production.

The qualities that German feature films did promote during the remainder of the decade were unconditional submission to the absolute authority of an infallible leader, love of the Fatherland, comradeship and self-sacrifice. The cycle chronicling the career of Frederick the Great from Ucicky's *Das Flötenkonzert von Sanssouci* (1930, *The Flute Concert at Sanssouci*) became known as the *Fridericus* films. Frederick appeared as an iron-willed proto-Hitler figure in *Der Choral von* Leuthen (1933, The Anthem of Leuthen), *Der Alte und der Junge König* (1935, *The Old and the Young King*) and *Fridericus* (1936).

Goebbels's view of historical films was that: 'Film subjects, even though they may go back into previous historical eras and draw from foreign countries, have to express the spirit of our time in order to speak to our time.'

The practical effect of this approach can be seen in *Das Mädchen Johanna* (1937, *Joan of Arc*), in which Joan of Arc becomes a female Führer figure reviving a depressed and occupied France, and in *Condottieri* (1937, *Knights of the Black Eagle*), a sort of fascist *El Cid*, in which black-shirted soldiers of fortune unify sixteenth-century Italy under the banner of a charismatic leader.

Hans Springer's poetic documentary, *Der Ewiger Wald* (1936, The Eternal Forest), dramatized the Nazi doctrine of *Blut und Boden* (Race and Soil), depicting German history through the life of the forest from primeval times to the present. It stressed the deep roots of love for the Fatherland and this love was given expression in a cycle of films about the desire of German exiles to return home from abroad: *Flüchtlinge* (1933, Refugees), *Ein Mann Will Nach Deutschland*

117

(1934, A Man Must Return to Germany) and *Friesennot* (1935, Frisians in Peril), for instance, showed the lengths to which patriotic Germans would go in order to get back to the homeland.

A glance down the list of *Staatsaufstragfilme* ('government contract films') reveals the prevalence of the themes of discipline, obedience, comradeship and self-sacrifice, usually against a background of the armed forces. The titles are stolid but self-explanatory: *Zwei Gute Kameraden* (1933, Two Good Comrades), *Soldaten-Kameraden* (1936, Soldier-Comrades), *Kameraden auf See* (1938, Comrades at Sea) and so on. One director who made a career out of popularizations of the Nazi ethos was Karl Ritter, who declared, 'My movies deal with the unimportance of the individual . . . all that is personal must be given up for our cause'. Typical of his films was *Unternehmen Michael* (1937, Operation Michael), in which he dramatized an episode from World War I with the specific intention of 'showing German youth that senseless, sacrificial death has its moral value'.

The popularity in Germany of war films at a time when hardly any were being made in Britain is, in itself, an interesting phenomenon and can be seen as part of the Nazi conditioning process – emphasizing nationalism and militarism. It was not until the outbreak of World War II, however, that the overtly anti-Jewish and anti-British films began to emerge. Indeed the English were sympathetically depicted in some films as, for example, in *Der Höhere Befehl* (1935, The Higher Command) in which they aid Prussian rebels against Napoleon.

It has been customary to argue that the majority of German feature films in this period were non-propagandist entertainments, but this is to take too narrow a view of propaganda. To quote Goebbels again:

'Even entertainment can from time to time perform the function of equipping the nation for its struggle for existence.'

Cinema, he emphasized, should be artistically meritorious and what he meant by art was, of course, German National Socialist art. As examples for the industry to emulate, he cited four films: Eisenstein's *The Battleship Potemkin* (1925), Lang's *Die Nibelungen* (1924)

Clarence Brown's *Anna Karenina* (1935) and Luis Trenker's *Der Rebell* (1932, The Rebel), all of which combined great visual beauty with a moral or message. By the same rule of course, it is possible to discern the ideology in even the most apparently unpolitical films of the Third Reich. The continuing series of frothy Viennese operettas, for instance, depicted the Austrians as effete, pleasure-loving dilettantes, who were, in contemporary terms, clearly ripe for takeover by Germany. The moody, atmospheric melodramas starring Swedish singing star Zarah Leander, particularly Douglas Sirk's *Zu Neuen Ufern* (*To New Shores*) and *La Habanera* (both 1937) portrayed women in society suffering great hardships uncomplainingly, something all women in the Reich would be called upon to do.

Ironically, the greatest works of art to come out of the German cinema at this time were the propagandist films of Leni Riefenstahl and Luis Trenker. Riefenstahl's *Triumph des Willens* and *Olympia* are treated elsewhere in this chapter. Equally forceful in translating the principles of National Socialist art were the films of Luis Trenker.

Left: The Flute Concert in Sanssouci; *the presentation of German history in such films lent weight to Hitler's theories about the nation's destiny. Above:* Condottieri (*or* The Knights of the Black Eagle) *was a German film of 1937 that dealt with the unification of Italy, thus reinforcing the German alliance with the Italian fascists. Below: death of a brownshirt in* SA-Mann Brand

His films, all of them starring himself, continued to give vibrant expression to the themes of 'Race and Soil' and to nature, mysticism and the leadership principle. *Der Verlorene Sohn* (1934, The Prodigal Son), the best of the 'returning exile' films had a Tyrolean mountain guide returning from the skyscrapers of New York to the glories of his native mountains. *Der Kaiser von Kalifornien* (1936, The Emperor of California) dramatized the struggle of a German pioneer to carve out a domain for himself in the United States. Stunningly shot on location and immaculately put together, Trenker's films give the lie to the myth that the Nazi cinema produced nothing of any artistic merit.   JEFFREY RICHARDS

Hollywood holds back

The movie capital meets the rise of fascism in Europe with apathy and compromise

The writer and humorist Dorothy Parker once remarked that the only 'ism' in which Hollywood truly believed was plagiarism. The comment was somewhat harsh since, in the Thirties, the film community contained many people who believed that they had a moral obligation, both as individuals and as members of an influential profession, to make known their radical views on the rise of fascism in Europe, as well as on domestic, social and economic conditions. Ultimately, however, after a great deal of posturing, the response of Hollywood to such problems was either apathetic or fatally compromised.

Most of the left-wing activists in Hollywood in the Thirties were European refugees or importations from the New York theatre. The writer of any successful Broadway play was inevitably offered a contract by one of the major film studios and among the key radical figures who made their way to the West Coast were Clifford Odets, John Wexley, John Howard Lawson, Lester Cole, and Albert Maltz (the last three later numbered in the

Hollywood Ten). Curious as it may seem in retrospect, the 'Workers Labor Theater' transferred almost en masse to the Burbank lot of the Warner Brothers to write pictures for Ann Sheridan and others. Clifford Odets' first script was for *The General Died at Dawn* (1936), an espionage thriller starring Gary Cooper. On leaving the premiere one of the writer's erstwhile supporters was heard to groan, 'Odets, where is thy sting?'

In response to such charges of political cowardice the writers pointed, in extenuation, to their new positions as the salaried employees of reactionary capitalist bosses. It was this particular dissatisfaction that prompted them to organize their own union, the Screen Writers' Guild. After five years of bitter wrangling – during which time the studios set up their own company union, called Screen Playwrights, threatening to blacklist any writer who did not join – the Screen Writers' Guild was eventually recognized in June 1938.

Parallel to the formation of this union, a similar struggle was taking place in the ranks

Above and above left: The Last Train From Madrid, *Paramount's lukewarm reaction to the Spanish Civil War. Top: altogether different was Warner Brothers'* Confessions of a Nazi Spy, *perhaps Hollywood's only serious denunciation of Hitler's regime before America joined World War II. Based on fact, it dealt with the cracking of a Nazi spy ring*

of the actors and directors. The leaders in the fight for guild recognition tended to be the people most active in such organizations as the all-embracing Anti-Nazi League. It is illuminating to note that the two questions posed to the Hollywood Ten during the HUAC (House Un-American Activities Committee) investigations in 1947 were 'Are you a member of the Screen Writers' Guild?' and 'Are you now or have you ever been a member of the Communist Party?' The leading members of the Communist Party, as well as the most prominent liberals, were invariably all strong trade-unionists, anti-Nazis, and supporters of the Republicans in the Spanish Civil War.

Above: Nils Asther and Barbara Stanwyck in
The Bitter Tea of General Yen, *banned
throughout the British Empire for scenes
suggesting miscegenation. Top: Madeleine
Carroll in* Blockade, *a Spanish Civil War film
from which all pro-loyalist content was cut.
Top right: Gary Cooper in* The General Died at
Dawn, *which lacked writer Clifford Odets'
usual left-wing venom. Above right:* Juarez,
*with Paul Muni, drew political parallels
between Maximilian's Mexico and the annexed
Czechoslovakia of 1939*

To these people, Hollywood in the Thirties
seemed to be a bastion of conservatism, an
impression the studios made few efforts to
correct. The movie moguls had all known
great poverty in childhood and great wealth in
middle age. Having sampled both they decided
that they preferred wealth, and they were
accordingly dedicated to the preservation of
their own fortunes. Two of the principal dangers which their activities faced were posed, on
the one hand, by the government, which
might capriciously decide to lop off a percentage of the studios' huge profits, and by the
various pressure groups such as the Knights of
Columbus, the Daughters of the American
Revolution, the American Legion or, most
powerful of all, the National Legion of
Decency. The latter was a body of Roman
Catholic film censors who, with the Church's
backing, graded all films from A1 to C (for
'Condemned'). The danger of an economic
boycott imposed by one of these groups led to
the granting of greatly increased powers to the
Hays Office, the industry's own self-censorship
body. In 1934 the Hays Office made its code of
practice mandatory and also promoted the
Catholic Joseph Breen to head of the Hollywood Production Code Authority. All films had
to obtain a Seal of Approval from the PCA, and
a fine of $25,000 could be imposed on a studio
that dared to release a picture without a
certificate.

The foreign problem

Another decisive factor that induced political
conservatism in Hollywood films was the
nature of the overseas sales market in which
the studios traditionally picked up their profits
(having recovered their production costs on
the North American rentals). During the
Thirties, foreign countries became increasingly sensitive to the way Hollywood films
caricatured them. Producers also had to bear
in mind the Japanese practice of censoring
every scene in which there was kissing, and
the British tendency to view any picture set in
one of its colonies with intense suspicion.
Frank Capra's *The Bitter Tea of General Yen*
(1932) was banned throughout the British
Empire because it showed miscegenation.

The uncertain political situation in Europe
was another matter. Mussolini's motion picture bureau banned *Clive of India*, *The Lives of a
Bengal Lancer* (both 1935), *Lloyds of London* and
The Charge of the Light Brigade (both 1936) on
the grounds that they contained British propaganda. Nazi Germany and, as the decade
progressed, the territories under its control
refused to exhibit pictures starring Mae West,
Johnny Weissmuller, Francis Lederer, Fred
Astaire and Ginger Rogers, Warner Oland,
George Arliss and Jean Hersholt for a variety of
racial and political reasons. These injunctions
worried the studio bosses who, dedicated as
they were to the unalloyed pursuit of entertainment, thought they had already driven
out of the movies any considered political
thought whatsoever.

The conclusive evidence to which Hollywood could point, if it required even more
reasons for steering away from the controver-
sies aroused by the rise of European fascism,
was the political mood of America itself in the
years leading up to World War II. Obsessed as
they were by their own economic depression,
Americans generally looked on Europe with
indifference and on the prospect of involvement in another war there with repugnance. A
Congressional investigation into the muni-
tions industry concluded that its leaders, in an
unholy alliance with international bankers
and businessmen, had been responsible for
dragging the country into the morass of World
War I. In the wake of the Pittman Neutrality
Resolution of August 1935 and the acquisition
of key Senate Committee posts by die-hard
isolationists, President Roosevelt failed to persuade the nation to take a more positive anti-
fascist stance.

Approaching Spain with caution

The invasion of Abyssinia by Italy in 1935 left
America noticeably unmoved, but the outbreak of the Spanish Civil War the following
year did prompt some cautious comment.
Paramount's *The Last Train From Madrid*
(1937) was simply another *Grand Hotel* on
wheels, however, and its depiction of Spain
during a civil war of unparalleled horror bore
as much resemblance to contemporary Europe
as David Selznick's Zenda. When Walter
Wanger, an independent producer releasing
through United Artists, tried to make a picture
about the war, his *Blockade* (1938), written by
John Howard Lawson, was so drastically altered by the Hays Office and Wanger's financial backers that the final version was simply

Above: James Cagney in Here Comes the Navy, *one of Lloyd Bacon's recruitment pictures for the American forces. Right: banned in Germany on the orders of Hitler – the films of Tarzan Johnny Weissmuller, a Jew; Fred Astaire and Ginger Rogers, for reasons undisclosed; and George Arliss, for his portrayals of Jewish characters like Shylock, Rothschild and Disraeli. Meanwhile* The Charge of the Light Brigade, *starring Errol Flynn, was banned in Mussolini's Italy for its 'British propaganda'*

confusing. Ironically, despite political censorship, *Blockade* still attracted controversy. The Fox West Coast chain of cinemas, under fierce pressure from Catholic groups who identified with anyone fighting the anti-clerical Republicans, declined to screen it at all and pickets from local churches managed to force the film out of various cities in Michigan, Nebraska, Louisiana and Ohio.

For entertainment only

As the Thirties drew to a close the fact that the prospect of war in Europe loomed ever larger was recognized, albeit reluctantly, in Hollywood. In 1938 the Hays Office's annual report on the film industry had given a grave warning that the public paid for entertainment at the box-office, not for propaganda disguised as entertainment. A year later it proclaimed that there was nothing incompatible between 'the best interests of the box-office and the kind of entertainment that raises the level of audience appreciation whatever the subject touched'. But for all these grand protestations of the Hays Office, a closer examination of the films being made in 1939 reveals that audience appreciation was principally raised by John Cromwell's *Abe Lincoln in Illinois* (a disastrous adaptation of Robert Sherwood's play), John Ford's *Young Mr Lincoln*, and Frank Capra's *Mr Smith Goes to Washington*.

Only two films produced in 1939 made abundantly clear America's contempt for the fascist regimes of Europe. The first to be released was *Juarez* in which Paul Muni plays the Mexican president elected by 'the people', and Brian Aherne plays the well-meaning Hapsburg autocrat placed on the throne by the army of Napoleon III. In its publicity material for the film the Press Department of Warner

Brothers drew a direct parallel between Mexico in 1863 and Czechoslovakia in 1939, an interpretation that was undoubtedly intended by the writers, self-proclaimed liberal and interventionist John Huston, and European refugee Wolfgang Reinhardt.

Warner Brothers' major anti-Nazi statement, however, was *Confessions of a Nazi Spy* (1939), adapted from the experiences of Leon G. Turrou, a former FBI agent who had cracked a Nazi spy ring hidden within the ranks of the German-American Bund (an American pro-Nazi organization). The film's production team was a microcosm of the Hollywood Popular Front: the screenplay was written by Milton Krims and John Wexley, both extreme left-wingers; the star was Edward G. Robinson, a Jew and leading Hollywood liberal; the director was Anatole Litvak, a refugee from Nazi persecution. *Confessions of a Nazi Spy* aroused intense hostility. Jack and Harry Warner both received telephone calls threatening their lives, and a cinema in the German-populated area of Milwaukee that dared to show the film was burned to the ground by an outraged band of Nazi sympathizers. Hans Thomsen, the German Chargé d'Affaires, denounced the film to Cordell Hull, the Secretary of State, as an example of the pernicious defamations that were poisoning German-American relations.

Death of a salesman

However tame it appears in retrospect, *Confessions of a Nazi Spy* was a notable landmark in the context of contemporary American foreign policy. It was also a logical culmination of the personal hatred both Jack and Harry Warner harboured against the Nazis – feelings that could be traced beyond the

activities of Hitler's regime to the murder of the chief Warner Brothers salesman in Germany by Nazi thugs in a Berlin backstreet. The picture, however, proved too strong a dose of anti-Nazism for the country and the film industry to digest, and the Warner Brothers thereafter restricted their comments on foreign policy to the minimum.

An entirely acceptable form of interventionist propaganda was the series of recruiting pictures calling for a strong national defence. *Here Comes the Navy* (1934), *Devil Dogs of the Air* (1935), *Submarine D-1* (1937) and *Wings of the Navy* (1939) were all directed by Lloyd Bacon, himself a naval officer in the Reserve, and financed by William Randolph Hearst's Cosmopolitan Productions. These films set the pattern for such wartime recruitment pictures as *Action in the North Atlantic* (1943), Bacon's appetizer for the Merchant Marines, and *Ladies Courageous* (dir. John Rawlins, 1944), a film encouraging enlistments in the Women's Auxiliary Flying Squadron.

However, in the space of ten days in the summer of 1939 the film colony's attitude to events in Europe was fundamentally reshaped. Until that time all the political pressures on Hollywood were exerted largely on the side of caution. But then on August 23 Ribbentrop and Molotov signed the Nazi-Soviet Non-Aggression Pact and on September 1 Germany invaded Poland. The first event split the alliance between the liberals and the Communists in Hollywood and resulted in the dissolution of the Anti-Nazi League. The outbreak of World War II unfeelingly jolted Hollywood into more than two years of anguish and indecision before America's intervention provided it with prime subjects for movies, patriotism and heroism.
COLIN SHINDLER

Modern Times

Directed by Charles Chaplin, 1936
Prod/sc/mus: Charles Chaplin. **photo:** Rollie Totheroh, Ira Morgan. **art dir:** Charles D. Hall, Russell Spencer. **mus dir:** Alfred Newman. **mus arr:** Edward Powell, David Raskin. **ass dir:** Carter de Haven, Henry Bergman. **r/t** 87 minutes. New York premiere, 5 February 1936.
Cast: Charles Chaplin (*Tramp*), Paulette Goddard (*working-class girl*), Henry Bergman (*café owner*), Chester Conklin (*mechanic*), Allan Garcia (*steelworks manager*), Lloyd Ingraham (*prison governor*), Louis Netheaux (*drug addict*), John Rand (*jailbird*), Stanley Sanford (*fellow conveyor-belt worker*), Hank Mann (*cellmate*), Mira McKinney (*prison chaplain's wife*), Richard Alexander (*prison chaplain*), Wilfred Lucas, Edward Kimball, Murdock McQuarry, (*fellow prisoners/workers*).

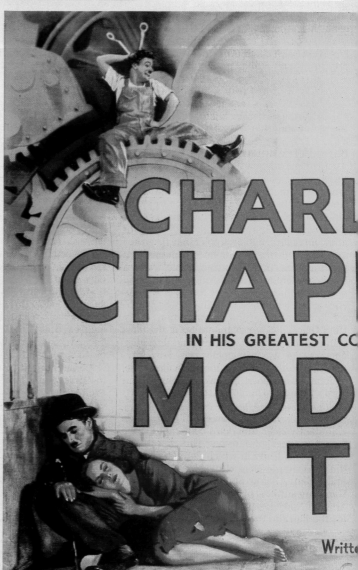

Chaplin regarded talking pictures as the ruin of 'the world's most ancient art, the art of pantomime. They annihilate the great beauty of silence'. *Modern Times* is conceived as a silent film. With the exception of the star's voice – heard for the first time on film when he sings a nonsense song – the only voices featured issue from television screens or loudspeakers. *Modern Times* was also the last appearance of Chaplin's Tramp figure – the little vagrant in a too-small Derby hat, too large boots, baggy pants, tight jacket, and a wing collar and sporty cane that proclaimed fallen gentility. This character first appeared on the screen 22 years before, in 1914, and achieved a universal acceptance such as no fictional image of a man had known before.

The film was poorly received by the critics of the time. Chaplin was charged with exceeding the proper function of the clown, of trying to set himself up as a popular philosopher. At the same time he was accused of being old-fashioned and cowardly in rejecting sound: after all, this was the era of the Marx Brothers, Mae West and W.C. Fields. In film technique, they said, he had learned little since 1914. Inevitably too, the film was charged with sinister political implications. It was banned in fascist Italy and Germany – and somewhat frowned upon in the USSR, on account of its satire on modern productivity. Protested Chaplin:

'Our only purpose was to amuse. It was just my old Charlie character in circumstances of 1936. I have no political aims whatever as an actor.'

'It started from an abstract idea, an impulse to say something about the way life is being standardized and channelized, and men turned into machines – and the way I felt about it. I knew that was what I wanted to do before I thought of any of the details.'

Chaplin's art has survived these criticisms. *Modern Times* looks perhaps even fresher today than on its original release. The film's chief quality – a characteristic of all of Chaplin's best work – is not so much its *modernity* as its *timelessness*. Chaplin's universe is not tied to a particular era, but seems to belong to all times. Though the world of *Modern Times* is the world of the American Depression, its characteristics – industrial regimentation, strikes, riots, drugs, demonstrations, urban pollution, the inhuman rigidity of bureaucratic social institutions – are all relevant and vivid to us today. And at the same time as the issues still seem topical more than forty years on, so the characters and sentiments often reach back to the ninteenth century. When Chaplin speaks of poverty and vagrancy, shows the child-care men snatching a child from a slum home, or shapes his vision of Paulette Goddard's sharp-faced little waif, he looks back to *The Kid* (1921), and beyond that to his own childhood in the slums and orphanages of Victorian London.

It is a film of brilliant set pieces, in which all the technical skills Chaplin had first learned in the English music halls are brought into play. W.C. Fields intended to insult him when he called Chaplin 'the best goddammed ballet dancer in the business', but it was only the truth: the conveyor belt sequence in the opening of tne film is a masterpiece of choreography. A moment's inattention to his mechanical task, when he brushes away a troublesome fly, causes chaos throughout the production line – and when finally he goes berserk, it is to dance his way into a beautiful mad ballet. demonically attacking with spanners anything that looks amenable to tightening, including the buttons of a busty lady who chances to be passing. There are comparable compositions of movement and mime in a scene where, having inadvertently swallowed a massive dose of 'joy powder', he pirouettes out of the prison dining-hall in the wake of a line of marching convicts; or in the miraculous, virtuoso sequence where he roller-skates, blindfold, on the brink of an abyss.

The full genius of Chaplin's comedy, however, appears in the scene where he obligingly picks up the red warning flag which has fallen off a passing lorry. He runs after it, quite unaware that a mass demonstration has formed up behind him. It is impossible to say whether the scene is comic or tragic. Either way, it remains one of the great symbolic representations of man as victim of his fate.
DAVID ROBINSON

122

Charlie plays a factory worker whose job is to tighten bolts of an endless series of machine parts on a moving belt (1). He is used as a guinea pig for a new aid to productivity – a machine that automatically feeds the men as they work. Finally he cracks under the strain, runs amok (2), and is sent to a mental hospital.

Discharged and part of the great army of unemployed, he helpfully picks up a red flag that has fallen from a lorry (3) – only to be arrested as a communist agitator. In prison, he accidentally averts a jailbreak and is given his freedom (4). Life outside prison is so fraught with perils, however, that he tries – vainly – to get arrested again. He attempts to take the blame when an orphaned waif, on the run from the child-care authorities, steals a loaf of bread (5). The two decide to join forces.

A job as a night watchman in a big store ends in disaster and jail again. Released, he returns to the factory, but a strike instantly puts him out of work and back on the streets. The girl is by this time a dancer in cabaret, where she finds him a job as a singing waiter. When this too ends in disaster (6), Charlie and the waif take off, the child-care men on their heels. They are last seen walking hand in hand down a country road (7).

3

4

5

6

7

Top Hat, White Tie and Tails

The story of Fred Astaire

Vincent Youmans, and *The Band Wagon* by Dietz and Schwartz – that brought the pair legendary status. Adele's retirement to get married in 1932 was the first real crisis in Fred's career: the team was great, but how would he make it on his own? The answer, in his next show, *Gay Divorce*, in which he starred with Clare Luce, proved to be: very nicely, thank you. But he was clearly ready for a real change, and offers from Hollywood seemed to provide it.

Shall we dance?

There still remained the problem of a partner. Though Fred usually had a speciality solo of some kind in his shows, the centre had always been the numbers he shared with his sister, who everyone agreed was his perfect complement in height, personality and technique. Someone had to be found for Fred's next film *Flying Down to Rio* (1933). Back at his own studio, RKO, he was only fifth on the bill below Dolores Del Rio (in very big letters) and (much smaller) Gene Raymond, Raul Roulien and Ginger Rogers.

Ginger Rogers was by no means a name to conjure with at this time. She had recently been put under contract by the same studio after singing and dancing in vaudeville and stage musicals. She had provided the romantic interest in a number of small movie comedies, and, on loan to Warner Brothers, had received tolerable reviews for her playing of hard-boiled chorus girls in *42nd Street* (1933) and *Gold Diggers of 1933* (1933). She was hard-working and resilient, but no-one thought she was a great dancer – or a great anything. But she *was* available, and thus easy to team with Astaire in a story which mainly concerned Dolores Del Rio trying to choose between the relative merits of Gene Raymond and Raul Roulien. Just as casually as that, one of the great romantic teams of the Thirties cinema came into being.

Against all expectation, the big success of the film was not its main romantic story but these two supporting players performing their one number together. Vincent Youmans' 'The Carioca'. At a time when Hollywood was quick to respond to audience reaction, the flood of letters and comments from ordinary movie-goers meant only one thing: Fred and Ginger

must be brought together as soon as possible in a film of their own. *The Gay Divorcee* (1934), a thorough reworking of Astaire's last stage success soon followed, and then in almost unbroken succession *Roberta* (1935), *Top Hat* (1935), *Follow the Fleet* (1936), *Swing Time* (1936), *Shall We Dance?* (1937), *Carefree* (1938) and *The Story of Vernon and Irene Castle* (1939). Throughout these years, the Astaire/Rogers films were RKO's most reliable box-office, performing the same bacon-saving function as the Mae West films did at Paramount and, a little later, Deanna Durbin films did at Universal. They also featured some amazing collaborators, especially on the musical side, with scores (often original scores) by Youmans, Cole Porter, Jerome Kern, the Gershwins and Irving Berlin – who, in particular, did much of his best work for *Top Hat*, *Follow the Fleet* and *Carefree*.

A fine romance, with no kisses

But the point was always Fred and Ginger. Though sentimental fans liked to fantasize real-life romances between their screen favourites – not always inaccurately, as in the case of Jeanette MacDonald and Nelson Eddy – Fred and Ginger's was a professional marriage of convenience. Socially they had little to do with each other outside the studio; but they worked perfectly together. It may be that a

Top: Fred, the epitome of elegance for his big solo number in Top Hat *– in which the chorus become targets in a mock shooting-gallery. Below: Fred poses with his sister Adele – his stage partner until her retirement in 1932 – in a Twenties publicity shot*

One of the best stories of Hollywood in the early Thirties tells of Fred Astaire's first screen test at RKO. An executive's report on it read: 'Losing hair. Can't sing. Can dance a little.' Happily, David O. Selznick, head of production, took a cheerier view: 'I am still a little uncertain about the man, but I feel, in spite of his enormous ears and bad chin line, that his charm is so tremendous it comes through even in this wretched test.' Astaire was promptly loaned out to MGM for a brief appearance in one of the big production numbers of the Joan Crawford vehicle *Dancing Lady* (1933). In this humdrum way began one of the most spectacular careers in the Hollywood cinema, spanning nearly five decades.

Fred Astaire was certainly no overnight sensation. His real name was Frederick Austerlitz and he was born on May 10, 1899. At the age of four and a half he was enrolled, along with his six-year-old sister Adele, in a dance school by his ambitious mother. From then on it was show business every inch of the way. By 1917 Fred and Adele had featured roles in a Broadway musical; five shows later, in 1922, they starred in *The Bunch and Judy*. Four big shows followed – *Lady, Be Good!* and *Funny Face*, both written by the Gershwins, *Smiles*, by

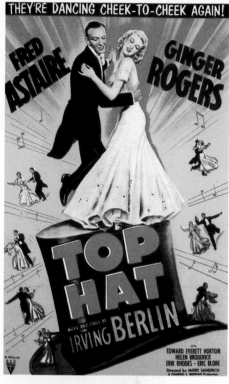

A matchless pairing of man about town with girl next door was the secret of Fred and Ginger's magic. A dance leads to a fine romance in Swing Time *(top left and below) and* Top Hat *(top right). In* Follow the Fleet *(above) Fred swaps a tailcoat for bell-bottoms*

measure of antagonism is good in such a relationship – certainly many of their most famous romantic numbers show them at first pulling away from each other and then drawing together, as if in spite of themselves. Similarly the plots of their films nearly always consisted of variations on the formula: boy meets girl, boy hates girl (and vice versa) – but since they are really deeply attracted to each other (hence the superficial hostility) everything turns out right in the end.

Someone (supposedly Katharine Hepburn, the other big RKO star at the time) said that the secret of their success together was that he gave her class, and she gave him sex-appeal. Certainly her bright, brash exuberance contrasted very well with his elegant understatement and ironic charm. Though he was the creative one behind the scenes – he would spend weeks working out the films' dance routines, rehearsing himself, her and everybody else involved within an inch of their lives to get it all exactly right – she was a quick and eager study, able, when shown how, to be not only a perfect foil for him but a full partner with a positive contribution to make. The films are consequently memorable, not only for his speciality dance solos but also for two similar but distinguishable kinds of dance duet: the straight romantic, and the love-hate kind.

Dancing cheek to cheek

It takes two or three films for the pattern to become perfectly established; in *The Gay Divorcee* the normal relationship between the partners is not yet clear, though the film does have a typical romantic number, 'Night and Day', and a novelty dance to introduce 'The Con-

tinental', in which 'you kiss while dancing'. In *Roberta* it is nearly there, though the main romantic interest resides in Irene Dunne and Randolph Scott – at least Fred and Ginger have a 'togetherness' dance number to 'Smoke Gets in Your Eyes' and an 'antagonism-rivalry' number in 'I'll Be Hard to Handle'. By *Top Hat* it is all there: Astaire's showy solo dancing on sand in 'No Strings', and again in the title number, where he 'shoots' a whole chorus of white-tied look-alikes; a love-hate number in 'Isn't This a Lovely Day?' with the two of them marooned by a freak thunderstorm on a bandstand in the park; and a classic love-love number with them dancing unmistakably 'Cheek to Cheek'.

From that point on Astaire's routines read like a roll-call of brilliant moments in the

Ginger Alone

Although Ginger Rogers was a virtual nobody when she first teamed up with Fred Astaire, she had plenty of ambition and a driving show-business mother, so it was not surprising that her career diversified more rapidly and radically than that of her dance-obsessed partner. She was, in fact, one of the busiest stars on the RKO lot, appearing in all kinds of thoroughly unmemorable dramas and

Below: Ginger in her Oscar-winning role of Kitty Foyle. Opposite page right: her good looks, twinkling feet and comic gift were all displayed in Roxie Hart. She plays a gold-digging chorus girl in the Twenties, who, as a publicity stunt, confesses to a murder she did not commit

Hollywood musical. He taps a sailor chorus to death in 'I'd Rather Lead a Band' (*Follow the Fleet*), dances blackface with an enormous chorus on a mirrored floor the size of Central Park in 'Bojangles of Harlem' (*Swing Time*), slaps 'that bass' (*Shall We Dance?*) and performs the most astonishing feats of golfmanship while dancing to 'Since They Turned Loch Lomond into Swing' (*Carefree*). Fred and Ginger clown and tussle in 'I'm Putting All My Eggs in One Basket' (*Follow the Fleet*) and 'A

Fine Romance' (*Swing Time*) and dance on roller-skates in 'Let's Call the Whole Thing Off' (*Shall We Dance?*). They are all elegance and restraint, but their passion is unmistakable, in the wonderful miniature ballet (he saves her from suicide after a gambling disaster) to the tune of 'Let's Face the Music' (*Follow the Fleet*). The same mood characterizes the numbers 'Never Gonna Dance' (*Swing Time*) and 'Change Partners' (*Carefree*).

Everything they did seemed effortless – it

was meant to seem that way. It was a meeting of disparate but equally genuine star personalities, whose encounters had a continuing spice and savour that survived changes of fashion. Even today, so long after the partnership broke up, and many years since their only return match in *The Barkleys of Broadway* (1949), people still tend to think of Astaire and Rogers as an indivisible entity, and it is generally accepted that Ginger was the best of all his partners.

comedies and always losing out on the roles she really wanted – like Mary Queen of Scots – to Katharine Hepburn. Her best film without Astaire during this period actually co-starred her with Hepburn: they both played young hopefuls in *Stage Door* (1937) – Rogers the apparently tough one with a vulnerable side.

Her first film after the break with Astaire was a successful comedy, *Bachelor Mother* (1939), about a shop-girl who takes in an abandoned baby which people assume to be her own. In 1940 she was in an eccentric comedy drama by Gregory La Cava, *The Primrose Path*, in which she was a shanty-town girl bent on escaping her awful family. She always counted this among her favourite films, along with *Kitty Foyle* (1940), a tale of conflict between love and money, for which, against unusually heavy competition, she won an Oscar. This was the high point of her career, though there was no immediate falling off, and the war years included three of her best comedies, *Tom, Dick and Harry* (1941), *Roxie Hart* (1942) and *The Major and the Minor* (1942), as well as her most lavish vehicle, an adaptation in colour of Gertrude Lawrence's Broadway success *Lady in the Dark* (1944).

In the decade after the war, she made quite a number of films, most memorably *The Barkleys of Broadway* (1949) – for which she was persuaded to renew her partnership with Astaire in place of an ailing Judy Garland – *Monkey Business* (1952), a comedy about rejuvenation with Cary Grant, *Forever Female* (1953), in which she played an ageing gangster's moll. Later she appeared frequently on the stage, notably in *Mame* in 1969. She usually played vivacious working-girls – as a 'lady' she seemed rather self-consciously on her best behaviour. It was this quality which made Graham Greene say that she would have been an ideal choice as the eccentric Augusta in the film adapted from his hilarious book, *Travels With My Aunt* (1972). The part went to Maggie Smith: sadly, roles of this quality too seldom came Ginger's way.

JOHN RUSSELL TAYLOR

Filmography
1929 Campus Sweethearts (short); A Night in a Dormitory (short); A Day of a Man of Affairs (short). **'30** Young Man of Manhattan; Queen High; The Sap from Syracuse (GB: The Sap Abroad); Office Blues (short); Follow the Leader. **'31** Honor Among Lovers; The Tip-Off (GB: Looking for Trouble); Suicide Fleet. **'32** Carnival Boat; The Tenderfoot; Hollywood on Parade, No 1 (short); The Thirteenth Guest; Screen Snapshots (short); Hat Check Girl; You Said a Mouthful. **'33** 42nd Street; Broadway Bad (GB: Her Reputation); Hollywood on Parade, No 3 (short); Professional Sweetheart (GB: Imaginary Sweetheart); Gold Diggers of 1933; A Shriek in the Night; Don't Bet on Love; Sitting Pretty; Flying Down to Rio; Chance at Heaven. **'34** Rafter Romance; Finishing School; 20 Million Sweethearts; Change of Heart; Upperworld; The Gay Divorcee (GB: The Gay Divorce); Romance in Manhattan. **'35** Roberta; Star of Midnight; Top Hat; In Person. **'36** Follow the Fleet; Swing Time. **'37** Shall We Dance?; Stage Door; Holiday Greetings (short). **'38** Having Wonderful Time; Vivacious Lady; Carefree. **'39** The Story of Vernon and Irene Castle; Bachelor Mother. **'40** The Primrose Path; Lucky Partners; Kitty Foyle. **'41** Tom, Dick and Harry. **'42** Roxie Hart; Tales of Manhattan; The Major and the Minor; Once Upon a Honeymoon. **'43** Tender Comrade; Show Business at War (short); Battle Stations (short). **'44** Lady in the Dark; I'll Be Seeing You. **'45** Weekend at the Waldorf. **'46** Heartbeat; Magnificent Doll. **'47** It Had to Be You. **'49** The Barkleys of Broadway. **'50** Perfect Strangers (GB: Too Dangerous to Love); Storm Warning. **'51** The Groom Wore Spurs. **'52** We're Not Married; Monkey Business; Dream Boat. **'53** Forever Female. **'54** Black Widow; Beautiful Stranger (USA: Twist of Fate) (GB). **'55** Tight Spot. **'56** The First Travelling Saleslady; Teenage Rebel. **'57** Oh, Men! Oh, Women! **'64** The Confession/Quick Let's Get Married/Seven Different Ways. **'65** Harlow.
Note: it is estimated that she made about a dozen shorts between 1929 and 1931 and several wartime shorts.

Let's call the whole thing off
All the same, they broke up – mainly, it seems, because she wanted to branch out as a dramatic actress, but it is not impossible that he was also growing restive with the limitations of their collaboration. In 1937, he had made one film outside the partnership *A Damsel in Distress* (1937), with a non-dancing partner, Joan Fontaine, whom he had to dance around – a not very satisfactory solution. But when (after the patchy biographical film *The Story of*

Vernon and Irene Castle) Ginger departed, a world of partners and possibilities opened up for him. Eleanor Powell in *Broadway Melody of 1940* (1940) and Rita Hayworth in *You'll Never Get Rich* (1941) and *You Were Never Lovelier* (1942) showed that Astaire was not necessarily tied to one partner, but was even 'improved' by variety.

Astaire made one serious attempt to retire, in 1946, but he was lured back to replace Gene Kelly – his only serious rival as a dancing star in films – in *Easter Parade* (1948) opposite Judy Garland. From then on he has never stopped working. He was part of the great heyday of colour musicals at MGM in the late Forties and early Fifties, appearing in some of the best, such as *Ziegfeld Follies* (1946), *Royal Wedding*

(1951), *The Band Wagon* (1953) and *Silk Stockings* (1957), as well as *Funny Face* (1957) at Paramount with Audrey Hepburn and Kay Thompson. As he got older he danced less in his films – partly also because the number of worthwhile musicals being made greatly diminished after 1960 – but he did several memorable television specials in which he sang and danced, and kept himself busy as an excellent comedian and a more than competent straight actor. Which is very much where he is today – he was even dancing, at the age of 77, in *That's Entertainment Part 2* (1976). There never has been anyone to touch him as a dancer; as a singer he was and remains still the only interpreter of many song classics, more of which he directly inspired than perhaps anyone else; and as an actor and personality he could always – and still can – charm the birds off the trees. Call him irreplaceable.   JOHN RUSSELL TAYLOR

Opposite page: Fred and Ginger dance to Kern's 'Lovely to Look at' in Roberta *(top left). Nanette Fabray and Jack Buchanan partner Fred for the hilarious 'Triplets' number from* The Band Wagon *(left). Astaire's first straight acting role was in* On the Beach *(1960) with Gregory Peck and Ava Gardner (right). This page: Fred was still dancing at the age of 69 in* Finian's Rainbow *(far left). He also waltzed (and escaped the flames) in* The Towering Inferno *(left)*

Change Partners and Dance

Fred Astaire and Ginger Rogers chose to go their separate ways in 1939 – she wished to further her career as a straight actress, he wanted to explore more fully the musical's potential.

Eleanor Powell (above centre), who could tap faster and kick higher than anyone else, was the first of his new partners, starring with him in Broadway Melody of 1940.

Rita Hayworth came from a family of professional dancers. Her youth, beauty and sheer vitality graced You'll Never Get Rich and You Were Never Lovelier (below).

In the mid-Forties, Fred made two films with Lucille Bremer – Ziegfeld Follies and Yolanda and the Thief (above left), which was supposed to make her a big star. But the partnership never quite worked and she soon retired.

Easter Parade provided Astaire with two partners – Ann Miller for the more classic

duos and Judy Garland for the comedy numbers, the highpoint of which was 'A Couple of Swells' (below right).

The next major sensation in Fred's career was Cyd Charisse – tall, statuesque, and in dance at least, smoulderingly sexy. Cyd and he were an explosive team, starring in The Band Wagon (above right) and Silk Stockings, Rouben Mamoulian's remake of Ninotchka.

Astaire's last two major partners, Leslie Caron in Daddy Long Legs (right) and Audrey Hepburn in Funny Face had both undergone ballet training. Their youth brought out a protective quality in Fred, and he provoked a special warmth in them.

Astaire has remained vague about who was his favourite partner: his stock answer is Gene Kelly, with whom he danced in Ziegfeld Follies and That's Entertainment Part 2.

Fred Astaire and Rita Hayworth–dancing and singing together!

Fan Magazines: gossip, gloss and good advice

♦ STAR'S HUSBAND IN HOLLYWOOD TO AID IN DEFENSE ♦

MARLENE DIETRICH DENIES
CHARGE SHE IS "LOVE THIEF"

ACCUSED BY WIFE OF JOSEF VON STERNBERG OF ALIENATING DIRECTOR'S
AFFECTIONS, STAR REFUSES TO SETTLE CASE OUT OF COURT

Picturegoer and Film Weekly. Registered at the G.P.O. as a newspaper   No. 462 (New Series). Vol. 9. March 30, 1940

Picturegoer
Incorporating Film Weekly 2d

Hedy LAMARR

Street-corners in London, New York and Paris were once bright with the colourful covers of American fan magazines, of *Photoplay, Motion Picture, Screenland, Silver Screen, Motion Picture Classic*. London also had its (less colourful) English weekly film papers.

The heyday of these magazines was the Twenties and Thirties when stars – the movie world's most marketable commodity – were revered by moviegoers as not only beautiful and desirable, but worldly-wise and omniscient. The studios in Hollywood had latched onto this idea early on and set about mobilizing the newly created, world-wide army of fans. They did this partly through fan clubs, but mostly through their own publicity departments which built up shelves of detail – factual and fictional – on rising stars for the magazines to publish. Increasingly, to suit studio policy in all its ramifications, the publicity departments rationed and regulated the supply of 'private life' stories, especially those of happy or threatened marriages.

The heart of the magazines was originally the illustration material that the publicity departments provided. Sometimes these were posed, sad pictures of frightened starlets, like the pathetic ones of Garbo, shortly after her arrival in Hollywood, crouching in a swimsuit to play tennis, or clutching a lion cub; or Gary Cooper or Joan Crawford in their tennis whites.

Even when the studios later provided good quality stills from their films, the magazines continued to swamp them in gossip. Most of the magazines carried several different gossip

features. In *Photoplay* there was 'Round the Studios with Cal York' and 'Close-Ups and Long Shots'. In *Motion Picture* there was 'Your Gossip Test' – a kind of quiz on intimate gossip, with answers, sometimes cruelly informative, at the back. *Motion Picture* also started with a 'Hot News Story of the Month'. Its report on the trial of Clara Bow's ex-secretary Daisy DeVoe, brought to court after exposing details of Clara's private life in a New York tabloid, was one sensational example. Through such items it was often easy to trace a consistent policy of pressure on a particular star.

At the beginning of the Thirties the focal points for Hollywood gossip were (publicly) the rapid decline since talkies of the great romantic silent star John Gilbert and (privately) his marriage to stage comedienne Ina Claire instead of Garbo, the 'Swedish Mona Lisa who alone seemed glamorous enough to tie him in the bonds of matrimony'. So we had 'The Girl Jack Married' and 'You'll Love Ina Claire Just as You Love Jack', and not a day's peace in print for 'Jack and Ina' until they were well and truly separated and divorced. Another target was Janet Gaynor's marriage to Lydell Peck after the fans' long expectations that she would marry her screen partner Charles Farrell. So Charlie's supposed heartbreak and Janet's restlessness became regular features. So, too, did the brief marriages of Gloria Swanson and Constance Bennett to French aristocrats, for Hollywood loves a title. Garbo was less enthusiastic about royalty – one of the most often repeated gibes at her

Above left: an article in Movie Classic *in the early Thirties feeds the Dietrich/Sternberg scandal; the star is pictured with her daughter, husband and Sternberg himself. Above: the English* Picturegoer and Film Weekly *dishing out sex-appeal in the form of Hedy Lamarr*

solitary habits concerned her declining to dine with the Mountbattens when they were visiting Hollywood.

An article on Robert Taylor asked: 'Can Robert Taylor escape the Hollywood Love Racket? Or will he, like Edward VIII, be prevented from marrying the woman he loves?' Another, discussing in general whether the male star should marry, concludes: 'If the girls who watch him think he is going home to his wife they will have more difficulty in thinking of him as their own Prince Charming.'

The studios, of course, needed to beg, buy and cheat their way out of involvement with the major tragic scandals – like that of Jean Harlow and Paul Bern for example. But they also had to keep from the magazines the more routine incidents that would also lead to adverse publicity. Even in England, where fan magazines – like movies – have never acquired the power and influence they have in America, a young studio publicity man could find himself compelled to cover up one morning for a talented starlet too dead drunk to keep an interview appointment. Above all, he would have to ensure that neither the star nor the magazine interviewer would involve his boss, the head of the studio, in any embarrassment.

Cedric Belfrage, the English Hollywood correspondent, wrote in *Motion Picture Classic* some sharp paragraphs about Hollywood's favourite income-tax adviser who had been asked in court to explain how she had come to put expenses for entertainment under the heading 'Publicity' in her noted clients' returns. Said Belfrage:

'Getting publicity in Hollywood is very largely a matter of keeping the various gossipers and tattlers well oiled . . . And it is well known that any star who gives a Press tea-party where the beverage is tea is taking the short cut to oblivion.'

More sinisterly, in a 1931 issue of *Motion Picture*, we read:

'There are probably not more than half a dozen stars of any magnitude who have not paid out money to avoid publicity . . . in some cases they may have real things to hide, but in many cases some unscrupulous person has played upon their dread of unfavourable publicity . . . Richard Dix once admitted in an interview that he had paid thousands of dollars over matters in which he was not to blame. So have many other stars.'

On the whole fan magazines saw their function as a central liaison between studio, stars and fans. They often adopted a warning, sometimes governessy, tone towards the stars, as when the editor of *Screenland*, Delight Evans, in her 'Open Letter to Clark Gable', reproved him for too much 'kiss and make-up' in his recent pictures. *Motion Picture*'s 'Here, There & Everywhere' once started a paragraph of warning to the fiery Mexican actress Lupe Velez:

'No more strong words . . . no more temperamental explosions on the set. She has compiled a list of forbidden phrases – swear words and other picturesque expressions she is not to use.'

Other pieces of reproof and gossip were less charitable. One magazine coyly captioned a harmless summer picture of Joan Crawford and Monroe Olsen with the words: 'Does your husband know, Joan, of this attractively posed picture with that smooth screen villain Monroe Olsen?' A gossip feature in *Silver Screen*, truthfully enough called 'Snooping in Hollywood', referred to 'Lana Turner who used to be Wayne Morris' girl (who hasn't) . . .'

To the fans the approach was cosy, with much good advice on how they should behave. 'How to Become a Hollywood Hostess' gave a table-plan for a score of Hollywood notables and concluded by coyly advising an invitation to those two glamorous and helpful bachelors, Ramon Novarro and Nils Asther. To the studios the magazines were fairly servile, with a wary look over the shoulder.

Into the morass of gossip most magazines slipped occasional pieces of technical information – about dubbing, sound systems, colour and so forth. And there were also the cash contests: $500 for a new name for the talkies; $5000 in prizes for a short story with a Hollywood background.

Meanwhile the more modest and generally more discreet and decorous British film magazines chugged along in the wake. There were four weeklies: *Film Weekly*, *Picture Show*, *Picturegoer*, and *Film Pictorial*. Despite the candid title of the monthly *Movie Fan*, the British magazines always seemed less shamelessly fan-orientated than the American, more concerned with the movies themselves. *Movie Fan*, though, did carry a remarkable 'Letter from Mary Pickford' on her future after *Kiki* (1931). For her next film Miss Pickford wanted 'a story very, very human . . . the character to be a human being and above all charming. I want the picture to have the scent of an old-world garden.'

The most serious of the British magazines, *Film Weekly*, never considered itself a fan magazine although it, too, inevitably carried a proportion of stardust and competitions. It had an excellent review service, and its editorial commentary and news attempted a genuine coverage of developments in the cinema. Its interviews and articles ventured analyses of the actors' and directors' work and their approach to it. For some years the magazine ran a weekly studio visit in the feature 'Words and Pictures'. Of the others the modest *Picture Show*, under its valiant editor Maude Hughes and her partner Edith Nepeane, kept up its chatty style until its demise in 1960. *Film Weekly* had a smaller circulation than the slightly glossier *Picturegoer* but both weeklies gave their staffs of

Above, left to right: magazines selling glamour and romance – with Clara Bow, Garbo and Gable, Anne Harding, Lilian Harvey, and Gary Cooper with Lupe Velez and Jean Arthur

young enthusiasts an honourable opportunity to learn about films by studying first-class filmmakers at work, and both played a part in helping to build an educated film public. Several respected British film critics did their stint on one or other magazine. (*Film Weekly* was amalgamated with *Picturegoer* on the outbreak of war in 1939.)

The French, too, had their own fan magazines. Like the French newspapers of the Thirties they were more uncouth in form than their English and American counterparts, but like French movies, much more sophisticated in content.

Mon Ciné, for example, would start with a competition about the eyes of such stars as Billie Dove, Colleen Moore and Clara Bow, and go on to a whole page about Eisenstein's *The*

STREET & SMITH'S
PICTURE PLAY
10 CENTS
OCTOBER

Art Plates of Lina Basquette, Dorothy Boyd, & Pat Aherne—Inside
Vol. 21 No. 529   JUNE 22nd, 1929.   every Saturday 2D
Picture Show
GARY COOPER here seen with LUPE VELEZ in "The Wolf Song." See page 16.
Hollywood's *Latest* "Sheik"

CAROLE LOMBARD on HOW I SELL MY PERSONALITY
Film Pictorial
2D Every Thursday
GARY COOPER IN "The Plainsman"
STORY AND PICTURES
Gary Cooper & Jean Arthur

General Line (1928) and a double spread on René Clair's *Sous les Toits de Paris* (1930, *Under the Roofs of Paris*). One issue of *Pour Nous* for 1930 – despite having the Dodge Sisters on the cover and a first page of fashion – devotes an inside page to *Westfront 1918* (1930) and a discussion on Pabst, with the adjoining column on Louise Brooks in *Prix de Beauté* (1930, *Miss Europe*). In addition there is a long article on the Russian actress Baranovskaya, star of Pudovkin's *Mother* (1926), her studi Moscow and her dedication to seeking harmony between movement, sensation, music. But the leading attraction is a full account – under the heading 'Mercy, Appeal and Theosophy' and above a still from *The Four Horsemen of the Apocalypse* (1921) – of

Below left and below: selling cigarettes and soap – magazine ads with Dolores del Rio and Barbara Stanwyck. Right: Joan Crawford, seldom out of the fan magazines, dispenses wisdom in an issue of Movie Mirror

an idolatrous get-together of Valentino-worshippers at the Salle Adja, headquarters of the Theosophy Society. Even these early specimens reveal that while playing lip- and eye-

service to the fans, French film papers already carried articles on the movies devoted to the serious discussion of ideas.

FREDA BRUCE LOCKHART

"I can help you win hearts...
says BARBARA STANWYCK

Lovely Warner Bros. star

"There's something about the charm of really exquisite skin men just can't resist" says this beautiful star.
"I have the sensitive skin that goes with red hair—yet for years my simple beauty care . . . Lux Toilet Soap . . . has kept it always soft and smooth. With a tempting, smooth skin you can win hearts and *hold* them. Try my beauty soap—you'll see!"

Scientists Explain: "Skin pores are reacting through the tended bars of common skincare. Some par fumes is to keep it youthful. Gentle Lux Toilet Soap, has been noticeable result, schools owners to see their feet form the skin."

Actually 9 out of 10 Hollywood stars use fragrant, white Lux Toilet Soap. Why don't you win new loveliness the Hollywood way? *Start today!*

LUX TOILET SOAP

For EVERY Type of Skin... dry... oily... in-between

"The trouble with Grand Passions," says Joan, "is that they don't allow for a sense of humor. You just can't find laughter in a cyclone."

From deep in her heart, she brings to you and me the new truths she has learned about human beings who are in love

By CARTER BRUCE

Joan Crawford [signature]

REVEALS
The Difference Between
FRIENDSHIP And LOVE

BLIND Love of which the poets sing . . . a soaring, comet-like love . . . heady as a cocktail . . . or—Romantic Friendship . . . like the coals of a glowing fire of sympathy and understanding before which lovers warm their hearts. . . .
Where lies the greatest happiness for a woman?
Hollywood knows much of Blind Love. It has found the inspiration of gossip columnists, Winchell rumors, most of the Yuma elopements and Reno hang-overs.
But Romantic Friendship, that seldom-reached state sometimes flippantly referred to as "Pals-in-love"—how many couples can be counted as the fortunate few, among the many Hollywood marriages, who have found this happiness?
These were the questions I put to Joan Crawford the day we lunched at the Ambassador during that last, hectic shopping-week before Christmas . . . and the answers she gave were an amazing insight into what romantic friendship has brought into Joan's life. To those Hollywood gossips who have hinted that Joan's glowing romance with Franchot Tone has "tumbled" from the romantic heights of hectic

love and "settled down" into a nice, calm friendship, she made the perfect observation:
"I'm afraid someone has mixed his terms a bit. People do not *settle down* to the happiness of romantic friendship. They soar to it!"

OVER a period of several years, I have frequently boasted that I knew this girl who sat across from me—a beautiful girl in smart, grey sports clothes and a chic hat that turned down on one side so that it almost obscured one eye. And, if acquaintance is to be counted on the clock, I presume I do know her. I've seen her and talked with her during most of her well-publicized Hollywood moods—from her dancing-contest days through her humorless marriage with Douglas Fairbanks, Jr., and on down to her separation and divorce. But each time I see her, I ask myself if I really know her at all. Not that I have been taken in with the hundred-and-one stories about the "New Joan Crawford," but I do not believe that the experiences of her life have tossed her about quite as recklessly as the sob sisters would have us believe. (*Continued*)

It Happened One Night

Nobody at Columbia wanted *It Happened One Night* – nobody, that is, except Frank Capra and his scriptwriter Robert Riskin. They had found the idea in a story called *Night Bus* by Samuel Hopkins Adams, which had appeared in *Cosmopolitan* magazine. They bought the story for a trifling sum and, engrossed in making *Lady for A Day*, forgot it. The events that follow are described by Capra in his autobiography, *The Name Above the Title*: Irving Thalberg wanted to borrow him from Columbia to make a film for MGM, but Thalberg became ill. Louis B. Mayer then vetoed the project and the loan of a director was off. Capra, thankfully back at Columbia, insisted that he now be allowed to make *Night Bus*.

A couple of 'bus' movies had flopped, so the title was changed to *It Happened One Night* and the script was rewritten to make the chief characters more attractive. Still nobody wanted the story. At last Columbia boss Harry Cohn gave his consent. Then they ran into casting problems. Myrna Loy turned down the female role, as did Margaret Sullavan, Miriam Hopkins and Constance Bennett. MGM, as the result of the Capra deal, still owed Columbia a star. Robert Montgomery said 'No', but Clark Gable was in Louis B. Mayer's bad books,

Directed by Frank Capra, 1934
Prod co: Columbia. **prod:** Harry Cohn. **sc:** Robert Riskin from the short story *Night Bus* by Samuel Hopkins Adams. **photo:** Joseph Walker. **ed:** Gene Havlick. **cost:** Robert Kalloch. **sd:** Edward Bernds. **ass dir:** C.C. Coleman. **r/t:** 110 minutes.
Cast: Clark Gable (*Peter Warne*), Claudette Colbert (*Ellie Andrews*), Walter Connolly (*Alexander Andrews*), Roscoe Karns (*Shapely*), Alan Hale (*Danker*), Ward Bond (*bus driver*), Eddie Chandler (*bus driver*), Jameson Thomas (*King Westley*), Harry Holman (*autocamp owner*), Maidel Turner (*his wife*), Irving Bacon (*gas station man*), Wallis Clark (*Lovington*), Arthur Hoyt (*Zeke*), Blanche Frederici (*Zeke's wife*), Charles C. Wilson (*Gordon*), Charles D. Brown (*editor*), Harry C. Bradley (*Henderson*).

1

and as a punishment was sent, grumbling, over to Columbia. Finally Claudette Colbert was approached. She was unfriendly: another 'bus' film? It took double her usual fee and the promise of only four weeks' shooting to persuade her.

During the making of the film Capra improvised constantly. One of the happiest passages – the singing in the bus of 'That Daring Young Man on the Flying Trapeze' – came out of an impromptu by a couple of bit-players; it was turned to narrative advantage by making the driver join in and neglect to look where he was going. Nobody, though, seems to have expected the film to be a radiant success, and when it appeared in February 1934 the critical reaction was only moderate. It was the public that went wild. In the

Academy Awards of the following year *It Happened One Night* won five Oscars: best picture, best actress, best actor, best screen adaptation and best director.

Capra's film was to be regarded as a pioneer of the 'screwball' comedies of the Thirties; and its success made it influential. Without it we might not have had *My Man Godfrey*, *The Awful Truth* or, come to that, Capra's own anti-authoritarian *Mr Deeds Goes to Town*. Possibly the hostilities which attended its inception created the right atmosphere for a comedy which opens in acrimony. At the outset Claudette Colbert and Clark Gable seemed to have an aversion to each other. Their early scenes needed to bristle – and did bristle! The casting could not have been better. Indeed the film develops into

a struggle between the two, not for domination – this is not the battle of the sexes – but for superiority in the business of the everyday world.

The journalist has the advantage at the start; after all, as the heiress says, when after their first night in the autocamp they have breakfast together, she has never been alone with a man before. He tries in a series of crucial scenes to assert his worldly experience. Taking off his shirt in the bedroom, 'This', he says, 'is how a man undresses'. At breakfast he demonstrates how to dunk a doughnut. However, his defeat comes when he proposes to hitchhike. He boasts to her of the eloquence of his thumb but the cars whizz negligently past. Only when the girl enters into competition, lifting her skirt to show a seductive leg, do the pair get a lift.

Shirt, doughnut, thumb versus leg: the stages in the co-education of the confident journalist and the 'spoiled brat', as he calls the heiress, are memorable. This is partly due to the successful combination of a tart social attitude with a sense of growing affection as conveyed by the two central characters; here Capra's gift for portraying warmth in human relations is never allowed to spill over into sentimentality. But there is another element in the pleasure of *It Happened One Night*. There is no waste in this comedy. Every incident, every phrase and gesture – from Ellie's flight from her father's yacht, to her escape from the wedding ceremony, bridal train flying behind her – is strictly devoted to narrative and the interplay of character and accident. After the passage of so many decades one still surrenders to the wit, the good humour and the charm of what is thought by many to be one of Capra's best films.

Finally, it is interesting to note that at a time when a star could be bundled off unceremoniously to another studio he could also affect the fashions of a nation. Gable, taking off his shirt, reveals no undervest; men all over the United States followed his lead. There is said to have been a disastrous slump in the undervest business.

DILYS POWELL

CLARK GABLE ** CLAUDETTE COLBERT in *It Happened One Night* A FRANK CAPRA PRODUCTION

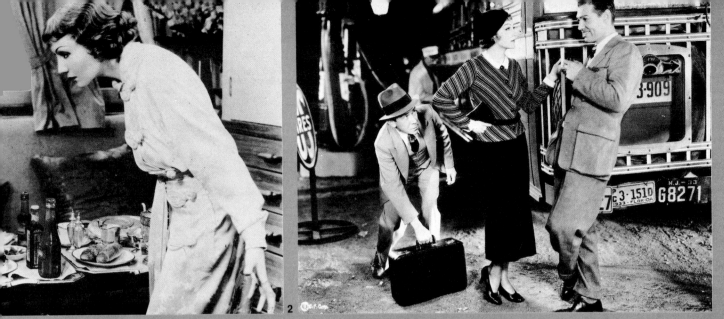

Ellie Andrews has married a mercenary playboy. Her rich banker father wants the unconsummated marriage annulled (1); defiantly she runs away to rejoin her husband. On a night bus she meets an out-of-work journalist, Peter Warne, who recognizes her (2); in return for his silence she agrees to give him her story. Dislodging an obnoxious passenger from the seat beside her, Peter claims that Ellie is his wife (3) and that night she is obliged to share his autocamp bedroom (4). He drapes a blanket over a cord to separate the two beds and calls the contrivance the walls of Jericho (5) – which, as he says, Joshua demolished by blowing a trumpet.

To avoid discovery they leave the bus and take to hitch-hiking (6), during which time they spend two blameless days and nights together; Ellie is now falling in love with him. He goes to borrow money so that he can justify proposing marriage. On waking, Ellie thinks she has been abandoned and telephones her father who, having now approved her secret marriage, wants to celebrate it with a formal wedding. When Peter returns he sees her driving away. She decides to go through with the loveless marriage. An embittered Peter demands repayment of his expenses, while admitting to her father that he loves her.

The wedding begins (7), the bride bolts, and a distant toy trumpet announces the fall of Jericho.

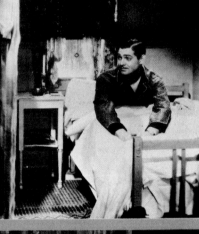

That Certain Cukor Quality

A stage director who became a true craftsman of cinema, George Cukor liberated the screen heroine from her role as incidental 'love interest'

Left: directing the emotional Judy Garland in A Star Is Born. *Above: Katharine Hepburn in* Little Women. *Below: Constance Bennett and Lowell Sherman play the waitress starlet and alcoholic film director in* What Price Hollywood? *(1932), one of the first realistic films about the movie business. Some 20 years later the same theme was reworked for Cukor's* A Star Is Born.

Back in 1933, George Cukor must have seemed an odd choice to direct *Little Women*. Already filmed twice during the silent era, Louisa May Alcott's classic (and to many highly sentimental) tale told the story of four young sisters (the March girls) and their mother, bravely coping while father was away from home fighting in the American Civil War. Nothing at the time indicated that Cukor would be particularly adept at handling this sort of family entertainment.

A native New Yorker, (born there in 1899) he was already an established Broadway director when he entered the film industry in 1929. At that time the studios were crying out for men and women with the requisite stage experience to coach actors in their delivery of lines. Cukor worked as dialogue director on *River of Romance* (1929) and Lewis Milestone's *All Quiet on the Western Front* (1930). He rose rapidly, making a few films as co-director, to become the fully-fledged director of such urbane, modern subjects as *Tarnished Lady* and *Girls About Town* (both 1931).

Cukor's career became linked to that of the producer David O. Selznick with whom he worked at Paramount. A joint migration to RKO resulted in such Selznick productions as *A Bill of Divorcement* and *What Price Hollywood?* (both 1932), and *Our Betters* (1933), which further stamped Cukor as a director attuned to repartee and conversant with such adult themes as divorce, adultery and the sexual inequalities of the double standard.

By the time *Little Women* was ready to start filming, Selznick had left this most cherished of his projects to join MGM, but Cukor stayed on. To the surprise of sophisticates and cynics, the Louisa M. Alcott spirit was lovingly preserved: even more important, some of the author's

flinty Yankee determination was allowed to infuse this chronicle of family life as lived in New England in the mid-nineteenth century.

Little Women also touched on serious matters that Depression-era moviegoers could relate to. It was set in the last bleak year of the Civil War and it acted as a subtle reminder that Americans had once lived through hardship and heartbreak and still managed to survive. There are uncanny similarities between this film and *Gone With the Wind*, another tale of families disrupted by the war – told this time

from the standpoint of the South – that suggests that *Little Women* served both Selznick and Cukor as an earlier draft – rougher but so much more heartfelt – for the most ambitious film project of the decade.

Of the four Alcott heroines, Cukor understandably concentrates on Jo (Katharine Hepburn), the spunky would-be novelist who (in the film) leaves home for New York, a literary career, and a foreign husband; and on Amy (Joan Bennett) the frivolous sister who settles down into the more traditional role of wife and

director reveals itself in his unique flair for establishing dramatic tension and relationships through his direction of actors. Thus, half the success of the overlong, overpopulated *David Copperfield* (1935) resides in the expert, fastidious, time-consuming casting resulting in the formidable Edna May Oliver as Great-Aunt Betsey Trotwood playing opposite Basil Rathbone's sneering, sadistic Murdstone. Around the central figure of the child David (Freddie Bartholomew) gravitates a collection of eccentric, larger-than-life Dickensian grotesques, each with a limited time in which to leave an impression on the viewer – a real challenge for a director who usually favours the gradual disclosure of character in long, sustained scenes.

After *Little Women*, Cukor followed Selznick to MGM where, save for occasional loan-outs to other studios, he remained for almost 25 years. From the start he was given 'plum' projects: the first film adaptation of *Romeo and*

society leader when she weds Jo's former beau.

Rather than lingering on the period detail – beautifully captured by Hobe Erwin in his set designs – Cukor retrieves whatever is relevant to a modern audience, assisted by Hepburn, whose presence, even in hoop-skirts, is an emblem of emancipation. The success of *Little Women* launched the trend of adaptations from classic novels. Cukor found himself typed now as a director with a flair for period drama – even when his versatility was being proven by the modern stories he managed to alternate with Dickens, Shakespeare and Alexandre Dumas *fils*, and which in retrospect seem to have lasted better: *Dinner at Eight* (1933), *Sylvia Scarlett* (1936) and *Holiday* (1938).

In both modes, Cukor's experience as a stage

Above: shot in 24 days, Dinner at Eight *brought out the comedienne in Jean Harlow. Right:* David Copperfield *made an instant star of Freddie Bartholomew, seen here with his mother (Elizabeth Allan) and the sadistic Murdstones (Basil Rathbone and Violet Kemble-Cooper). Below: Robert Taylor with Garbo in the final moments of* Camille

Juliet since the arrival of sound, and the most ambitious (and arguably most successful) of Garbo's vehicles, *Camille*, (both 1936). The former's dramatic moments were isolated between the useless pageantry and vacuous posturing that characterize Shakespearean adaptations of the Thirties. *Camille*, on the other hand, is that rare instance where a director's vision is embodied in the leading lady. Without Garbo, this would be just another overstuffed period piece; with her as the focus, Cukor goes straight to the essence of play-acting. The most coveted courtesan of mid-nineteenth century Paris is a perfect metaphorical role for the most sought-after screen presence of her generation.

Since the Thirties mark the apogee of the star system, Cukor's status was inevitably linked to his performers – specifically to actresses like Katharine Hepburn, Constance Bennett, Norma Shearer, Greta Garbo and Joan Crawford, all of whom gave perhaps their finest performances under his direction. However, Cukor's designation as a 'woman's director' is limiting when not patronizing – especially when one considers that his career spans 50 years and embraces every Hollywood genre

save the gangster film. However, it is undeniable than an emotional commitment to the Twenties and Thirties lingers in the later work: the sense of craft, a taste for the scene that plays well, a passion for performance. Coming from the theatre, then a medium more intellectually and socially aware than the motion picture, Cukor makes the 'woman's picture' and the drawing-room comedy a valid context for problems of manners and morals. In retrospect, his films – and to a degree, those

Left: clever editing was needed to conceal Marilyn Monroe's *acting lapses in* Let's Make Love. *Below left: Hepburn understudied the lead in the 1928 Broadway play but starred in the movie version of* Holiday. *Below: with* Philadelphia Story *Hepburn left behind her 'box-office poison' tag, but James Stewart won the Oscar. Above: Tracy and Hepburn, unbeatable comedy team in* Pat and Mike

GLADYS GLOVER   WENDY BARRIE

of Frank Borzage, John M. Stahl, and Gregory La Cava – represent the more sensitive, liberal side of Hollywood; the theme of an emergent feminine sensibility appears nowadays more acceptable, certainly more generous, than the aggressive politics the film industry espoused in support of the American success myth.

Cukor's typical heroine is a spirited, idealistic woman with a mind of her own – far removed from the sweet, comforting creature or posturing vamp of Victorian fiction and many Hollywood movies. Her eyes are fixed on goals that lie beyond empty respectability. In proclaiming her own identity, she forces the hero to question his blasé assumptions of superiority; he, in turn, is puzzled, confused, chastened and therefore humanized. Cukor's films thus offer a revitalized vision of the possibilities of relationships between the sexes – a lasting camaraderie of shared experience that goes beyond the shallow role-playing of romantic convention.

To the standard misogynous situation of the hero corrupted by a wicked woman, Cukor opposes the predicament of a woman married to the wrong man, whether a fascist, as in *Keeper of the Flame* (1942), or a psychopath, as in *Gaslight* (1944). The self-destructive heroines of *Edward, My Son* (1949) and *A Life of Her Own* (1950) reveal the director's most pessimistic view of woman's condition.

In the late Forties, Cukor began a successful set of comedies – built by screenwriters Garson Kanin and Ruth Gordon, jointly or separately, around the mature charms of Spencer Tracy and Katharine Hepburn or the off-beat personality of Judy Holliday. They mark a democratization of drawing-room comedy

Above left: in It Should Happen to You *Judy Holliday played Gladys Glover, a nobody who shot to media fame as the Average American Girl. Above: Ava Gardner gave a sensuous performance in* Bhowani Junction, *from John Masters' novel set in the India of 1946. Below: Audrey Hepburn's performance in* My Fair Lady *helped Cukor to win a personal Oscar for this highly stylized film*

(*Adam's Rib*, 1949) a nostalgic return to New England small-town life (*The Actress*, 1953), even a belated but delightful incursion into madcap comedy (*It Should Happen to You*, 1954). Yet they contain nothing that suggests the colourful expansiveness of Cukor's films in the mid-Fifties. However, *A Star Is Born* (1954) upsets every preconception about the director's personal style. Often criticized for excessive good taste, Cukor here throws restraint to the wind, allowing Judy Garland to take emotional risks only this side of embarrassment; a self-proclaimed custodian of the dramatic text, Cukor now employs the unwieldy resources of CinemaScope like a visual master. Fairly busting the seams of the musical genre, *A Star Is Born* boldly mixes confessional biography with Hollywood chronicle, and may be a definitive statement on the grandeur and servitude of performers.

Over a quarter of a century has elapsed since then, and there have been new, unexpected twists in Cukor's career: exotic adventures like *Bhowani Junction* (1956) and *Justine* (1969), a Western, *Heller in Pink Tights* (1960), and musicals like *Les Girls* (1957) and *My Fair Lady* (1964). The latter won the director a belated personal Oscar (after he had guided James Stewart, Ingrid Bergman, Ronald Colman, Judy Holliday and Rex Harrison to theirs). Sheer energy and intellectual curiosity made this runaway from the stage a grand old man of the movies – one who is not afraid of television either, as proven by *Love Among the Ruins* (1975). His influence has been acknowledged by Ingmar Bergman and Eric Rohmer among others. For these foreign directors, so far removed from the Hollywood experience, Cukor is both a pioneer and a master: he showed them that a storm in a teacup can mirror a metaphysical upheaval, and taught them to keep close watch on a woman's face.

CARLOS CLARENS

Filmography

1929 River of Romance (dial. dir. only). **'30** All Quiet on the Western Front (dial. dir. only) Grumpy (co-dir. only); The Virtuous Sin (GB: Cast Iron) (co-dir. only); The Royal Family of Broadway (co-dir. only). **'31** Tarnished Lady; Girls About Town. **'32** What Price Hollywood?; A Bill of Divorcement; Rockabye; One Hour With You (dial. dir. only); Une Heure Près de Toi (French version of One Hour With You); The Animal Kingdom (add. dir. uncredited). **'33** Our Betters; Dinner at Eight; Little Women. **'35** David Copperfield. **'36** Sylvia Scarlett; Romeo and Juliet; Camille. **'38** Holiday (GB: Free and Easy/Unconventional Linda). **'39** Zaza; The Women; Gone With the Wind (uncredited contribution). **'40** Susan and God (GB: The Gay Mrs Trexel); The Philadelphia Story. **'41** A Woman's Face; Two-Faced Woman. **'42** Her Cardboard Lover; Keeper of the Flame. **'43** Resistance and Ohm's Law (short). **'44** Gaslight (GB: The Murder in Thornton Square); Winged Victory; I'll Be Seeing You (add. dir. uncredited). **'47** Desire Me (uncredited). **'48** A Double Life. **'49** Edward, My Son (GB); Adam's Rib. **'50** A Life of Her Own; Born Yesterday. **'51** The Model and the Marriage Broker. **'52** The Marrying Kind; Pat and Mike. **'53** The Actress. **'54** It Should Happen to You; A Star Is Born. **'56** Bhowani Junction. **'57** Hot Spell (add. dir. uncredited); Les Girls; Wild Is the Wind. **'60** Heller in Pink Tights; Let's Make Love; Song Without End (uncredited). **'62** The Chapman Report; Something's Got to Give (unfinished). **'64** My Fair Lady. **'69** Justine. **'72** Travels With My Aunt. **'76** The Bluebird (USA/USSR).

Frank Capra's American Dream

'I would sing the songs of the working stiffs, of the short-changed Joes, the born poor, the afflicted. I would gamble with the long-shot players who light candles in the wind, and resent with the pushed-around because of race or birth. Above all, I would fight for their causes on the screens of the world.'

Frank Capra, when writing these words in 1971 about downtrodden workers ('the working stiffs') was not just repeating the flattering

Above, left to right: James Stewart and Jean Arthur in Mr Smith Goes to Washington; *Gary Cooper, with tuba, in* Mr Deeds Goes to Town, *and with Barbara Stanwyck in* Meet John Doe. *Tall, lean men of integrity, Stewart and Cooper perfectly conformed to Capra's idea of the populist hero. Left and below left: early Capra comedies included* The Strong Man, *with the childlike Harry Langdon, and* Platinum Blonde, *with Jean Harlow as a sexy 'society girl' seeking a husband*

comments critics had made about his films. While other successful Hollywood directors in the Thirties were content to coast along on the charms of stellar performances and glitteringly unreal plots, Capra made a clear stand for films with a recognizable basis in the world the audience lived in or, more accurately, the world they wanted to live in. These were films that – along with the romantic clinches, chases and slapstick – provided idealism.

A dream comes true

Capra himself was born poor and pushed-around, one of seven peasant children, in Sicily in 1897. By 1903 the bulk of the family had emigrated to Los Angeles, and Capra began his determined climb up the ladder of success in the fabled land of opportunity. The fable in his case proved spectacularly true: Capra even writes that he thought of his films as one way of saying 'Thanks' to America, its people and history. In the Twenties he became a gagman for Mack Sennett and directed two celebrated films – *The Strong Man* (1926) and *Long Pants* (1927) – starring the baby-faced comic Harry Langdon. Langdon's ego subsequently got the better of his talent and his career declined; Capra's ego and talent fortunately developed at the same rate. Once ensconced at Columbia – the Poverty Row studio ruled by Harry Cohn, a man of drive, independence, and scant tact – Capra's career shot upwards. He cannily leapt at subjects with 'headline' appeal – an airship's crash in the Antarctic in *Dirigible* (1931) a bank crisis in *American Madness* (1932).

In this last film Capra was warming to his theme and to his technique. In the chaos of the Depression the bank president, played by Walter Huston, appeals to the virtues of good neighbourliness against the vices of blind self-interest. Thus encouraged, his customers earnestly rush to return the money they had

Capra was Hollywood's arch-populist: his films championed the typical American whom he believed to be endowed with innate goodness and wisdom and possessed of the inviolable right to seek happiness

previously rushed to take out. But everyone was rushing: beginning with this film Capra deliberately speeded up the dialogue, made speeches overlap, cut out all dawdling camera fades and character entrances. The dialogue itself was written by Robert Riskin, a former playwright who collaborated with Capra throughout the Thirties and had an acute ear for the twists and turns of everyday speech. He also shared many of Capra's own beliefs about the rights of America's ordinary citizens.

The delectable *It Happened One Night* (1934) provided another stepping-stone for Capra. He had long set his sights on the Oscars, Hollywood's ultimate accolade of success, and with this comedy he secured an armful for himself, his stars, and his writer. He also achieved a new spontaneity in his direction: scenes between Clark Gable, the snappy news-paperman, and Claudette Colbert, the run-away heiress he pursues first for a story and later for love, had an almost improvisational ease. And Capra had now departed decisively from the drawing-room setting of earlier com-edies like *Platinum Blonde* (1931). The action takes place in a cross-country bus, along the highways, inside the motels. The haughty Colbert character can't but be humanized by the experience; even her father, played by Walter Connolly, proves to be a plutocrat with a heart of gold, allowing her to run away all over again with honest, down-to-earth Gable rather than marry a dull, wealthy aviator.

Good Deeds

Elements of the Gable character – his un-complicated decency, his fondness for homely pursuits like dunking doughnuts in coffee or giving piggybacks – reappear in bolder form with Gary Cooper's Longfellow Deeds in *Mr Deeds Goes to Town* (1936). Deeds is catapulted by an uncle's inheritance from small-town

peace in Mandrake Falls to New York turmoil. His simple habits – tuba-playing, writing greeting-card verses – provoke scorn and derision, while lawyers, creditors and opera committees jump on him for every penny. He finally puts his money to work for the country's impoverished farmers in a self-help scheme, giving them a cow, a horse, some seed and some land. The cream of New York society responds by declaring him insane; the sub-sequent courtroom trial provides a perfect setting for Capra and Riskin's brilliantly en-gineered debate on the values of American life.

Road to Utopia

Capra's next film, *Lost Horizon* (1937), may at first glance seem an unlikely venture. But this lavish fantasy, based on James Hilton's book, provided an opportunity for the director and writer to create an abstract version of the Utopia their Longfellow Deeds and other good citizens were working towards. The Utopia of Shangri-La is located in a Himalayan monas-tery, where all strife and all old age have been eradicated. But without strife, without Capra's usual endearing characters and rushing crowds (the benign lamas walk very slowly), the film's visual and dramatic interest sinks dangerously low.

Capra quickly worked himself back towards his top form with an adaptation of another popular success – Kaufman and Hart's play *You Can't Take It With You*, filmed in 1938. Typically, the adaptation strengthens the characters and the beliefs they espouse. An-thony P. Kirby (Edward Arnold), the man who wants to take as much of it with him as possible, is made more of a grasping, villainous ogre, while those for whom money and worldly goods mean nothing – the Vanderhof family and assorted guests (like the iceman who delivers ice and just stays) – are made less

whimsical, more forthright. And, as in *It Happened One Night*, the obstructive plutocrat is finally humanized, joining in the music-making at the Vanderhof's home-grown Shangri-La, joyfully playing 'Pollywolly-doodle' on a harmonica.

With *Mr Smith Goes to Washington* (1939) Capra returned to the proven formula of *Deeds*, but deployed it over a larger canvas. Now his unassuming all-American hero was tilting not just at snobbish, money-grabbing New York society – but at the whole government mach-ine in Washington DC. Jefferson Smith (James Stewart), pet-shop owner and Boy Scouts leader, is voted to the Senate on the strength of his gullibility (there is a pocket-lining deal coming up involving the construc-tion of a dam). His bird-calls cause as much laughter as Longfellow Deeds' poetry, yet he proves a sterner customer than his Party overlords anticipated. He proposes building a National Boys' Camp on land that would be flooded by the dam, and argues its merits – along with much else – in a filibuster speech lasting almost a day: a clear parallel with Deeds' courtroom trial.

Government of the people

Capra had pushed his concern for the rights of 'the working stiffs . . . the short-changed Joes' straight into the political arena with *Mr Smith*. Yet his own political position in his films was vague in the extreme – they would hardly have had such a wide success had it been otherwise. Their motivating beliefs were simple, naive even, but Capra's picture of America as a continent of small communities helping each other to prosperity and happiness held great attraction in the Thirties. This wasn't Roosevelt's vaunted New Deal, with its elab-orate network of Government bodies guiding, marshalling, even creating work. Rather it

Above: in A Hole in the Head *Sinatra plays a down-and-out Miami hotelier who tries to get his wealthy brother to bail him out. Capra was at his best when he sent his characters in search of less tangible goals, such as happiness; in the Shangri-La of* Lost Horizon *(above left) with John Howard, H.B. Warner and Jane Wyatt; in the communal life of small-town America in* You Can't Take It With You *(left) with James Stewart and Jean Arthur; in life itself in* It's a Wonderful Life *(below left) with Stewart, Thomas Mitchell and Donna Reed*

Filmography

1922 The Ballad of Fultah Fisher's Boarding House/Fultah Fisher's Boarding House (short). **'24** The Wild Goose Chaser (short) (co-sc.). **'25** The Marriage Circus (short) (co-sc. only); Plain Clothes (short) (co-sc. only); Super Hooper-Dyne Lizzies (short) (co-sc. only); Breaking the Ice (short) (co-sc. only); Good Morning, Nurse (short) (co-sc. only); Cupid's Boots (short) (co-sc. only); Lucky Stars (short) (co-sc. only); There He Goes (short) (co-sc. only). **'26** Saturday Afternoon (short) (co-sc. only); His First Flame (co-sc. only); Tramp, Tramp, Tramp (co-sc; + uncredited dir. and prod); Fiddlesticks (short) (co-sc. only); Soldier Man (short) (co-sc. only); The Strong Man. **'27** Long Pants; For the Love of Mike. **'28** That Certain Thing; So This Is Love; The Swim Princess (short) (co-sc only); The Matinee Idol; The Way of the Strong; Say It With Sables; The Burglar/Smith's Burglar (short) (co-sc. only); The Power of the Press; Hubby's Weekend Trip (short). **'29** The Younger Generation; The Donovan Affair; Flight. **'30** Ladies of Leisure; Rain or Shine. **'31** Dirigible; The Miracle Woman; Platinum Blonde. **'32** Forbidden; American Madness; The Bitter Tea of General Yen. **'33** Lady for a Day. **'34** It Happened One Night (+ prod); Broadway Bill (GB: Strictly Confidential). **'36** Mr Deeds Goes to Town (+ prod). **'37** Lost Horizon (+ prod). **'38** You Can't Take It With You (+ prod). **'39** Mr Smith Goes to Washington (+ prod). **'40** The Cavalcade of Academy Awards (doc) (sup. only). **'41** Meet John Doe (+ prod). **'42** Divide and Conquer (doc*) (co-dir; + prod). **'43** Prelude to War (doc*) (+ prod); The Battle of Britain (doc*) (prod. only); The Nazis Strike (doc*) (co-dir; + prod); Battle of Russia/Battle for Russia (doc*) (prod. only). **'44** Arsenic and Old Lace (+ prod); Know Your Ally: Britain (doc) (prod. only); Tunisian Victory (doc) (co-dir; + prod); The Negro Soldier (doc) (prod. only); The Battle of China (doc*) (co-dir; + prod). **'45** Know Your Enemy: Germany (doc) (prod. only); Two Down and One to Go! (doc) (+ prod); War Comes to America (doc*) (prod. only); Know Your Enemy: Japan (doc) (co-dir; + prod). **'46** It's a Wonderful Life (+ co-sc; + prod). **'48** State of the Union (GB: The World and His Wife) (+ prod). **'50** Riding High (+ prod). **'51** Here Comes the Groom (+ prod). **'59** A Hole in the Head (+ prod). **'61** Pocketful of Miracles (+ prod). **'64** Rendezvous in Space/Reaching for the Stars (short).

* *Why We Fight war documentary series. Capra also worked as a gag writer on six films in 1924.*

was an Old Deal, the deal of Abraham Lincoln, Thomas Jefferson and other statesmen (duly mentioned and revered in the scripts) whose lives and beliefs showed the strengths of the pioneer spirit and individual initiative untrammelled by faceless authorities interfering from on high.

As the decade came to a close, however, the threats to Capra's American dream became more perilous. As one critic has pointed out, even Capra couldn't stop Hitler's evil designs armed with a harmonica. And in *Meet John Doe* (1941) the ordinary man is almost defeated and duped out of existence. Long John Willoughby (Gary Cooper), a former baseball player, is publicized as an incarnation of the folk hero John Doe by a publisher and would-be President bent on fascist domination. When Willoughby learns he is just a puppet he decides to enact the suicide threat that sparked off the whole campaign – by falling to his death

from the top of City Hall (at Christmas-time) too!). Capra and Riskin found themselves in a quandary about the ending: their final choice, with Doe's supporters persuading him to carry on fighting for his ideals, fails to convince – though it is difficult to imagine what could bring this ambitious, garrulous, awkward film to a satisfactory conclusion.

Liberty's last fling

When Capra returned to feature films as an independent director-producer in 1946, after a notable career supervising the wartime documentary series *Why We Fight*, the hysteria that marred *Meet John Doe* had evaporated. But Capra's ideals were clearly no longer quite intact: George Bailey, the despairing, philanthropic hero of *It's a Wonderful Life* (1946), is brought to the point of suicide. And it takes divine intervention by an angel to save George (James Stewart) and show him what a grim, garish, materialistic town Bedford Falls would have become if he had never existed. For all its prolixities and whimsies, the film remains a stunning example of Capra's consummate technical skills and his unbounded love for small-town America. It is the last example, too, for after making the hectic *State of the Union* (1948) – with an election candidate involved in more political buccaneering – Capra's independent company Liberty Films was sold to Paramount, and Capra lost his liberty indeed.

Pushed into a tight corner, Capra responded with the kind of films he produced in the years before *Deeds* when he was still evolving his style and subject-matter. *Riding High* (1950), starring Bing Crosby and various horses, was a flaccid remake of his earlier film *Broadway Bill*

(1934); *Here Comes the Groom* (1951) featured Crosby in another weak comedy romance – about a reporter who adopts war orphans.

After eight quiet years Capra returned – in Cinemascope and colour – with *A Hole in the Head* (1959), a rancid sentimental comedy with Frank Sinatra. But with *Pocketful of Miracles* (1961), a remake of another of his early films, *Lady for a Day* (1933), Capra rallied. The screen once again teemed with lovable, eccentric characters – mostly Broadway types rushing about to help Bette Davis' Apple Annie, the apple-seller whose daughter has been led to expect a society queen for a mother. It was Capra's last display of good neighbourliness in action. Following this he prepared a science-fiction subject, *Marooned* (1969), eventually directed by John Sturges. The title was sadly suitable, for Capra himself had become marooned in post-war Hollywood – a place where working stiffs and short-changed Joes wanted their songs sung in far more harsh and complex ways than Capra could possibly manage.   GEOFF BROWN

Gary Cooper
The Gentle Giant

'Wyatt Earp, now, he hardly ever shot a man. But he frequently used to hit them between the eyes with the butt of his pistol. Don't know how he got away with it.'

He learned to sit tall in the saddle because of a road accident which damaged his hip. The doctor advised him that the best therapy would be horse-riding, a pastime at which he became skilled.

During his time at college – where he also developed his skill as a cartoonist – he thought he'd like to join the staff of a newspaper. By then his parents were living in Los Angeles, and Cooper was strolling down Hollywood Boulevard when he met a couple of chums who were playing extra roles in cheap Westerns for $10 a day. He decided to join them.

From 1925 Cooper appeared briefly in countless films. Then in 1927, Clara Bow – who had been having a much-publicized romance with Cooper – managed to secure him a minor role in *Wings*, directed by William Wellman, where he played an easy-going but doomed young flyer in World War I. The idea of heroically dying for one's country and the philosophy that what will be will be, were easy for Cooper to convey. In barely more than five minutes screen time he communicated a magnetism

More than any other actor, Gary Cooper epitomized the quiet, staunch, gallant virtues of the pioneer American as portrayed in the cinema. The Western hero of *The Virginian* (1929) and *High Noon* (1952) was, in principle, not so different from the rebellious adventurer of *The Lives of a Bengal Lancer* (1935) or the hick-from-the-sticks who becomes a crusading millionaire in *Mr Deeds Goes to Town* (1936).

Within a certain range, from comedy to near-documentary drama, he was a peerless film performer. Ernest Hemingway insisted he play the lead in *For Whom the Bell Tolls* (1943) because he was the perfect Hemingway hero, a man who could fight the good fight and still retain his own integrity and dignity.

John Barrymore observed: 'That fellow is the world's greatest actor. He can do with no effort what the rest of us spent years trying to learn – to be perfectly natural.'

Certainly he was one of the first actors who achieved an instant rapport with the camera.

At the height of his popularity in the Thirties and Forties, he tended to be regarded as a 'personality' actor, who always played the same role in different settings. Later, his performances were reassessed. Because he appeared so 'natural', the public and even the critics believed he was simply playing himself. But, as countless stars have said, playing yourself is the most difficult art in the cinema.

He was born in 1901, the son of British immigrants. His father was a judge who owned a ranch. Gary was christened Frank, the name Gary being bestowed on him later by an agent. They lived in Helena, Montana, which Cooper remembered when it was a gold-mining town – called Last Chance Gulch. During the making of his penultimate film, *The Wreck of the Mary Deare* (1959), he reminisced about the old days:

'I saw a gunfight once; a couple of characters had had a fight, gone home and thought about it, then they met up in town and shot it out. My pal and I were standing on the street outside the saloon. Darn near got shot, too.'

He never liked the idea of Westerns which were based on the legend of the fastest draw:

Previous page: Cooper in The Westerner (1940). *Top:* Wings *gave him the vital break at Paramount. Above: he played a similarly dashing young hero in* The Lives of a Bengal Lancer. *Below:* The Plainsman *(1936) put Cooper's horsemanship to good use.*
Below right: in the court drama Souls at Sea *(1937) Cooper refused to defend his killing of men who were about to capsize a rescue boat carrying women and children*

who was only concerned about how his protégée, Dietrich, would look.

Hollywood didn't really know what to do with Cooper in the Thirties. Incredibly handsome, he also conveyed a toughness that was evident in his eyes. Helen Hayes – who co-starred with him in the first film version of Hemingway's *A Farewell to Arms* (1932) – remembers him as 'the most beautiful man I have ever met'.

In 1936 he established a professional relationship with director Frank Capra which extended from the classic *Mr Deeds Goes to Town* (1936) to the tougher *Meet John Doe* (1941). The characters remained true to type and true to Cooper: men of integrity faced with

Above: Cooper with Helen Hayes in A Farewell to Arms, *after which he became a close friend of author Ernest Hemingway. Top left: he was chosen by Hemingway to star in* For Whom the Bell Tolls, *which led to his fourth Oscar nomination for his role as a Loyalist fighter in the Spanish Civil War. Top right: in 1941 Cooper had won an Oscar for* Sergeant York, *becoming an idol of an America recently plunged into World War II. Right: a typical stance from* The Real Glory *this was perhaps his most violent film. Centre top and bottom: High Noon won Cooper a second Oscar in 1952 for his intense portrayal of the lone and bitter sheriff*

that made the audience sit up and take notice.

Paramount signed him up and he worked non-stop. As the uncompromising lawman in *The Virginian* (1929) he followed the code of good versus bad, allowing no deviation in his search for justice. It was in this film that he coined that famous misquoted phrase 'when you call me that, smile!' Cooper believed that this was his best Western, although:

'I liked *The Plainsman*, the one I did for Cecil B. DeMille. But, of course, it was romanticized. Wild Bill Hickok, the character I played, wasn't really a very nice man.'

He then co-starred with Marlene Dietrich in *Morocco* (1930) but loathed Josef von Sternberg

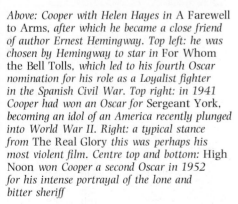

himself in love with his co-star Patricia Neal, but Cooper's wife – being an ardent Catholic – would not give him a divorce. In 1951 the romance, a very discreet affair, was over. In the meantime Warners starred Cooper in action films such as *Task Force* (1949), a routine naval drama, because they felt that the public would not accept Cooper in his usual spotless-hero guise until the adverse publicity died down.

After a period in the doldrums, he won his second Oscar for his performance in *High Noon* (1952) which revitalized his screen career. He couldn't quite understand why: 'It was just a good story of the policeman who had to do a job and the townsfolk who were prepared to let him do it alone. But it was a good script and we

Left: Cooper urges an astonished Dana Andrews to fight in Ball of Fire *(1941). Below:* Ten North Frederick *(1958) showed fans an ageing Cooper. Bottom: The last film released before his death was* The Wreck of the Mary Deare *(1959) with Charlton Heston*

the nauseous machinations of big business or big politics.

In 1941 Cooper won his first Oscar for his performance as the conscientious objector who becomes a war hero in *Sergeant York*, and in *Ball of Fire* (also 1941) he put his shy manner to fine use in a comedy role in which he played a meek professor researching slang who pursues a gangster's moll and finds himself in trouble.

The Fountainhead (1949), based on Ayn Rand's novel about an idealistic architect and his fight against big business, was a turning point in his private life. Married to a New York socialite Veronica Balfe since 1933, he found

had a fine director, Fred Zinnemann. I really didn't see it as a psychological Western.'

In the last two years of his life he was surprised that he should be regarded as a Western hero, not having made many Westerns. He recalled with more affection films like *The Court-Martial of Billy Mitchell* (1955), about an American general brought before a judicial court for accusing the war department of criminal negligence, and *Ten North Frederick* (1958), where the members of a dead man's family look back on the events of his life. In both films Cooper played characters wrestling with the realities of contemporary life.

Before he died in 1961, he was awarded an honorary Oscar for his services to the film industry. As a screen actor, Cooper had the same fundamental idea as all the great stars:

'You have to go through the mill first. It's not good to become a big star with your first film. An actor has to have lived a little.'

Cooper lived a lot and died too soon.

MARGARET HINXMAN

Filmography

1923 Blind Justice. **'25** The Thundering Herd; Wild Horse Mesa; The Lucky Horseshoe; The Vanishing American (GB: The Vanishing Race); The Eagle; Tricks; Lightnin' Wins (short). **'26** Three Pals; The Enchanted Hill; Watch Your Wife; The Winning of Barbara Worth. **'27** It; Children of Divorce; Arizona Bound; Wings; The Last Outlaw; Nevada. **'28** Beau Sabreur; Doomsday; Legion of the Condemned; Half a Bride; The First Kiss; Lilac Time (GB: Love Never Dies); The Shopworn Angel. **'29** Wolf Song; Betrayal; The Virginian. **'30** Seven Days Leave/Medals; Only the Brave; Paramount on Parade; The Texan; A Man from Wyoming; The Spoilers; Morocco. **'31** Fighting Caravans; City Streets; I Take This Woman; His Woman. **'32** Make Me a Star (guest); Devil and the Deep; If I Had a Million; A Farewell to Arms; The Stolen Jools (GB: The Slippery Pearls) (guest) (short); Voice of Hollywood (guest) (short). **'33** Today We Live; One Sunday Afternoon; Alice in Wonderland; Design for Living. **'34** Operator 13 (GB: Spy 13); Now and Forever. **'35** The Lives of a Bengal Lancer; Star Night at the Cocoanut Grove (guest) (short); The Wedding Night; Peter Ibbetson. **'36** Desire; La Fiesta de Santa Barbara (guest) (short); Mr Deeds Goes to Town; Hollywood Boulevard (guest); The General Died at Dawn; The Plainsman. **'37** Lest We Forget (guest) (short); Souls at Sea. **'38** The Adventures of Marco Polo; Bluebeard's Eighth Wife; The Cowboy and the Lady. **'39** Beau Geste; The Real Glory. **'40** The Westerner; North West Mounted Police. **'41** Meet John Doe; Sergeant York; Ball of Fire. **'42** The Pride of the Yankees. **'43** For Whom the Bell Tolls. **'44** Memo for Joe (guest) (short); The Story of Dr Wassell; Casanova Brown. **'45** Along Came Jones (+ prod); Saratoga Trunk (begun in '43). **'46** Cloak and Dagger (final reel removed before release and never restored). **'47** Variety Girl (guest); Unconquered. **'48** Good Sam. **'49** The Fountainhead; Snow Carnival (guest) (short); It's a Great Feeling (guest); Task Force. **'50** Bright Leaf; Dallas; It's a Big Country. **'51** You're in the Navy Now/USS Teakettle; Starlift (guest); Distant Drums. **'52** High Noon; Springfield Rifle. **'53** Return to Paradise; Blowing Wild. **'54** Garden of Evil; Vera Cruz. **'55** The Court-Martial of Billy Mitchell (GB: One Man Mutiny); Hollywood Mothers (guest) (short). **'56** Friendly Persuasion. **'57** Love in the Afternoon. **'58** Ten North Frederick; Man of the West; The Hanging Tree. **'59** Alias Jesse James (guest); They Came to Cordura; The Wreck of the Mary Deare. **'61** The Naked Edge; The Real West (TV doc) (narr. only). **'76** Hollywood on Trial (featured in doc. footage).

King Vidor

One of America's most distinguished directors, King Vidor was preoccupied with the plight of ordinary men and showed his concern in films like *The Big Parade, The Crowd* and *Our Daily Bread*

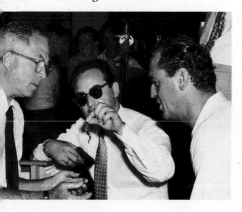

Back in the Twenties and Thirties, Hollywood directors were seldom crusaders. Although some were of humble origin, by the time they had 'made it' to the top of their profession they were earning thousands a week. When they travelled it was always first class – so they rarely encountered 'the common man'. Yet many of them put his story on the screen with skill and sensibility.

King Vidor was among the finest practitioners of such films. He was a director who survived five decades within the Hollywood system, yet managed to make uncompromising and challenging films. Not all the time, of course. He walked a tightrope between what he wanted to do and what he was permitted to do. Yet few film-makers can look back at such a record of courage and concern.

As a boy in Texas – he was born in Galveston in 1896 – Vidor fell in love with the cinema. He worked in a nickelodeon and, when he was 15, managed to borrow a camera and set himself up as a newsreel cameraman – 'the only one in Southwest Texas'. In 1915 Vidor and his wife Florence, an aspiring actress, decided to travel across country in a Model-T Ford 'to go where the action was', to the expanding movie colony in Hollywood.

Vidor served his apprenticeship there with determination; he wrote 52 scenarios, all of which had been rejected before the Vitagraph company bought one. His first opportunity to direct came from a juvenile-court judge anxious to make a series of two-reelers about errant youth. When the judge ran into financial problems, Vidor was out of work again. But he embarked on a feature of his own – *The*

Turn in the Road (1919) – a Christian Science subject which had the curious distinction of being backed by a group of doctors who also played extras and donated props. The picture was a surprise hit and Vidor was instantly in great demand. But with characteristic integrity he felt that he owed the doctors something and stayed to direct films for them for a year before starting his own small studio.

The man in the trenches

The modest pictures he turned out at Vidor Village in Hollywood were warmly greeted by the public, but it was not until Vidor joined Metro that critics sensed the emergence of a new and important talent. *The Big Parade* (1925), a study of war through the eyes of an ordinary soldier, established him among the world's greatest directors. That Vidor was able to mount an epic, without losing hold of the fragile strands of an intimate story, was an achievement as impressive as anything in the American cinema.

'I was strictly anti-war,' said Vidor, 'and I was doing as much as I could to speak against war in that film. And it has a lot of things that we thought could not be shown in regular theatres . . . if you made anything that discouraged enlistment, the government would not permit it to be shown. Yet we had surprising support. One of the top men from Dupont, the armament people, told me that if we had any trouble, he would arrange for it to be shown throughout the country in tents.'

The star was John Gilbert, accustomed to playing Great Lovers. Vidor changed his romantic image, dirtied him down, and Gilbert

Above: Vidor, with megaphone, directing Hallelujah *(1929). Left: producer Dino De Laurentiis gives Vidor a lucky charm before shooting begins on* War and Peace *(1956)*

played the role with profound conviction; it is one of the half-dozen finest performances of the silent screen. *The Big Parade* was received with wild acclamation and made more money than any other MGM film. Vidor followed it with a dignified production of *La Boheme* (1926); it starred Lillian Gish whom he had much admired in D.W. Griffith's pictures.

'Lillian Gish was and is the greatest actress and the greatest lady of the American cinema, certainly the most extraordinary actress I have ever worked with. Gilbert and I were both in love with her after the first couple of days shooting.'

The Crowd (1928) was about an ordinary man struggling with ordinary problems. The American obsession with success was an undercurrent throughout the film. The man courts a girl, marries her, and they move into a tiny apartment. The wife goads him to get a better job and he loses the one he has. He fails to hold down the simplest job thereafter – he even fails at suicide.

The Hallelujah trail

For his first sound film Vidor tackled a subject that had long been taboo – the Negroes. Of *Hallelujah* (1929), he later said:

'That's a record of an era. The black people have made progress since then – fantastic progress – but that's the way they were then. There's nothing in that film I don't remember from my own experience in Texas . . . Even before sound came in, I had tried time and again to get MGM to give me permission to make a film about black people. They kept turning me down.

'Well, I went to Europe in '28, and I was sitting in a Paris cafe when I read in the newspaper that all pictures were turning to sound. I took an earlier boat home because I felt that now was the time to put *Hallelujah* over. I stopped in New York to visit Nicholas Schenck – the President of Loew's Inc. and the head of MGM. He was sceptical and wouldn't go for it. Finally, I said I'd do the picture for nothing – contribute my salary to the budget. "Well," said Schenck, "if that's the way you feel about it, I'll let you make a picture about whores." That was his attitude . . .'

MGM and Vidor were undoubtedly emboldened by the Broadway success of *Porgy*, the all-Negro musical. Vidor made his film – a melodrama about a cotton-worker who kills, repents, and becomes a revivalist preacher – equally stylized and operatic. He approached it exactly as if it were silent (the sound trucks failed to turn up at the Memphis location) so it was free of the deadly static quality of so many 1929 talkies. Vidor used sound with great imagination – although matching pictures shot on location with sound recorded in the studio was unbelievably hard, and the editor had a nervous breakdown.

In his best films Vidor always subdued technique to the vital job of conveying emotion. *The Champ* (1931) is a story about an ageing boxer (Wallace Beery) and the son who idolizes him (Jackie Cooper). Vidor filmed it laconically in long-held dialogue scenes, avoiding any technical fireworks that might detract from the emotion. The final scene, when the Champ dies, is among the most amazing directorial achievements in Vidor's career. The boy bursts into tears of anger, yelling 'I want the Champ!' stamping his foot and hitting the wall. Only when his mother comes in does his rage die down. She then carries him away like a baby – the one moment in the film he behaves like a child.

Down on the farm

Vidor's most dazzling technical achievement was the meticulously timed climax to *Our Daily Bread* (1934). His courage as a film-maker was put to a stern test with this picture:

'During the Depression, I had very strong feelings about what was happening . . . Hoovervilles [shanty towns], milk trucks overturned, people going hungry, farm mortgages being foreclosed . . . I thought a film should be made about the situation. I read a magazine article called "Looks Like We'll All Have to Go Co-operative", about cutting out money and going back to barter, and used it as the basis for the script. The studios were firmly entrenched in the glamour cycle, and the bankers were foreclosing on the very farmers I was showing in the film. So they all turned it down. I was close to Chaplin and he told me I would get a release through United Artists if I could get the money for the picture. I just took what stocks and real estate I had, offered them as collateral, and borrowed the money outright from a company that specialized in motion picture loans.'

Fortunately for Vidor the film did not lose money and, although seldom revived, it has become celebrated. Its climax shows how a co-operative farm is saved from annihilation

James Murray and Eleanor Boardman as the beleaguered couple in The Crowd *(left); hungry soldiers Tom O'Brian, John Gilbert and Karl Dane in* The Big Parade *(below left); farmers of America in* Our Daily Bread *(below). Vidor's later films included the lavish* A Duel in the Sun *(above) with Lillian Gish and Lionel Barrymore;* Solomon and Sheba *(above right) with Gina Lollobrigida;* Northwest Passage *(right) with Spencer Tracy;* War and Peace *(below right) with Henry Fonda. But* The Fountainhead *(far right) revealed his abiding interest in the problems of ordinary men*

when the hero stumbles upon a stream high in the mountains. He organizes the commune into one last, massive effort to bring the water to their parched corn. Superbly directed and edited, the sequence demonstrates Vidor's inbred sense of cinema.

Strong medicine

There was a left-wing bias to *The Citadel* (1938), which Vidor made in England. Based on the A. J. Cronin novel about a young doctor (Robert Donat) confronted with the twin corruptions of poverty and riches, it contained a passionate plea for socialized medicine – a message which Vidor did not dilute. The film also portrayed the medical profession with a brutal realism – Vidor's distrust of doctors owing more to his Christian Science beliefs than his politics.

Although he welcomed the chance to work abroad, Vidor's preoccupations as a film-maker were with America. He kept a map of the USA and marked on it all his locations. He always said that his favourite themes were war, wheat and steel. *An American Romance* (1944) is his 'steel' – or industrial – picture. It is the story of an immigrant who rises to a position of power yet never loses his humanity:

'I wanted to show how a man can become a major figure, and still put on a pair of overalls and fix something when it goes wrong.' Unfortunately the MGM Front Office cut vital sequences and, in Vidor's opinion, ruined it. But his fascination with individualism was given further expression in *The Fountainhead* (1949) from Ayn Rand's novel about an idealistic architect who clashes with big business.

'When I made the picture, I thought the hero's action was too extreme in blowing up an apartment building because it had been a travesty of his original concept. Now I'm not so sure.

'You see, I can look at some of my old movies now and whenever there was a compromise, I can see it. Stands out like a scar, no matter what it was: compromises in casting, in script, in budget . . . the times when I couldn't do what I knew what had to be done . . .'

God speed the plough

After the massive *War and Peace* (1956) and *Solomon and Sheba* (1959), Vidor retired and bought a ranch at Paso Robles, California, where he had shot part of *Ruby Gentry* (1952).

For a long time he has had another film in mind – one of his favourite themes:

'It's about a man – a motion picture director – who gets to a point in his career in Hollywood and doesn't want to go on making films that don't express his own ideas and feelings. He feels a responsibility to the public and he stops. In searching his soul, his integrity, he goes back to his small town and most of the picture concerns this search.

'I'll shoot a lot of it on my ranch. Farms and ranches have always been my favourite locations. I used to be kidded about having a plough in every film. I guess it meant a new cycle of life, a new generation going on – you know, the plough turning over the earth. It has a great deal of meaning for me. Maybe that's why I live on a ranch now.'

KEVIN BROWNLOW

GARY COOPER
PATRICIA NEAL

"No man takes what's mine!"

THE FOUNTAINHEAD

The great best seller made greater on the screen by WARNER BROS.

All About Bette

'What a fool I was to come to Hollywood where they only understand platinum blondes and where legs are more important than talent'

On December 3, 1930, Bette Davis arrived in Hollywood. Originally from Lowell, Massachusetts (she was born in 1903), she had studied drama at the John Murray Anderson school, acting in summer repertory. She had won a modest but growing reputation as a promising young actress in two Broadway plays – *Broken Dishes* and *Solid South* – and had come to the attention of Universal studios, who put her under contract.

It was hardly an auspicious time for someone like Davis to break into films; she was pretty enough, in an odd way, but hardly fitted any of the moulds by which either the studios or the public judged beauty. The fact that she was, or wanted to be, a serious actress was irrelevant, if not actually a handicap to success. When she got off the train, no-one from the studio was there to meet her. In fact, a representative *had* been at the station but later reported that he had seen 'no-one who looked like an actress.' When head of the studio Carl Laemmle saw the first film in which she was cast, *Bad Sister* (1931), he said, 'Can you picture some poor guy going through hell and high water in a picture and ending up with *her* at the fade-out?'

Five undistinguished films later, Universal dropped her contract. Just as she and her

Above: even in publicity portraits Bette Davis avoided the glamorous extravagances of most other Hollywood actresses. Right: The Man Who Played God provided her with a prestigious role as the fiancée of a concert pianist (George Arliss)

mother were packing to return to New York and the theatre, George Arliss, then a leading star at Warner Brothers telephoned. A friend of his, Murray Kinnell, had worked with Davis in her fifth film *The Menace* (1932) and had thought she might be right for Arliss' upcoming *The Man Who Played God* (1932). In his autobiography, Arliss recalled:

'I did not expect anything but a nice little performance. But . . . the nice little part became a deep and vivid creation . . . I got from her a flash that illuminated mere words and inspired

them with passion and emotion. That is the kind of light that cannot be hidden under a bushel.'

Warners, however, either didn't see that light, or didn't care; she was put under contract, but given a series of roles in mediocre pictures which today have few, if any, redeeming qualities except Davis' presence.

She was, of course, noticed by critics and the public, and her reputation as a solid actress continued to grow. She was a convincing vixen in *Cabin in the Cotton* (1932), and man-

aged to make even the most ludicrous Southern dialogue – 'Ah'd luv ta kiss yo, but ah jes washed mah hayuh' – sound believable. She fought with director Archie Mayo over the way she should play her mad scene in *Bordertown* (1935); she won, as she often did in battles with directors, and was proved right, as she often was in such cases, when the film was well received. Critics pointed to the subtlety of her portrayal of 'a fiery-souled, half-witted, love-crazed woman' (*Film Weekly*) in their reviews.

Davis has claimed that 'There wasn't one of my best pictures I didn't have to fight to get.' *Of Human Bondage* (1934), from the novel by Somerset Maugham, was one of the first. Director John Cromwell wanted her for the role of Mildred, a scheming waitress who ensnares a sensitive medical student, but Warners was reluctant to loan her to RKO for the film. Bette hounded Jack Warner every day for six months, and he finally gave in simply to be left in peace. She recalled in her autobiography *The Lonely Life*:

'My employers believed I would hang myself playing such an unpleasant heroine . . . I think they identified me with the character and felt we deserved each other.'

It is, seen now, perhaps not one of Davis' best performances; her Mildred is so constantly overwrought and nasty that one begins to wonder what even the obsessed student Philip Carey (Leslie Howard) could see in her. Put in historical perspective, however, the performance is both effective and courageous; at a time when 'movie star' meant glamour and sympathy, Davis had dared to look terrible and to be unsympathetic. All were surprised when

she was not even nominated for an Academy Award. When she won an Oscar for *Dangerous* (1935), she claimed it was given her because she had been overlooked the previous year.

In spite of the acclaim she received for *Of Human Bondage*, Warners threw her into five melodramas of variable quality before giving her the script of *Dangerous*. Davis says that she thought it 'maudlin and mawkish, with a pretense at quality', and that she had to work hard to make something of her role as an alcoholic actress bent on self-destruction. She is undoubtedly right about the screenplay, but she gives a performance of such intensity that one overlooks everything that is going on around her on screen.

Those critics who had begun to complain that she was fast developing a set of mannerisms and was playing too broadly for the screen were suprised at her tender and restrained Gaby in *The Petrified Forest* (1936). Yet, in spite of her obvious power at the box-office and her critical standing as a serious actress, Warners insisted that she make an empty comedy, *The Golden Arrow* (1936), and a flat and confused version of Dashiell Hammett's *The Maltese Falcon* called *Satan Met a Lady* (1936). Davis was understandably angry. To preserve her self-respect and her popularity, she wanted to make fewer films each year and to act only in those with scripts she thought intelligent. Warners reply was to cast her in something called *God's Country and the Woman* (made in 1936 with Beverley Roberts as the female lead), with the promise that if she made it she could have the part of Scarlett O'Hara in *Gone With the Wind* (1939). She refused and the studio put her on suspen-

Left: a role Davis fought to get – Mildred in Of Human Bondage, *co-starring Leslie Howard. Centre: Davis (with Miriam Hopkins) in* The Old Maid *– a study of repressed love. Top left:* Dark Victory *was one of her strongest melodramas; Humphrey Bogart played a minor part. Top: as the rich flirt Madge, she bewitched her father's employee Marvin (Richard Barthelmess) in* Cabin in the Cotton

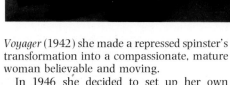

sion for three months. She held out, refusing two other scripts offered her, with the comment 'If I continue to appear in mediocre pictures, I'll have no career worth fighting for'.

With the Davis–Warners feud at an impasse, Ludovico Toeplitz, who produced films in England, offered her a two-picture contract at £20,000 for each film, with script approval. She signed, but upon her arrival in London found herself under injunction from Warners. They claimed that she was contracted to work exclusively for that studio and was not allowed to make films for others. The entire film industry watched the ensuing court battle (which all actors applauded) as the outcome would determine how the studio system would work in the future. Davis lost her suit and was forced to return to Warners or to give up films until her long-term contract expired – but she

'I have never known the great actor who . . . didn't plan eventually to direct or produce. If he has no such dream, he is usually bitter, ungratified and eventually alcoholic'

did not lose out in the long run. Warners paid her legal fees and began to take her more seriously; the standard of her material temporarily rose.

Her first film upon her return to Hollywood was *Marked Woman* (1937), an above-average social-problem (prostitution) film which gave her a chance to show a wider range of emotion than usual. *Jezebel* (1938) began a long series of films specially tailored for Davis. They were for the most part what was then called 'women's pictures', melodramatic soap operas turning on romantic conflict and sacrifice. It would be a mistake, however, to dismiss them in the

light of the wider freedom of expression allowed in today's films. In the Thirties and Forties such films were taken seriously and accorded more than a little respect. The best of them attempted to illuminate areas of emotion, sexuality and human situation which could not be portrayed on the screen at that time in any other way. Those that Davis made were certainly among the best – she continuously fought for a certain level of intelligence in plot and dialogue, and insisted on as much realism as possible in her portrayals of disturbed or troubled women.

In *Jezebel* she was convincing as a wilful Southern belle who is made to suffer for her own strange peversity. In *Dark Victory* (1939) she alone lifted a maudlin tale of a woman slowly dying into an illuminating study of human understanding and sacrifice. In *Now*

Voyager (1942) she made a repressed spinster's transformation into a compassionate, mature woman believable and moving.

In 1946 she decided to set up her own production company with the films thus made to be released through Warners. A single film came from her company – *A Stolen Life* (1946) in which she played twins, one good, one evil, both in love with the same man. She found she was uncomfortable in the role of producer: 'I never really *produced*,' she said, 'I simply meddled as usual. If that was producing, I had been a mogul for years.'

From 1946 onward, Davis seemed to have a problem finding suitable material, and her popularity began to slip. *Winter Meeting* (1948) is a talky film about a poetess meeting a naval

Left: Bette with William Dix in The Nanny, *one of her best later roles. Above left: Her performance as stage star Margo Channing (here with Celeste Holm and Hugh Marlowe) helped* All About Eve *achieve a record of 14 Academy Award nominations (it won six). Above: Davis in full regalia as* The Virgin Queen *– her second portryal of Elizabeth the First*

officer who wants to be a priest. *Beyond the Forest* (1949) was forced upon her by Warners in spite of her warning that 'I'm too old and too strong for that part'. The film was savaged by the critics and the public stayed away. Nonetheless, it is one of the most enjoyable bad movies ever made. ('There never was a woman like Rosa Moline, a twelve-o'clock girl in a nine-o'clock town.') Davis pulls out all the stops and turns in one of the finest Bette Davis caricatures ever seen. She asked for her release from the studio and got it, although Jack Warner was considering her for Blanche in *A Streetcar Named Desire* (later made in 1951).

She was completing a rather ordinary melodrama about divorce, *Payment on Demand* (1951) at RKO, when she was offered the part of ageing actress Margo Channing in *All About Eve* (1950). Davis later recalled:

'I can think of no project that from the outset was as rewarding from the first day to the last . . . It was a great script, had a great director, and a cast of professionals all with parts they liked . . . After the picture was released I told Joe [Mankiewicz, the director] he had resurrected me from the dead.'

Davis was never better in a role that allowed

'There was more good acting at Hollywood parties than ever appeared on the screen'

---

her to play an actress larger than life, and at the same time to reveal the self-pity and vulnerability beneath. But this upswing in her career was not maintained; throughout the decade she was cast in poor roles.

Still, as had happened with *All About Eve*, a film came along which once more revitalized her career: Robert Aldrich's *What Ever Happened to Baby Jane?* (1962). She obviously more than enjoyed playing 'Grand Guignol', and the film was overwhelmingly popular everwhere in the world. Perhaps the one unfortunate aspect of its success was that, in spite of minor

Left: Bette became one of the murderer's victims in the whodunnit Death on the Nile. *Above: as the crazy, former child star in* What Ever Happened to Baby Jane? *she slowly destroyed her crippled sister*

forays back into 'women's films' such as *Where Love Has Gone* (1964), she was offered and accepted a series of ghoulish roles in progressively worse movies.

Davis' most notable recent achievement was an Emmy award for the TV series *Strangers: the Story of a Mother and Daughter*. She also tours the lecture circuit with her older films, and remains the determined figure she always was:

'I'll never make the mistake of saying I'm retired. You do that and you're finished. You just have to make sure you play older and older parts. Hell, I could do a million of those character roles. But I'm stubborn about playing the lead. I'd like to go out with my name above the title.'

She is still known as 'the finest actress of the American cinema'. There are those who have disputed that she acted at all, maintaining that all the characters she played were drowned by her own strong personality. It is a moot point, depending upon one's standards and definition of screen acting, although one could reply that she has played the widest range of roles in the widest range of mood of any actress ever to work in American films. Whatever the final judgment of her abilities as an actress, however, it cannot be denied that, whatever she does on the screen, it is impossible to take one's fascinated eyes off her.   DAVID OVERBEY

Quotations from The Lonely Life, *by Bette Davis (New York, G.P. Putnam's Sons, 1962)*

Filmography

1931 Bad Sister; Seed; Waterloo Bridge; Way Back Home (GB: Old Greatheart). **'32** The Menace; Hell's House (reissued as: Juvenile Court); The Man Who Played God (GB: The Silent Voice); So Big; The Rich Are Always With Us; The Dark Horse; Cabin in the Cotton; Three on a Match. **'33** 20,000 Years in Sing Sing; Parachute Jumper; Ex-Lady; The Working Man; Bureau of Missing Persons. **'34** The Big Shakedown; Fashions of 1934 (GB: Fashion Follies of 1934; USA retitling for TV: Fashions); Jimmy the Gent; Fog Over Frisco; Of Human Bondage; Housewife. **'35** Bordertown; The Girl From 10th Avenue (GB: Men on Her Mind); Front Page Woman; Special Agent; Dangerous. **'36** The Petrified Forest; The Golden Arrow; Satan Met a Lady. **'37** Marked Woman; Kid Galahad (USA retitling for TV: The Battling Bellhop); That Certain Woman; It's Love I'm After. **'38** Jezebel; The Sisters. **'39** Dark Victory; Juarez; The Old Maid; The Private Lives of Elizabeth and Essex. **'40** All This and Heaven Too; The Letter. **'41** the Great Lie; Shining Victory (uncredited guest); The Bride Came COD; The Little Foxes; The Man Who Came to Dinner. **'42** In This Our Life; Now, Voyager. **'43** Watch on the Rhine; Thank Your Lucky Stars; Old Acquaintance. **'44** Mr Skeffington; Hollywood Canteen. **'45** The Corn is Green. **'46** A Stolen Life; Deception. **'48** Winter Meeting; June Bride. **'49** Beyond the Forest. **'50** All About Eve. **'51** Payment on Demand; Another Man's Poison (GB). **'52** Phone Call From a Stranger; The Star. **'55** The Virgin Queen. **'56** The Catered Affair (GB: Wedding Breakfast); Storm Center. **'59** John Paul Jones; The Scapegoat (GB). **'61** Pocketful of Miracles. **'62** What Ever Happened to Baby Jane? **'63** La Noia (IT). **'64** Dead Ringer (GB: Dead Image); Where Love Has Gone; Hush . . . Hush, Sweet Charlotte. **'65** The Nanny (GB). **'67** The Anniversary (GB). **'69** Connecting Rooms (GB). **'71** Bunny O'Hare. **'72** Lo Scopone Scientifico (IT) (USA: The Scientific Cardplayer). **'76** Burnt Offerings. **'78** Return From Witch Mountain; Death on the Nile (GB).

Joan Crawford
self-made Star

Jazz-baby Joan

When Joan Crawford first really became that magic being, a star, she had already made at least 19 films. Discovered as a chorus girl in a Broadway show called *Innocent Eyes* she began her film career as an anonymous double for Norma Shearer. She worked her way up through bit parts to female lead in low-budget films, or played opposite male stars, such as Harry Langdon in *Tramp, Tramp, Tramp* (1926), or Lon Chaney in *The Unknown* (1927), who were important enough not to need a real co-star. With *Our Dancing Daughters* (1928), however, the die was cast; she was flaming youth, a jazz-baby who lived life to the full without caring for the consequences (until, of course, bitter experience made her care). She was also a star. She was 24 years old (most probably: ten years later her official birthdate was abruptly changed from 1904 to 1908), under contract to MGM for three years and well on the way to becoming a complete product of the studio system. In later years, when it became fashionable for stars and ex-stars to complain about their 'slavery' and the autocratic rule of Louis B. Mayer, she always stoutly defended Mayer as an understanding father-figure and captain of a generally happy ship.

Above: Joan keeps a close watch on what the fan magazines are saying about her. Her intense relationship with her fans began in the Twenties when MGM organized a competition to find a new name for their starlet Lucille LeSueuer – Joan Crawford was the result. Top and above left: George Hurrell's striking portraits helped her to win forceful roles

Movie mannequin

All the same, she was ambitious and had ideas of her own. She became increasingly conscious of the rough edges in her manners and personality, for which she blamed her humble background (when she left home to go on the stage, her mother, twice divorced, was working in a laundry), and set out to 'improve' herself. She began dating Douglas Fairbanks Jr and then, despite some parental objections, married him. She began moving in the smartest social circles around Pickfair, the home of Fairbanks Sr and his wife Mary Pickford, and she learned quickly. At work, too, she was learning and planning. She toyed with various images (for a while in 1930 she looked alarmingly like Jean Harlow, her hair briefly platinum blonde), before setting on the look which became her trade mark: the broad, full mouth

Joan Crawford was nothing if not a star. Others might have had more varied acting abilities, have sung and danced better, have been more statuesquely beautiful or sweetly pretty or unashamedly sexy, but they lacked Joan Crawford's naked will to stardom. Like the characters she played in so many of her films, she fought her way up from the bottom; she modelled and remodelled herself tirelessly to match changes of taste and fashion, she built her own personality, polished her party manners, refined her dress sense and became a lady. She learned how to act – surprisingly well – and, more importantly, to know and abide by her own limitations. And she worked: morning, noon and night; she was totally the star, living for her public and her fame.

In other words, she was every shop-girl's dream come true. The secret of her appeal lay in her apparent ordinariness. However hard a girl tried, however far she stretched her imagination, she could never really be a Garbo or a Dietrich; but she could, conceivably, be a Joan Crawford. If simple little Lucille LeSueur (Crawford's real name) from San Antonio, Texas, could become the biggest thing in Hollywood, then so could anyone. Or that, at least, was the easy fantasy.

emphasized with heavy lipstick; the eyes – her best feature – madeup to look even larger than they were; the rest of her face became a boldly sculpted classical mask. She persuaded George Hurrell, the leading studio photographer, to take a series of striking pictures of her, virtually without makeup, to prove to the studio bosses that she could be convincing in strong melodramatic roles. She persuaded

As Sadie Thompson in Rain *(above) her appearance was termed 'bizarre'. Joan was more at ease as a hopeful show girl in* Dancing Lady *(above right) co-starring Clark Gable. By the Forties, she had matured into an actress of great power. Both* A Woman's Face *(right) and* Strange Cargo *(below right) provided her with strong roles;* Mildred Pierce *(below) won her an Oscar. In this scene she is falsely confessing to the murder of her husband to save the real culprit – her daughter who had killed him in a jealous rage*

Adrian, chief designer at the studio, to design a complete wardrobe for her. He particularly stressed her broad, square shoulders; soon, all across the USA women were copying her.

And so emerged a new 'mature' Joan, ready to play meaty roles in films like *Paid* (1930), in which she is imprisoned for a crime she did not commit and sets out to get even; and *Letty Lynton* (1932), where she is not imprisoned for a crime she *did* commit (poisoning an insanely ardent lover) and somehow manages to live happily ever after. Best of all was *Grand Hotel* (1932), in which she was genuinely touching as the hotel stenographer Flaemmchen – and managed to steal the picture right away from Garbo, a couple of Barrymores and others of similar standing.

Rain (1932), directed by Lewis Milestone at United Artists, was a mistake, since Sadie Thompson was a role which needed more than poise and personality to play, but she seldom made such a mistake again. From 1933 onwards her films were generally vehicles for her, and very sleek, finely tuned vehicles at that. True, she seemed in danger of becoming little more than a clothes-horse in some of them – but what a clothes-horse, and what clothes!

In film after film at this period – *Today We Live* (1933), *Chained*, *Forsaking All Others* (both 1934), *Love on the Run* (1936), *The Bride Wore Red* (1937) – she had nothing much to do except look gorgeous while two or three or more of the most eligible men in Hollywood fought for her favours. Often it was Clark Gable who finally won them. For good reasons she nearly always played modern roles – when she tried a period role in *The Gorgeous Hussy* (1936) critics immediately noted that 'century-old costumes do not go well with the pronounced modernity of her personality'. And indeed, through all her various incarnations, she did seem to belong unmistakably to the twentieth century: Aldous Huxley once said that she looked like a still-unnamed Dupont product. In 1938 she was pronounced 'box-office poison' – along with, admittedly, most of the biggest stars of the time – but no one seems to have bothered very much and she forged on into the Forties as hardly-disputed queen of MGM.

Her crown's awry

But her films were getting odder, as though behind the scenes nobody knew quite what to do with her. In 1935 you would have known exactly what to expect from a Crawford film; by 1940 it was almost impossible to guess – and this is a very alarming situation for a star, a real star, to be in, since it is consistency above all that counts. There could hardly be a more assorted group of films than *The Shining Hour* (1938), about a nightclub dancer who marries into a family of society neurotics; *The Ice Follies of 1939* (1939); *The Women* (1939), in which a society woman outmanoeuvres an ambitious shop-girl to keep the love of her (unseen) husband; *Strange Cargo* (1940), the story of a dance-hall girl who joins a band of convicts escaping from a French penal colony in the tropics; *Susan and God* (1940), a sophisticated comedy-drama about a nitwitted society woman who tries to convert her family and friends to a cranky religious movement; and *A Woman's Face* (1941), in which a hideously scarred criminal becomes converted to love and virtue after an operation on her face. Crawford is, in fact, very good in several of them – particularly *The Women*, where she

turns in a marvellously unsparing portrait of a vicious schemer – but it was becoming evident that her rule at MGM must be nearing its end, and that making a graceful transition to middle age might prove to be a problem for her.

A couple more films, and she left MGM, in her own words, 'by the back door'. She was put under contract to Warner Brothers, who brought her in perhaps as a handy rival to keep their top female star, Bette Davis, in line. They could not come up with a suitable property for her, and, apart from one brief guest appearance, she did not work for two years.

Then, in 1945, came *Mildred Pierce* which

GABLE
Joan
CRAWFORD *in* Strange Cargo

gained her an Academy Award and revitalized her career. In *Mildred Pierce* she was still glamorous and sexually desirable, but, at the same time, old enough to have a troublesome teenage daughter and so suffer the pangs of despised mother-love as well. She had all the qualities for agonizing in the grand manner. In this and her next pictures – *Humoresque* (1946), *Possessed* (1947), *Flamingo Road* (1949) and *The Damned Don't Cry* (1950) – she might play a bitch, but always a somewhat sympathetic one: you knew what had made her that way, and suffered along with her. She had usually been born on the wrong side of the tracks, made her own way to the top by baking pies or building empires for her menfolk, and then found that luxury and glamour were vain without the love of a good man (or a good child, or both) – a secretly satisfying conclu-

Above: Crawford gave a superb performance in Humoresque *playing a rich socialite desperate for the love of a violinist (John Garfield) but incapable of coping with it. Right: as Vienna, a tough saloon owner in* Johnny Guitar, *she successfully fought a duel to the death. Below: one of her last parts – as a circus owner in* Berserk! (1967)

sion for those of her audience who might aspire to such wealthy heights but were unlikely ever to attain them.

She had assumed such a powerful – some would say overpowering – persona by this time that few of the shrinking, malleable men in her films could stand up to her: these were 'women's pictures' *par excellence*, products of an era when film-going was still the major spare-time occupation of the American public and a large proportion of this vast audience was female. Women generally either went by themselves to matinées or decided what their boyfriends or husbands should take them to. As television began to threaten this state of affairs, the audiences for Crawford's films began to tail off.

A tough and ruthless thriller, *Sudden Fear* (1952), gave her career another shot in the arm, and then she was back at MGM with *Torch Song* (1953) – starring in a musical, of all things, and showing that she still had fabulous

legs. She then made a series of disastrous films: shooting it out with Mercedes McCambridge at the end of *Johnny Guitar* (1954), Crawford's first and only Western; being threatened with murder by another woman (what man would dare?) in *Female on the Beach* (1955); and getting a typewriter thrown at her by a young psychopath in *Autumn Leaves* (1956).

After that came an apotheosis of a sort with *What Ever Happened to Baby Jane?* (1962), in which she starred with her old arch-rival Bette Davis as one of two sisters, both Hollywood has-beens, in a gleefully Grand Guignol piece. It was her last film of note: afterwards, she refused to take parts that suited her age, thereby missing many mature roles that she could have played very well. Instead she was confined to incidental parts in big films and leading roles in ever more tatty shockers, after the last of which, *Trog* (1970), she retired to concentrate on public relations for Pepsi-Cola, for which her fourth and final husband, Alfred Steele, had been an important executive.

Very much a recluse by the end of her life, she died in New York in 1977 – one of the last stars from an era when they really had faces.

The camera and Crawford

What more did she have than a face? A lot more acting talent than she has ever been given credit for. Apart from rare aberrations like *Rain*, her performances really do not date. Compared with Norma Shearer her greatest rival at MGM during the Thirties, Crawford comes live off the screen – however foolish the context – and Shearer does not. Bette Davis, Crawford's great rival at a later stage, could be wonderful with the right role and the right director, but without one or the other she is often mannered to the point of absurdity. Crawford is simpler, more direct in style, and absolutely consistent.

But then acting ability has little to do with star quality. Joan Crawford loved the camera so much that it just had to love her back. It fulfilled for her every childhood dream just as she did, vicariously but vividly, for millions of women in one-horse towns and anonymous cities all over the USA. After her very earliest days she was never much of a pin-up star for men: she was a woman's star, and especially an American star, who lived out a series of specifically American women's dreams. Vibrant, glamorous, self-made and self-sufficient, Joan Crawford was not so much *a* star as *the* star – the perfect summary of just what Hollywood in its heyday was all about.

JOHN RUSSELL TAYLOR

Filmography

1925 Lady of the Night (double for Norma Shearer); 'Miss MGM' (short); Proud Flesh; Pretty Ladies; The Only Thing; Old Clothes; Sally, Irene and Mary. **'26** Tramp, Tramp, Tramp; The Boob (GB: The Yokel); Paris (GB: Shadows of Paris). **'27** Winners of the Wilderness; The Taxi Dancer; The Understanding Heart; The Unknown; Twelve Miles Out; Spring Fever; West Point (GB: Eternal Youth). **'28** The Law of the Range; Rose-Marie; Across to Singapore; Four Walls; Our Dancing Daughters; Dream of Love. **'29** The Duke Steps Out; The Hollywood Revue of 1929; Our Modern Maidens; Untamed. **'30** Montana Moon; Our Blushing Brides; Paid/Within the Law. **'31** Dance, Fools, Dance; Laughing Sinners; This Modern Age; Possessed. **'32** The Stolen Jools (GB: The Slippery Pearls) (short) (guest); Grand Hotel; Letty Lynton; Rain. **'33** Today We Live; Dancing Lady. **'34** Sadie McKee; Chained; Forsaking All Others. **'35** No More Ladies; I Live My Life. **'36** The Gorgeous Hussy; Love on the Run; Screen Snapshots No 12 (short). **'37** Parnell (guest); The Last of Mrs Cheyney; The Bride Wore Red; Mannequin. **'38** The Shining Hour. **'39** The Ice Follies of 1939; The Women. **'40** Strange Cargo; Susan and God (GB: The Gay Mrs Trexal). **'41** A Woman's Face; When Ladies Meet. **'42** They All Kissed the Bride; Reunion/Reunion in France (GB: Mademoiselle France). **'43** Above Suspicion; For Men Only (short). **'44** Hollywood Canteen (guest). **'45** Mildred Pierce. **'46** Humoresque. **'47** Possessed; Daisy Kenyon. **'49** Flamingo Road; It's a Great Feeling (guest). **'50** The Damned Don't Cry; Harriet Craig. **'51** Goodbye, My Fancy. **'52** This Woman is Dangerous; Sudden Fear. **'53** Torch Song. **'54** Johnny Guitar. **'55** Female on the Beach; Queen Bee. **'56** Autumn Leaves. **'57** The Story of Esther Costello (GB); The Best of Everything. **'62** What Ever Happened to Baby Jane? **'63** The Caretakers (GB: Borderlines); Strait-Jacket. **'65** I Saw What You Did. **'67** Berserk! (GB). **'70** Trog (GB).

BUSINESS IS BOOMING

In Britain the cinema expanded, though a slump in British film production allowed Hollywood to extend its empire to England. Meanwhile in the USA finance flooded back into production

By the late Thirties the superficial boom in British production was nearly ended. The old Quota Act was coming up for renewal in 1938, and in anticipation of this American producers set about making top-class films in England.

The crucial necessity of selling films in the USA had already defeated both Michael Balcon and Basil Dean. The only producer who still had a chance of breaking into the American market was the larger-than-life Alexander Korda. In 1937 Korda made a bid for equal co-ownership of United Artists with Sam Goldwyn. Had the deal come off it would have given him a vital foothold in America, but at the eleventh hour it fell through.

Korda's production empire included real assets such as a large studio, contract players and some of the most outstanding talent in the business. The enterprise made glossy and enjoyable films and was heavily backed by the Prudential Assurance Company along conventional shareholding lines.

At the same time as Korda was pursuing this orthodox production practice, a small and virtually unknown group had been channelling vast sums of money into film production through an elaborate system of bank loans secured by guarantees from marine underwriters. In this way many production units without capital, studios or personnel of their own – 'tramp' producers as they have been called – were extravagantly financed on a film-by-film basis without any supervision from their backers in London's business world. Financiers were speculating on film production.

Korda had set the fashion for lavish production but he always kept his books in order. The day of reckoning was bound to come, however, for a number of the 'tramp' producers whose spending was on a scale comparable to that of Korda. Unfortunately the financial scandal that resulted from movie speculation came to light. The bad publicity and the resulting reluctance on the part of businessmen to invest in production harmed Korda as much as the rogue producers. Shorn of control of his studios, and confined to making more economical pictures, Korda now had little chance of regular American distribution.

After a decade of the quota regulations, the potential had gone out of British production companies. On the other hand the cinema business was booming. Throughout the Thirties audiences grew and grew. Funds poured into the exhibition side of the business which remained profitable even during the Depression. Gaumont-British and Associated British Cinemas both became highly profitable circuits and were organized as large vertical combines, with their own production, renting and exhibition branches.

Gaumont-British Picture Corporation, run by the Ostrer family, was made up of three companies: the Gaumont and Gainsborough studios in London, a nation-wide film distribution network and the Gaumont-British cinema circuit. By 1929 the company controlled 287 cinemas throughout Britain. Their chief competitor was ABC, headed by the tough, aggressive John Maxwell, who later tried to wrest control of Gaumont-British from the Ostrer family. At the beginning of the Thirties ABC owned 88 cinemas, the prolific British International Pictures studio at Elstree and the distribution firm Wardour Films. During the winter of 1933–34, the company was reorganized as the Associated British Picture Corporation and by 1938 it had increased its number of cinemas to 325.

Another major film exhibitor was the energetic and likeable Oscar Deutsch, whose chain of Odeon cinemas was built up over the decade, his first cinema having been built at Perry Bar, Birmingham in 1930. A new approach to urban planning in the Thirties created large suburbs which contained ideal sites for the new Odeons. These cinemas were broadly uniform in their functional art-deco appearance and created a modern brand image for the circuit.

In 1937 Odeon merged with County Cinemas to form a circuit of 250 cinemas and had first call on all United Artists and Korda films. At this point Odeon became the third circuit in size and worth £6 million as a company. Towards the end of 1939, the Odeon board was enlarged to include two members of the new General Cinema Finance Corporation; one of them was the future mogul J. Arthur Rank.

A Methodist millionaire with flour-milling and other business interests, Rank had entered films in the early Thirties to improve the production of religious films. In 1936 his company moved into feature production and studio ownership. His arrival on the board of Odeon and was his first step into exhibition – a business he all but monopolized.

While film exhibition was flourishing, production was depressed. A government committee under the then Lord Moyne studied the problem and tried to accommodate the opposing interests of the big combines (Gaumont-British and ABC) and the independent producers like Basil Dean. The problem continued to be the quality of British films and the difficulty of selling them in America. The new Quota Act was finally passed in 1938. The committee who had framed the legislation had attempted to ensure higher quality in British films by insisting

Above: MGM stamped its familiar lion logo on its British films. Below: Conrad Veidt and Annabella played nobles in Richelieu's France in the black and white romance Under the Red Robe. Bottom: Henry Fonda, Annabella and the crew of Wings of the Morning

that a film should meet certain minimum costs in order to be eligible for distribution as a quota film.

As might have been hoped, the introduction of the minimum-cost clause killed off the cheap 'quota quickie'. It also put a premium on expensive films and led to the production of some high-quality pictures. But film production as a whole did not revive. In the first year of the new quota regulations, no feature films emerged from eight of the British studios. The labour union claimed that unemployment among technicians stood at 80 per cent. Fewer 'quota quickies' meant, moreover, that film production continued to decline numerically.

Worse still for those who had hoped for a truly national picture-making industry, statistics revealed that all but 25 per cent of films made in 1938 were American productions of one kind or another. The dilemma central to the British film industry remained unsolved: quality films were expensive and to cover their costs they had to be exported to the USA. Once again the effort to achieve this had put the industry in the hands of the American major companies.

In order to forestall the British government's moves against them, the American majors had begun serious production in Britain on a large scale. Twentieth Century-Fox made a horse-racing drama, *Wings of the Morning* (1937), that had the distinction of being the first British film in Technicolor. The film starred Henry Fonda and the popular French star Annabella and was produced by Robert T. Kane, who had been Paramount's chief in Paris at the start of the Thirties. Kane retained Annabella for his next English production, *Under the Red Robe* (1937). This historical romance was another prestige picture, with Conrad Veidt starring opposite Annabella. The film brought together the great talents of cameramen Georges

Above: filming A Yank at Oxford with (left to right) American director Jack Conway, British producer Michael Balcon and star Robert Taylor. Right: John Maxwell, a Scottish solicitor turned film mogul. Below: Conrad Veidt and Valerie Hobson who had been a hit in The Spy in Black were teamed here in a similar wartime spy film, Contraband. Top right: There Ain't No Justice was a story of bribery in the ring. Far right: Robert Donat in Vidor's The Citadel

BIGGEST *Personality*
of **BRITISH FILMS**

The Spectacular Success of John Maxwell

The final article in our series dealing with British Film Personalities tells of the phenomenal achievements of the Chairman of British International Pictures, who certainly seems to be the leader for whom the British Film Industry has waited so long

by the EDITOR of "FILM WEEKLY"

Périnal and James Wong Howe, under the direction of the Swedish director Victor Sjöstrom.

Columbia embarked on production at Korda's Denham studio, making several good thrillers, among them *Q–Planes* and *The Spy in Black* (both 1939), which promoted the beautiful Valerie Hobson into a star, after she had been neglected for several years by British producers.

MGM made perhaps the biggest impact of all. The plans they announced when Michael Balcon joined them as head of production early in 1937 included *A Yank at Oxford* and one film he was to make in Hollywood. But Balcon and MGM were to part company within 18 months of agreeing a long-term producer's contract.

A Yank at Oxford (1938) was a big undertaking involving a mixed American/British cast. A vast and varied collection of writers including John Monk Saunders, Sidney Gilliat, Hugh Walpole, Ben Travers, Herman J. Mankiewicz and F. Scott Fitzgerald had a shot at the script. Jack Conway was the director and the film sold well on both sides of the Atlantic.

Balcon's old friend Victor Saville took a different approach to MGM. As an independent producer he had prudently acquired the film rights to A. J. Cronin's recent best-selling novel *The Citadel*, a book that MGM wished Balcon to produce. Saville was not inhibited by the MGM regime and he soon found himself producing both *The Citadel* (1938) and *Goodbye, Mr Chips* (1939). Once again the directors, King Vidor and Sam Wood, were American but the main star of both was the British actor Robert Donat. These two films were highly successful and earned Saville his passport to Hollywood where he was to remain when MGM pulled out of Britain at the outbreak of war.

During the late Thirties other top British film-makers like Hitchcock, Wilcox and Korda found their way to Hollywood. Balcon, however, turned his back on the American market and was to spend the rest of his career in the British cinema. He stepped into Basil Dean's shoes at Ealing Studios where Dean had come under increasing criticism from the board. Balcon assembled many of his former Gaumont team and continued the Ealing tradition of providing vehicles for music-hall comics, but in certain other films he introduced a more realistic treatment of ordinary people and themes. *There Ain't No Justice* (1939), an unassuming film starring Jimmy Hanley as a young boxer, was scarcely noticed as a forerunner of what later became known as the Ealing style.

By the end of the decade, British film technicians and directors, who had proved themselves in the tough training school of 'quota quickies' and documentary film production, were ready to undertake the difficult task of filming the war. On its own the 1938 Quota Act is unlikely to have fostered a prosperous national industry. Early in 1939, an important daily newspaper carried the headline 'Films Act Has Failed'. The following day its correspondence columns had a letter from Basil Dean saying bitterly, 'I told you so'. Whether the making of quality American films would have expanded in the Forties is hard to say; with the outbreak of war the American majors withdrew from Britain and the character of the native industry was to change beyond recognition.   RACHAEL LOW

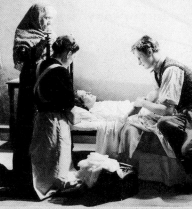

Hollywood invades Britain

The foreign invasion of British films in the Thirties was on a large scale. Indeed, so many Europeans were employed by Alexander Korda at Denham studios that the trio of Union Jacks hoisted outside the building was said to stand for the only three British workers in the place. But it was the Americans who aroused the strongest feelings in Britain. They were feared as potential economic invaders who might take over the more profitable parts of the home film industry; they were envied for the greater popularity of their films, even with British audiences; and they were admired for their greater technical expertise.

Here come the Yanks

During the decade British companies continued the well-established practice of luring American stars across the Atlantic. The first feature made at Pinewood, *Talk of the Devil* (1936), starred Americans Ricardo Cortez and Sally Eilers – though otherwise it was an entirely British production. Helen Chandler, Sylvia Sidney and Fay Wray, Bela Lugosi, Raymond Massey and Edward Everett Horton were other stars who worked in Britain.

The really big stars almost never made the crossing: they had more important commitments in Hollywood. But stars who had passed their peak or who had never shone that brightly in the Hollywood firmament were happy to work in Britain. Ruth Chatterton's last two films, *The Rat* (1937) and *A Royal Divorce* (1938), were both British, as was Cary Grant's *The Amazing Quest of Ernest Bliss* (1936), made when he was still a rising star. Exceptionally, Edward G. Robinson was in great demand back home when Warners loaned him out at such short notice for *Thunder in the City* (1937) that it seems to have been one of that studio's many tactless exercises of authority over its contract players.

Hollywood directors who worked in Britain were often in decline. Among them was William Beaudine, a top director of silents (including Mary Pickford's *Sparrows* of 1926). Beaudine settled down to making bright British

comedies – like *Windbag the Sailor* (1936) with Will Hay – before returning to Hollywood and the Bowery Boys. Another director past his best, William K. Howard, whose films had included *Transatlantic* (1931) and *The Power and the Glory* (1933), was entrusted in Britain with *Fire Over England* (1937). It was a lavish historical costume picture climaxing in the defeat of the Spanish Armada, and to photograph it Howard recruited his favourite American cameraman, James Wong Howe. William Cameron Menzies was a major American art director when Alexander Korda tempted him over with an offer to direct the spectacular *Things to Come* (1936) – based on an H.G. Wells novel about an apocalyptic world war and requiring strong pictorial stylization.

At the time of the 1927 Films Act, several American companies went into 'quota-quickie' production for themselves, appointing American executives to oversee output. The films made by Paramount British, under Walter Morosco, included *Service for Ladies* (1932), the first to be directed in Britain by Korda. Fox British, under Albert Parker (formerly a leading director), made a stream of economical 'quota quickies' at Wembley and discovered James Mason – giving him his first role in the crime story *Late Extra* (1935).

Warners at Teddington

But it was Warner Brothers that made the biggest move into British production, vastly improving the existing studios at Teddington in 1931 and promising that major pictures of international appeal would be made with top stars. George Arliss was one scheduled to make films in Britain but the company lost his services soon afterwards when he joined Darryl F. Zanuck at 20th Century, and Teddington was only used for low-budget films that were rarely released in the USA. Irving Asher headed production and made some important acting finds that he sent on to Hollywood; they included Errol Flynn, Ian Hunter and Patric Knowles who were put into major Warner films like *The Adventures of Robin Hood* (1938).

Ever economical, Warners remade some of their Hollywood successes in Britain – *The Man*

Above: Robert Donat in Goodbye, Mr Chips, *a triumph for Anglo-American collaboration. Left: Annabella and Henry Fonda in the race-track romance,* Wings of the Morning

Above: Bristol-born Cary Grant returned to Britain in 1936 to film The Amazing Quest of Ernest Bliss. *Above right: James Mason in his first film,* Late Extra. *Right: Laurence Olivier defeating the Spanish Armada in* Fire Over England. *Below: Victor McLaglen as a boxer and Gracie Fields as his wife, a singer, in* We're Going to be Rich

From Blankley's (1930), a mild comedy, was repeated as *Guest of Honour* (1934) with Henry Kendall taking the part that John Barrymore had played in the original. American directors like Beaudine, William McGann and John Rawlins were given plenty of work at Teddington, and players like Laura La Plante, Glenda Farrell, and James Finlayson were active there. But Warners also used many British directors and stars, and one exceptional murder thriller, *They Drive by Night* (1939), with Emlyn Williams, had little or no American participation, while Max Miller's films gave the company its biggest successes.

With *Wings of the Morning* (1937), 20th Century-Fox's British outpost, offered an early example of a frequent ploy to widen a film's appeal in Britain and the Empire by making the American star (here Henry Fonda) play a Canadian. Fox also tried to make an international star of Gracie Fields by starring her in a South African 'Western', *We're Going to be Rich* (1938), before returning her to the indigenous subjects that made her so popular with British audiences.

The MGM lesson

MGM, who also announced major production plans in Britain, retained its traditional methods of big-budget film-making. The script of *A Yank at Oxford* (1938) eventually called upon some thirty writers, working both in Britain and Hollywood. The film had an American director (Jack Conway), cameraman (Hal Rosson) and supervising editor (Margaret Booth), while Robert Taylor played the lead supported by Maureen O'Sullivan and Lionel Barrymore. British participation was secondary (though Vivien Leigh was striking in a small role) and American production procedures provided a useful lesson for British technicians in such areas as dubbing.

MGM's subsequent pictures did give more scope to British talent and especially to Robert Donat who was persuaded to sign for six films in England. But he was still directed by and co-starred with Americans: King Vidor on *The*

Citadel (1938) with Rosalind Russell, and Sam Wood on *Goodbye, Mr Chips* (1939) with Greer Garson. The pictures could as easily have been filmed at Culver City as Denham: the Welsh mining village of *The Citadel* was a studio creation, not location work; and Irving Thalberg had originally bought *Chips* as a vehicle for Charles Laughton, who would have made it in Hollywood as he did *The Barretts of Wimpole Street* (1934).

War calls a halt

The two films were world-wide successes, gaining Donat Oscar nominations for Best Actor: he won for *Chips*, beating MGM's reigning star, Clark Gable, who was nominated for *Gone With the Wind*. MGM's British programme was proving a winner; for its fourth picture, *Busman's Honeymoon* (1940), Robert Montgomery came over to play Dorothy L. Sayers' sleuth, Lord Peter Wimsey. He was accompanied by the director Richard Thorpe and co-star Maureen O'Sullivan, but the declaration of war caused a temporary suspension of production and Thorpe and O'Sullivan hurried back home. Montgomery stayed on to work under the talented British director Arthur Woods who had made *They Drive by Night*. But *Busman's Honeymoon* was Woods' last picture: an RAF pilot, he died in action soon afterwards.

Montgomery had also planned to make *The Earl of Chicago* (1939) with Richard Thorpe in Britain, but it was transferred back to Hollywood along with other MGM British projects in the pipeline. MGM's only other British picture of the war period was *Adventures of Tartu* (1943), directed by Hollywood's Harold S. Bucquet, and starring Robert Donat – as a British spy in Czechoslovakia – after he had been taken to court to enforce his contract.

Warners meanwhile continued filming in Britain, responding to the outbreak of hostilities with such propaganda efforts as *The Prime Minister* (1941) – starring John Gielgud as Disraeli – and *Flying Fortress* (1942), with Richard Greene as a Yank in the RAF. Then on July 5, 1944, a flying bomb wrecked the Teddington studios: after 152 films Warners' British output came to a halt. Other Hollywood companies like RKO were active in the war years and it was probably Columbia that did most to keep up British spirits by putting George Formby into such comedies as *Much Too Shy* (1942), *Get Cracking* and *Bell Bottom George* (both 1943).   ALLEN EYLES

Robert Donat

Charles Laughton called him 'the most graceful actor of our time'. Graham Greene said he was 'the best film actor we possess'. Sadly Donat's career was brutally cut short

Above: The Citadel gave Donat the part of a young doctor who must amputate a trapped miner's arm to save his life; he encounters greater difficulty, later, in maintaining his professional ideals in high society.
Right: Donat and Eugene Pallette haunted by the 'Glourie Ghost' in The Ghost Goes West

Robert Donat had everything an actor could hope for – except health. Beneficent spirits, attending his cradle, endowed him with good looks, a fine voice, exceptional elegance of demeanour. A malevolent spirit gave him chronic asthma.

Born in 1905 of mixed parentage – a Yorkshire mother and a Polish father who had settled in Manchester – Donat came to the screen in a period when it was the poor sister of the stage in Britain. It was natural that he should long for the theatre, and indeed he was to become one of its notable players. He made his stage debut in Birmingham in 1921 and by 1930 had reached the West End. But he was made for the cinema. Alexander Korda recognized Donat's gifts and in 1933 cast him, after a few banal roles, as Thomas Culpeper in *The Private Life of Henry VIII*. Donat was overshadowed by the bravura of Charles Laughton as the King; but looking back one sees how much his grace and easy charm added to the film. A year later he was in Hollywood playing the lead role in *The Count of Monte Cristo* and rags and beard could not disguise his qualities. In 1929 Donat had married Ella Annesley but they were to divorce in 1946.

Back in Britain Donat was Richard Hannay in Alfred Hitchcock's *The Thirty-Nine Steps* (1935), then starred in René Clair's comedy *The Ghost Goes West* (1935) as both the young owner of a Scottish castle and his ghost-ancestor, who is doomed to haunt the castle when it is transported to the USA. Clair was brought over to England by Korda, as was Jacques Feyder, director of *Knight Without Armour* (1937) – in which Donat played the Englishman faced with the job of getting a widowed countess (Marlene Dietrich) to Moscow after the revolution.

Always Donat was the romantic hero, resourceful, brave, the ideal star of the Thirties and Forties. Perhaps if health had not handicapped him he might have gone back in triumph to Hollywood and become a truly great star. As it was, his illness, increasing diffidence and self-doubt, and contractual problems combined to cost him the lead roles in such prestigious films as *Captain Blood* (1935), *Anthony Adverse* (1936), and *The Adventures of Robin Hood* (1938). Instead he stayed to work in Britain and there had a brief period of glittering fame in the late Thirties.

He had not been happy in Hollywood in any case, but he had made an impression and when MGM extended their empire to include production in Britain they made him one of their leading players. King Vidor directed him in *The Citadel* (1938) and drew from him a performance of considerable range as the young doctor who moves from Wales to fashionable London. In 1939 came the film with which the name of Robert Donat has been linked ever since: Sam Wood's *Goodbye, Mr Chips*. Insisting on the role, he audaciously broke away from the smooth, confident face; the easy, elegant movements of the ideal film star. He played a master at an English public school, at first helplessly ragged by his pupils, then taught self-assurance by his beautiful wife (Greer Garson), desolate as a widower and finally a whiskery old sentimentalist. It was a character of fantasy, but still solid enough for Donat to deliver a superb performance and win the Best Actor Oscar. Decades afterwards, Donat's Chips is still remembered.

He never did as well again. Turned down for military service, he gave a decent but uninspired performance in the flag-waving *The Young Mr Pitt* (1942); and returned to action in *Adventures of Tartu* (1943), a piece of flummery in which he played a wartime British sabotage agent. It was not worthy of his powers. But increasingly Donat was engaged in the fight against illness. He was unremarkable as the husband who resumes marriage with Deborah Kerr after war-enforced separation in *Perfect Strangers* (1945) – both his and Korda's last film for MGM – but more commanding as the defence counsel in *The Winslow Boy* (1948). In 1949 he produced, adapted (from Walter Greenwood's play), directed and starred in a tame but pleasant Northern comedy *The Cure for Love* for Korda. Donat played a soldier pursued by a coarse, overbearing fiancée (Dora Bryan) and a sweeter girl (Renée Asherson) who wins him in the end; in 1953 Donat married Miss Asherson in real life but they parted in 1956.

He was touching as the film pioneer Friese-Green in the Festival of Britain picture, *The Magic Box* (1951) but, by now very ill, had to refuse roles in *No Highway* (1951) and *Hobson's Choice* (1954). Oxygen cylinders were kept in the wings for him when he acted in T.S. Eliot's play *Murder in the Cathedral* in 1953 and there was mordant irony in his casting as the dying country parson in *Lease of Life* (1954). In 1958 he summoned up the last of his strength to play the mandarin in *The Inn of the Sixth Happiness*. A month later he was dead.

Donat could have been one of the universal stars of cinema. Illness, however, corroded the latter years of his comparatively brief life. It could not destroy his brilliant gifts but it shortened his career and, one might say, blunted it.

DILYS POWELL

Filmography
1933 Men of Tomorrow; That Night in London (USA: Overnight); Cash (USA: For Love or Money); The Private Life of Henry VIII. **'34** The Count of Monte Cristo (USA). **'35** The Thirty-Nine Steps; The Ghost Goes West. **'37** Knight Without Armour. **'38** The Citadel. **'39** Goodbye, Mr Chips. **'42** The Young Mr Pitt. **'43** Adventures of Tartu (USA retitling for TV: Tartu). **'45** Perfect Strangers (USA: Vacation From Marriage). **'47** Captain Boycott (guest). **'48** The Winslow Boy. **'49** The Cure for Love (+ dir; + co-sc; + prod). **'51** The Magic Box. **'54** Lease of Life. **'56** The Stained Glass at Fairford (short) (voice only). **'58** The Inn of the Sixth Happiness (USA).

Harry Cohn

'I don't have ulcers-I give them'

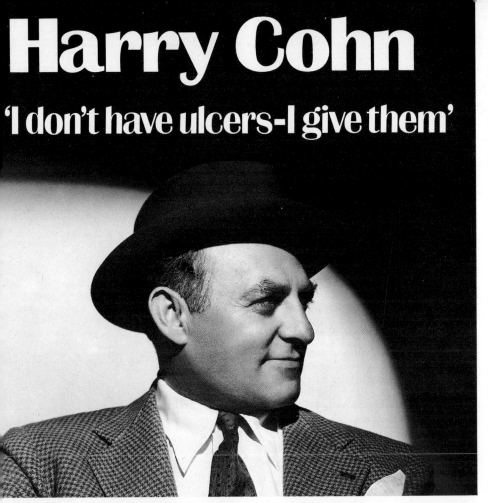

Harry Cohn, one of Hollywood's most successful moguls, hauled Columbia studios from Poverty Row into the big time. He was a man whose ruthlessness kept his employees in a state of constant fear, who regarded the business of movie-making as 'better than being a pimp'

The great days of the studio system were richly populated by colourful figures. Yet Harry Cohn barged to the front of them – more energetic and ruthless, and more enigmatic as a character than any of his extraordinary contemporaries. He was a man who inspired every emotion except indifference.

Harry Cohn was born in 1891, shortly before the movies. He lived through their greatest years, dying in 1958 during their decline. He came from a family of orthodox Jews, son of a German immigrant who worked as a tailor on the East Side of New York. By the time Cohn was 30, he had founded CBC (later Columbia Pictures), of which he was to be head of production and President. He was the only person to hold both positions in a major Hollywood film company.

But CBC (named after co-founders Cohn, Joe Brandt, and Harry's brother Jack Cohn) did not begin life as a major company – and here lies the true fascination of Cohn's career: he represents what was once – and for many people still is – the American Dream. He hauled himself and his studio from poverty. Columbia never rivalled MGM or Paramount for glamour during the golden Thirties and Cohn remained in constant awe of Mayer, but when the economic tide turned against the big studios, Columbia – one of the small studios in the area known as 'Poverty Row' – remained secure.

In January 1924, four years after it was founded, CBC became Columbia and within a further two years had offered shares on the open market. Slowly the company gained respectability, though Cohn insisted that it should remain in the heart of the 'Row'. It would expand, but only in the vicinity of its original Hollywood headquarters – an area Cohn knew only too well. He first acquired a small, two-stage studio in Gower Street. Over the next decade Columbia nibbled away at the surrounding blocks, buying up lot after lot; building sound stages, additional offices and workshops, and making the company self-contained. Although still small by the standards of the five majors, Columbia emerged as the most important of the minor studios.

Honest Harry

During the formative Twenties, Cohn retained iron control over the West Coast development while his brother controlled the New York side of the business. The distance of several thousand miles kept them from each other's throats – but the telephone lines were 'blue' with their exchanges.

What seems most remarkable about Harry Cohn's rise to power and wealth is that it appears to have been achieved without dishonesty. He paid his taxes scrupulously and accounted – with devastating accuracy – for all studio expenditure. He bargained and wheedled to get the best deal for the studio. Many actors and actresses found themselves loaned out to another studio, but the colossal cash gains from this went into Columbia's coffers, not the stars' bank accounts. The reasons for this respectability and penny-pinching stem from Cohn's childhood; his parents believed in unremitting hard work and honesty, and in those far off days there was no room for wastage. In addition, their son was gifted with the one quality that all self-made millionaires share – tireless energy. Cohn's working day was, literally, that. And once the studio day ended, the entertaining he did at home was concerned purely with business. His entire life was spent controlling all aspects of studio policy and production. He took lunch in the studio, visited the sets and viewed every movie. He would fine someone for leaving on an unnecessary light and negotiated major contracts personally.

In such matters, Cohn – whose dictatorship was absolute – was ruthless. His treatment of those unable – or, like Jean Arthur, unwilling – to contest his bullying was utterly heartless. Careers could be smashed, and artists given ten minutes to get out of the studio. No women's liberationist would complain of Cohn's attitude, since he treated his actresses and other women with the same contempt as he treated the men. He preferred to deal with men as he could not bear tears, and an actor such as Glenn Ford, who retaliated physically to Cohn's abuse, was subsequently treated better both professionally and socially.

Cohn modelled his office on that of the fascist dictator Benito Mussolini whom he had visited in Rome. It was not so much that Cohn admired Il Duce's politics, but he liked his style. Cohn's office was long and dominated by a massive desk – the lighting favoured him, shining intimidatingly at his visitors who had probably already been kept waiting in an outer office for hours. Once inside they would be told of their next assignment, of a loan-out to another studio, whether they could get married,

Rod Steiger (left) as the tyrannical movie producer in The Big Knife, *and (below, on the left) Broderick Crawford as the millionaire junk-dealer in* Born Yesterday – *both portrayals were inspired by Harry Cohn*

or even see the person they loved. Kim Novak found her romance with Sammy Davis Jr terminated when Davis, a coloured entertainer and therefore considered 'bad' for her image, was told to choose between working in lucrative nightclubs or continuing the affair. He preferred to carry on singing.

Working with Capra

In building Columbia, Cohn naturally had valuable help – and strokes of good fortune. The most significant of these was his early association with writer-director Frank Capra who first worked for Columbia on silent movies. Most importantly, he helped usher the studio into the sound era and it was at this time, according to Capra's autobiography *The Name Above the Title*, that his boss stopped calling him 'Dago'. Cohn learned respect for the man, if not for his Sicilian ancestry, and the two shared an artistic collaboration throughout the late Twenties and the Thirties. Other great directors worked with Cohn: Hawks on *The Criminal Code* (1931) and the masterpieces *Twentieth Century* (1934) and *Only Angels Have Wings* (1939); Ford on *The Whole Town's Talking* (1935); even Welles on *The Lady from Shanghai* (1947). But only Capra worked consistently and fruitfully for Columbia.

After the runaway success of *It Happened One Night* (1934), most of the ensuing Columbia–Cohn–Capra pictures of the Thirties were also successful, and the studio acquired a respectability from which its location on Poverty Row could not detract. Many of the fifty-plus Oscars that found their way behind Cohn's massive desk resulted from these halcyon days.

Despite such success, Cohn lost Capra (who left and formed his own company in the Forties) as he had lost the wonderful Barbara Stanwyck and the equally talented Jean Arthur who was terrified by his manner. She refused to have direct contact with him, was frequently suspended and finally ceased working for the studio: hardly surprising for a sensitive actress who could find herself in a conversation with a man liable to walk off to the private bathroom adjoining his office and urinate with the door open so that the chat could continue. The action typifies a man who had a daily manicure, dressed in the most expensive clothes and was obsessed with personal cleanliness, yet behaved like a hoodlum.

Lovely Rita

Cohn, however, was to find a replacement for Barbara Stanwyck and Jean Arthur. If not his greatest actress, beautiful Rita Hayworth became his greatest star. She came to prominence in *Only Angels Have Wings* (1939), co-starring with Arthur who was then in comparative decline. At the time Hayworth was receiving only $250 a week – a salary that was to rise ten-fold in the following years as she entered the realms of the great Hollywood love goddesses. Working for Columbia, and on loan-out, in dramas, comedies and musicals, Hayworth earned Cohn a fortune, but his interference with her love life – typically, he supervised her contract, her work and her lifestyle – alienated her. He also alienated his male leads, Glenn Ford and William Holden. He groomed them, paid them handsomely and seemed genuinely fond of the trio – his 'children' – yet resented their independence. By the late Forties and the Fifties, he had lost control of these and other artists.

Hayworth's swansong for Cohn and Columbia was *Pal Joey* (1957). The wheel had come full circle and she was to be replaced as the studio's top star by the latest Cohn discovery, Kim Novak, who supported her in the film just as Rita herself had supported Jean Arthur 18 years previously. Frank Sinatra, Hayworth's other co-star on *Pal Joey*, remarked that, for him, Hayworth *was* Columbia – 'She gave them class'.

Cohn did nothing in a small way. He gambled furiously, often as much as $10,000 a day. This obsession was halted by the money men in the East when the total losses for one single season reached $400,000. His lifestyle was modified only by his certain 'knowledge' that he would die in his sixties, but during the last decade of his life Cohn refused to relinquish control of the studio, since the only alternative he could envisage was an even earlier death. He resented the independence of producers and directors such as Stanley Kramer and Fred Zinnemann as much as he did that of his stars, yet he could not resist the tide of a changing Hollywood.

Cruel but kind

Boorish and bullying, Cohn was also capable of great kindness. Even his most intimate colleagues and workers could be struck dumb by his outbursts of cruelty, only to find on another occasion that a mammoth hospital bill for an ageing mother had been settled by Cohn personally. Cohn would accept no thanks for such an action and would warn the recipient never to tell anyone of his generosity. Also, as the studio gradually slimmed down its personnel, Cohn made sure that the old Columbia staff had jobs to go to.

He was the model for Broderick Crawford's politician in *All the King's Men* (1949) and his crude junk-dealer in *Born Yesterday* (1950) – both Columbia pictures – and Rod Steiger's studio boss in *The Big Knife* (1955). Cohn remains an enigma. He has never been described as a happy man, and his cruelty became legendary. But at his gaudy funeral, the tributes flowed with a mixture of affection, hypocrisy and disbelief that the man had finally succumbed. It is said that most people attended it to make sure he was dead. In the history of the cinema, however, Harry Cohn and Columbia deserve a prominent place.

BRIAN BAXTER

Some of the actresses Cohn's Columbia loved and lost: Jean Arthur (top left), overjoyed when her contract expired; Kim Novak (top) whose love-life was ruled by the studio; Barbara Stanwyck (above) who sued for more money; Rita Hayworth (below with Harry) who angered Cohn by eloping with Aly Khan

TECHNIQUE AND TRICKERY

Colour film is as old as the cinema itself and there is nothing new about wide-screen presentation, but the Thirties saw the perfection of these and other technical triumphs

From the earliest days of the cinema, film-makers had sought to add colour to moving pictures. In the spring of 1896, soon after motion pictures had been projected before the public for the first time, hand-coloured films were also presented.

Each frame in the film was coloured by hand using two, three or sometimes even four colours. The task was made more difficult by the small size of each frame – 25mm by 19mm – and the fact that nearly 1000 frames had to be coloured for a film lasting less than a minute. Nevertheless, hand-colouring remained in use for several years until the increasing length of film productions and the demand for many more copies made it impractical.

In 1905 the Pathé company adopted a method which had long been in use for colouring postcards. A series of prints of the film were made, one for each colour to be applied. From each frame in each print areas were cut out corresponding to a particular colour. These stencil films were run in turn through a staining machine in close contact with another (uncut) print in accurate synchronism. The print received colour from rotating brushes, a different dye being applied through another stencil film each time the print passed through the machine. Up to six stencils might be prepared for an elaborate effect. This was a very lengthy process, but once the stencils had been made many other prints could be coloured at high speed. The Pathécolor stencil process, and similar methods operated by rival companies, remained in use until the Thirties.

Less complex methods were used to produce general colour effects. Passing the film through a bath of dye had the effect of tinting it with an overall wash of colour. The tints were chosen to suit the subject or mood of the shot – green for landscapes, blue for night, red for fire, yellow for lamplight etc.

Chemical toning was also used, whereby the black and white silver image was converted to one in colour. In this case the image itself was coloured while the lightest parts of the picture remained white; the effect was the reverse of that produced by the tinting process in which the image remained black and white but the highlights were coloured.

While these systems gave general colour effects, the result on the screen in no way reproduced the colours of the original scene. Photographic analysis of the colours was necessary for this. The principles of colour photography are based on a theory proposed by James Clark Maxwell and demonstrated by him as early as 1861. He showed that by an appropriate mixture of red, green and blue light all the other colours could be reproduced. By superimposing three photographs (red, green and blue) projected by three lanterns onto a single screen, a recognizable reproduction was made of the original, in this case a tartan ribbon.

Initially, the direct application of Maxwell's method to the production of moving pictures presented problems, and the first commercially successful motion-picture colour process was based on the use of two colours only.

The English pioneer film-maker George Albert Smith invented the Kinemacolor process in 1906. By this method successive frames of film were exposed alternately through red and green filters held on a rotating disc in front of the film. A black and white print from the negative was run in a projector also fitted with a filter wheel. The film was set up so that the red exposure was projected through the red filter, and the green exposure through the green. The film ran at 32 frames per second (twice the normal speed) and at this speed the alternating red and green impressions blended to give the illusion of a continuous coloured image.

The range of colours which could be reproduced by such a two-colour system was limited; blues and purples in particular were impossible. But for most subjects a pleasing reproduction was achievable, although colour 'fringing' was apparent on rapidly moving objects.

The Kinemacolor process was launched commercially in 1908 and operated with great success until well into World War I. Other two-colour processes followed, in which two objects were photographed simultaneously through red and green filters and using complicated optical devices. The projector was fitted with similar lenses or devices to enable the two pictures to be projected through appropriate filters and superimposed on the screen. Unfortunately such processes always showed some colour 'fringing' on the screen. Two-colour processes which had limited commercial application included Colcin (1913), Cinechrome (1921), Busch Colour (1926) and Raycol (1929).

The Gaumont company extended the idea to a full three-colour reproduction in their Chronochrome process which they demonstrated in 1912. A triple-lens camera simultaneously recorded the subject through red, green and blue filters. A

Top: hand-tinted colour from an unidentified French film of the 1890s. Centre: stencil colouring circa 1909. Above: two-colour Technicolor from Ben Hur *(1925). Below: tinting for atmosphere in* Intolerance *(1916) and* Dante's Inferno *(1924)*

Top: red uniforms provide a splash of colour in Mamoulian's Becky Sharp (1935) – an otherwise muted colour movie. Above: Technicolor conquers the musical in The Dancing Pirate. Top right: Magnacolor was one of many new colour processes to appear in the Forties

projector with three lenses combined the results of this process on the screen and contemporary reports suggest that the colour reproduction was quite good.

These methods of adding two or three pictures together through separate lenses still produced some degree of colour 'fringing', even when the projectionist took the greatest care in adjusting the lenses. A British process overcame this problem by incorporating the red, green and blue filters into the film itself; it was called Dufaycolor and was first demonstrated in 1931. The Dufaycolor process had a regular pattern of minute red, green and blue filters on the surface of the film base. The sensitive emulsion was coated onto this filter mosaic, and was exposed through it in the camera. The processed film carried a complete record of the colours of the scene, as a pattern of coloured dots and lines. Seen from a reasonable distance, the dots and lines blended to give a continuous full-colour image. Dufaycolor was used for a number of shorts and sequences in feature films in the Thirties, and for one entire feature film, Maurice Elvey's Sons of the Sea (1939).

In common with all the other 'additive' processes. Dufaycolor suffered from one inherent drawback. The red, green and blue filters through which the images had to be projected eliminated all but a third of the light from the projector; consequently a rather dim picture was produced as compared with a black and white film projected on the same machine.

An alternative method of colour photography, the 'subtractive' principle, overcame this problem. Here, three negatives were produced, recording the red, green and blue content of the scene. These negatives were used to make three transparent positive images, coloured cyan (blue-green), magenta and yellow respectively. Since these colours were complementary to those used to record the scene, their purpose was to control the amount of the primary colours reaching the screen. For example, cyan absorbes red light, and will thus subtract red light from white light passing through it. A cyan image, therefore, varies the amount of red light reaching the screen, in the same way as does the black and white positive and the red filter in the 'additive' process. The magenta image controls green light, and the yellow the blue light. Thus three subtractively-coloured positives superimposed on the film will give a full-colour image with no great light loss and no need for complicated optical devices on the projector.

As with the additive processes, the first subtractively coloured movies were made by two-colour reproduction. The first demonstration of such a method was made by the Cinecolorgraph process in 1912 and many other two-colour processes followed in the course of the next 40 years: two-colour Kodachrome (1915), Prizma Color (1919), Polychromide (1918), Multicolor (1928), Ufacolor

(1930), Cinecolor (1932) and Trucolor (1946).

Despite its limitations two-colour photography made by the subtractive process was desirable, but there were considerable practical difficulties at first. The Technicolor company, founded in 1915 by Dr H. Kalmus, D.F. Comstock and W. Westcott, developed a practicable, two-colour subtractive system. A camera was fitted with a beam-splitting device behind the lens so that red and green exposures could be made simultaneously. These two-colour 'recordings' were printed onto separate, thin positive films in such a way as to make relief images in the gelatin coating. The lightest parts of the image were represented by a very thin gelatin layer and the darker parts by a thicker one. The two relief images were cemented back to back and dyed to produce a red-orange on one side and a green on the other.

Technicolor put an end to hand-tinting and stencilling and brought colour movies to the millions

The first film made in the so-called 'cemented positive' Technicolor process was The Toll of the Sea (1922). Other films wholly or partly in the new process included: The Ten Commandments (1923), Ben Hur (1925), The Wanderer of the Wasteland (1924) and, most successful of all, the Douglas Fairbanks movie The Black Pirate (1925). The cemented positive prints, however, tended to buckle in the projector. Technicolor therefore developed a new printing process that did not require the images to be cemented together but depended upon dye images being transferred from a 'matrix' film (bearing a relief image) to a final print film. This latter principle (known as imbibition printing owing to the absorption of dye) formed the basis of the Technicolor process from 1928.

Early Technicolor productions included: The Broadway Melody, On With the Show, Gold Diggers of Broadway (all 1929). Since the new process could be used to print three colours as well as two, Technicolor developed a camera in which three negative films could be exposed simultaneously. The three processed negatives were used to make matrix relief films which transferred the cyan, magenta and yellow dye images to the print film. The same print carried the soundtrack and, in the early Technicolor films, a black and white 'key' image to improve the definition. The new process was first used by Walt Disney for his Silly Symphony Flowers and Trees in 1932, and subsequently for many other Disney cartoons. The first live-action, three-colour Technicolor production was a short film La Cucaracha (1934) and the first full-length feature was Mamoulian's Becky Sharp (1935).

The 'three-strip' cameras remained in use until

the early Fifties, when the introduction of modern colour-negative films made them obsolete. Finally the imbibition printing process was discarded in the mid-Seventies, when the demand for prints dropped to an uneconomic level.

The idea of creating an illusion of reality by using a very large picture, filling most of the visual field of the observer, is much older than the cinema. It was the impulse behind the panoramic paintings popular in the late eighteenth century. Magic lantern shows giving a 360° picture on a cylindrical screen were presented in the 1890s.

The Frenchman Raoul Grimoin Sanson was the first to try to adapt the idea for the cinema. His Cinéorama method used ten linked cine cameras facing outward in a circle so as to cover the whole horizon. Films shot from the basket of a balloon ascending over Paris were shown on a cylindrical screen, using ten synchronized projectors at the great Paris Exposition of 1900.

In the same Exposition the Lumière brothers used a special 75mm-wide film to show the pictures on a 19.2m (65 feet) wide screen to huge audiences. Apart from these rather special shows, no significant development of wide-screen methods occurred until the early Twenties. The Widescope process of 1922 involved using a camera which recorded two films side by side. When shown in two linked projectors, the films gave a panoramic picture of twice the normal width. This process, however, did not get beyond the stage of trade demonstrations.

The Magnascope system, developed by Lorenzo del Riccio in 1926, was intended to heighten the dramatic effect of certain sequences in conventional films. The cinema was fitted with a screen much larger than normal; for most of the time the screen was restricted to the usual proportions by movable masking which was withdrawn to uncover the full screen just before the beginning of a special sequence that would then appear on the full screen at four times the size of the rest of the film. The Magnascope effect was used, for example, for the elephant stampede in *Chang* (1927), the naval battle in *Old Ironsides* (1926) and the aerial sequences in *Wings* (1927).

The French director Abel Gance used a multiple film system (designed by André Debrie) for his film *Napoléon* (1927). A screen three times normal width was used; certain sequences were shown either as a triptych of three different images, or as a single panoramic image, screened by three projectors. The film aroused great interest among film-makers, especially in America, and may well have influenced the development of wide-screen methods during the next few years. The same principle formed the basis of the Cinerama process of the Fifties. In 1927 the French scientist Henri Chrétien described a new lens design which was to have a great influence, years later, on the development of the wide screen.

His Hypergonar lens distorted the image in the camera, compressing it laterally but not vertically; thus a circle would be photographed on the film as an oval. In this way twice the normal horizontal angle of view would be recorded on the film. A similar lens, fitted to the projector, corrected the distortion and gave a panoramic picture on the screen of twice the normal width.

Chrétien's invention came into its own much later when 20th Century-Fox adopted it for their Cinema-Scope process, and the so-called 'squeeze' lens formed the basis of many wide-screen methods that were to follow.

Ever since the introduction of Edison's Kineto-scope in the 1890s the standard width of film had been 35mm. When new systems of wide-screen presentation proliferated towards the end of the Twenties they were based on the use of wider than normal film. The first to appear was Spoor and Berrgren's Natural Vision process that used a film 63.5mm wide. RKO adopted the process and used it for *Dixiana* and *Danger Lights* (both 1930).

Natural Vision had several drawbacks: the projector was very noisy, and since the soundtrack was carried on a separate film running at a different speed, any breakdown provided severe synchronization problems.

The Grandeur system developed by 20th Century-Fox went one better by using a 70mm-wide film. It was demonstrated in September 1929 with a sound newsreel and a 70mm version of *Fox Movietone Follies of 1929*. Fox then shot two of their features, *Happy Days* (1929) and *The Big Trail* (1930), on 70mm as well as on the conventional 35mm. Warner Brothers, United Artists and MGM plumped for a 65mm film with an integral soundtrack.

Warners had their own wide-screen process called Vitascope which was used for *Kismet* (1930). The film was shot in 65mm and shown in that format in a few large cinemas, but was reduced to a 35mm format for most presentations. United Artists made *The Bat Whispers* (1930) in both 35mm and 65mm versions, and MGM's Realife process was used for their Western *Billy the Kid* in the same year.

Following the example of Warners, MGM made 'reduction' prints from the 65mm negative films for release in cinemas that only had the facility for 35mm projection. Paramount, to be different, adopted a 56mm film process developed by del Riccio and christened Magnafilm. But after their first demonstration film *You're in the Army Now* (1930), Paramount made little use of the Magnafilm process.

These wide-film developments came at a time when cinemas had scarcely recovered from the cost of re-equipping with sound systems, and it was a time of general recession. It is hardly surprising that so few cinema owners were willing to incur the costs of larger projectors and new screens. By 1931, the early wide films were obsolete and interest did not revive until the advent of television prompted the search for further technical innovations.

BRIAN COE

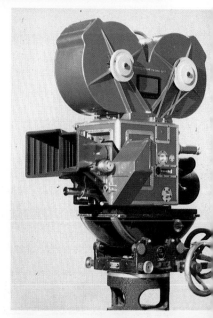

Top left: Marlene Dietrich holds up a colour test card for The Garden of Allah *(1936). Top: colour frame from* The Trail of the Lonesome Pine *(1936), the first Technicolor feature shot on location. Centre: a Technicolor camera of 1938. Above: a test film for the Fox Grandeur wide-screen system.*

a

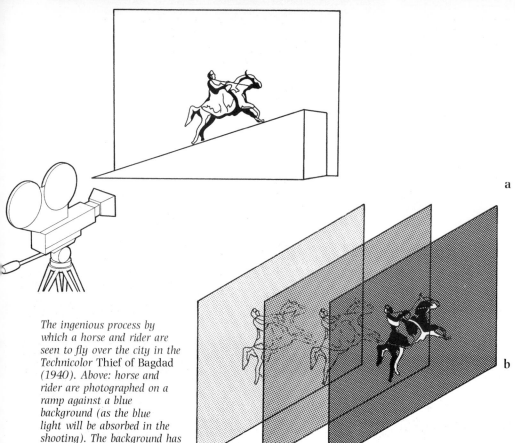

The ingenious process by which a horse and rider are seen to fly over the city in the Technicolor Thief of Bagdad *(1940). Above: horse and rider are photographed on a ramp against a blue background (as the blue light will be absorbed in the shooting). The background has to be the same size as the final image area, so the backing screen is erected against the actual set*

b

Above: three separate colour records (blue, red, and green) are obtained via the process described below (camera diagram). On the three strips the horse and rider register as negative images. Separately two mattes are then derived from the negative: (a) a transparent horse against an opaque background and (b) an opaque horse against a clear background

Special effects

The advent of talkies made open-air shooting a complex business and shooting sound in the studios was preferable for a while. There was, therefore, an increasing need to combine action recorded in the studio with exterior background scenes. Moreover the trend towards bigger productions, especially musicals and historical epics, called for the extension of studio sets by technical trickery rather than by actually building bigger sets. Towards the end of the Thirties the greater use of colour photography added its own special demands.

Back projection for example, was widespread: the background scene (previously photographed) was projected from behind onto a translucent screen in front of which the foreground action was performed. The camera thus recorded both foreground and background at the same time.

For a static background a large transparency on a glass plate was used. But for backgrounds showing movement a movie projector running a film print was required and had to be exactly synchronized with the camera mechanism. There were practical problems: the background had to appear absolutely steady in relation to the foreground actors; it also had to be projected large enough to cover all the actors' movement and to be uniformly illuminated at a bright enough level for it to be re-photographed satisfactorily. Special projector mechanisms were devised to ensure the steadiness of the back image, and screen materials were developed that gave a uniform distribution of light, though the difficulty of achieving adequate brightness remained.

During the early days of the three-colour Technicolor process the most powerful back projectors could only cover a screen 1.8m (6 feet) wide. This was sufficient for the moving background seen through a car or train window, but hardly adequate for a complete outdoor scene.

Towards the end of this period, however, both Paramount and Warners invented so-called 'triple-head' systems of projection by which three separate projectors each superimposed their own copy of the background picture on the same screen. In this way the brightness was greatly increased and the apparent graininess of the image was reduced.

By the late Thirties Paramount's *Men With Wings* and Warners 'outdoor' features *Gold is Where You Find it* and *Valley of the Giants* (all 1938) proved that back projection could now be used on screens of more than 10 metres (33 feet) wide, and with Technicolor photography.

Another method combining foreground action with moving backgrounds was the Dunning process, originated by Lionel Dunning about 1928. A camera loaded with two films (known as a bi-pack) was used in this process. The front film in the camera was a previously exposed positive image in yellow-orange dye of the background scene. Behind, and running in contact with it, was an unexposed negative film.

On the set the foreground action was lit with yellow light only and was played against a brightly illuminated blue backdrop. In the camera the yellow dye image of the background scene was exposed on the negative by the blue light from the backdrop, but was transparent to the yellow light from the foreground action which was recorded at the same time.

The glass shot, or painted matte, was a much used way of extending the apparent size of a studio set. This process required a large sheet of optical glass to be firmly mounted in front of the camera. On the glass sheet were painted additional details of the scene which matched the actual set. The set itself

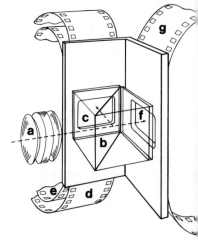

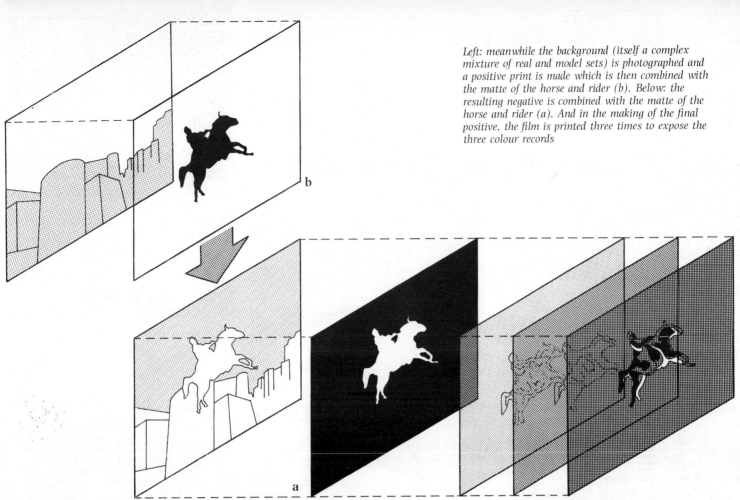

Left: meanwhile the background (itself a complex mixture of real and model sets) is photographed and a positive print is made which is then combined with the matte of the horse and rider (b). Below: the resulting negative is combined with the matte of the horse and rider (a). And in the making of the final positive, the film is printed three times to expose the three colour records

Left: diagram of the three-strip Technicolor camera developed in the late Thirties. Light from the subject photographed passes through the lens (a) and enters the beam-splitting prism (b), where part of the light is reflected to the gate (c) that carries a bi-pack of two films – the front film (d) is blue-sensitive and the rear film (e), red-sensitive. The remaining light is transmitted to the aperture (f) and exposes the green-sensitive film (g). In this way, separate red, green and blue records are obtained

would have been built just large enough to contain the live action. When complete, the painting was illuminated and photographed at the same time as the actors in front of the real portion of the set seen through the glass. In the hands of a skilled artist, the results could be most effective: for example, the upper parts of buildings could be 'added on', a sky could be placed above a street, and so on. Naturally enough, glass shots brought about great economy in studio set construction.

For exterior shots it was not normally possible to match the character of the scene by painting in advance. Instead the practice was to reserve the area to be painted by masking off a portion of the glass when the camera was shooting through it. The partly exposed negative was then kept undeveloped except for a few short test lengths, which were processed so that the artist could match the scenes in his painting. When the painting was complete, the film would be double-exposed with the original scene on the retained negative.

Another method of combining studio live action with paintings or models at the time of shooting was the mirror shot, or Schüfftan process. Named after its German inventor, the cameraman Eugen Schüfftan, this technique worked on the following principle: a large silvered mirror was mounted at 45° in front of the camera on the set, so as to reflect the model in its field of view. Parts of the reflecting surface were then carefully removed so that the live-action sequences could be photographed through the mirror (lined up with the model).

In the early days of cinema, film-makers had very limited means of making transitions from one scene to another. All such effects had to be done in the camera at the time of photography: a scene would be faded in or out, for example, by opening or closing the lens diaphragm or camera shutter.

As better-quality duplicating films were introduced by film-stock manufacturers, it became the practice to make effects after the event by using an optical printer. This machine was effectively a movie camera aligned to photograph (frame by frame) a positive-print film in a projector.

Fades were made by opening or closing the shutter of the camera head. Simple wipes (a line moving across the film indicating change of location or time) were achieved by mechanically moving a metal blade across the projector aperture. More elaborate wipes with complex edge patterns (for example, wiggly lines) required the use of a matte process whereby a secondary strip of film (with opaque areas corresponding to the progressive wipe) would be run in contact with the positive of the first scene to reserve the appropriate portions of the picture. A complementary matte (clear where the first was opaque) was used when exposing from the second scene.

In principle a matte is merely a mask, used either in original photography or in optical printing to expose one area of the film image and leave the rest unexposed so that 'trick' shots may be executed.

Originally, matte shots were done by placing a stencil box in front of the camera and shooting through it, as in the case of the 'keyhole' or 'binoculars' effect. More frequently the matte is a photographic image on film that is placed in the light path of the optical printer to expose only one part of the picture, so that paintings or other moving images may be photographed on the unexposed part of the film to achieve trick juxtapositions.

With the availability of the optical printer, advanced forms of combination trick effects involving the use of travelling mattes became possible even for productions in Technicolor. At the end of the Thirties, Alexander Korda's production of *The Thief of Bagdad* (1940) exemplified the peak of special-effects film-making.

BERNARD HAPPÉ

167

In Glorious Technicolor

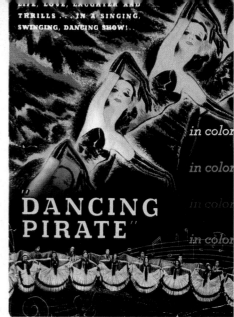

The full emergence of Technicolor as the pre-eminent name in colour film-making dates from 1932 with the development of the three-strip process. Where previously only two primary colours – red and green – had been possible, the third, blue, was now introduced. As a result 'natural' colours were possible for the first time.

Despite the increase in expense – filming in Technicolor added about fifty per cent to the negative cost – Hollywood was eager to experiment with the new medium. With varying degrees of success, every kind of film – costume pictures, musicals, Westerns, even screwball comedy – was seen by audiences for the first time 'In Glorious Technicolor'.

Disney paved the way with the animated film *Flowers and Trees* (1932). Then in 1935 Rouben Mamoulian, another film-maker always eager to try something new, completed the feature which is acknowledged as the first modern colour film – *Becky Sharp*. Mamoulian had definite theories concerning the aesthetic role of colour. In *Picturegoer Weekly* of July 13, 1935 he wrote:

'. . . there is a definite emotional content and meaning in colour and shades . . . the director of a colour picture must be acutely aware of, and take advantage of, the emotional implications of colours and use them to enhance the emotional in dramatic effectiveness of a scene or situation.'

Virtually the whole of *Becky Sharp* is confined to studio interiors, allowing Mamoulian and designer Robert Edmund Jones exceptional control over colour and mood. However, Mamoulian's anti-realistic, symbolic approach was misunderstood or was not entirely successful; *Becky Sharp* had little immediate influence on future colour productions.

The effectiveness of Technicolor in capturing the colours and textures of natural settings was first exploited in *The Trail of the Lonesome Pine* (1936). Critics were quick to praise the film's colour landscape photography. *Today's Cinema* of April 18, 1936 commented that 'the colouring of mountain, forest and lake is in many cases supremely beautiful'. The actors did not come off so well – the same review noted that they appeared 'flushed or unpleasantly anaemic . . . It seems impossible to produce the red that is correctly suggestive either of health, blood or fire; black too seems difficult . . . for most dark-haired players sport all the iridescence of the beetle's wing.'

The Trail of the Lonesome Pine was followed in 1936 by a diverse group of colour films which have been largely forgotten. These include the first three-strip Technicolor musical, *The Dancing Pirate* produced by Pioneer Pictures/RKO

(of which no prints appear to survive); *Ramona* from 20th Century-Fox, *The Garden of Allah* produced by David O. Selznick, and Warner Brothers' *God's Country and the Woman*. Thus each of the major studios (apart from MGM) had made an attempt to jump onto the colour bandwagon. However, *Ramona*, *The Garden of Allah* and *God's Country and the Woman* were all adapted from weak stories and failed at the box-office; *Garden of Allah*, in particular, was a financial disaster having cost over $2 million. Selznick was quick to redeem his reputation, with *A Star Is Born* and *Nothing Sacred* (both 1937, and both directed by William Wellman). *A Star Is Born* was nominated for seven Oscars and won two – for best original story (Wellman) and a special award for colour cinematography. In both films colour was used in a restrained and realistic way in keeping with their stories about contemporary life in America, providing a unique picture of what the world of the Thirties looked like in colour.

For most film companies 1937 was a boom year; the recession which followed in 1938 hit the industry hard. Despite this, the number of Technicolor films grew steadily throughout the late Thirties and early Forties. Perhaps the novelty value of colour was regarded as a means of fighting the slump – certainly the three aspiring majors, Fox, Paramount and Warners, saw colour as a means of competing in prestige with the top company MGM, where the attitude was, 'if our films make money in black and white, what do we need colour for?'

Warners first big prestige colour film was *The Adventures of Robin Hood* (1938) which cost over $1.5 million. The striking colour photography – with much of the picture filmed on location – was achieved by Sol Polito, Tony

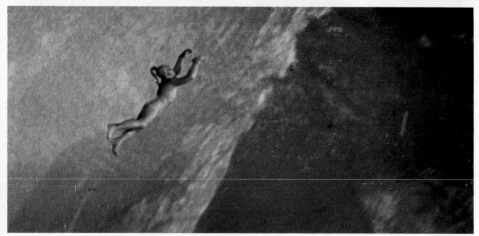

Gaudio and W. Howard Greene. The film strikes an ideal balance between intimate moments, spectacle and action sequences, and between a toned-down, restrained use of colour and the brighter, more lavish scenes featuring the costumes of Milo Anderson.

Despite all this, the reaction of film audiences at the time was disappointing; the picture hardly managed to recoup its substantial cost. A new incentive for filming in colour – with a new emphasis on musical fantasy – was supplied by the smash success of Disney's *Snow White and the Seven Dwarfs* (1937). In addition Selznick finally embarked on filming *Gone With the Wind* (released in 1939).

From the beginning of his work on the project, Selznick had been firmly committed to colour. He was particularly insistent that the film should not be confined to the kind of neutral and pastel shades favoured by the colour consultants assigned to the project by the Technicolor company. He commented:

'This picture in particular gives us the opportunity occasionally to throw a violent dab of colour at the audience to sharply make a dramatic point.'

The film's director, Victor Fleming, accomplished the remarkable feat of making the other most famous movie of 1939 – *The Wizard of Oz*, MGM's most expensive film up to that date. In view of its substantial cost the film was not a commercial success on its initial release, reinforcing MGM's prejudice against the added cost of Technicolor.

In marked contrast to MGM's reluctance, the producer Darryl Zanuck had, towards the end of 1938, embarked on a series of Technicolor pictures at 20th Century-Fox which continued into the Forties and averaged five or six films per year. This represented the first substantial and lasting commitment to colour by any of the major studios and established the pattern of colour-filming for the Forties. Although he concentrated on musicals and Westerns, Zanuck nevertheless provided the opportunity for a number of important directors to express their individual styles in colour for the first time, including John Ford (*Drums Along the Mohawk*, 1939), Fritz Lang (*The Return of Frank James*, 1940), Ernst Lubitsch (*Heaven Can Wait*, 1943) and Busby Berkeley (*The Gang's All Here*, 1943).

Ford in particular made effective use of location filming with the emphasis on a tonal range of greens and browns, of heavily wooded forests and log cabins. The peace of the community is disrupted by the appearance of enemy redskins, with the striking image of home and crops on fire – the red and the orange flames outlined against a pale blue sky.

Wings of the Morning (1937), produced by 20th Century-Fox, was the first British Technicolor film. A story of horse-training and racing, it is memorable mainly for some outstanding photography of Irish locations. During the following years only a small number of British productions were filmed in colour. The one producer of note in this respect was Alexander Korda. His company was allied with the Technicolor corporation for the production of five features between 1938 and 1940. The most successful were *The Four Feathers* (1939) an action-packed tale of the British Empire, and *The Thief of Bagdad* (1940). Despite a strong cast, the real stars of *The Four Feathers* were the four cameramen who teamed with the art director Vincent Korda to give the film a stunning appearance – especially in the sequences filmed in Egypt and the Sudan, including a spectacular battle climax.

Korda was equally successful with *The Thief of Bagdad*, co-directed by Michael Powell, Ludwig Berger and Tim Whelan. The combination of cameraman Georges Périnal and Vincent Korda produced colour effects which matched the fantasy and spectacle of this story, inspired by *The Arabian Nights*. The film spawned a host of imitations in Hollywood during the early Forties. Inevitably the outbreak of war seriously affected British production of colour films – even *The Thief of Bagdad* had to be completed by Korda in the USA.

The preference for escapist entertainment during the war meant that colour films were predominantly musicals or other lightweight fare. Many of the leading directors of the Forties avoided colour entirely, including Capra, Cukor, Huston and Wyler, while Hawks, Sturges, Welles and Wilder directed only one minor colour film apiece. Even Ford, Lang, and cameraman James Wong Howe, all of whom had done some distinguished colour work during the late Thirties, returned to black and white.

The first substantial move into colour did not take place until the early and middle Fifties to counteract the effects of TV on movie audiences. There remained a widespread prejudice against colour for certain types of film – particularly gangster pictures and psychological dramas. Both from an artistic point of view and also from 'realistic' considerations – owing perhaps to the fact that documentaries were filmed in black and white – colour was frequently disparaged by critics. A typical comment was made by James Agee:

'Colour is very nice for costume pieces and musical comedies, and has a great aesthetic future in films, but it still gets fatally in the way of any serious imitation of reality.'

The contradictions inherent in this statement would not be realized for several years.

JOEL FINLER

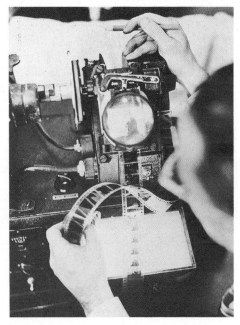

The sound of change

Above and left: a cutter at work at MGM, where cutting rooms were very similar to those Robert Parrish knew at the RKO studios. The cutter here is viewing his film through the magnifying glass of the movieola – chinagraph pencil poised to mark his cutting point. Behind him (on the left) are the film bins on which the trims are hung

Robert Parrish is the complete movie man. As a child actor he tormented Chaplin in *City Lights* and tore up the town with Our Gang. At the age of 35 he turned director, making an impressive debut with *Cry Danger* (1951). The intervening years, however, were spent as a cutter. He was, indeed, one of the best film editors in the business, winning an Academy Award for *Body and Soul* (1947). Here he remembers hard times in the cutting room – when sound arrived

The cutting rooms at RKO had been built, before the advent of sound pictures, as working areas for two people – the cutter and his assistant. There was a work-bench for each, two or three chairs, racks for cans of film, several film bins with wire hooks on which to hang trims (left-over bits of film) and a 'silent' movieola.

The movieola is an editing machine through which the positive print of the film is run. It magnifies the moving images so that the cutter can select the sections he wants to use. It was called a 'silent' movieola only because the images under the magnifying glass didn't talk. The machine itself sounded like a Thompson sub-machine gun.

When sound came in, everything doubled, tripled or quadrupled – except the size of the cutting rooms. Now there was not one piece of film (the picture), there were two pieces of film (dialogue and picture). Later there was even more film, for music and sound effects.

With the new pieces of film arrived new experts: dialogue writers, sound-effects editors, music editors, composers, conductors, dance directors and many others. At one time or another they all seemed to find their way into the cutting room – the same ten-foot-square cubicle where the cutter and his assistant formerly led their quiet, isolated lives.

In these early days, music was the cutter's biggest headache. The cutter was at that time considered at best a technician. Although some were educated, a few even musically educated, most cutters from the silent era had come up through the ranks of the young motion-picture industry. They were former stunt men, prop men, extras and grips. They worked hard, but were often allowed the freedom to work when and as they wished as long as they completed their work when it was required.

In any event, they resented the sudden influx of strangers into their cutting rooms. They especially resented the musicians because they came in droves, loaded down with arrangements, metronomes, stop watches and, most annoying of all, expert advice on exactly where the music, and therefore the picture, must be cut.

One real expert who spent a good deal of time in the cutting room at RKO was Fred Astaire. Astaire was not only a great dancer, a fine singer and actor and a delightful man, he was also a perfectionist – especially about the sound-synchronization and quality of his dancing 'taps'. After he had rehearsed a dance thoroughly he would make several recordings of the taps alone – without music. Then he would sit in a projection room with George Emick, or one of the other music cutters, and select the best recorded taps for each section of his dance. After this was done, he and the music cutter would cut the chosen bits of film together. When they had what they considered the best possible complete 'tap track', they would go to the dubbing room and listen to it with the music track and (if Astaire also sang in the number) the vocal track. Once this was done, he would summon the musical director and his covey of colleagues and they would descend upon the clutter in his ten-foot-square cutting room.

The climax in the cutter–versus–musician conflict at RKO came at 1.30 am on Sunday, August 8, 1935. *Top Hat* had been previewed at the Pantages cinema on Hollywood Boulevard. Like the previous Astaire–Rogers films (and the ones that came after), *Top Hat* was a glorious success. The producers, executives, stars, their agents, the musicians and their followers gathered on the sidewalk in front of the cinema to congratulate each other. The director, the cutter and his assistant remained in the foyer for a serious talk.

The cutter said that Ginger's solo number in reel two dragged, and the director agreed. The cutter suggested cutting one and a half choruses. The director thought he was right, but didn't think it would be possible because he had promised that the negative of the picture would be shipped to New York over the weekend. He reminded the cutter that only musicians could cut music, and that musicians wouldn't work on Sunday. The cutter said that was the best news he had heard since the days of silent films, and that he would cut the music himself.

He ordered ten prints of Ginger's number, cut it where it suited the picture, and listened to it on the movieola. The first seven experiments were unsuccessful. The cuts 'bounced'. Even the non-musical cutter realized that. He studied the music track and chose another frame. The result of the eighth experiment sounded fine, so he had the negative cut and shipped to New York on Sunday night. The film was a huge commercial success and the cutter was established as an expert on musicals. Thereafter musicians were admitted to his cutting room by invitation only.

ROBERT PARRISH

Animating the Ape

Filming *King Kong* involved many ingenious trick effects. Ray Harryhausen, world-famous special-effects man, describes the film's technical innovations

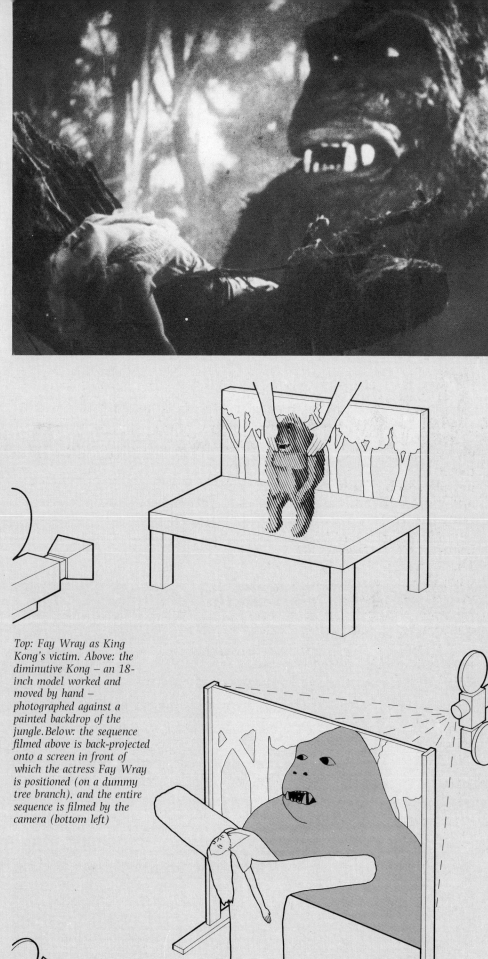

In 1933 RKO presented *King Kong* as 'the Eighth Wonder of the World'. Of course audiences knew that he was not actually alive. Yet Kong, like his prehistoric companions, looked so amazingly lifelike that the public, for almost half a century, has credited him with a reality and personality of his own.

The illusion was basically achieved by the extensive use of the process of stop-motion animation. Successive still poses are photographed on motion picture, frame by frame. The process is similar to that of the animated cartoon, but unlike the cartoon the subject to be given movement is made in a full three-dimensional form; and this dimension gives an appearance of greater reality.

Over the years I have come to prefer the word 'Dynamation' for this process capable of giving the illusion of a living form to something which could in all probability not be found in nature, or photographed in the ordinary way. I have adopted this term because Charles Schneer, my associate for many years, and myself found so often that the word 'animation' was interpreted to mean the use of cartoon animation.

On screen King Kong appears 50 feet (15.24m) tall. In reality he stood a mere 18in (45cm) – a scale model. He was the creation of Willis J. O'Brien, a wizard at technical effects since 1914, who had devised the prehistoric creatures for *The Lost World* in 1925. The great ape's interior skeleton was constructed of steel, with complicated friction ball-and-socket joints. His flesh was of rubber; and his exterior was covered in clipped rabbit fur (which gave the animators some problems because it tended to show their finger-marks). The figure would hold in any position in which he was placed: to keep him upright, as his weight moved from foot to foot, required a baseboard with holes into which he could be firmly fixed and yet remain mobile.

For some close-up scenes – for instance where Fay Wray is held in the creature's hand, or actors are seen struggling as he grips them in his teeth – full-size animated sections of the beast were required. For the scene where the ape chews people, a huge model was constructed, and operated by motors and compressed air. It required 40 bear hides to cover it,

Top: Fay Wray as King Kong's victim. Above: the diminutive Kong – an 18-inch model worked and moved by hand – photographed against a painted backdrop of the jungle. Below: the sequence filmed above is back-projected onto a screen in front of which the actress Fay Wray is positioned (on a dummy tree branch), and the entire sequence is filmed by the camera (bottom left)

Above: Kong shaking people off a tree trunk. The ape model is worked by hand against a painted backdrop and the sequence is filmed through a painted glass plate edged with real foliage. The whole sequence is printed together with the matte shots (top left) of actors walking up a ramp

and four men to make it move convincingly. The eyebrows raised or lowered at will; the great 'twelve-inch' eyeballs rolled and blinked, and the jaws seemed to change expression as they clamped down on the unfortunate natives. Similarly, internally operated sections of arms and legs were built in full-size, all to maintain the impression of Kong's gargantuan appearance.

To combine these disparate elements, so different in scale, required some very elaborate mathematical work, and the use of the whole repertory of special photography as it was then known – though the work on *Kong* in itself developed the range of special effects. A usual method was to obscure a part of the camera lens with a painted glass while filming one element of the scene – perhaps the animated miniature. The 'blackout' would mean that a certain portion of each frame remained unexposed. The film could therefore be run back to the start; a different mask was placed over the lens to correspond to the material already shot; and the film was then exposed for a second time, to photograph the setting.

This technique is the basis of the 'matte' shot; and already in 1933 very much more sophisticated developments of the system were available, using colour filters. The principle was that an image photographed under orange-yellow light would pass through orange-dyed positive film and print as normal on the negative film. On the second exposure, blue light reflected from the scene's background

would be blocked out by the image on the (orange-dyed) positive film and register as a negative image on the negative film. Through this technique, for example, figures could be made to interact with backgrounds in a way that could not have been filmed normally.

King Kong was one of the earliest – at RKO the first – films to use much back projection. This technique, employed extensively in the later Thirties and Forties, involved projecting a filmed background onto a large translucent screen, while the actors performed and were filmed in front of it. *King Kong* made use of a new form of cellulose back-projection screen which won its inventor, Sidney Saunders, an Academy Award. Previously sand-blasted glass screens had been employed, and apart from giving rather poor technical results, exposed actors and crew to grave peril from breakage.

Almost an inversion of this process was the projection of live-action shots of actors onto a tiny screen within a miniature model of the setting. This was used for the sequence in which we see Fay Wray dangled from the Empire State Building by Kong. Subsequently known as 'miniature projection' the technique was used again by Willis J. O'Brien in another gorilla movie, *Mighty Joe Young* (1949).

The spectacular jungle scenes were achieved by the use of paintings on three or four separated planes of fine plate glass. Miniature sets – trees made of paper and lacquer, thin copper, the twisted roots of old vines – were then sandwiched in between them. The technique was probably to an extent influenced by the work of early Victorian illustrators, in which the impression of depth is achieved by a dark foreground, a medium-toned middle ground and a pale, diffused background. The method produced an illusion of great depth in the fabulous, mystic jungles.

Thus it was that a team of twentieth-century necromancers employed all the magic of the painter, the model-maker, the camera, the laboratory, and the tricks of the animator – as well as intense patience – to achieve a work of magnificent scenic value and fantastic imagination that has stood the test of time. They had achieved a milestone in the creation of the grand illusion.   RAY HARRYHAUSEN

Above and right: in this scene of the ape on the rampage in New York, the illusion of perspective is achieved by matching a painted backdrop of the Hudson River shoreline to a glass painting of skyscrapers and in turn to the model of Kong. The model aircraft were moved on wires, and a doll replaced Miss Wray

The Art of Animation

Reynaud's skipping girl bounce slightly each time her feet hit the ground.

Thus, when moving pictures proper arrived, there was a pre-existing tradition of animation. It took slight ingenuity and the example of Georges Méliès' magic films to suggest the idea of photographing series drawings onto film, frame by frame, to give movement to the cartoonist's creations.

Above: Winsor McCay's Gertie the Dinosaur. *Left: Dave Fleischer's feature* Gulliver's Travels. *Below left: the Phenakistiscope, a toy demonstrating a primitive form of animated cartoon in the 1830s. Below: Disney's* Snow White and the Seven Dwarfs

Animation is older than cinema itself. There were moving drawings long before the days of *The Great Train Robbery*. But film made many new techniques available to artists and cartoonists, and by the mid-Thirties animated films in many different styles were being produced all over the world

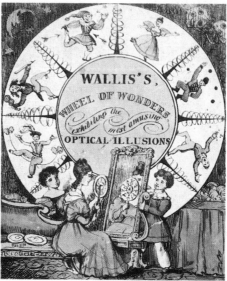

Animation is the oldest art of moving pictures. In the eighteenth century crude mechanical movement was produced in the images projected by the magic lanterns of travelling showmen. Sixty years before the Kinetoscope and the Cinématographe, scientists demonstrated the basic optical principles from which the cinema was to be developed by means of toys which used short sequences of cartoon drawings to produce the illusion of movement. In these toys – the Phenakistiscope and Stroboscope of 1832 and the Zoëtrope, first described in 1834 – the essential principle of the animated cartoon is already fully stated.

In the 1880s the Frenchman Emile Reynaud (1844–1918) succeeded in projecting onto a screen the moving drawings produced by his invention the Praxinoscope; and by 1892 he was able to present his Pantomimes Lu-

mineuses – little plays performed by animated cartoon characters, the direct forerunner of modern film animation.

Apart from his technical ingenuity, Emile Reynaud, as an artist, was the first great animator, accurately reproducing in his little drawings the sense of real-life movement. A present-day animator, Richard Williams, still marvels at the lifelike way that the braids of

(1907), experimented with giving life to normally inanimate objects. In 1910 Emile Cohl made *Le Tout Petit Faust* (*The Little Faust*) in which little dolls or puppets were animated instead of drawings. The great master of puppet animation, however, was the Russian Ladislav Starevitch (1892–1965) who made a series of delightful films of anthropomorphic insects and animals that recalled the work of the nineteenth-century French illustrator Grandville. In the Soviet Union Starevitch's most notable follower was Alexander Ptushko (b.1900) whose feature *The New Gulliver* (1935) achieved international reputation. In this, as in his later *The Little Gold Key* (1939), Ptushko combined live actors with his animated dolls.

Ptushko's example inspired a whole school of puppet animation in the Soviet Union and, much later, in Czechoslovakia. Elsewhere the practice was sporadic. In France Jean Painlevé and René Bertrand used plasticine dolls for *Barbe Bleue* (1938). In Britain Len Lye and Humphrey Jennings collaborated on *Birth of a Robot* (1936). In Holland production was more consistent thanks to the work of the Hungarian Georg Pal (b.1908) and Joop Geesink (b.1913), their work often being sponsored

Early this century the English-born pioneer of American cinema, J. Stuart Blackton (1875–1941), originally a newspaper cartoonist, made *Humorous Phases of Funny Faces* (1906) and *The Magic Fountain Pen* (1909). More significant, however, was the work of Emile Cohl (1857–1938), a well-known newspaper cartoonist in Paris and already 50 years old when he made his first cartoon film, *Fantasmagorie*, in 1908. In the course of the next ten years, first in France and then in the USA, Cohl made hundreds of short films. Working in the most basic of graphic styles, he had a gift for giving vigorous characterization to little creatures who were often no more than circles, lines and dots traced on the film.

From strip to screen
These pioneer days of the cinema coincided with the great period of the comic strip, and newspaper cartoonists in every country – in England, for example, Harry Furniss and Tom Webster – undertook the laborious work of bringing their characters to life on the screen. The most successful was the American artist Winsor McCay (1871–1934) whose masterpiece was *Gertie the Dinosaur* (*c*.1909), originally filmed for use in a vaudeville act in which McCay talked to, petted and fed the large, flirtatious and bashful prehistoric beast.

Other characters, even before Mickey Mouse and his entourage, rivalled the status of live film stars. Prototypes were: Baby Snookums, originated between 1912 and 1914 by Emile Cohl and George McManus; Colonel Heeza Liar, John Randolph Bray's skit on Theodore Roosevelt; Bud Fisher's long-lasting Mutt and Jeff; George Herriman's Krazy Kat; and Max

Fleischer's Koko the Clown and Betty Boop. The greatest cartoon star of silent films, however, was Felix the Cat, created by the Australian-born Pat Sullivan (1887–1933).

Mickey Mouse, animated for Disney by Ub Iwerks, came in 1928; and his popularity and the success of the first Silly Symphonies enabled Disney to effect a revolution in animation. Throughout the Thirties Disney dominated the field, and his technical and industrial innovations and achievements culminated in the first cartoon feature film, *Snow White and the Seven Dwarfs* (1937), followed by the innovatory *Fantasia* (1940).

No-one could rival Disney; but the audiences now demanded cartoons in every cinema programme, and each major company established its own animation production. Fired by Disney's success with *Snow White*, the Fleischer studio later embarked on feature production with the admirable *Gulliver's Travels* (1939); but after the commercial failure of *Mr Bug Goes to Town* (1941) the Fleischers concentrated on the production of shorts.

Puppet masters
There were other styles of animation. Influenced by the trick films of Méliès, a number of early film-makers, including Segundo de Chomon in *El Hotel Electrico* (1905, The Electric Hotel) and J. Stuart Blackton in *Haunted Hotel*

Top: Disney's Fantasia *combined cartoon and classical music to remarkable effect. Above right: Alexander Ptushko's* The New Gulliver. *Right: the animal puppets of Ladislav Starevitch. Below: cartoon images drawn by Emile Reynaud for his Praxinoscope*

by big industrial firms. After 1940 Pal worked in the USA, lending his ingenuity to science fiction films like *Destination Moon* (1950).

Lotte Reiniger (b.1899), whose creative career now spans more than sixty years, went back to one of the most venerable forms of light show, the oriental shadow theatre. Even before she began her first experiments in 1918, other film-makers had used crude cut-out silhouettes for film animation; but Reiniger, an artist of genius, transformed the style. Using scissors as

freely as other artists might use pen or brush, she created a world of exquisite, filigree beings who were animated, step by step, on a 'trick table' largely developed by herself and her collaborators – husband Carl Koch (1892–1963), Walter Ruttmann and Bertold Bartosch. In 1926 Reiniger made the first *true* feature-length animated film, *Die Arbenteuer des Prinzen Achmed* (*The Adventures of Prince Achmed*), a work whose quality has not diminished more than half a century later. With the coming of sound she experimented with music and her *Harlekin* (1931, *Harlequin*), *Carmen* (1933) and *Papageno* (1935) are perfect choreographic creations. Since World War II she has worked in Britain and, occasionally, Canada.

Making waves
Reiniger's main creative collaborator on *Prince Achmed* was Bartosch (1893–1968) who excelled in producing effects of atmosphere, snow scenes, sea waves and the like. Before working with Reiniger, Bartosch had made a number of advertising films. Afterwards he went on to make his masterpiece *L'Idée* (1932, *The Idea*), a tragic, symbolist allegory of man's struggle for the Ideal, based on illustrations by Franz Masereel and with music by Arthur Honegger. Bartosch combined cut-out silhouettes on the lines of the Reiniger technique with subtle effects achieved by control of photographic exposure and diffusion of the light source.

It was watching Bartosch at work on *L'Idée* that stimulated the Russian emigré illustrator Alexandre Alexeieff (b.1901) to try his hand at animation. Working with his future wife, Claire Parker, he made his most remarkable contribution with the 'pinboard' – a soft board studded with thousands of headless pins which are raised or deflected so that the reflection of light on their surfaces produces an image

Above: some of the animated cut-out silhouettes created by Lotte Reiniger. Above right: Len Lye and Humphrey Jennings' Birth of a Robot. Right: one of Georg Pal's characters from his Puppetoon series

that may be subtly changed. The technique enabled Alexeieff and Parker to give the i̇ es of their *Une Nuit sur le Mont Chauve* (1933, ht on *a Bare Mountain*) the range and subtlety of a dry-point etching. Later they were to use their pinboard for *En Passant* (1943), made for the National Film Board of Canada, *Le Nez* (1963, *The Nose*) and *Pictures at an Exhibition* (1972).

The early work of Bartosch and Alexeieff was among the most sophisticated animation of the inter-war period, comparable with the abstract films made in Germany in the early Twenties. The earliest abstract animated film appears to have been *Opus I* shown by the painter Walter Ruttmann (1887–1941) in 1921. It is now not quite clear what system of animation Ruttmann used for this 'absolute' film and its successors, *Opus II*, *Opus III* and *Opus IV*, which occupied him between 1921 and 1925. Ruttmann also provided the 'Hawk Dream' sequence of Lang's *Die Nibelungen* (1924), and later worked with Lotte Reiniger.

Meanwhile, two other painters, who had been associated with the Dada group in Zurich, were also seeking a form of dynamic graphic art through animated film. Viking Eggeling (1880–1925), a friend of Modigliani and Arp, completed only one film, *Diagonal Symphonie*,

which had its first public show in Berlin at the moment he was dying of blood poisoning. For his contemporaries the film revealed new spatial relationships in abstract art.

Hans Richter (1888–1976) was deeply involved with Eggeling and his experiments. Both, in Richter's words, 'saw in the completely liberated (abstract) form not only a new medium to be exploited, but the challenge towards a ''universal language'' '. Richter's *Rhythmus 21*, completed in 1921 (the year that Eggeling had made the first version of *Diagonal Symphonie*) was followed by *Rhythmus 23*, *Rhythmus 25* and *Rhythmus 26*. Later Richter incorporated his experiments into advertising films, and for the rest of his life – especially after his emigration to America in 1940 – was an inspirational figure for the young avant-garde film-makers of successive generations. Oscar Fischinger (1900–67), an engineer and draughtsman, was inspired by the work of Eggeling and Richter to embark on his series of eight *Studies* (1927–32), numbered 5 to 12.

Lye's painted film
The film work of Len Lye (b.1901), a New Zealander, was altogether more intuitive. He had been variously inspired by Oceanic Island art, Australian travelogues and Soviet art, and spent a year on a South Sea island before making his way to England in the mid-Twenties. The Film Society helped him with the costs of a ten-minute cartoon, *Tusalava* (1929); then he managed to interest John Grierson in his revolutionary (and attractively inexpensive) notion of painting directly onto film. The results were *Colour Box*, *Kaleidoscope* (both 1935) and *Trade Tattoo* (1937).

Lye moved to the USA in 1944. Though he later seemed discouraged by lack of interest in his work, he resumed film-making in the late Fifties. His influence has, perhaps, been strongest through the work of his successor, Norman McLaren, who followed him to John Grierson's GPO Film Unit in 1937, and whose work in abstract film has been seminal to the development of animation since the beginning of the Forties.
DAVID ROBINSON

IMAGES OF FRANCE

Outside of Hollywood, the Thirties belonged to the French cinema, and the atmosphere of romantic fatalism created by France's famous directors seemed appropriate to the prevailing mood of the time

The structure of the film industry in France changed markedly with the arrival of sound in 1930. The extra costs of talkie production eliminated many of the smaller film companies, though others continued to proliferate throughout the decade, albeit undercapitalized and short-lived; in 1936 alone, for example, 175 new film companies were founded.

Financial considerations also led to the creation of two massive and vertically-integrated companies (embracing production, distribution and exhibition) formed out of the pioneering companies of Charles Pathé and Léon Gaumont. Both the resulting companies, however, withdrew from film production in the mid-Thirties, partly as a result of the illegal financial manipulations of Bernard Natan who had taken over the Pathé company in 1929.

From an output of some fifty feature films in 1929, French film production doubled by 1931 and more than tripled by 1933. But the native film industry never supplied any more than 25 per cent of the movies distributed annually in France. Moreover these were years of chaos and disorder in the industry: technical crews struggled with the limitations of unwieldy new sound-recording equipment; cinema owners required considerable capital to convert their buildings to sound; and producers contrived to add sound to projects conceived originally as silent films. For a while the cumbersome business of multi-language shooting occupied the studios until dubbing and subtitling enabled French films to be distributed abroad with ease. In retrospect it seems almost a miracle that the cinema survived at all.

Certainly in the confusion of the early years of the decade, much of the specifically French quality of the national film production was lost. France had a slow start in talkies since patent rights to the most successful sound systems were owned by American and German companies. The early Thirties had also seen the establishment of large-scale multi-language production in Paris, both on the part of the American Paramount company and the German Tobis company, operating from suburban studios at Joinville and Epinay respectively.

The upheavals of sound were followed, from the middle of the decade onwards, by further crises which reflected the contradictions of contemporary French society as much as the inherent problems of the film industry itself.

In this climate a sense of national identity was difficult to achieve and sustain even after the era of multi-language production had come to an end. Germany, in particular, was a major foreign influence. On the one hand co-productions with Ufa at the Neubabelsberg studios in Berlin continued to provide work for French directors, writers and actors throughout the decade. On the other hand, the advent of Hitler to power in 1933 caused a mass emigration to Paris of German producers, directors and technicians. Figures as important as Erich Pommer, Fritz Lang, Billy Wilder, Robert Siodmak, G.W. Pabst and Eugen Schüfftan worked, some of

them for several years, in the French film industry. It has been estimated that up to a third of French cinema in the Thirties was strongly shaped and influenced by emigrés like, for example, Max Ophuls who spent eight years in France during the decade.

In the new situation of sound-film production, many of the characteristic features of earlier French cinema were lost, in particular the visual experiment associated with the various avant-garde movements of the Twenties.

The interaction of film with Surrealism in France had reached a climax by 1930 with the premiere of Luis Buñuel's *L'Age d'Or* (*The Golden Age*), a masterly indictment of society which provoked riots when first shown in Paris. In the same year the Vicomte de Noailles financed Jean Cocteau's *Le Sang d'un Poète* (1930, *The Blood of a Poet*), but with the increased costs of sound-film production this kind of private patronage of independent film-making came to an end. *Le Sang d'un Poète* was Cocteau's first venture into film and though attacked and derided by the Surrealists on its first appearance, the film now stands as a major achievement and a statement of the personal vision which would be fully orchestrated in *Orphée* (1950, *Orpheus*) some twenty years later.

Sound meant that other key figures of French silent cinema, such as Abel Gance, Marcel l'Herbier and Jean Epstein were reduced to merely commercial film-making. Gance, for example, alternated remakes of some of his earlier successes – he made a sound version of his famous *Napoléon* in 1935 – with routine assignments which offered only rare opportunities to show his full talents. L'Herbier made a couple of lively thrillers, adapted from the novels of

Above left: if any one face typified the look of French cinema in the Thirties it was that of Jean Gabin; in this film he played a fugitive from the law. Top: Jean-Louis Barrault as Napoléon, and Jacqueline Delubac as Josephine, in Les Perles de la Couronne. Above: Fernandel in his first serious role in Pagnol's Regain

Above: Abel Gance's J'Accuse *was a 1937 sound version of his 1919 anti-war classic. Right: Jean Grémillon's* Gueule d'Amour *was a Hollywood-style romance with Gabin at the mercy of a femme fatale. Below: poster for* Marius. *Bottom: in* La Kermesse Héroïque *a Flanders town is occupied by Spanish troops who are first seduced and then routed by the townswomen. Bottom right: the delightfully nostalgic* Un Carnet de Bal *related a woman's search for the beaux of her youth*

France for 12 years except for a brief period during 1939 when he began, but failed to complete, *Air Pur* (Pure Air).

Another great loss to the French film industry was that of Jean Vigo, who died in 1934 at the age of 29. Vigo was one of France's most talented and promising young film-makers, whose entire output amounted to two documentaries and two longer fictional works.

After a penetrating study of Nice, *A Propos de Nice* (1930), which blends documentary and surrealist elements, and a short film about a champion swimmer, *Taris* (1931), Vigo made the two films on which his reputation principally rests. Both were dogged by misfortune. The 47-minute *Zéro de Conduite* (1933, *Nought for Behaviour*) was banned by the French censor until 1945, and the feature-length *L'Atalante* (1934) was re-edited and redubbed by its producers while Vigo himself lay dying.

Through both films runs a unique vein of poetry. The world of childhood has seldom been so accurately captured as in *Zéro de Conduite* and the combination in *L'Atalante* of realistically detailed barge life with larger-than-life elements (such as the figure of the mate, brilliantly played by Michel Simon) is a splendid fusion of fantasy and reality.

The outstanding film-maker throughout the decade, however, is Jean Renoir – the son of the painter Auguste Renoir. Like Clair, he had worked extensively during the silent period but the Thirties, when he made some fifteen films, were the richest years of his career. His work is enormously varied and combines elements drawn from his father's Impressionist style and from the naturalism of the nineteenth-century novel or theatre.

Renoir's work during the early years of the decade is marked by his collaborations with the actor Michel Simon. The first film they made together was a farce called *On Purge Bébé* (1931, Purging Baby). Next they did two splendidly amoral tales designed to exploit the actor's remarkable talents: Simon excels as Legrand in *La Chienne* (1931, The Bitch), a timid cashier turned painter who murders his faithless mistress and allows her lover to be executed for the crime. He is equally impressive as Boudu, the tramp in *Boudu Sauvé des Eaux* (1932, *Boudu Saved From Drowning*) who rewards his rescuer by seducing both his wife and his mistress. The anarchism celebrated in the figure of the tramp links the Renoir film with Vigo's *L'Atalante* and to some extent with the mood at the end of Clair's *A Nous la Liberté*. It is a measure of Renoir's versatility that he could subsequently follow adaptations of Simenon – *La Nuit du Carrefour* (1932, Night at the Crossroads) and Flaubert's *Madame Bovary* (1934) – with *Toni* (1934) a sober study of migrant workers shot on location and in a style which anticipates some aspects of post-war Italian neo-realism.

In the great theoretical debate about sound, and particularly talking pictures, two highly successful French dramatists declared themselves opposed to

Gaston Leroux, – *Le Mystère de la Chambre Jaune* (1930, The Mystery of the Yellow Room) and *Le Parfum de la Dame en Noir* (1931, The Perfume of the Lady in Black). Otherwise l'Herbier's output was restricted to dull historical spectacles, while Epstein's work of the Thirties was equally compromised by unsuitable scripts and financial restraints.

One thread of continuity is provided by the career of René Clair, the master of silent cinema whose writings of the late Twenties opposed the notion of sound (and particularly talking) films but who was one of the first in France to exploit the new form with wit and inventiveness.

The five Clair comedies released in the early Thirties create a distinctive universe where the entanglements of his characters are presented with good-humoured sympathy, and where good eventually triumphs over evil. His first sound film, the internationally successful *Sous les Toits de Paris* (1930, *Under the Roofs of Paris*) with its treatment of characters living on the fringes of society, is an early precursor of what was later to be called 'poetic realism'. Generally, however, Clair's comedies are much lighter and involve a great use of the interplay of dream and reality.

Clair is at his weakest when attempting abstract statements about society, as at the end of *A Nous la Liberté* (1931), or politics, which form the background of *Le Dernier Milliardaire* (1934, *The Last Millionaire*). But despite the reticence and restraint which characterizes all his work, Clair's films of the early Thirties remain genuinely moving and affectionate works.

He left for England in 1935 and was absent from

the traditional view of the primacy of the image. Sacha Guitry and Marcel Pagnol both initially turned to the cinema simply as a means of recording their own work written for the theatre. Both of them had plays adapted for the cinema by other directors in 1931 and then began to direct their own work for the screen a few years later. The results were paradoxical. Their best films, far from being stage-bound, show a freedom shared only by Renoir among their contemporaries.

Guitry was a prolific dramatist who wrote some hundred and thirty plays; most of his Thirties films are simple adaptations, but in his original work written for the screen he shows a freedom of construction, a light and playful style of performance and an inventive approach to the relationship of image and sound which would later be acknowledged as an influence by post-war directors like Alain Resnais. Among Guitry's notable films are: *Le Roman d'un Tricheur* (1936 Story of a Cheat), *Les Perles de la Couronne* (1937, Pearls of the Crown), *Remontons les Champs-Elysées* (1938, Let's Go Up the Champs-Elysées) and *Ils Etaient Neuf Célibataires* (1939, They Were Nine Bachelors).

The work of Pagnol, too, has its surprises. His first contact with the cinema was through his own adaptations of his famous Marseilles trilogy – *Marius* (1931), *Fanny* (1932), and *César* (1936, directed by Pagnol himself). He later made his own film adaptation of his play *Topaze* in 1936, which has subsequently been much filmed.

The success of these works in the tradition of filmed theatre allowed Pagnol to build his own studio and exercise total control over production, even to the extent of completely remaking films that displeased him, either through defects of sound, as in *Merlusse* (1935) or in *Cigalon* (1935).

Pagnol's major films of the Thirties, however, were all adapted not from his own plays, but from novels and stories by the popular author Jean Giono. *Angèle* (1934) and *Regain* (1937, Harvest) with Fernandel, and *La Femme du Boulanger* (1938, The Baker's Wife) with the great Raimu, were filmed away from the studios on location in Provence so as to make the most of the landscape. The construction and the direction of these films is characterized by a freedom that now strikes us as extremely modern and undated.

Less successful in the Thirties, despite his enormous talent, was the director Jean Grémillon who experienced difficulties in establishing himself in feature film production.

His first sound film, *La Petite Lise* (1930, Little Lise), was a box-office failure and from then on he was condemned to make films that were guaranteed commercial projects or, subsequently, to seek work abroad in Spain and Germany.

Working at the Ufa studios in Berlin, Grémillon made two films from scripts by Charles Spaak. Both *Gueule d'Amour* (1937) starring Jean Gabin and *L'Etrange Monsieur Victor* (1937, The Strange Mr Victor) with Raimu had considerable merits. It was,

Left: in Sans Lendemain *Edwige Feuillère played a typically tragic Max Ophuls heroine who makes desperate sacrifices to retain her lover and her small son. Above: the director Julien Duvivier. Below:* Le Parfum de la Dame en Noir: *the heroine is 'haunted' by her first husband, whom she believes dead. Below: Raimu at the centre of a typical peasant group in* La Femme du Boulanger. *Bottom left: scene from* Pépé-le-Moko, *an early film noir set in North Africa*

however, typical of Grémillon's ill-fortune that when, in 1939, he had the opportunity to direct the ideal couple of the period – Jean Gabin and Michèle Morgan – in Jacques Prévert's scenario *Remorques*, the plan to make the film was disrupted by the outbreak of World War II.

While Grémillon was forced to seek work abroad, the French studios were filled with refugees from Germany. Max Ophuls achieved some impressive melodramas that portrayed the misfortunes of beautiful women: *Divine* (1935), *La Tendre Ennemie* (1935, Tender Enemy), *Yoshiwara* (1937), and *Sans Lendemain* (1939, No Tomorrow).

What distinguished the French cinema of the Thirties artistically was its sheer literacy. The lead was given by Jacques Feyder, the Belgian-born director who returned from Hollywood to make three films that re-established his European reputation (first acquired during the silent era). The films were *Le Grand Jeu* (1933, The Great Game), *Pension Mimosas* (1934) and *La Kermesse Héroïque* (1935, Carnival in Flanders) and the team of technicians Feyder assembled to make them included the designer Lazare Meerson, the photographer Harry Stradling and a young assistant, Marcel Carné.

All three films starred Feyder's wife, Françoise Rosay, and were scripted by Charles Spaak, another Belgian who had earlier worked with Feyder on *Les Nouveaux Messieurs* (1928, The New Gentlemen). The writer's contribution, not only to the surface brilliance of the dialogue but also to the structural organization of the plot, was vital. It was to be the first of several writer-director collaborations that characterized the French cinema of the period.

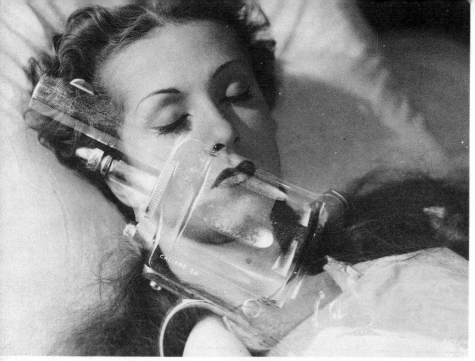

Above: surrealistic images found their way into mainstream cinema – here a dream sequence with Daniéle Darrieux in Anatole Litvak's Mayerling *(1936). But the overtly surrealist films appeared earlier in the decade.*
Right: Le Sang d'un Poète *was Jean Cocteau's first film; using trick shots and bizarre images like the 'animated' statue of the poet's muse, he explored the act of artistic creation. Below right and bottom: the dream-like imagery of Buñuel's* L'Age d'Or; *the first shot illustrates his anti-clerical sentiments and the second his erotic fetishism*

Spaak himself went on to work with another veteran of silent cinema, Julien Duvivier. They made two films starring Jean Gabin: both *La Bandera* (1935) and *La Belle Equipe* (1936, The Fine Team) captured the confused aspirations of the period when the left-wing Popular Front government came to power in France.

Duvivier's other major script collaborator was the more superficial but nonetheless brilliantly witty writer Henri Jeanson. Together they worked on the gangster film *Pépé-le-Moko* (1936), a striking example of the romantic pessimism of the time, starring Jean Gabin and the nostalgic *Un Carnet de Bal* (1937, *Christine*) in which a woman seeks out all the men whose names appear on an old dance card to discover what fate has befallen them.

To return to the work of Jean Renoir in the latter half of the Thirties is to confirm him as the greatest director of the decade. He was, in every sense, the complete author of his films and was far less dependent than either Feyder or Duvivier on the quality of scripts written by others.

Many of his greatest films like *Une Partie de Campagne* (1936, A Day in the Country), *La Bête Humaine* (1938, *Judas was a Woman*) and *La Règle du Jeu* (1939, *The Rules of the Game*) were made from his own scripts. *Le Crime de Monsieur Lange* (1935, *The Crime of Monsieur Lange*), however, announces a new orientation for his work since it was made in collaboration with the poet and scriptwriter Jacques Prévert.

The two of them captured the essential socialist optimism of the Popular Front period and subsequently Renoir found himself caught up in political activity to the extent of making *La Vie Est à Nous* (1936, *People of France*), an explicit propaganda piece for the Communist Party.

The following year he made *La Grande Illusion* (1937, *The Great Illusion*), a passionate anti-war statement and a triumph of human observation, controlled rhetoric and total professionalism. At the end of the decade Renoir completed his masterpiece *La Règle du Jeu*, a perceptive dissection of a divided society which amounts to his personal statement on the eve of world war.

If the genius of Renoir is of a kind that defies classification and generalization, the talent of Marcel Carné, by contrast, is defined by a single period and style. Carné was the protégé of Feyder and had proved himself a brilliant organizer of artistic collaborators like the designer Alexandre Trauner and the composer Maurice Jaubert. Before he was 30, Carné had completed five star-studded features, four of them from scripts by Jacques Prévert.

After his debut with *Jenny* (1936), he made the striking comedy *Drôle de Drame* (1937, *Bizarre, Bizarre*), a comparatively rare example of Prévert's purely comic gifts. Carné and Prévert's two master-pieces *Quai des Brumes* (1938, *Quay of Shadows*) and *Le Jour se Lève* (1939, *Daybreak*) are both fatalistic pieces in which Jean Gabin loses all chance of happiness with the woman he loves after a confrontation with two personifications of evil, respectively portrayed by Michel Simon and Jules Berry. The combination of Prévert's anarchic poetry and Carné's technical prowess creates an unforgettable mixture that is echoed in the Carné-Jeanson collaboration *Hôtel du Nord* (1938).

The achievements of Clair and Vigo in the early Thirties and, later in the decade of Feyder, Duvivier, Renoir and Carné, together with their writers Spaak, Jeanson and Prévert, combine to make this a seminal period in the development of French cinema. Its influence extends not only to post-war France but also to Italian neo-realism.

ROY ARMES

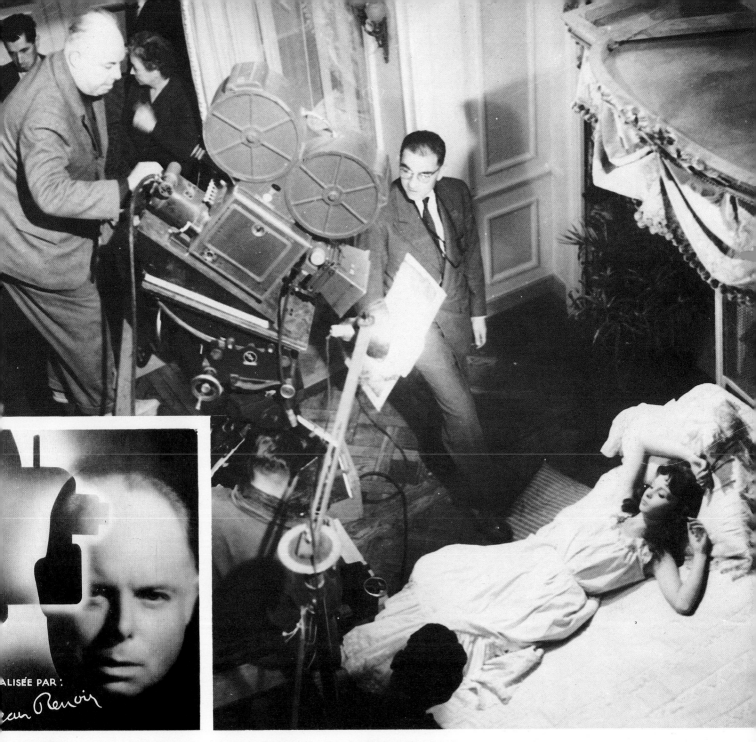

The artistry of Jean Renoir

Jean Renoir died on February 12, 1979 at his Beverly Hills estate. He was 84. Hardly anyone today would question that he was the greatest French film director. His work and his vision of the world, no less than his personality, have delighted several generations of moviegoers

Above: even in his seventies, Renoir was eager to involve himself in every aspect of direction. Here he checks a high-angle shot of Françoise Arnoul for a scene from what was to be his last film Le Petit Théâtre de Jean Renoir. She plays Isabelle, a pretty, young wife, who cuckolds her rich old husband in the third episode of the film

Renoir's career, more than that of any other director, summarizes the whole evolution of the cinema, from the first hesitant steps of silent films to the French *nouvelle vague* (of the late Fifties), encompassing advances in sound recording, colour and even television techniques. At each stage of his life he was open to suggestions from those around him, while retaining a fine sense of his own artistic integrity. The critic and theorist André Bazin has written that Renoir always knew 'how to adapt to the evolution of the cinema and the taste of his contemporaries' – not out of some vain opportunism but because 'the need to renew himself was part of his genius'. The 38 films which he directed between 1924 and 1969 have profoundly influenced the art of the screen and most have stood the test of time.

That said, Renoir's work curiously defies investigation and confounds the kind of critic who is fond of attaching labels to works of art. It seems to advance without any guiding line or internal logic; it cannot be pigeon-holed. Renoir would change his style without warning and cheerfully contradict himself from one film to another – if not within the same film.

Between 1931 and 1939 (his most prolific period) he tackled every type of film with

181

Top left and top right: Catherine Hessling, Renoir's first wife, dances in Nana *and dies in the snow in* La Petite Marchande d'Allumettes *their last film together. Above left and left: Rodolphe (Jacques Borel) flirts with Mme Dufour (Jeanne Marken) in* Une Partie de Campagne *(1936). Above: Jean Gabin as engine driver Jacques Lantier in the grim railway setting of* La Bête Humaine

equanimity: naturalistic melodrama in *La Chienne* (1931, The Bitch), thriller with *La Nuit du Carrefour* (1932, Night at the Crossroads), broad farce in *Boudu Sauvé des Eaux* (1932, *Boudu Saved From Drowning*), respectful adaptations of great writers such as Flaubert, Maupassant, Gorky and Zola, examinations of French society like *La Vie Est à Nous* (1936, *People of France*) and *La Marseillaise* (1937), moving human dramas like *La Grande Illusion* (1937, *The Great Illusion*), culminating in that modern sequel to the enchantments of Beaumarchais and Marivaux that is *La Règle du Jeu* (1939, *The Rules of the Game*). Though superficially a 'mad imbroglio', it is a perfectly constructed film which (with Orson Welles' *Citizen Kane*, 1940) is the source of everything of importance in modern cinema. With a couple of exceptions, all these films were, in

their day, received with total incomprehension by both public and critics.

It seems almost impossible, therefore, to encompass Renoir's multiple, abundant, unclassifiable and contradictory *oeuvre* – its broad contrasts are an expression of its richness. If one sees Renoir as a sensualist, it immediately becomes apparent that he does not disdain general ideas, abstraction or intellectual rigour. He could be sarcastic, good-natured, licentious, nonchalant, endearing – according to subject, mood and circumstances. In a film like *Le Testament du Docteur Cordelier* (1959) he seemed obsessed by human failings and sought to place spiritual pursuits beyond the whims of the flesh. Immediately afterwards he made *Le Déjeuner sur l'Herbe* (1959, *Picnic on the Grass*), which was a hymn to nature and to the joy of living. The 'mixture of irony and

tenderness, humour and sensuality' which Renoir discerned in his father, the painter Auguste, applied equally well to himself. Renoir was, as it were, a cross between a peasant, whose temperament and work had their roots in the soil, and an artist, whose vocation was universal. His comedies were caustic, his dramas light-hearted. His life, too, was in the image of his films – one of constant wandering, of inspired disorder.

'I must insist on the fact that I set foot in the world of the cinema only in order to make my wife a star, intending once this was done to return to the pottery studio. I did not foresee that once I had been caught in the machinery I should never be able to escape'

It was long believed that the adjective 'realist' sufficed to account for the diversity of his gifts. Historians and critics wished (and still wish) to make Renoir the leader of a so-called French 'realist' school, including personalities as unlike him as Carné, Duvivier, Grémillon and Pagnol. No doubt his path at some time crossed theirs. He made, for instance, at least

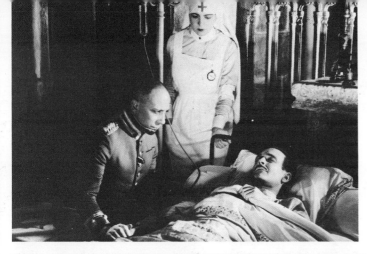

one film strongly influenced by the theories and sensibilities of Pagnol – *Toni* (1934). But this does not prove that Renoir was a realist. If one means by realism the direct, objective reproduction of reality, without any reworking, the kind of reproduction whose logical conclusion was the invention of first photography and later cinema (whose initial claim was to describe 'life as it is'), it is clear that Renoir was not a realist in that sense. He never ceased to affirm the primacy of the narrator over the narration, the painter over the painting, man over nature. Contrary to those mediocre directors naively concerned with 'getting close' to the reality (psychological, social, political) of their time, it would appear that Renoir contrived to get as far away from it as possible. He saw such a reality as a constraint. He did not so much wish to destroy it as to restructure it in a more agreeable and harmonious fashion. Renoir's early films twisted reality, were all flights into imaginary worlds and fairy-tales.

Early in his career, Renoir demonstrated that the vocation of cinematography lay in fantasy, even science fiction (*Charleston*, 1927), bending plots and characters to fit the conventions of fantasy. So the heroine of *La Fille de l'Eau* (1924, *The Whirlpool of Fate*), recklessly

Top left: Rauffenstein, the prison commandant (Erich von Stroheim), visits the bedside of Boeldieu (Pierre Fresnay) in La Grande Illusion. *Top right:* La Marseillaise – *a re-creation of the French Revolution. Above right: Renoir's first American film –* Swamp Water. *Right: the Tucker family contemplate their devastated home in* The Southerner. *Above: boats on the Ganges – a scene from* The River

takes refuge in escapist day-dreaming to console herself for the indignities of everyday life, just as the main character in *La Petite Marchande d'Allumettes* (1928, The Little Match Girl), will do one cold Christmas night. In the same way *Nana* (1926) is firmly ensconced in a self-made woman's mythomania, while *Mar-*

'In my view cinema is nothing but a new form of printing – another form of the total transformation of the world through knowledge'

---

quitta (1927), a humble street-singer, imagines she is a grand-duchess. As for the madcap soldiers of *Tire au Flanc* (1928, Skiver), their substitute for the dull routine of the barracks is

rowdyism, irreverence, wrangling, lechery and finally a wild Bacchanalia.

Almost all of Renoir's characters seek comfort in dreams: Maurice, the wretched clerk of *La Chienne*, fleeing the drab greyness of his middle-class life and seeking solace in art and a doomed love affair; the federates of *La Marseillaise* heroically pursuing a revolutionary ideal which never ceases to elude them; Monsieur Lange, who, in *Le Crime de Monsieur Lange* (1935, *The Crime of Monsieur Lange*) creates a romantic universe made to his own measure; *Madame Bovary* (1934) and her romantic fancies, and *Toni* with his unrequited love for the beautiful, fickle Josefa. What are the prisoners of *La Grande Illusion* looking for if not to escape, to regain their freedom even if they know that by doing so they will only be plunged back into a chaotic world at war.

In each case, for better or for worse, imagination attempts to triumph over reality. For some characters, indeed, the price to be paid for this relentless quest will be their own lives. In the later films, fantasy, humour, gaiety – the 'superior form of civilization', as one of the characters in *Eléna et les Hommes* (1956, *Paris Does Strange Things*) calls it – will carry the day. Camilla in *Le Carrosse d'Or* (1952, *The Golden Coach*) and Nini in *French Cancan* (1955), will find their vocation in art: they have both understood that they are not made 'for what is called life', that their place is 'among the acrobats, the clowns, the mountebanks', that their happiness lies not in the petty concerns of reality but in the *grande illusion* of the stage. Renoir shared with his father the conviction

---

'To a film director who will take the trouble to use his eyes, everything that constitutes our lives has a magical aspect. A metro station can be as mysterious as a haunted castle'

---

that the task of a true artist is not to copy nature, however faithfully, but to re-create it. He has commented:

'What will remain of any artist is not his imitation of nature, since nature is changeable and transient; what is eternal is his approach to nature, what he can achieve by the reconstruction, and not the imitation of nature.

In *The River* (1951) Renoir asked his director of photography, his nephew Claude Renoir, to paint the turf, as he found it 'not Indian enough'. In *La Bête Humaine* (1938, *Judas Was a Woman*) Renoir compared the locomotive to 'a flying carpet in the Arabian Nights', and wanted to retain only the poetic side of Zola's original novel to the detriment of its naturalistic message. Neither of these actions or statements can possibly be described as being realist in motivation. Renoir has declared more than once: 'It's by not being realistic that one has the greatest chance of capturing reality', and has said, even more dogmatically, 'All great art is abstract'. This so-called realism, which a whole critical tradition hoped to attach to his work at any price, is for Renoir, only the façade of fantasy, a mask which must be ripped off to uncover the work's true dimension. Life is a dream, a 'rich comedy with a hundred different acts'; and the film-maker (like every artist) must try to feel the upsurge of the imaginary at the heart of the real, the quest for the irrational that makes the world go round. This is the key to Renoir's aesthetics and philosophy. At the opposite pole to realism, his art is an art of magic and fantasy.

Renoir's last film *Le Petit Théâtre de Jean Renoir* (1969, The Little Theatre of Jean Renoir) gives a crucial insight into the director's genius. It is just the film one would expect from a creator whose *oeuvre* is complete and who chooses nonchalantly to recapitulate its principal themes, as one might leaf through an

Above: the finale of French Cancan. *Opposite page, top left: a gust of wind scatters the picnickers in* Le Déjeuner sur l'Herbe. *Top right: a scene from* The Golden Coach. *Right: Jean-Louis Barrault in* The Testament of Dr Cordelier. *Far right: Jean-Pierre Cassell and Jean Carmet in* The Vanishing Corporal

album of memories. The film's premise is put in a nutshell by wise old Duvallier who introduces each section of the film. 'Life', he exclaims, 'is only bearable because of constant

---

'I was afraid, and still am, of photographing Nature as it is. I think one has to look very hard, and by means of camera-angles and lighting enlarge the significance of a setting, a countryside or a human face'

---

little revolutions . . . revolutions in the kitchen . . . in bedrooms . . . on village squares . . . storms in teacups.' This is, according to Renoir, the way of the world: in his films the bonds of society are slightly stretched, irregularities are committed by certain characters who are cleverer than others, risks are calmly taken by free spirits. Some find undreamed of happiness by the end, some die pointlessly; it hardly matters since, as Duvallier says, all that will remain when all is said and done are the lyrics of a bitter-sweet song, which generations to

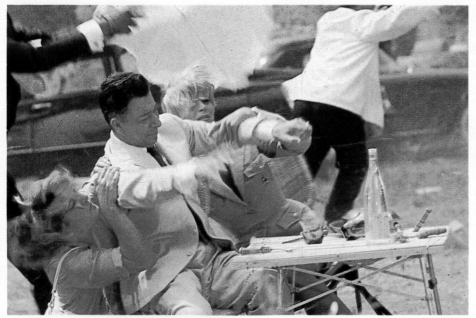

come will sing in chorus:

> When everything is ended
> When your hopes have died
> Why lament the days gone past
> Why regret the vanished dreams . . .

The discreet exit that Renoir contrived with *Le Petit Théâtre de Jean Renoir* is in keeping with his character. The film critic Jean Collet wrote:

'When the red curtain falls on the stage of the Little Theatre, as it fell at the end of *The Golden Coach*, we have the feeling that Renoir is leaving us with a fragile secret, a secret that was lost and found again a thousand times.'

Renoir said something similar about his father's work, at the end of the painter's life. As he looked with emotion at his father's 'extremely simplified palette' composed of 'a few tiny droppings of colour' it seemed as if the artist had been approaching 'the secret of universal harmony as if it were the most natural thing in the world'.

CLAUDE BEYLIE

Quotations from My Life and My Films, *by Jean Renoir, translated by Norman Denny, (Collins, 1974).*

Filmography

1924 Une Vie Sans Joie (re-edited and shown in France as Catherine in 1927) (sc. only); La Fille de l'Eau (GB: The Whirlpool of Fate) (+prod; +des). '26 Nana (+prod). '27 Charleston/Sur un Air de Charleston/Charleston-Parade (unfinished) (+prod); Marquitta (+prod); La P'tite Lili (actor only). '28 La Petite Marchande d'Allumettes (co-dir; +co-prod; +sc); Tire au Flanc (+co-sc). '29 Le Tournoi/Le Tournoi dans la Cité (+sc); Le Petit Chaperon Rouge (actor only); Le Bled. '31 On Purge Bébé (+sc); La Chienne (+sc). '32 La Nuit du Carrefour (+sc); Boudu Sauvé des Eaux (USA: Boudu Saved From Drowning (+sc). '33 Chotard et Cie (+sc). '34 Madame Bovary (+sc); Toni (+co-sc). '35 Le Crime de Monsieur Lange (USA: The Crime of Monsieur Lange) (+co-sc). '36 La Vie Est à Nous (USA: People of France); Une Partie de Campagne (+sc; +act) (not released until 1949). '37 Les Bas-Fonds (USA: The Lower Depths) (+co-sc); La Grande Illusion (USA: Grand Illusion; GB: The Great Illusion) (+co-sc); Terre d'Espagne (+comm; +sc; +narr) (French version of USA doc. Spanish Earth); La Marseillaise (+co-sc). '38 La Bête Humaine (USA: The Human Beast; GB: Judas Was a Woman) (+sc; +act). '39 La Règle du Jeu (USA: The Rules of the Game) (+co-sc; +act). '40 La Tosca (+co-sc) (some scenes only) (IT). '41 Swamp Water (GB: The Man Who Came Back) (USA). '43 This Land Is Mine (USA) (+co-sc). '44 Salute to France (short) (co-dir; +co-sc) (USA). '45 The Southerner (+sc) (USA). '46 The Diary of a Chambermaid (+co-sc) (USA); The Woman on the Beach (+co-sc) (USA). '51 The River (+co-sc) (IN). '52 Le Carrosse d'Or/La Carozza d'Oro (GB: The Golden Coach) (+co-sc) (IT-FR). '55 French Cancan (USA: Only the French Can) (+sc). '56 Eléna et les Hommes (USA: Paris Does Strange Things; GB: The Night Does Strange Things (+sc; +lyr); L'Album de Famille de Jean Renoir (short). '59 Le Testament du Docteur Cordelier (USA: The Testament of Doctor Cordelier; GB: Experiment in Evil) (+sc; +narr); Le Déjeuner sur l'Herbe (USA: Picnic on the Grass; GB: Lunch on the Grass) (+sc; +co-prod). '62 Le Caporal Epinglé (USA: The Elusive Corporal; GB: The Vanishing Corporal) (+co-sc). '68 Le Direction d'Acteurs par Jean Renoir (as himself) (short). '69 Le Petit Théâtre de Jean Renoir (+prod; +sc; +narr) (FR-IT-GER); The Christian Liquorice Store (actor only) (USA).

"Le plus important film français jamais réalisé"

La Critique Internationale

LA RÈGLE DU JEU

Le chef d'oeuvre de **JEAN RENOIR**

A weekend party assembles at the château of the Marquis de la Chesnaye (1). Among the guests are André, an aviator, who is in love with Christine (the Marquis' wife), Geneviève, the Marquis' mistress and Octave, an old friend of the family.

When his gamekeeper captures a notorious poacher (2), the Marquis, on a whim, decides to employ the poacher as a servant.

The weekend diversions include a morning hunt and an evening fancy-dress masquerade (3). During the former the Marquise is shocked to learn of her husband's infidelity. She tells André that she is willing to go away with him, but when the Marquis surprises them together, a fight breaks out between the two men (4). At the same time, the gamekeeper becomes aware of the poacher's attentions to his flighty wife (5), Lisette, and chases him through

the château with a gun (6).

Christine decides that, after all, she would prefer to go away with Octave who has always loved her. However, Lisette points out to Octave that he is far too old to satisfy Christine. He feels the truth of this and sends André out into the garden to meet her.

Christine, wearing a coat borrowed from Lisette, is spotted by the gamekeeper, who has now become reconciled with the poacher. The gamekeeper mistakes her for his wife and shoots André, believing that he is making love to Lisette. The Marquis explains to his guests that the gamekeeper has shot André having mistaken him for a poacher. The guests feign belief but privately decide that it was the Marquis who did the shooting to rid himself of a dangerous rival. They file back into the château (7).

7

6

Directed by Jean Renoir, 1939

Prod co: La Nouvelle Edition Française. **prod:** Claude Renoir. **sc:** Jean Renoir, Carl Koch. **photo:** Jean Bachelet, Jean-Paul Alphen, Alain Renoir. **ed:** Marguerite Renoir, Marthe Huguet. **art dir:** Eugène Lourié, Max Douy. **cost:** Coco Chanel. **mus:** Roger Desormières, Joseph Kosma, from Mozart, Monsigny, Saint-Saëns. **sd:** Joseph de Bretagne. **ass dir:** Carl Koch, André Zwoboda, Henri Cartier-Bresson. **r/t:** 113 minutes. Paris premiere, 7 July 1939. Released in the USA as *The Rules of the Game*.

Cast: Marcel Dalio (*Robert, Marquis de la Chesnaye*), Nora Gregor (*Christine de la Chesnaye*), Jean Renoir (*Octave*), Roland Toutain (*André Jurieux*), Mila Parély (*Geneviève*), Paulette Dubost (*Lisette*), Julien Carette (*Marceau, the poacher*), Gaston Modot (*Schumacher, the gamekeeper*), Pierre Magnier (*the General*), Eddy Debray (*Corneille, the major-domo*), Pierre Nay (*Saint-Aubin*), Odette Talazac (*Mme de la Plante*), Richard Francoeur (*La Bruyère*), Claire Gérard (*Mme de la Bruyère*), Anne Mayen (*Jackie, Christine's niece*), Léon Larive (*cook*), Lise Elina (*radio reporter*), Nicolas Amato (*South American*), Tony Corteggiani (*Berthelin*), Camille François (*radio announcer*), André Zwoboda (*engineer at Caudron*), Henri Cartier-Bresson (*English servant*), Jenny Hélia (*kitchen servant*).

In a currently distributed print of *La Règle du Jeu*, a mysterious caption has been inserted at the beginning claiming that the film 'is intended as entertainment not as social criticism'. It seems that, even today, the nature of this potent work is still misunderstood. In *My Life and My Films*, Renoir recalled:

'During the shooting of the film I was torn between my desire to make a comedy of it and the wish to tell a tragic story. The result of this ambivalence was the film as it is.'

Of all the characters that assemble at the Marquis' château, only two act without duplicity and guile. One is the aviator André, a romantic idealist infatuated with Christine, the Marquis' beautiful wife. He has just made a spectacular crossing of the Atlantic, and was upset that Christine did not welcome him in Paris. The other, Octave (played by Renoir himself), is a friend of the Marquis and his wife, with a special fondness for the latter. However, in procuring for André an invitation to the house party he is not entirely without blame for the eventual tragedy. Indeed it may be said that none of the characters acts with any really malicious intent – but are simply weak or incapable of controlling their wayward caprices. Even the gamekeeper, whose jealousy results in André's accidental death, cannot help himself. Yet the characters' excusable – even at times endearing – fallibilities stem finally from selfish irresponsibility. In the dissolute social world the film depicts, the 'rules of the game' solely concern the hollow observance of 'appearances'; any idea of living according to a stable form of morality has been lost.

When the film was first shown in Paris, in July 1939, it caused a riot and attempts were made to burn down the cinema. The distributors called for cuts in certain offending scenes, but even when these were made, the public found others to jeer at. The film ran for a mere three weeks. In October of that year the French government banned it, claiming it was morally unacceptable. The ban was lifted some months later but re-enforced when the Germans occupied Paris, and it remained in existence until the end of World War II. Though it was championed by a few discerning French critics, most found the film's mixture of drama, comedy and farce unpalatable and chaotic, while others viewed it as a calculated attack on the *haute bourgeoisie*. Moreover, owing to the presence in the cast of the Jewish actor, Dalio, and Nora Gregor, an Austrian refugee, the film was attacked by both the anti-Semitic and the nationalist press.

At the end of the war it was feared that a complete version of the film was lost for ever. Then, by a series of chance discoveries and the dedicated work of two young French enthusiasts under Renoir's supervision, it was re-assembled. With hindsight, it is easy to see why Renoir's film met with such violent antipathy: France was about to find herself plunged into war, into a conflict which she was not to prove herself capable of sustaining for long – perhaps due to the very debilitating social inconsistencies that Renoir had depicted in his film.

Renoir's original choice for the role of the Marquise had been Simone Simon, but the film's limited budget precluded her participation. Then, by chance, at a theatre Renoir met Nora Gregor, the Austrian stage actress. Despite his colleagues' vigorous opposition (her French was far from perfect) he insisted on engaging her for the role. Renoir's obstinacy seems justified: the actress' statuesque bearing is extremely effective in the scene where her aviator lover arrives at the château; whereupon she rises to the occasion to deliver a homily to her other guests on the beauties of platonic friendship. Also effective is the moment when, elegantly scanning the scene of the hunt through binoculars, she chances to see her husband embracing his mistress.

The hunt is splendidly executed. Shot in greyish light and using natural sounds, it turns into a savage, senseless massacre of wild life. This is followed by a ball where, with unconscious irony, many of the guests opt to wear skeleton costumes and cavort in a dance of death. The intrigues of the guests and the underlings intermingle. Few of the residents seem unduly surprised when the jealous gamekeeper causes havoc by chasing his rival through the house with a gun; they treat the incident almost as an entertaining diversion and remain obsessed with their own petty intrigues. Occasionally the film's underlying theme is illuminated by a casual remark: 'Sincere people are such bores', or 'We live in a time when everything is a lie'.

In the final scene – when the gamekeeper sees the aviator in the grounds of the château with the woman he takes to be his wife, and shoots him – the guests are quick to rationalize the event according to their own ethics. They feel that the murder was surely committed by the Marquis who was justified in preventing the aviator eloping with Christine.

After *La Règle du Jeu*, Renoir went to Italy to begin work on *La Tosca* (1940). Renoir was forced to abandon the film after a few days, owing to the worsening political climate, and left for the USA.

With *La Règle du Jeu* he had made his most personal statement about a society he knew well. Although received acrimoniously, the film's accuracy and validity have been established over the passing years.
DEREK PROUSE

The Epic Entertainments of

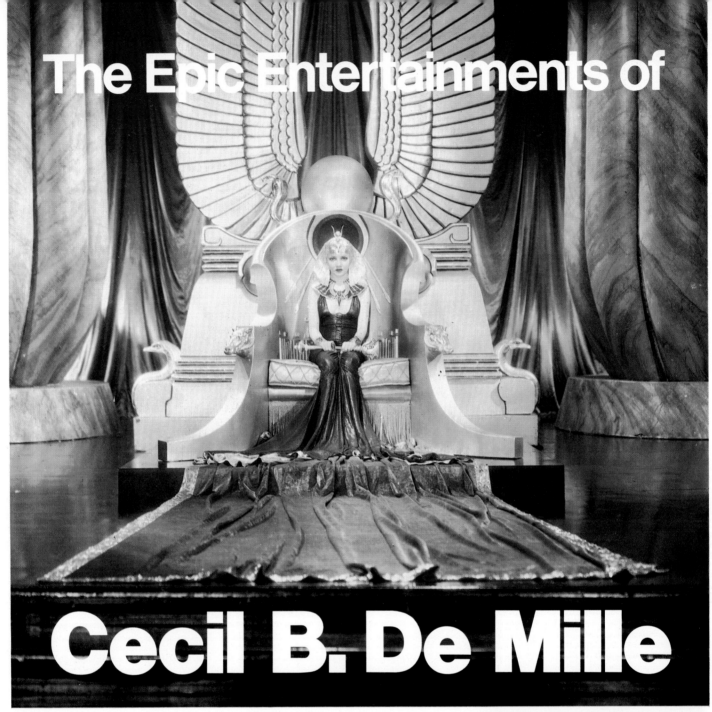

Cecil B. De Mille

During the Thirties DeMille rescued his floundering career with grand re-creations of the power and debauchery of Ancient Rome and with Westerns that celebrated the American pioneering spirit

When sound first came to the movies, the career of Cecil B. DeMille, Hollywood's greatest showman, had reached an unprecedented crisis. From his first film, *The Squaw Man* (1913), he had unerringly mirrored changing fashions in public taste. During World War I he made contemporary war stories like *The Little American* (1917), which depicted the sinking of the *Lusitania*. Thereafter, in the changing moral climate of the early Twenties, he specialized in spicy marital dramas such as *The Affairs of Anatol* (1921), visions of opulence centring on the bathroom and bedroom. He

then undertook his most ambitious project to date, *The Ten Commandments* (1923), a blockbusting epic costing $1.5 million.

Although he was a household name, DeMille's professional position was far from secure. Arguments over the cost of *The Ten Commandments* initiated a widening rift between DeMille and his business associates at Famous Players-Lasky – especially Adolph Zukor. DeMille left under a cloud to form his own company in 1925. However, despite the success of an epic life of Christ, *The King of Kings* (1927), many of his company's films failed at the box-office and his backers and partners lost confidence in him. As DeMille explained himself in his autobiography:

'The trouble in 1928 was that I did not have

Above: DeMille's Cleopatra*; the star, Claudette Colbert, was one of his favourite leading ladies in the Thirties. Right: Cecil Blount DeMille in favourite directorial garb – riding boots, jodhpurs and open-necked shirt*

DeMille contracted to make three pictures with MGM. *Dynamite* (1929) was made in both silent and sound versions (he still was not convinced): *Madame Satan* (1930), a musical, was a box-office flop, and in something of a panic he attempted to repeat earlier successes with his third version of *The Squaw Man* (1931), but this, too, failed disastrously. At this time DeMille attempted to form an organization known as the Directors' Guild with Lewis Milestone, King Vidor and Frank Borzage. The Guild's aim was to place creative control of picture-making with the directors rather than the financiers. DeMille claimed:

' . . . the conditions under which motion pictures are now generally produced are not conducive to the best creative work, and must, if long continued, result in a deadly uniformity of ideas and methods, thus seriously retarding the highest commercial and artistic development of the craft.'

This move by DeMille highlights one of his fundamental contradictions: by forming the Guild he was attempting to gain for himself an artistic freedom from financial constraint which was impossible in such a highly capita-

enough 'picture money' to be completely independent and make only the kind of pictures I wanted to make.'

In 1928 he embarked upon *The Godless Girl*, a moral tale set in a girl's reform school. The shooting of this film is a typical example of DeMille's methods. His production team spent months researching reform schools and a realistic set was constructed on the lot. True to DeMille's passion for authenticity this set was to be burnt down at the end of the film with the actors (literally) escaping the flames – a procedure which was planned to the second. Despite the fine timing, when one wing of the set fell down on cue (pulled by special wires) two girls were trapped. They luckily managed to escape by climbing up a gable and down the other side.

DeMille was convinced that the success of *The Jazz Singer* (1927) was only temporary and that *The Godless Girl*, which he had shot silent, would be a hit, but his backers insisted that sound should be added. The quarrels that ensued finally prompted him to sign with MGM. On his departure a soundtrack was added to the film.

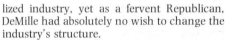

Top: Charles Laughton as the Emperor Nero, with Claudette Colbert and Fredric March, in The Sign of the Cross, *one of DeMille's finest epics. Above:* The Plainsman *marked DeMille's successful return to the Western. Below: the last spike is hammered in to complete the Western Union railroad in* Union Pacific

lized industry, yet as a fervent Republican, DeMille had absolutely no wish to change the industry's structure.

Louis B. Mayer, head of MGM, was, not surprisingly, unhappy about this move; his unhappiness was compounded by DeMille's box-office failures. After an extended trip to Russia and Europe, lack of money forced DeMille to mortgage his property and swallow his pride; he approached his first company (which had, in the meantime, become the Paramount Pictures Corporation) and Lasky and Bud Schulberg (the head of production on the West Coast) persuaded Zukor to let DeMille back into the fold. He was assigned to direct a Roman epic entitled *The Sign of the Cross* (1932) on a budget of only $650,000; he received a meagre salary of $450 per week. (In 1916 DeMille had been drawing a salary of $1000 per week plus a share of the profits.) DeMille was forced to adopt a more rigorous production operation: Nero's palace, far from being an authentic, life-size reproduction, was largely constructed in miniature with special flights of stairs and ramps of sufficient size for the cast to walk on. DeMille was not allowed to marshal thousands of extras as he had in the old days; instead, the cameraman used a prism lens which gave the effect of doubling the number of people in a crowd. However the Roman circus was genuinely full-size; it seated

189

7500 and had a vast arena. DeMille brought the picture in on budget (apparently stopping shooting in the middle of a take so as not to exceed it) and it was a box-office smash.

Clearly a great deal of this success was due to the film's sexual content, which included the attempts of Poppea (Claudette Colbert) to seduce Marcus Superbus (Fredric March) and his futile efforts to seduce a Christian girl called Mercia (Elissa Landi) in the course of which he forces her to attend an orgy with him. DeMille writes that William Hays, the industry's moral guardian, was very upset about a dance in the orgy scene and telephoned to ask him what he was going to do about it. 'Not a damn thing,' DeMille replied, and didn't. DeMille's insistence that 'I will always resist, as far as I am able, the claim of any individual or group to the right of censorship' is ironic in view of his support of Hays' appointment, which he defended on the grounds that some pictures were '...bad art as well as bad morals and bad taste'.

The film's success reinstated DeMille within the industry. After two pot-boiling films (*This Day and Age* in 1933 and *Four Frightened People* in 1934) he launched himself into another epic, *Cleopatra* (1934). This time DeMille's passion for authenticity was rampant – even Cleopatra's hairpins were museum copies – in addition to his pleasure in sexual symbolism and innuendo, which he justified on commercial grounds. A slave girl danced almost naked with and on a golden bull, and the film was a box-office if not a critical success. From then on, with the exception of *The Greatest Show on Earth* (1951), all DeMille's films were historical.

His position at Paramount was now assured, not only because of these successes but also because Ernst Lubitsch had become production director at the studio (both Lasky and Schulberg had long since departed) and he was a great admirer of DeMille's silent films. Lubitsch's presence was a godsend; although DeMille's next picture, *The Crusades* (1935), failed miserably, he was able to abandon the ancient world for a while to make *The Plainsman* (1936), based on the lives of Wild Bill Hickok and Calamity Jane – but *not* with any historical accuracy in terms of events. DeMille built sets covering six acres of the Paramount lot and was once again able to use as many extras as he wanted for the battle scenes. Reviewing the film, *Variety* weekly wrote: 'It's cowboys and Indians on a broad, sweeping scale: not a *Covered Wagon* but realistic enough.' Realistic or not, it was a financial success, as was his later *Union Pacific* (1939) which dealt with the construction of the Western Union railroad. His researchers went through the company's records going back 70 years. In Utah he built a complete reproduction of the town of Cheyenne and imported by bus over a thousand Navajo and Cheyenne Indians. During shooting, DeMille was taken ill and after an emergency operation he directed from a stretcher, but large sections of the film had to be shot by Arthur Rossen and James Hogan. The film's enormous success led Paramount to grant him a four-year contract and virtual independence. His next two films, *North West Mounted Police* (1940) and *Reap the Wild Wind* (1942) were both hits, the latter breaking Paramount's record for grosses at the box-office previously held by DeMille's silent version of *The Ten Commandments*.

DeMille then became carried away with the idea of filming the story of a missionary and naval commander, Dr Corydon E. Wassell, who had run a Japanese blockade in order to rescue nine wounded sailors despite orders to abandon them. The subject especially appealed to DeMille, who practised what would today be described as something of a 'macho' lifestyle. Prior to his film career he had loved attending Pennsylvania Military College, where the regimen included daily Bible readings and cold baths; until his last years he went every day for a nude swim in his pool. The film he made, *The Story of Dr Wassell* (1944), was a success, but the critics, as DeMille admits, did not like it. In

Top left: Loxi Claiborne (Paulette Goddard) sights a ship running on the rocks in Reap the Wild Wind, *a seafaring drama set in Georgia in the 19th century. Right: Charlton Heston as Moses in DeMille's second version of* The Ten Commandments, *his last biblical epic. Below: Samson (Victor Mature) brings the house down on his Philistine captors at the climax of* Samson and Delilah

ploying some 12,000 extras and 15,000 animals for the Exodus scene alone. DeMille was, of course, well versed in the organization and control of huge productions. He habitually directed from a platform, with a megaphone, and in sequences with thousands of extras used to communicate his instructions to his assistant directors in amongst the action by radio telephone. The film's final cost was $13 million and by the end of 1959 it had grossed over $83 million and been seen by more than 98 million people.

DeMille's career is significant for his production of Biblical epics and other films on a grand scale. He acknowledged the influence of the silent Italian epics on his work, and his contribution to the genre was both formative and substantial. However the artistic value of his films, of which he himself was quite convinced, probably lies in his silent work, not simply because, despite his Christian beliefs, he undoubtedly began to serve Mammon in his later work, but also because his despotic professional personality blinded him to the possibilities of fine art on small budgets. The *New Yorker*'s review of *Samson and Delilah* read:

'It may be said of Cecil B. DeMille that since 1913, when he teamed up with Jesse Lasky to create *The Squaw Man*, he has never taken a step backward. He has never taken a step forward either, but somehow he has managed to survive in a chancy industry where practically everybody is incessantly going up, down, or sideways . . .'

This, sadly, probably sums up his career.

SHEILA WHITAKER

Below: DeMille's career was financially successful, but not until The Greatest Show on Earth *did a film of his win a Best Picture Oscar. Here, the circus manager (Charlton Heston), injured in a train crash, is tended by a murderer (James Stewart) who, to escape dectection, wears the makeup of a clown*

the *Nation* James Agee wrote:

' . . . Cecil DeMille's [film] is to be regretted beyond qualification. It whips the story, in every foot, into a nacreous foam of lies whose speciousness is only the more painful because Mr DeMille is so obviously free from any desire to alter the truth except for what he considers to be its own advantage.'

This is an interesting point with regard to DeMille's complex character. His devout Christian beliefs and adherence to the Episcopalian Church, his increasingly right-wing political opinions and his somewhat unusual sex life – he was a foot fetishist and openly maintained relationships with two mistresses (Jeanie Mac-Pherson and Julia Faye) for many years – combined with his strict moral sense, inevitably produced violent contradictions in himself, his actions and his films.

DeMille's devotion to the American way of life led him to become passionately involved in the anti-communist movement that took hold in the USA after World War II. He was one of the first to name the respected left-wing writer John Howard Lawson as a leader of communist infiltration.

DeMille's career ended in grand style: *Samson and Delilah* (1949), *The Greatest Show on* Earth and *The Ten Commandments* (1956). The script of this film took three years to write and it was shot in Egypt after two years' preparation. It was a monumental production, em-

Alexander Nevsky

Eisenstein's picture of heroism

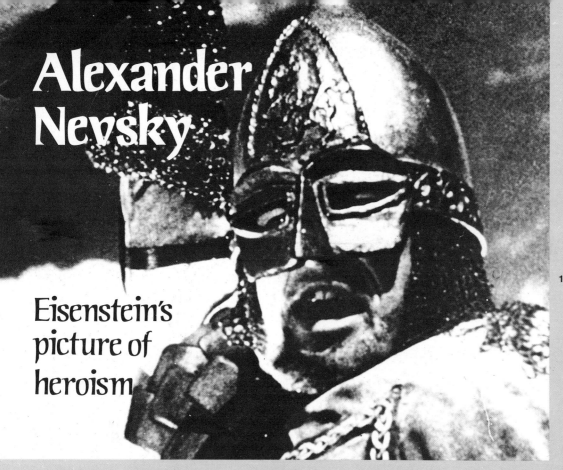

'. . . a completely contemporary picture, so close are the feelings that inspired the Russian people in the thirteenth century in repulsing the enemy to the feelings that inspire the Soviet Russian people now, and doubtless to all the feelings that inspire all those towards whom the grasping claw of German aggression is spreading . . . Let them not cringe before fascism, let them not kneel before it without protest, let them stop the unending policy of concession and appeasement towards this insatiable mon-

Directed by Sergei Eisenstein, 1938
Prod co: Mosfilm. **sc:** Sergei Eisenstein, Pyotr Pavlenko. **photo:** Eduard Tissé. **art dir:** Isaak Shpinel, Nikolai Solovyov, Konstantin Eliseyev, from drawings by Eisenstein. **mus:** Sergei Prokofiev. **ass dir:** Dmitri Vasiliev, Boris Ivanov, Nikolai Maslov. **r/t:** 112 minutes. Moscow premiere, 23 November 1938.
Cast: Nikolai Cherkasov (*Alexander Nevsky*), Nikolai Okhlopkov (*Vasili Buslai*), Alexander Abrikosov (*Gavrilo Olexich*), Dmitri Orlov (*Ignat*), Vasili Novikov (*Pavsha, governor of Pskov*), Vera Ivasheva (*Olga*), Nikolai Arsky (*Domash*), Varvara Massalitinova (*Amelfa*), Anna Danilova (*Vasilisa*), Vladimir Ershov (*Grand Master of the Teutonic Order*), Sergei Blinnikov (*Tverdilo*), Lev Fenin (*bishop*), I. Lagutin (*Ananias*), Naum Rogozhin (*black monk*).

Alexander Nevsky was the first film to be completed by Eisenstein since *The Old and the New* (1928) as well as being his first sound film. It offered an opportunity for the realization of the ideas on sound expressed in the 1928 *Declaration* by Eisenstein, Pudovkin and Aleksandrov. In this the authors warn that a mere:

'. . . *adhesion* of sound to pieces of montage reinforces their inertia.

'*Only a contrapuntal use* of sound in relation to the piece of visual montage offers new possibilities for the development and perfection of montage. *The first experiments with sound must be directed towards a sharp contrast between it and the visual images*. And only such a ''storm'' will produce the sensation needed to create a new *orchestral counterpoint* of visual and sound images.'

This concept of 'orchestral counterpoint', is exemplified in the Battle on the Ice sequence by the interaction between Eisenstein's powerful imagery and Prokofiev's dramatic musical score.

Alexander Nevsky was also the film that marked Eisenstein's return to official respectability. After *October* (1927) and *The Old and the New* Eisenstein had gone abroad, but his film projects there remained unfinished. Returning to the USSR, he fell foul of Boris Shumyatsky, administrative 'tsar' of the Soviet film industry. When he was eventually permitted to begin filming *Bezhin Meadow* the project was halted by Shumyatsky in March 1937, after two million roubles had already been spent on its production. This was an expensive mistake, not only for Soviet film art, but also for Shumyatsky: he was purged as a 'captive of the saboteurs' in January 1938.

This gave Eisenstein his opportunity. He began filming *Alexander Nevsky* on June 7. The film had its premiere a fortnight later. In the process of its rapid editing Eisenstein fell asleep one evening. While the director slept, an incomplete print was removed to the Kremlin and shown to Stalin, who was eager to see it. He liked what he saw, and this made it difficult for Eisenstein to add the missing sequences. Thus his most success-

ful film remained for him the most unsatisfactory — at least from an artistic point of view. At the time, Eisenstein noted:

'*Nevsky* is brazenly effective despite *itself*. *Everyone* can see its staginess *above all*, its length, the rhythmic breaks and failures. *Everyone* can see them, not just the specialists . . . And it is effective *nonetheless*. Why? . . . There's only a single thought and everything revolves around a *single* thought. There's not a word, a remark, an episode or a scene where the dialogue and the plot are not concerned with the enemy and the need to defeat him.'

The story of the Russian people's successful struggle against the Teutonic Knights was an allegorical warning to the Nazis. Alexander's final address to the liberated citizens of Pskov renders this explicit:

'Go and tell all in foreign parts that Rus lives. Let people come to us as guests without fear. But he who comes with the sword shall perish by the sword. On this Rus stands and will stand forever!'

Alexander Nevsky was, in Eisenstein's words:

5

2

3

ster. Let the sceptics remember that there is no force of gloom and darkness that could stand against the combined efforts of all that is best, healthiest, most progressive and forward-looking in mankind.'

The article in which Eisenstein penned these words was called 'Patriotism Is My Theme': it remained unpublished in the USSR because, in August 1939, the Nazi–Soviet Pact was signed. The film no longer served a useful political purpose and was removed from circulation. But by then both

the director and Nikolai Cherkasov, who played Alexander, had been awarded the Order of Lenin, the highest order that the Soviet Union can bestow.

Following the German invasion of the USSR on June 22, 1941, *Alexander Nevsky* was re-released. It is a tribute to both Eisenstein and his politically most successful film that the Soviet government soon instituted a new battle honour for bravery at the front – the Order of Alexander Nevsky.

RICHARD TAYLOR

Thirteenth-century Russia is laid waste by the Mongol hordes from the East, while the Teutonic Knights (1) invade from the West, capturing the ancient city of Pskov and committing atrocities against the population (2). The men of Novgorod call on Alexander Nevsky to lead the Russian forces. The people take arms (3).

On the eve of battle, Ignat entertains the men with the tale of the hare and the vixen: as the hare cannot outpace her, he runs between two closely planted tree

trunks. Following him, the vixen is trapped and the hare deflowers her. This tale inspires Alexander's battle strategy. The Russian armies lie in wait (4), luring the Teutonic Knights (5) onto the frozen surface of Lake Peipus (6); the weight of their armour cracks the ice and they drown in the freezing water. This is the famous Battle on the Ice.

At the head of his victorious forces, Alexander enters Pskov to be fêted by the population (7). Russia is free.

7

6

Action! The films of Michael Curtiz

'Curtiz liked blood so much, he insisted the tips be taken off the swords.' Errol Flynn's viewpoint of Michael Curtiz's temperament was possibly coloured by the mutual antipathy that finally split up their successful partnership; but it is supported by Olivia de Havilland's assertion that 'Curtiz was, until his later years, always an angry man'. Certainly his own attempts at self-promotion were clumsy and arrogant: a manic-depressive by nature, he seldom allowed himself the luxury of any social contact, but his addiction to work combined with an efficient, economic and rapid productivity, made him a perfect craftsman for Warner Brothers. Between 1930 and 1939, Curtiz directed 46 features.

Born Kertész Mihály in Hungary in 1888, he entered the Hungarian film industry in its infancy and directed some of the country's first feature films, *Az Utolsó Bohém* (The Last Bohemian) and *Ma és Holnap* (Today and Tomorrow) in 1912. His career was interrupted in 1919 when he became a political exile and fled to Austria. Jack Warner saw his *Die Slavenkönigen* (1924, *Moon Over Israel*) and invited the director to America. He rapidly acclimatized himself and began to churn out films in all genres, with particular success in horror movies whose suspense was created through ghoulish humour and Expressionistic lighting.

First blood

In 1935 Michael Curtiz (as he was known as in the USA) was assigned a large budget and expensive sets, and Robert Donat was approached to star in *Captain Blood*. Curtiz had filmed many romantic love stories and costume dramas in Hungary, and was the ideal choice to bring to the screen the grandeur and dramatic sweep of Sabatini's novel of a gentleman pirate. Pirate films had not been in vogue since the heyday of Douglas Fairbanks Sr, the athletic swashbuckling hero of silent films, but Warners realized their excellent potential for giving Thirties audiences plenty of action and excitement.

When Donat withdrew owing to illness and contractual misunderstandings, Curtiz remembered a young actor who had worked with him on a B feature, *The Case of the Curious Bride* (1935), and Errol Flynn was summoned back from his honeymoon to test for a role which catapulted him to overnight stardom. Flynn's screen presence as the dashing, inspiring, devil-may-care hero outweighed his limited experience as an actor, compensated for in any case by the excellence of Basil Rathbone and Olivia de Havilland. The narrative – Peter Blood, a doctor, is forced into piracy when he opposes James II – was concise and well-paced. Curtiz also engineered a remarkable technical collaboration that brought ingenious process photography and miniature work, precise editing, and an outstanding first score by Erich Korngold to the film. *Captain Blood* established a highly successful formula that the studio returned to constantly during the next decade, but it was also to prove a typecasting trap for Flynn who was unable to break away from his swashbuckling image for the rest of his career.

The oversized personality of the hero was one of the staple ingredients of the swashbuckler, which had no pretensions to great art but an instinctive appeal to child, critic and intellectual alike. Its genesis lay in the novels of Dumas and Sabatini, and its realization flourished in the hands of Belgian fencing masters and European expatriate directors and musicians. The success of the genre in talkies depended largely upon the contributions from Hollywood's 'English' colony – including Flynn (a Tasmanian with an English accent), Rathbone and Ronald Colman – who carried

off their roles with grace and bravado, presenting the tongue-in-cheek material with balanced earnestness. Curtiz summed up the basic appeal of this type of film: 'I don't see black and white words in a script when I read it, I see action.'

He applied the formula to other swashbucklers, Westerns and comedies with Flynn but their working relationship became increasingly strained and tense. Their next collaboration, *The Charge of the Light Brigade* (1936), involves some awkward romantic entanglements, while titles used as establishing shots slow the pace; but the final charge is a supreme technical achievement.

Colour photography was in more frequent use by 1938 when Flynn starred as Robin Hood. It was the logical and ultimate embellishment of the swashbuckler; and the sharper, primary colours of the three-colour stock that was used gave *The Adventures of Robin Hood* a wonderfully rich texture. The film had been begun by William Keighley and second-unit director B. Reaves Eason (best known for filming the famous chariot race in the 1925

Ben Hur). But after completing most of the Sherwood Forest scenes in six to seven weeks, Keighley was taken off the film by producer Henry Blanke, who felt that his approach was too light-hearted. Curtiz was called in and shot some additional exterior footage as well as all the interiors.

The result was a classic: lavishly bedecked, brilliantly photographed, with a jolly, rousing score by Korngold; and its highlight is the superbly orchestrated final duel between Flynn's Robin and Guy of Gisborne (Basil Rathbone). The playing – Flynn, Rathbone and Olivia de Havilland were excellently supported by Claude Rains, Alan Hale, Eugene Pallette, Ian Hunter and Patric Knowles – was a combination of enthusiasm and total conviction. Flynn's daredevil charm and assurance were enough to carry a variable performance, but the final triumph belonged to Curtiz's professional skill.

Good Queen Bette
Curtiz's *The Private Lives of Elizabeth and Essex* (1939) was a much less satisfying experience

Below: Curtiz staged the climax of The Charge of the Light Brigade *in the San Fernando Valley, California; one man and many horses were killed during filming. Above left: Errol Flynn, Curtiz and David Niven discuss the script. Above: Flynn as Sir Geoffrey Thorpe in* The Sea Hawk, *tenth of 12 films he made with Curtiz*

for Flynn; action took second place to words and he was acted off the screen by Bette Davis as the ageing Elizabeth I. The ambiguous screen relationship between the Queen and her courtier, bedevilled by court intrigue, was certainly more 'Hollywood history' than textbook fact, but Davis' performance was sensitively shaped – the tempestuous outward nature of the monarch tellingly counterpoints her tender, feminine inner-self, while the makeup is determinedly unattractive. Offscreen, Flynn was well aware of his disadvantaged role, and he felt correctly that the action scenes – such as the opening triumphant return from Cadiz, Essex's ill-fated campaign in Ireland, and the storming of the

palace – were not enough to compensate. He is also reputed to have behaved badly towards Davis during filming. He did manage to have the title changed before release to include the name of his character, but to little avail as the praise went to Bette Davis' performance and to Curtiz's effective presentation of the scheming courtiers.

The final Flynn–Curtiz swashbuckler, *The Sea Hawk* (1940), again had its basis in a Sabatini novel – about English captains loyal to Elizabeth I (Flora Robson) who wage an undeclared war with Spain. Korngold supplied the music and the climax was another spectacular duel – between Flynn and Henry Daniell – but contemporary propaganda also crept in with some veiled allusions to the need for opposing military aggression.

Above: Claude Rains, Paul Henreid, Humphrey Bogart and Ingrid Bergman in Casablanca, *filmed by Curtiz without a script so that the end was not decided until the final shooting*

The Casablanca story
By the time America entered World War II, Flynn had begun a new partnership with Raoul Walsh. Curtiz was able to establish himself as Warner's resident 'prestige' director, promoting patriotism and the war effort in the musicals *Yankee Doodle Dandy* (1942) and *This Is the Army* (1943), and in high-powered dramas like *Casablanca* (1942) and *Mission to Moscow* (1943). *Casablanca* has proved an ageless film, beautifully constructed, superbly played and carrying an emotional impact of continuing relevance.

Multi-faceted characterization of all protagonists, major and minor, binds a gripping plot through which the action is perfectly distributed; precise editing ensured the constant tempo and the elimination of any irrelevance. Curtiz's master-stroke was in giving full rein to Bogart's jaded, worldly-wise cynical appeal as the bitter lover with little faith in the general good, who chooses to sacrifice his love for Ilsa (Ingrid Bergman) in favour of her and

her husband's lasting happiness. Bogart does so with the immortal words:

'I'm no good at being noble, but it doesn't take much to see that the problems of three little people don't amount to a hill of beans in this crazy world.'

Another form of choice – the overriding ambition of a mother that destroys her marriage, alienates her vicious daughter, and involves her in murder, blackmail and corruption – provided Joan Crawford with an Oscar-winning showcase in *Mildred Pierce* (1945). The more sordid aspects of Mildred Pierce's dealings with Monty Berrigan (Zachary Scott) were handled with particular taste.

The last of Curtiz
The latter half of the Forties provided Curtiz with a change of pace, initiated by *Life With Father* (1947), a beautifully observed cameo of family life in New York during the 1880s, scripted by Donald Ogden Stewart. But although Curtiz remained active for another 15 years, his career had reached a summit and the assignments slipped from prestige pictures to minor musicals, remakes and some absolute 'turkeys'. The break up of the studio system, culminating in Curtiz's departure from Warners in 1954, directly affected this decline, aided by a poor business sense. He continued to work steadily with stars like Cooper, Holden, Bacall, Ladd, Loren and Wayne, but little of his output – with the notable exceptions of *The Best Things in Life Are Free* (1956), *The Proud Rebel* (1958) and *The Comancheros* (1962) – was worthy of his name or time. He died in Hollywood in 1962.

Although Michael Curtiz has never really achieved the critical stature of John Ford, Alfred Hitchcock and Ingmar Bergman, there is no disputing the craftsmanship and skill with which he packaged his films. Many of them epitomize the best film-making to emerge from Warners in the Thirties and Forties.

KINGSLEY CANHAM

Filmography
Films made in Hungary as Kertész Mihály: **1912** Az Utolsó Bohém; Ma és Holnap. **'13** Hazasodik az Uram; Rablélek; Atlantis (act; + ass. dir) (DEN). **'14** A Hercegnö Pongyolában; Az Éjszaka Rabjai (+ act); Aranyáso; A Kölcsönkért Csecsemok; A Tolonc; Bánk Bán. **'15** Akit Ketten Szeretnek (+ act). **'16** Doktor ur; A Fekete Szivarvany; A Magyar föld ereje; Az Ezust Keckse (+ co-sc); Farkas; Karthausi; A Medikus; Makkhetes. **'17** A föld Embere; A Karuzslo; A Béke Utja; A Senki Fia; A Szentjóbi Erdö Titka; A Vörös Sámson; Arendás Zsidó; Az Utolsó Hajnal; Az Ezredes; Halálcsengö; Zoárd Mester; Egy Krajcár Története; Tartárjárás (+ sc); Tavasz a Télben. **'18** Szamárbör; Alraune (co-dir); A Csunya Fiu; A Napraforgós Hölgy; A Skorpió; A Wellingtoni Rejtély; Az Ördög; Judás; Kilencvenkilenc; Lu, A Kokott; Lulu; Varázskeringö; Vig Özvegy (+ sc). **'19** Jön Az Öcsem; Liliom (unfinished). *Films made in Austria as Michael Kertesz:* **'19** Die Dame mit dem Schwarzen Handschuh. **'20** Boccaccio (+prod); Die Dame mit den Sonnenblumen (+ sc); Die Gottesgeisel; Der Stern von Damaskus. **'21** Cherchez la Femme; Dorothys Bekenntnis/ Frau Dorothys Bekenntnis; Mrs Tutti Frutti (A-IT); Wege des Schreckens/Labyrinth des Grauens. **'22** Sodum und Gomorrah/Die Legende von Sünde und Strafe (Pt 1: Die Sünde) (+ co-sc); Sodum und Gomorrah/Die Legende von Sünde und Strafe (Pt 2: Die Strafe) (+ co-sc); Samson und Delila, der Roman Einer Opernsängerin (prod. ass. as Kertész Mihály only) (GB: Samson

and Delilah). **'23** Der Junge Medardus (co-dir); Der Lawine (USA: Avalanche); Nemenlos/Der Scharlatan/Der Falsche Arzt. **'24** Harun al Raschid; Die Slavenkönigen (USA: Moon Over Israel). **'25** Das Spielzeug von Paris (A-FR) (USA: Red Heels). **'26** Der Goldene Schmetterling (A-DEN) (USA: The Road to Happiness); Fiaker Nr 13 (A-GER). *All remaining films in USA as Michael Curtiz:* **'26** The Third Degree. **'27** A Million Bid; Good Time Charley; The Desired Woman. **'28** Tenderloin; Noah's Ark. **'29** The Glad Rag Doll; The Madonna of Avenue A; The Gamblers; Hearts in Exile. **'30** Under a Texas Moon; Mammy; The Matrimonial Bed (GB: A Matrimonial Problem); Bright Lights; A Soldier's Plaything (GB: A Soldier's Pay); River's End. **'31** Damon des Meeres (GER. language version of Moby Dick, USA 1930); God's Gift to Women (GB: Too Many Women); The Mad Genius. **'32** The Woman From Monte Carlo; Alias the Doctor (with scenes by another director); The Strange Love of Molly Louvain; Doctor X; The Cabin in the Cotton (co-dir). **'33** 20,000 Years in Sing Sing; The Mystery of the Wax Museum; The Keyhole; Private Detective 62; Goodbye Again; Female (co-dir); The Kennel Murder Case. **'34** Mandalay; The Key; Jimmy the Gent; British Agent. **'35** The Case of the Curious Bride; Black Fury; Front Page Woman; Little Big Shot; Captain Blood. **'36** The Walking Dead; The Charge of the Light Brigade; Stolen Holiday. **'37** Kid Galahad (retitling for TV: The Battling Bellhop); Mountain Justice; The

Perfect Specimen. **'38** Gold Is Where You Find It; The Adventures of Robin Hood (co-dir); Four Daughters; Four's a Crowd; Angels With Dirty Faces. **'39** Dodge City; Sons of Liberty (short); Daughters Courageous; The Private Lives of Elizabeth and Essex (retitling for TV: Elizabeth the Queen); Four Wives. **'40** Virginia City; The Sea Hawk; Santa Fe Trail. **'41** The Sea Wolf; Dive Bomber. **'42** Captains of the Clouds; Yankee Doodle Dandy; Casablanca. **'43** Mission to Moscow; This Is the Army. **'44** Passage to Marseille; Janie. **'45** Roughly Speaking; Mildred Pierce. **'46** Night and Day. **'47** Life With Father; The Unsuspected. **'48** Romance on the High Seas (GB: It's Magic). **'49** My Dream Is Yours (+ exec. prod); Flamingo Road (+ exec. prod); It's a Great Feeling (guest appearance as himself only); The Lady Takes a Sailor. **'50** Young Man With a Horn (GB: Young Man of Music); Bright Leaf; The Breaking Point. **'51** Jim Thorpe – All American (GB: Man of Bronze); Force of Arms. **'52** I'll See You In My Dreams; The Story of Will Rogers. **'53** The Jazz Singer; Trouble Along the Way. **'54** The Boy From Oklahoma; The Egyptian; White Christmas. **'55** We're No Angels. **'56** The Scarlet Hour (+ prod); The Vagabond King; The Best Things in Life Are Free. **'57** The Helen Morgan Story (GB: Both Ends of the Candle). **'58** The Proud Rebel; King Creole. **'59** The Hangman; The Man in the Net. **'60** The Adventures of Huckleberry Finn; Olympia (IT-USA) (USA: A Breath of Scandal). **'61** Francis of Assisi. **'62** The Comancheros.

From Peasant to President

The Career of Henry Fonda

Lean, tough and likeable, with a steady lulling drawl, Henry Jaynes Fonda has gracefully aged from portrayals of doomed youths on the wrong side of the tracks and Western heroes to convincing studies of politicians, generals and presidents. He has reached these heights and held his position by avoiding the adulation and studio-processing that nurtured stars like Robert Taylor, Tyrone Power and Alan Ladd, who were then discarded when their box-office draw was fading. 'Hank' Fonda's career continues to grow in stature and to diversify at a staggering pace.

He was born on May 16, 1905, in Grand Island, Nebraska, where his father owned a printing company. Fonda pursued an early ambition to be a writer, majoring in journalism at the University of Minnesota, but he dropped out after two years as he was having to work to pay his tuition fees and could not find enough energies for his studies. Mrs Marlon Brando Sr introduced him to the Omaha Community Theatre where he spent three years, totally stage-struck and often

unpaid, before entering vaudeville and appearing in a series of sketches, which he had written himself, with an old Abraham Lincoln impersonator, George Billinger.

Moving on again he joined the University Players, a New England stock company whose members included Joshua Logan, James Stewart and Margaret Sullavan (who became Fonda's first wife). At this stage of his acting career he was equally interested in scenic design but, landing the lead part in the play *The Farmer Takes a Wife* in 1934, his future was decided. Brooks Atkinson, theatre critic of the *New York Times*, realized exactly in which qualities the actor's strengths resided: 'Henry Fonda . . . gives a manly, modest performance of captivating simplicity.' Recalling that shuffling, clean-cut, all-American boy whose naive idealism was matched by his resolute strength of character, Fonda has commented:

'This shy self-conscious boy was not at all self-conscious on the stage. I was behind a mask fashioned by a playwright, and I could do anything because it wasn't me on that stage.

John Ford used Henry Fonda to embody the American spirit of liberty – as the pioneer farmer in Drums Along the Mohawk *(above left) with Claudette Colbert, and as the future President in* Young Mr Lincoln *(above)*

The audiences weren't looking at me. They were looking at whoever my character was.'

He has always prided himself on this anonymity, part of his intuitive instinct for drawing out a character:

'Usually, I don't have a method . . . I either like a part in a script, or I don't, and if I like it, I'll probably do it. I think the writer has done the homework that's necessary to get the specifics of a character, and he's put it there.'

Fonda entered into a contract with Walter Wanger that stipulated he make two films a year, but which allowed him to continue acting on the stage. He was only third choice for the film version of *The Farmer Takes a Wife* (1935), but neither Gary Cooper nor Joel McCrea was available. Fonda has never forgotten the director Victor Fleming's advice on the

197

different techniques involved in projecting oneself as a film actor as opposed to acting on the stage. Insistent on getting the right parts, he has often had to be talked into a role – he only appeared in Fritz Lang's *The Return of Frank James* (1940) after taking the advice of his friend, director Henry Hathaway.

During the Thirties Fonda made a mixed bag of action and romantic films, society comedies and socially committed stories such as *You Only Live Once* (1937); although the latter was a success, he loathed working with Lang, its director, whom he described as 'a master puppeteer'. But he came into his own with three films for Ford – 'Ford's communication was to chew you out to stop you from acting' – namely *Young Mr Lincoln*, *Drums Along the Mohawk* (both 1939) and *The Grapes of Wrath* (1940). They were all made at 20th Century-Fox, as was Henry King's *Jesse James* (1939), in which he perceptively accepted the second lead to Tyrone Power as he realized that it was the meatier characterization.

At the time, Fonda achieved greater acclaim

Above left: Fonda's first film role was that of an Erie Canal farmer of the 1800s in The Farmer Takes a Wife *with Janet Gaynor. Above: in Vincent McEveety's moody Western* Firecreek *(1968), he played a wandering badman gunning for the town sheriff (played by Fonda's old friend James Stewart)*

for his portrayal of Lincoln than for his Tom Joad in *The Grapes of Wrath*, though his wily studio boss, Darryl F. Zanuck, had used the role of Joad as the bait to lure Fonda into a long-term contract. With the single exception of *The Ox-Bow Incident* (1943), Fonda loathes all the films he made at the studio in this period and was much happier on loan, making *The Lady Eve* (1941) for Paramount and *The Male Animal* (1942) for Warners. Zanuck then delayed Fonda's entry into active naval duty so he could make *The Immortal Sergeant* (1943).

Finally freed by the studio, Fonda served with distinction in the Central Pacific, winning a Bronze Star and a Presidential Citation, and attained the rank of Lieutenant (Senior Grade). After the war he returned to Fox and Ford, scoring a great critical success as a gentle, thoughtful Wyatt Earp in *My Darling Clementine* (1946). But he had an increasing yen to go back to the stage and, after appearing as the disciplinarian cavalry Lieutenant-Colonel Owen Thursday in *Fort Apache* (1948), left the screen until 1955, apart from a guest appearance and some narrations for documentaries.

'I haven't seen over half my films, but in the ones that I have seen, even those that were received well critically, and those that have won awards, I wish I had had the chance to rehearse more. It is the building of the part that matters; you don't know what you could have done had you done it 18 more times, or 1800 more times.'

Fonda certainly had the chance to perfect *Mister Roberts*, with three years on Broadway and on tour in this famous comedy of life on a battleship during World War II. He then starred in two other Broadway hits, *Point of No Return* in 1951, and *The Caine Mutiny Court Martial* in 1955. There was an outcry when Warners offered Brando the *Mister Roberts*' role in the 1955 film version, and Ford, who was assigned to direct, insisted on Fonda for the part. Sadly, they fell out over interpretation with Fonda complaining about the injection of what he considered too much low comic relief,

and reputedly blows were struck. Ford, in any case, was ill and had to be replaced.

Although he has never sought publicity, Henry Fonda has never been far away from the public eye – with a string of failed marriages and his stormy relations with his gifted children, Peter and Jane. Off screen, Fonda can be a moody and often angry man, but he kept his cool remarkably when one tactless wife of a producer asked him: 'What was it like to be married to all those women and two of them committed suicide?' He answered softly:

'Well, I loved them all – in a way I still do. I could not have saved one of them and they could not save me. Everyone has to save himself.'

He reached another peak in his career with *Twelve Angry Men* (1957), in which he plays a juror with a dissenting voice of reason who persuades the other jurors to waive a verdict of guilty on a defendant in a murder trial. Fonda

set up his own company to make the film:

'The one chance I had in the cinema was with Sidney Lumet, making *Twelve Angry Men* . . . we got the artists together, most of them theatre actors, and we rehearsed for two weeks like a play . . . the actors had the benefit, and the thrill, of building their parts from the beginning to the end like a graph.'

Henry Fonda is a committed actor. When the strains of a sustained programme of film-making, Broadway, stage touring and a one-man television show proved physically over-taxing, he entered hospital to have a heart pacemaker inserted, and was back on stage within the week. As to the future, he simply intends to carry on as before:

'I'm not sure I have any goals as an actor, other than to be good and real. All any actor can do with the part is to be as good as he can, try to think it out as much as he can, suggest as much as he can.'   KINGSLEY CANHAM

Above: Fonda and Jackie Cooper in the 1940 sequel to Jesse James. *Above right: as the malicious killer taken unawares by Charles Bronson in* Once Upon a Time in the West *(1968). Below right: with William Powell and Jack Lemmon in* Mister Roberts. *Below left: as 'Juror No. 8' in* Twelve Angry Men

The Clark Gable Story

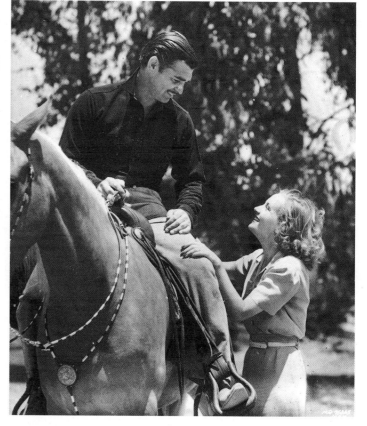

There was no nonsense with Gable. He was rough, tough and ready for anything. And when it came to women . . . well, frankly, he didn't give a damn. But who would have guessed that the King of Hollywood owed his early breaks as an actor to the care and encouragement of the women who wooed him?

When the age of talking pictures dawned in Hollywood, the two greatest romantic male stars of the silent era – Wallace Reid and Rudolph Valentino – were already a memory. Douglas Fairbanks Sr was ageing fast; so was Richard Barthelmess; and that other cavalier, John Gilbert, was in decline. The kings of the silents were all dead or dying. It was time to push the young princes forward and cry out 'Long live the King!'

The most promising heir apparent, ignored at first because he had protruding ears, became the public's choice for King. Twelve Clark Gable pictures were released during 1931, and there was little doubt that MGM, the studio that made most of them, was grooming him for stardom. In the second of those films, *Dance, Fools, Dance*, Gable played a brutal gangster giving Joan Crawford a bad time, and in his seventh role that year, in *A Free Soul*, he beat up Norma Shearer. In the silent days he would have been an out-and-out villain, but the film heroines of the Thirties were showing masochistic tastes, and thought of rugs as something not just to be walked on but dragged over.

William Clark Gable was born in Cadiz, Ohio, on February 1, 1901, the only child of farmer and oil-driller William H. Gable and his wife Adeline. His mother died when he was just seven months old, and his grandparents looked after him for two years until his father married again. William Jr's stepmother, Jennie Dunlap, was the best thing that could ever have happened to him; always a rough diamond, he learned from her the strength of tenderness. He worshipped her.

When young Gable finished his sophomore year at high school, he wanted to go to Akron with an older friend and work in a tyre factory, and his stepmother persuaded her husband to let the boy go. All through his life, women (usually older ones) put him on the right track and helped him forward. It was in Akron that he saw his first stage play, and he was entranced. He went backstage afterwards and got an unpaid job after factory hours as a call boy at the theatre, and was even sometimes given a few small parts with lines.

Gable was hooked. Not even when his stepmother died and his father compelled him to work with him in the Oklahoma oil fields could he forget the magic of the theatre. When he was 21 his grandfather gave him $300 and Gable took off for Kansas City, where he joined a company known as the Jewell Players.

The image everyone associates with Gable is such a virile one, and he played so many cowboys, reporters, oil-men, truckdrivers, auto-racers, boxers and soldiers in his time that he never had any trouble convincing his audiences and fans that he was anything but a hard-working male with square ideas. Certainly no-one would have guessed that at an early age he had drunk of theatre wine and really had little interest outside the stage. He was eager to learn more of the show world, and again it was the women he met who helped him. Among them was Franz Dorfler, an aspiring young actress who took him home to her parents when his stock company failed in Oregon, and saw to it that he was looked after. He marked time in Portland where he was variously employed, first by a newspaper and then a telephone company, until he got a job with an acting group. It was headed by actress and stage director Josephine Dillon, 14 years his senior, who was aware of what he had to offer as an actor and helped him refine his talents. She took him with her to Hollywood, where, on December 13, 1924, they were married.

Gable learned more about the craft of acting from her than he did from anybody else. She taught him physical grace so that he did not move like an oil-rigger; his deportment, both on and off stage, was exemplary. She bought him clothes, took him to a dentist so that he could smile unashamedly, showing off the deep dimples at the sides of his mouth, and persuaded him to drop the name 'William', and call himself Clark Gable. She also got him his first roles in films – mostly as an extra, though he did receive his first screen credit when he played Alice Joyce's brother in *White Man* (1924), and also had a bit part in *The Plastic Age* (1925), with Clara Bow.

Gable was aware that he needed more finesse as an actor and returned to the stage. He played juvenile for Lionel Barrymore in a production of *The Copperhead*. Then, separated from his wife, he let the ladies of the theatre take turns sponsoring him. Jane Cowl took him on as a spear-carrier in her production of *Romeo and Juliet*; Pauline Frederick cast him as the public prosecutor in her revival of *Madame X*, and as a nightclub owner in *Lucky Sam McCarver*. Gable often accompanied Miss Frederick socially; she bought him a new suit and paid for the further expensive dental work he needed. Apart from acting he had other duties to perform, as he grumpily explained, 'Miss Frederick is forever complaining she has a sore back. She likes me to rub it for her.'

After other minor roles he made his debut on the Broadway stage on September 7, 1928, in *Machinal*, playing the star's lover and attracting very good notices. On tour with another play in Texas, he met Mrs Ria Langham, a Houston socialite and several times a divorcee. She was very wealthy, and she liked what she saw when she looked at Clark Gable and followed him back to New York. Like others before her, she took him on as a 'special project'. Josephine Dillon had given him the essentials, but Mrs Langham, 17 years older than Gable and blessed with social contacts, gave him the polishing touches. She took him to the best tailor, the best bootery, the best barber, the best everything. He developed manners, confidence and ease. After they saw Spencer Tracy in the play *The Last Mile*, Mrs Langham decided that the role of Killer Mears was custom-made for Gable. Reputedly, she arranged for him to take the part in the West Coast production of *The Last Mile*, and he was a sensation. As a result, Darryl F. Zanuck tested him for *Little Caesar* but complained about the shape of his ears, and did not sign him to a contract. Minna Wallis, however, did. She was not only a top agent but also the sister of the producer Hal Wallis. She got him the role of a nasty young villain in a Pathé Western, *The*

Painted Desert (1931), with William Boyd and Helen Twelvetrees. She then persuaded William Wellman to hire him for the part of a villainous chauffeur in Warner Brothers' *Night Nurse* (1931), in which he gave Barbara Stanwyck such a brutal beating that audiences were left gasping.

The release of *Night Nurse* was delayed for over a year, and by the time it came out Minna Wallis had got Gable a two-year contract, with options, at MGM. His first picture there was in a small role as Anita Page's husband, a hardworking laundryman in *The Easiest Way* (1931). His success in the part led him directly into *The Secret Six* (1931), in which he and John Mack Brown played reporters investigating underworld crime. The studio was pushing Brown because he had been a top athlete before entering films and had big movie star potential. Frances Marion, however, the scriptwriter of *The Secret Six* and the highest-paid person in her profession at that time, immediately saw Gable's galactic potential. Her husband, George Hill, was the film's director, and they quietly decided to give the stronger lines and better scenes to Gable rather than to Brown. The ruse worked. Gable's rough, tough, but sympathetic role was made to fit. Studio interest was diverted from Brown to Gable and the order went out to give him the big star build-up.

He fitted in well at MGM; his best friends there were the public relations man Howard

Far left: Gable as Rhett Butler in Gone With the Wind. *Left: with his third wife Carole Lombard. Above left: the rising star of 1931 in* A Free Soul *with Norma Shearer and Leslie Howard and* Possessed *(above) with Joan Crawford and Skeets Gallagher. Below: Fletcher Christian to Charles Laughton's Bligh in* Mutiny on the Bounty

Strickling and the director Victor Fleming, in whose company he frequently hunted and fished, golfed and sailed. The studio paid for the perfect set of dentures it was finally necessary for him to have; and also paid for surgery to pin back his ears.

Meanwhile Josephine Dillon had agreed to a divorce. She spoke of him with reluctant but calculated reticence:

'Clark told me frankly that he wished to marry Ria Langham because she could do more for him financially. He is hard to live with because his career and ambition always come first.'

Ria Langham became the second Mrs Clark Gable in New York on March 30, 1930, and they were married a second time in California on June 19, 1931, because of a legal hitch. Ria Langham queened it in Beverly Hills film society, which was fitting enough because by the end of 1931 her husband was the acknowledged King of Hollywood. He was a star who would be in the box-office top ten from 1932 to 1943, again from 1947 to 1949 after he

had returned from the war, and for one more year in 1955.

Most of the time MGM reserved Gable, drawing on his powerful masculine image, to co-star with their galaxy of female stars, and he developed powerful screen partnerships with three of their greatest stars. Joan Crawford and he were together in eight features, Myrna Loy was with him seven times, and Jean Harlow was with him six times.

Gable's off-screen relationships with Miss Loy and Miss Harlow were always platonic, friendly but strictly professional. Miss Crawford later confessed, however, that on several occasions when they were both free from personal obligations they nearly ran away and married, but on each occasion came to their senses in time – their careers mattered more.

Gable also starred with Lana Turner in four films, with Norma Shearer in three, with Rosalind Russell in three, Constance Bennett twice, and Helen Hayes twice. He made one appearance each with Greta Garbo and Jeanette MacDonald. He was, in fact, at some time or another teamed with every MGM female star except Marie Dressler.

Gable was at his best, however, in a man's world, leading the *Mutiny on the Bounty* (1935), sorting out the problems of the Air Force in *Command Decision* (1948), scouting Indian country in *Across the Wide Missouri* (1951). Also, say the name of Clark Gable and to most people it means Rhett Butler in *Gone With the Wind* (1939), or Peter Warne, the newspaper reporter he played in *It Happened One Night* (1934); yet he hadn't wanted to play them or *Bounty's* Fletcher Christian. These were the three pictures for which he was honoured with Oscar nominations (winning for *It Happened One Night*) – virtually the only three he fought against playing.

During the filming of *Gone With the Wind*, Gable was more excited when Ria divorced him for a settlement of $286,000. He was a free man before shooting was finished and drove with Carole Lombard to Kingman, Arizona, where they were quietly married on March, 29, 1939. They had known each other for nearly three years; it was no secret that they had been living together for most of that time, and were both still ecstatically happy. They bought a ranch in Encino and settled down; it seemed as if they would always be the perfect couple. World War II came, however, and Lombard threw herself into war work. She went out on the first War Bond tour after Pearl Harbor in 1942. Returning home, the plane crashed into a mountainside and everybody on it was killed.

Gable was half-crazy with grief. Lombard had teased him about getting involved in the war and now it was all he wanted to do. He took time off from the nearly completed *Somewhere I'll Find You* (1942) to get a firm hold of himself. Then he finished the picture, and eventually joined up in August 1942. He was assigned to Officers Candidate School in Miami, Florida, and went overseas with the Eighth Air Force in 1943. Seven months later he received the Distinguished Flying Cross and Air Medal for 'exceptionally meritorious achievement while participating in five separate bomber combat missions' over Germany. Gable was promoted to the rank of major and, discharged shortly afterwards, returned to work for MGM.

The studio did not know what to do with him: Gable had changed – so had the image of the movie hero. *Adventure* (1945), his comeback film co-starring him with Greer Garson, was a tedious, manufactured comedy. *The Hucksters* (1947), with Deborah Kerr and Ava Gardner, had its moments but was largely a bore. Next to *Parnell* (1937), *Homecoming* (1948) – his third post-war film – is probably his most tiresome and embarrassing picture. The next two were better: Gable seemed to be at ease in uniform with an all-male cast in *Command Decision* (1948); and in *Any Number Can Play* (1949), here as a casino owner. Most

Above left: Gable and Jean Harlow in Wife vs Secretary *(1936). Above: on the set of* Lone Star *(1952) with Ava Gardner. Above right: in* Across the Wide Missouri *(1951). Below, far left: with Spencer Tracy and Myrna Loy in* Test Pilot *(1938). Below left: with Barbara Stanwyck in* To Please a Lady *(1950). Below right: with (back row) Eli Wallach, Arthur Miller, John Huston, (front) Montgomery Clift, Marilyn Monroe, while making* The Misfits – *the last film for both Gable and Monroe*

of his later films were disappointing, however. Even *Mogambo* (1953), Ford's remake of *Red Dust* (1932), with Ava Gardner and Grace Kelly, which did very well at the box-office, was tame in comparison to the earlier version and had little 'bezazz' except Miss Gardner.

Gable was bitterly discontented during this period. He was also lonely, and committed a terrible and expensive error when, on December 21, 1949, he married a fourth time. The bride was Lady Sylvia Ashley, the widow of Douglas Fairbanks Sr. It is said that three weeks after the wedding Gable knew that he'd made a mistake. They were not divorced, however, until 1951 – an event which cost Gable a neat bundle. That same year Dore Schary replaced Louis B. Mayer as head of production at MGM. The stars began falling out of the MGM heavens and Gable's contract, expiring in 1954, was not renewed.

He became the most expensive freelance actor in the business, working for a percentage of the gross. His pictures, though largely ineffective, were better than any he had made at MGM after returning from the war, and they made money. Gable also fell in love, and married for the fifth time. His new wife was beautiful Kay Spreckels; there was much about her that was not unlike Carole Lombard and for the first time since Lombard's death Gable was really happy.

His last film, *The Misfits* (1961), written by Arthur Miller and directed by John Huston, was one of the best pictures he ever made. He played an ageing cowboy who is seeking one

Filmography
1923 Fighting Blood (series). **'24** White Man; Forbidden Paradise. **'25** Déclassée/The Social Exile; The Pacemakers (series); The Merry Widow; The Plastic Age; North Star. **'31** The Painted Desert; Dance, Fools, Dance; The Easiest Way; The Finger Points; Laughing Sinners; The Secret Six; A Free Soul; Night Nurse; Sporting Blood; Susan Lenox: Her Fall and Rise (GB: The Rise of Helga); Possessed; Hell Divers. **'32** Polly of the Circus; Strange Interlude (GB: Strange Interval); Red Dust; No Man of Her Own. **'33** The White Sister; Hold Your Man; Night Flight; Dancing Lady. **'34** Men in White; It Happened One Night; Manhattan Melodrama; Chained; Forsaking All Others. **'35** After Office Hours; Call of the Wild; China Seas; Mutiny on the Bounty. **'36** Wife vs Secretary/Wife versus Secretary; Screen Snapshots No. 10 (short); San Francisco; Cain and Mabel; Love on the Run. **'37** Parnell; Saratoga. **'38** Test Pilot; Too Hot to Handle. **'39** Idiot's Delight; Gone With the Wind. **'40** Strange Cargo; Boom Town; Comrade X. **'41** They Met in Bombay; Honky Tonk. **'42** Somewhere I'll Find You. **'43** Combat America (military training short); Wings Up (propaganda short, incorporating footage from Combat America); Aerial Gunner (military training short). **'45** Adventure. **'47** The Hucksters. **'48** Homecoming; Command Decision. **'49** Any Number Can Play. **'50** Key to the City; To Please a Lady. **'51** Across the Wide Missouri; Callaway Went That-a-Way (guest) (GB: The Star Said No). **'52** Lone Star. **'53** Never Let Me Go (GB); Mogambo. **'54** Betrayed. **'55** Soldier of Fortune; The Tall Men. **'56** The King and Four Queens. **'57** Band of Angels. **'58** Teacher's Pet; Run Silent, Run Deep. **'59** But Not for Me. **'60** It Started in Naples. **'61** The Misfits.

last perfect moment on earth and finds it in a beautiful divorcee (Marilyn Monroe).

Gable had a good time making *The Misfits* but it was not an easy picture to work on. Filming it on location in Reno, the cast and crew had to put up with weather conditions of sheer hell – it was usually over 105°F. The action was far too strenuous for a man of Gable's years but he refused a double; Monroe, meanwhile, was exasperatingly difficult, never on time and unprofessional. But Gable was content. His wife was pregnant, and he went around announcing, 'It's going to be a boy'.

It was a boy – named John Clark Gable – but his father never lived to see him. Two days after completing his part in *The Misfits*, Clark Gable suffered a massive heart attack and died on November 16, 1960, aged 59.

Between 1957 and 1961 many of the screen heart-throbs of the Thirties and Forties died, including Ronald Colman, Gary Cooper, Tyrone Power, Errol Flynn and Humphrey Bogart. But it was Gable's death that really signified the end of that generation of all-male, all-action movie heroes – for Gable alone had been the King of Hollywood.

DeWITT BODEEN

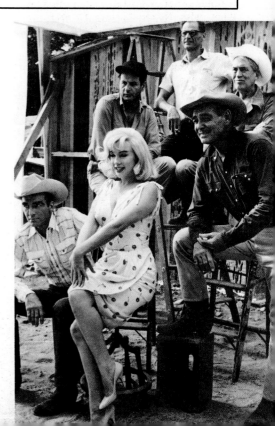

That Scarlett Woman!

Vivien Leigh's legendary rise to stardom can be traced back to the evening of December 10, 1938, when Atlanta – simulated by a group of old sets – was going up in flames a second time. The long-delayed filming of *Gone With the Wind* (1939) was finally under way, even though the Scarlett O'Hara role remained to be cast – an extraordinary risk for producer David O. Selznick to run. Between setting up the takes, Myron Selznick, one of Hollywood's foremost agents, approached his brother, beckoning from the shadows of the old Pathé back-lot a slender young woman with beautiful eyes. 'Dave,' uttered Myron, for press agents, film fans and raconteurs to quote slavishly for decades to come, 'I want you to meet Scarlett O'Hara.'

That, at least, is the story of how Vivien Leigh came to be cast in the role coveted or claimed at one time or another by every rising, established or waning female star in Hollywood. Perhaps the only exceptions were Barbara Stanwyck (who was aware that her screen persona made her unsuitable for the part) and Hedy Lamarr (whose Viennese accent cancelled her out).

The carefully orchestrated three-year search ended in a *coup de théâtre* with the revelation that an English actress, with only a few films to her credit, was to play the Southern heroine of the novel that, since 1936, had outsold the Bible in the USA. The fact that Vivien Leigh was not American failed to outrage the many

Scarlett O'Hara fan clubs in the Deep South; the unforgivable miscasting would have been to let a Yankee play the role!

After diction lessons, Vivien Leigh successfully added the right touch of molasses to her clipped English delivery. She was also coached (at first officially, later privately) by George Cukor, Selznick's original choice to direct *Gone With the Wind*. She battled constantly with Victor Fleming (the director who replaced Cukor after three weeks), failed to make friends with co-star Clark Gable, threw tantrums on the set and off, and won an Oscar.

The truth about Scarlett?

Her achievement still stands, even if there remains some doubt as to how she came to play the role. Another version of the story is that Victor Saville, the British director who had directed Leigh in *Storm in a Teacup* (1937) rang her London flat one day and said:

'Vivien, I've just read a great story for the movies about the bitchiest of all bitches, and you're just the person to play the part.'

Resolved to try for the part of Scarlett, Leigh

Convent-educated, married at the age of 19 to Ernest Leigh Holman, a man of retiring habits, Vivian Hartley (alias Vivien Leigh) claimed to have little in common with the role of Scarlett O'Hara (top right). But her bewitching blend of innocence, beauty and guile fitted the character like a glove

followed Laurence Olivier – then her paramour, later her husband – to California, where he was to play Heathcliff in Samuel Goldwyn's production of *Wuthering Heights* (1939).

It seems that she was probably seen by – and made a strong impression on – David O. Selznick and Cukor, and was kept under wraps while the continuing search for Scarlett garnered a million dollars' worth of publicity. She was then made to appear, like a rabbit out of Myron Selznick's hat, to snatch the part.

The English rose of Hollywood

At 26 she became a priceless commodity in the industry. David O. Selznick, the sole proprietor of her contract, doled out her talents parsimoniously: first to MGM for *Waterloo Bridge*

(1940), then to Alexander Korda, who had originally discovered Leigh in Britain, for *That Hamilton Woman!* (1941). There followed an absence from the screen dictated by war and sickness. She reappeared as Bernard Shaw's Egyptian kitten of a queen in *Caesar and Cleopatra* (1945), looking ravaged and mature enough to play Shakespeare's Cleopatra.

She was Tennessee Williams' own choice for the part of Blanche DuBois in his play *A Streetcar Named Desire*. The play was filmed in 1951, and this time Leigh's Southern drawl was so convincing that it seemed to issue from a dark, bruised recess of her being. A sense of inevitable decline is captured in the curtain line: 'After all, I've always depended on the kindness of strangers' – a melancholy echo of that other famous exit line: 'After all, tomorrow is another day', which summed up the headstrong, vixenish, egotistical Scarlett.

Living close to the edge

Various screen tests for Scarlett have survived and been screened: Leigh's has disappeared into some clandestine collection, but we have Cukor's word that no-one, not even Leigh herself during the actual shooting of the film, could match her miraculously intuitive approach on that first brush with the part.

Bottom: Alexander Korda capitalized on Leigh and Olivier's much-publicized affair by casting them as Lady Hamilton and Lord Nelson in That Hamilton Woman! *Above right: severe bouts of depression marred her performance as Anna Karenina which failed to match Garbo's earlier portrayal. Centre right: Leigh as the Egyptian queen in* Caesar and Cleopatra. *Bottom right: Blanche in* A Streetcar Named Desire, *clinging to her fading beauty and her dreams of romance in a brutal world, was her last great screen appearance. The film's sexual frankness caused a storm of controversy*

Around her Scarlett one perceives, even now, not just the whims and caprices of a spoiled beauty, but real hovering demons; the same which would overwhelm her later in her private life. As early as *Fire Over England* (1937), she seemed a needlessly neurotic lady-in-waiting, but while she was young such traits could be taken as eccentricities. Watching Vivien Leigh glow in inferior pictures like *The Roman Spring of Mrs Stone* (1961) or *Ship of Fools* (1965), there is the strong impression of a trained performer drawing perilously close to lived experience; in *The Deep Blue Sea* (1955), she is almost too genuine for comfort playing a woman caught between suicide attempts.

Vivien Leigh's own life had been one of extremes. Born in 1913 in India, separated in childhood from her mother, she struggled with bouts of hysteria and depression before contracting tuberculosis in 1945. She fought the disease throughout her life until finally succumbing to it in 1967. But these bare facts do not explain her peculiar 'poetic' nervousness.

Tennessee Williams celebrated a certain breed of women as 'ladies who died when love was lost'. This definition, though it misses Scarlett, encompasses Blanche, Anna Karenina, Mrs Stone and Mrs Mary Treadwell of *Ship of Fools*, and may stand as a fitting, if melancholy, epitaph for Vivian Leigh herself.

CARLOS CLARENS

Filmography
1935 Things Are Looking Up; The Village Squire; Gentleman's Agreement; Look Up and Laugh. **'37** Fire Over England; Dark Journey (cut version issued as The Anxious Years); Storm in a Teacup; (USA: 21 Days Together). **'38** A Yank at Oxford. **'39** St Martin's Lane (USA: Sidewalks of London); Gone With the Wind (USA). **'40** Waterloo Bridge (USA). **'41** That Hamilton Woman! (GB: Lady Hamilton) (USA). **'45** Caesar and Cleopatra. **'48** Anna Karenina. **'51** A Streetcar Named Desire (USA). **'55** The Deep Blue Sea. **'61** The Roman Spring of Mrs Stone (USA). **'65** Ship of Fools (USA).

David O. Selznick
Memos of a Movie-making Mogul

Driving ambition and a passionate interest in every aspect of film-making were the chief characteristics of David O. Selznick. On the road to becoming one of Hollywood's most powerful independent producers, he furthered the careers of George Cukor, William Powell and Myrna Loy, and virtually discovered Fred Astaire and Katharine Hepburn. But *Gone With the Wind* was the achievement of a lifetime

In 1931, when David O. Selznick was 29 years old, he sent one of his famous memos to his employers at Paramount complaining that he had not been granted sufficient control:

'A motion picture is like a painting. Instead of oil paints, it uses talents and personalities to tell its story. But each artist must paint his own picture and sign it.'

Selznick never doubted whose signature should appear on each of the films he was associated with. Indeed, when younger he had spent some time in creating a signature dignified enough for the films he intended to produce. His parents had neglected to give him a middle name, so he went through the alphabet until the letter 'O' (which he later claimed stood for Oliver) struck him as giving the proper tone to plain David Selznick.

His insistence throughout his career that *his* should be the decisive voice, that *his* vision and taste should dominate the films he produced no matter who the original author or director, came from his belief that he understood both films and audiences better than anyone else. He had, after all, grown up in the industry.

He began by working for his father's own Selznick Pictures, where he did everything, at one time or another, from designing advertising posters to editing and directing. This gave him a supreme self-confidence and convinced him that in the American production system everyone hired became part of a team to be managed by and to carry out the producer's will. It also made him uneasy with employers and partners, especially after his father had been manipulated by business competitors into a state of bankruptcy.

David O. Selznick subsequently became the archetypal 'creative producer'. He was involved in every aspect and every detail of each film he produced, from the basic structure of the narrative to the colour of the nail varnish worn by the leading lady. In spite of current attitudes in film criticism which stress the importance of the director's vision and style, the films of Selznick indicate how much American cinema could be a producer's cinema. For his major films, he often replaced director after director, writer after writer, and set designer after set designer, until he found those people

who could give him exactly what he wanted. He soon became notorious for his long memos (often running as long as the scripts for the films themselves) which described in great detail what *should be done* or what was wrong with what *had been done*. The films which he produced thus resemble one another; the style, the production values, the performances, all have in common the 'Selznick touch'.

'It is my opinion, generally speaking, and from long observation, that there are only two kinds of merchandise that can be made profitably in this business – either the very cheap pictures or the expensive pictures'

His ambition – to have his own studio and to be a power in Hollywood – was realized with the creation of Selznick International in 1936, just 12 years after he had made his first independent low-budget feature, *Roulette* (1924). During those dozen years, he had put his unflagging energies, his sure knowledge of every part of film production, and his imagination to work towards that ambition. After his father's company had failed, he followed his brother Myron to Hollywood, where he at first took what jobs he could find (assistant editor at MGM, for instance) as a pretext for demonstrating his greater abilities to his employers. While at MGM he managed to produce two Tim McCoy Westerns for not much more than the price of one. He was soon hired by Paramount, first as assistant to the studio head B.P. Schulberg, and then as a producer in his own right. He brought his pictures in on schedule, and often turned 'programmers' into profit-making main features. He also made a number of professional and personal contacts at Paramount, including directors John Cromwell and Merian C. Cooper, whom he would take with him when the time came to move on. That time came in 1931 when he fully understood that no matter how highly regarded he might be at Paramount, all important decisions would continue to be made by others.

David Sarnoff's Radio Corporation of America had just acquired RKO studios, and

Above: newlyweds David and Irene Selznick with the bride's parents, Mr and Mrs Louis B. Mayer. Top: Ingrid Bergman lays a friendly hand on Selznick's shoulder as he jokes with Shirley Temple and his future second wife, Jennifer Jones

Sarnoff hired Selznick as head of production, with a promise that he would be able to do as he liked. In addition to a young and talented production team, Selznick surrounded himself with writers and directors he had observed at

---

'RKO had an amazing faith in me at a time when my previous employers did everything to run me down, and when very few other companies in the business had an appreciable respect for my ability'

---

work at Paramount. He made dialogue director George Cukor into a fully-fledged film director. While Selznick retained, as ever, the right to make final decisions, he listened to the opinions of those around him. Thus, although he at first found Katharine Hepburn unattractive and unpromising, he listened to Cukor and helped to make her into a major star. Selznick also hired Fred Astaire despite advice that the

Left: Selznick confers with Jennifer Jones on the set of A Farewell to Arms. *Above: Ingrid Bergman, seen by Selznick in the Swedish version of* Intermezzo, *starred in his remake and gained international fame. Below left: Powell and Loy were teamed by him for the first time in* Manhattan Melodrama

gramme at Selznick International falls under the gigantic shadow of his *Gone With the Wind* (1939), that programme included *A Star Is Born, Nothing Sacred* (both 1937), *Intermezzo* (1939) and Alfred Hitchcock's first American film, *Rebecca* (1940).

After the release of *Gone With the Wind*, Selznick spent the rest of his career trying to find a project with which he could top it. In 1944, he met Jennifer Jones, a young actress

---

'I am getting to the end of my patience with criticism based on the assumption that actors know more about scripts than I do'

---

working in his *Since You Went Away* (1944). She was to remain a constant obsession. Even on those films in which she acted and he did not produce, Selznick sent off to their directors a never-ending stream of memos about how Jones should look, act and be treated.

In 1946, Selznick decided he had found a novel which could be turned into a film with the epic scope of *Gone With the Wind* – Niven Busch's novel *Duel in the Sun*. The film was released in 1946 with much hyperbolic fanfare. It was laughed at by most critics, some of whom dubbed it 'Lust in the Dust', but it was also hugely successful at the box-office and revitalized the careers of Jennifer Jones and Gregory Peck, its two stars. Seen now, this Western holds up very well indeed as an operatic and melodramatic entertainment; its production matches its content, with the oversaturated colours of every sunset somehow fitting exactly the over-saturated emotions of the characters.

Although there were a number of projects which were never realized (including *War and Peace*), Selznick continued to search for bigger and 'more important' subjects, especially those which had a part for Jones, now Mrs Selznick. While waiting for the right property to turn up, he personally produced two smaller films after *Duel in the Sun* – Hitchcock's *The Paradine Case* (1947) and Dieterle's *Portrait of Jennie* (1948). The latter reveals Selznick's creative state of mind at the time. Although the story is modest,

---

young dancer was unphotogenic. He encouraged Merian C. Cooper and Ernest Schoedsack to develop the film to which he himself gave the title *King Kong* (1933). While he personally produced or supervised a number of hit films, many of them now classics, such as *What Price Hollywood?, A Bill of Divorcement* (both 1932) and *Topaze* (1933), he again found himself at odds with RCA executives who had no intention of allowing Selznick to use RKO merely as an instrument for releasing his own productions. Selznick again resigned.

Although he had earlier married Irene Mayer, daughter of MGM chief Louis B. Mayer, Selznick had refused to play the Hollywood game of nepotism. Now, however, Mayer found himself in need of someone to take charge of MGM production as his previous production head, Irving Thalberg (with whom Mayer never got along anyway) was seriously ill. With a huge salary and access to MGM's full roster of stars and technicians, Selznick accepted the offer and began to turn out expensive, star-filled melodramas based on plays and novels – *Dinner at Eight* (1933), *David Copperfield* and *Anna Karenina* (both 1935). He brought Cukor to MGM (where the director had a long and successful career), 'discovered' Mickey Rooney (for *Manhattan Melodrama* in 1934) and was the first to co-star William

Powell and Myrna Loy (in the same film). But even with his own production unit at MGM, Selznick was still not his own boss; his decisions might always be overridden by Mayer or by Loew's head office in New York. Once more he resigned.

Making a deal by which his own productions would be released through United Artists, he assured himself that films he produced would reach cinemas, most of which were

---

'I hear rumours that Miss Hepburn is under twenty-one, which we should take immediate action to confirm, to find out whether it is necessary to get the approval of the courts. I understand she is prone to exaggerate her age and likes to be thought much older than she is'

---

then controlled by the major studios. Not surprisingly his taste in the projects he chose to undertake, and the style in which he made them, differed little from that shown at MGM. He continued to transfer classic and popular novels and plays to the screen, producing them in glossy and expensive style, and casting them with a combination of established stars and his own discoveries. Although his production pro-

Above: Gregory Peck and Jennifer Jones in Duel in the Sun. *Above right:* A Farewell to Arms, *set in Italy during World War I, was Selznick's last production. Below: Selznick hired Alfred Hitchcock to direct* Rebecca *in Hollywood; it won an Oscar for Best Film in 1940. Bottom: Jones and Montgomery Clift in* Indiscretion of an American Wife, *the director De Sica's first English-language film*

concerning a man falling in love with the portrait of a girl from an earlier time, the film has an epic climax – a full-scale hurricane. Even in his smaller films, then, the ghost of *Gone With the Wind* continued to haunt him.

Selznick also became involved in several co-productions throughout the late Forties and Fifties. Although he did not 'interfere' much with *The Third Man* (1949), he had whole sequences of Michael Powell's *Gone to Earth* (1950) re-shot in Hollywood by Rouben Mamoulian for release in the USA. He also expressed interest in working with one of the Italian neo-realist directors. He once approached Roberto Rossellini, perhaps in an effort to protect his star Ingrid Bergman, perhaps in a misguided attempt to recapture the prestige which had eluded him for at least a decade. Certainly nothing could be more opposite to the aims of neo-realism than Selznick's own glossy productions; nonetheless he proceeded to co-produce (with Columbia) *Stazione Termini* (1953, *Indiscretion of an American Wife*), directed in Italy by Vittorio De Sica and starring Jennifer Jones. The result was a critical and financial disaster.

Selznick's final film was a co-production with 20th Century-Fox, an expensive epic adaptation of Hemingway's *A Farewell to Arms* (1957), directed by Charles Vidor (who had earlier done the first sequences of *Duel in the Sun*) and starring Jennifer Jones and Rock Hudson. One can again assume that the ghost

of *Gone With the Wind* appeared to the producer, for the new film diminished its personal story to make way for battles and marches through snow-covered mountains. Its lack of success with critics and public caused Selznick to retire from film production.

Still, it is not by those last few films that one should judge Selznick's career. He worked in every genre except horror and science fiction, and in each created at least one recognized classic. He knew how to entertain mass audiences, and yet do it with a certain sensitivity and taste.   DAVID OVERBEY

Quotations from Memo From David O. Selznick, *edited by Rudy Behlmer. Copyright © 1972 Selznick Properties, Ltd (New York, Viking, 1972)*

Filmography

1923 Will He Conquer Dempsey? (short); Rudolph Valentino and His 88 American Beauties (short). **'24** Roulette. **'27** Spoilers of the West. **'28** Wyoming (GB: The Rock of Friendship); Forgotten Faces (sup. only). **'29** Chinatown Nights (assoc. prod. only); The Man I Love (assoc. prod. only); The Four Feathers (assoc. prod. only); The Dance of Life (assoc. prod. only); Fast Company. **'30** Street of Chance; Sarah and Son; Honey; The Texan; For the Defense; Manslaughter. **'32** Lost Squadron/The Lost Squadron; Symphony of Six Million (GB: Melody of Life); State's Attorney (GB: Cardigan's Last Case); Westward Passage; Roar of the Dragon; What Price Hollywood?; The Age of Consent; Bird of Paradise; A Bill of Divorcement; The Monkey's Paw; The Conquerors; Rockabye; The Animal Kingdom (GB: The Woman in His House); The Half-Naked Truth. **'33** Topaze; The Great Jasper; Our Betters; Christopher Strong; Sweepings; Dinner at Eight; Night Flight; Meet the Baron; Dancing Lady; King Kong (exec. prod.). **'34** Viva Villa!; Manhattan Melodrama. **'35** David Copperfield; Vanessa, Her Love Story; Reckless; Anna Karenina; A Tale of Two Cities. **'36** Little Lord Fauntleroy; The Garden of Allah. **'37** A Star Is Born; The Prisoner of Zenda; Nothing Sacred. **'38** The Adventures of Tom Sawyer; The Young in Heart. **'39** Made for Each Other; Intermezzo: a Love Story (GB: Escape to Happiness); Gone With the Wind (+uncredited sc; +uncredited dir). **'40** Rebecca. **'44** Since You Went Away (+ sc); I'll Be Seeing You. **'45** Spellbound. **'46** Duel in the Sun (+ uncredited dir). **'47** The Paradine Case (+ sc). **'48** Portrait of Jennie (GB: Jennie). **'49** The Third Man (co-prod. only) (GB). **'50** Gone to Earth (USA: The Wild Heart) (co-prod. only) (GB). **'53** Stazione Termini (USA: Indiscretion of an American Wife; GB: Indiscretion) (co-prod. only) (IT-USA). **'57** A Farewell to Arms (co-prod. only).

LONESOME TRAIL

After a big-guns opening to the sound era, Westerns fell from popularity in the Thirties until 1939's bumper crop of cowboy pictures proved that old genres never die

In the Western actions usually spoke louder than 'words', but when the sound revolution occurred the craze was for films with plenty of dialogue – comedies and musicals. So in the early days of talkies the immediate outlook for the Western was bleak. To make matters worse the sound engineers claimed that recording outdoors would be difficult, if not impossible.

In the ensuing uncertainty, the big Western stars of the silent cinema – Tom Mix, Ken Maynard, Tim McCoy – were dropped by their studios. Only Universal persevered, pumping out more of its Hoot Gibson Westerns and later snapping up Maynard and McCoy. But it was the director Raoul Walsh and the crew of *In Old Arizona* (1928) who quashed any reservations about applying sound to outdoor subjects.

The film was a modest Cisco Kid drama based on a story by O. Henry with a typical twist in which the Kid neatly revenges himself on a double-crossing señorita and outwits the law at the same time. The incidental sounds were laid on somewhat heavily, but audiences were thrilled at the clear recording of lips being smacked after a character had swallowed a drink, of eggs and bacon frying, and of horses' hoofs fading away as riders departed. There was also a zestful performance by Warner Baxter as the laughing bandit who serenaded his faithless señorita with the song 'My Tonia'. Baxter won the Academy Award in 1929 for Best Actor and *In Old Arizona* was the smash hit that restored

Westerns to favour.

The same year saw Victor Fleming's painstaking screen version of the thrice-filmed story *The Virginian* (1929) in which Gary Cooper made a suitably laconic hero forced to hang the friend who has turned cattle-rustler.

The Western was so strong a box-office prospect that by 1930 it was seen as a suitable candidate for wide-screen experimentation. MGM made *Billy the Kid* (1930) which was shot in the 70mm Realife process; Fox released its epic *The Big Trail* (1930) which ran 158 minutes in its Fox Grandeur version and 125 minutes in the standard 35mm version (both were shot simultaneously). Warners contributed *The Lash* (1930), a romantic adventure set in the California of the 1850s with Richard Barthelmess as a Spanish nobleman who turns bandit in order to overthrow a crooked American land commissioner. This movie was released in yet another wide-screen process: 65mm Vitascope.

Despite the resurgence of interest in Westerns, these three films flopped at the box-office owing to resistance on the part of exhibitors to the cost of installing wide-screen systems in their cinemas. Experimentation with 65mm and 70mm film gauges had raised the production cost enormously, and because of their failure the Western was once again brought into disrepute as far as the big producers were concerned.

Billy the Kid (dir. King Vidor) was a straightforward, slow, austere account of the young outlaw's

Top: William S. Hart, the foremost star of silent Westerns, hands over to the talkie star, John Mack Brown. The gun used for this historic occasion is reputed to have belonged to the real-life outlaw Billy the Kid. Left: Indian chiefs survey the range in Raoul Walsh's The Big Trail

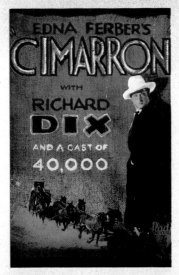

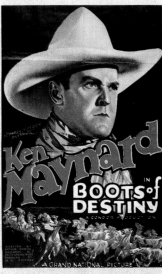

Top: Cimarron *portrayed the life of an Oklahoma family between 1890 and 1915. Above: Ken Maynard, an early cowboy star, continued well into the Thirties in B pictures like this 1938 Western. Below: wagons roll westwards in* The Big Trail

life, using the Grand Canyon for its locations. Although the film altered the facts by allowing a reformed Billy to go off with his girl at the end, the high death count up to that point set a harsh tone that did not appeal to audiences. John Mack Brown played Billy but it was not a role that suited him and he was to gain more charisma later in the decade as a star of series Westerns.

The Big Trail (dir. Raoul Walsh) was made to celebrate the centenary of a pioneering wagon-train journey that had set out from Independence, Missouri. The movie was shot under conditions almost as gruelling as those endured by the original travellers. It contained spectacular scenes of a buffalo hunt, a massive Indian attack on a circle of wagons, the fording of a swollen river and the lowering of cattle and wagons down a sheer cliff-face, in settings ranging from rainstorms and blizzards to desert heat. Unfortunately the human-interest was feeble and the casting of the unknown John Wayne as the wagon-train scout was a gamble that did not pay off at the box-office, although Wayne acquitted himself well. The final image fittingly celebrates the might of nature – the film's most impressive theme – as Wayne strides out of frame to be reunited with the heroine (Marguerite Churchill) and the camera tilts upwards to take in the towering trees of the forest setting.

The only Western ever to win the Academy Award for the year's Best Picture was *Cimarron* (1931). But this was more than a Western: based on one of Edna Ferber's vast, sprawling, generation-spanning sagas, it was an epic about the development of Oklahoma. It began with a spectacular reconstruction of the Cherokee Strip land-rush and continued through to the oil boom of the twentieth century. The success of *Cimarron* spawned such imitations as *The Conquerors* (1932) with the same star, Richard Dix, and *Secrets* (1933), with Mary Pickford and Leslie Howard. The latter film was the only main feature Western among the sixty or so released in 1933.

Before the genre went into the wilderness of the B movie there was one notable, medium-scale Western, *Law and Order* (dir. Edward Cahn, 1932) which drew heavily on the story of Wyatt Earp bringing law to Tombstone and of the gunfight at the OK Corral. Walter Huston brought his usual authority to the central role and the script was written in part by his son John Huston. Cahn's direction provided some powerful sequences as, for example, the coverage of a lynch mob's arrival on horseback, townsfolk thronging the balconies around the jail-house, then edging forward slightly (the camera edging with them) to press in on Huston who is waiting on the steps outside. Cahn composed a striking finale to the film, shooting the march towards the final showdown with his camera set low, tracking backwards in front of Huston and his men as they stride purposefully forward.

After this production, however, it was left to the B picture units and the Poverty Row studios to keep the Western alive, though usually in the series format. In 1935, however, minor Westerns doubled in number in response to public demand, and two important developments in the genre occurred. First there was the arrival of Gene Autry, a former radio singer, who made his debut as a singing cowboy in the serial *The Phantom Empire* and the feature *Tumbling Tumbleweeds* (both 1935). Songs and comedy became major ingredients in Autry's work and his bland easy-going personality set the tone for the relaxed quality of his films which non-metropolitan audiences found especially to their liking. His stories were set in a fantasy land where contemporary and period details merged – aircraft, for example, could co-exist comfortably with old-fashioned stagecoaches.

The second key development was the Hopalong Cassidy series starring William Boyd as the blond knight of the range. Boyd was an accomplished performer who could handle action as ably as he could deliver lines; responding to a query about his guns in *Bar 20 Rides Again* (1935), he says, 'I just wear them to keep my legs warm'. The Hopalong Cassidy series was a success and encouraged Para-

mount, who had distributed it, to venture into big Westerns again.

So in 1936 King Vidor made *The Texas Rangers* with Fred MacMurray as the former stagecoach robber who joins the lawmen and brings an old partner (played by Lloyd Nolan) to justice. More significant, however, was Cecil B. DeMille's *The Plainsman* (1936) a lavish pot-pourri that starred Gary Cooper as Wild Bill Hickok, Jean Arthur as Calamity Jane, James Ellison as Buffalo Bill, John Miljan as Custer and Frank McGlynn Sr as Abraham Lincoln. Its robust action scenes, filmed by the second-unit director Arthur Rosson, blended awkwardly with studio close-ups of the stars firing at back-projections of marauding Indians. There were also moments of light relief as, for example, when a bullet was fired into a water-keg to provide a stream of water for a man lying wounded underneath – but at least DeMille insisted on a factual conclusion with Hickok being shot in the back and dying. Paramount followed this slice of comic-strip history with Frank Lloyd's static *Wells Fargo* (1937), starring Joel McCrea, and James Hogan's livelier *The Texans* (1938), with Randolph Scott, Joan Bennett and Walter Brennan.

Surprisingly, although three-strip Technicolor was being used by Paramount and other studios on outdoor subjects it was not used in Westerns until *Jesse James* (1939), although a number of Warners' outdoor films – *God's Country and the Woman* (1936), *Gold is Where You Find it* and *Heart of the North* (both 1938) – were almost Westerns. Then two films, Fox's *Jesse James* and Paramount's De-Mille extravaganza *Union Pacific* (1939) triggered a great Western boom; the trade paper *Variety* noted the trend early in 1939.

'Out of Hollywood from now until the end of the present production year in midsummer, will flow the rootin', tootin', shootin'est, bowie-knife wielding bunch of ride 'em cowboy, major budget Westerns the picture business has witnessed in a decade. Some $15,000,000 worth of shooting, scalping, train and stagecoach robbing, hypoed with gentle love, mad brawls for the protection of honour and "curse you, Jack Dalton" villains has been budgeted.'

Variety's explanation for the revival of the genre was the cyclical nature of the business and the copy-cat techniques of the studios; all of them were making Westerns for fear of being left out of a forthcoming box-office bonanza. But other factors may have come into play. *Variety*'s report of a 'surge of Americanism' in film subject-matter was only to be expected as the European situation worsened. Key foreign markets were threatened or already lost, and films with strong domestic appeal made sense at the box-office.

Furthermore, cinema attendance figures in the United States had become static despite the rise in population and the studios were consequently making changes in film content in the hope of building new audiences.

One picture has come to stand out from all the rest in the bumper crop of 1939: *Stagecoach*. It was John Ford's first Western since *Three Bad Men* (1926) but was not an outstanding success commercially. *Variety* announced:

'*Stagecoach* at the box-office has not sustained the enthusiastic reviews it received from the press. Lack of strong names in the cast and a trite title are the reasons given for the *Stagecoach* fade.'

But the praise heaped on the film and the evident skill of Ford's direction did have a strong influence on other film-makers: it made the Western a respectable subject for quality films. If the year had not been dominated by *Gone With the Wind*, the film would have won more Oscars than the two it did.

In a dramatic sense *Stagecoach* was not essentially a Western – its carefully assorted band of passengers could have been assembled in any setting and exposed to an equivalent danger to show their reaction under stress. And almost all the scenes involving the leading players were filmed in the studio. But besides John Ford's inimitable use of Monument Valley and his striking chase sequence across salt flats, there was his masterful treatment

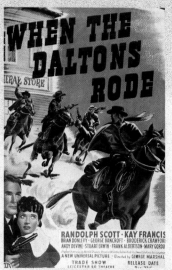

Top: Randolph Scott, Kay Francis, Brian Donlevy and Andy Devine were among the familiar names in popular Westerns; here they were teamed in a version of the Daltons legend. Above: the singing cowboy Gene Autry made his feature-film debut in the Western with songs, Tumbling Tumbleweeds

Gun Fights!
Thundering herds!
Prairies ablaze!
Romance!

SAMUEL GOLDWYN presents

GARY COOPER

THE WESTERNER

directed by WILLIAM WYLER

with WALTER BRENNAN · DANA ANDREWS

Top: on location with The Texans. *The large circular disc is designed to reflect sunlight on the couple in the buckboard – Joan Bennett and Robert Cummings. Top right: Ronald Reagan and Errol Flynn prepare to shoot it out in* Santa Fe Trail. *Above: Wyler's prestige Western based on the life of Judge Roy Bean. Below: Tyrone Power in* Jesse James

of the traditional gunfight on main street. Moreover the dynamic performance of John Wayne, in such moments as the halting of the runaway stage or when he dives to the ground to fire on his opponents in the climactic shoot-out, assured the actor of the front-rank stardom that had eluded him since *The Big Trail.*

Both *Jesse James* and *Dodge City* (1939) eclipsed *Stagecoach* in box-office terms; they had top stars and were in Technicolor. *The Oklahoma Kid* (1939) was another success. James Cagney wore a ten-gallon hat and brought his city-slicker mannerisms to the role of the Robin Hood of Oklahoma, and Humphrey Bogart, dressed in black from tip to toe, played the dastardly villain, but the movie was tongue-in-cheek and deserved its success. *Jesse James* was a romanticized depiction of the celebrated outlaw's life with sympathetic portrayals from both Tyrone Power as Jesse and Henry Fonda as his brother Frank; the two of them take up robbery only after the railroad's representative (played by Brian Donlevy) has burnt down the family farm and killed their mother. Jesse's actual death (he was shot in the back) was retained but the newspaper editor, acting as chorus or commentator, gave the film an upbeat ending eulogizing Jesse:

'We ain't ashamed of him – I don't think even America is ashamed of Jesse James. Maybe it was because he was bold and lawless like all of us like to be sometimes, maybe it's because we understand a little that he wasn't altogether to blame for what his times made him . . .'

The cue had been given for the Old West's other badmen to be covered in Hollywood whitewash. MGM remade *Billy the Kid* (1941) with Robert Taylor; Gene Tierney appeared as the notorious *Belle Starr* (1941) and Universal told of *When the Daltons Rode* (1940).

In contrast *Dodge City* was merely an actionful Western with Errol Flynn dispensing the heroics to a zestful score by Max Steiner. Michael Curtiz's direction displayed its usual panache but the script by Robert Buckner was rather weak. The same combination of star, composer and director were brought in to liven up two more Buckner screenplays: *Virginia City* and *Santa Fe Trail* (both 1940).

DeMille's *Union Pacific* was the epic story of the construction of the first transcontinental railway. No expense was spared to give the film an authentic look: the top track-laying crew of the actual Union Pacific company was recruited to perform in front of the cameras, and there was a spectacular Indian attack on a moving train, staged by Arthur Rosson. The main plot featured Joel McCrea as the overseer fighting saboteurs (led by Brian Donlevy, the period's most hard-working screen villain) while avenging the death of a friend at the same time. The narrative was stronger than that of *The Plainsman* and DeMille gained some inspiration from John Ford's *The Iron Horse* (1924) which had the same historical background.

Even Republic, the leading source of B Westerns, with its singing cowboys Gene Autry and Roy Rogers, decided the time was right to move up-market. Borrowing a star, Richard Dix, a director, George Nichols Jr, and a supporting actress, Joan Fontaine, they made *Man of Conquest* (1939), the story of the pioneer Sam Houston, that culminated in a rousing reconstruction of the battle of San Jacinto. So contagious was the fever for big Westerns that even the 'quality film' specialist Sam Goldwyn succumbed and hired William Wyler to make *The Westerner* (1940), Goldwyn's second (and last) horse opera. The film was a cleverly written account of the relationship between an honest cowpoke (played by Gary Cooper) and the wily Judge Roy Bean (Walter Brennan in an Oscar-winning portrayal).

At the turn of the decade the Western was in such strong shape that it even encouraged the satirical treatment of George Marshall's *Destry Rides Again* (1939), a light-hearted re-working of a Max Brand story that had been filmed straight in 1927 as Tom Mix's first sound film. James Stewart played the apparently naive and helpless Destry who helps clean up a town while Marlene Dietrich was the saloon singer who fell for his good looks and innocent charm.

The astonishing recovery of the genre put it back on its feet for good, but the excitement and vitality of the Westerns of the 1939–41 period was only short-lived.

ALLEN EYLES

How John Ford's West was Won

The heroes of John Ford's films are the frontiersmen, pioneers and peacemakers who dedicated themselves to the founding of the homes and communities that make up America. Ford's vision is a folk vision: a celebration of the ideals that sent wagon trains of settlers westwards in search of freedom and opportunity, but couched in the homeliest of terms – where a dance or a gathering round a graveside speaks volumes more than the dramatic battles and gunfights that were also waged in the winning of the West

Above: Stagecoach, in which John Ford (inset) first made use of the spectacular mesas of Monument Valley, Utah. The film itself was a landmark in the career of one of the most respected directors in world cinema. Ford (1895–1973) directed his first feature, Tornado, in 1917. Born Sean Aloysius O'Feeney, thirteenth child of Irish immigrant parents, in Maine, he had come to Hollywood after failing to get into naval college. He worked his way up as prop man, stunt man and actor

By the end of the Thirties John Ford already had a hundred films to his name. Whereas a lesser director would have probably burned himself out, the best years for Ford were still ahead. His 'golden age' spanned nearly three decades. It began in 1939 with two films, *Stagecoach* and *Young Mr Lincoln*, and encompassed along the way such milestones as *She Wore a Yellow Ribbon* (1949), *Wagonmaster* (1950) and *The Searchers* (1956). These films are packed with unforgettable sequences and images: the young Lincoln (Henry Fonda) climbing a hill in a storm; Nathan Brittles (John Wayne), the old cavalry captain in *She*

Wore a Yellow Ribbon, riding out of the fort for a final mission and furtively shielding his face from the sun, or Brittles going to his wife's grave in the evening to 'talk' to her. There is the moment when the showgirl Denver (Joanne Dru) flashes a mysterious look at the wagon-train leader Travis (Ben Johnson) in *Wagonmaster*; or when Ethan (Wayne) lifts up and cradles the niece (Natalie Wood) he has sought to kill in *The Searchers*, understanding in those few instants the uselessness of his hatred; or Frank Skeffington (Spencer Tracy) returning home alone after failing to be re-elected as the mayor in *The Last Hurrah* (1958). These

sublime moments in Ford's films reveal more than a thousand critical post-mortems that his art is above all meditative – one might even say symphonic.

The contemplative nature in Ford has rarely been understood. In France, for example, his Westerns have been promoted with pompous phrases like 'heroic charge', 'hellish pursuit' and 'fantastic journey' which suggest that the films somehow belong to the epic genre. Nothing is further from the essence of these fundamentally peaceful works of art. And although Voltaire's assertion that 'Epic authors had to choose a hero whose name alone

problems in so far as they overlap those of society at large; whereas in Howard Hawks' Westerns, for example, adventure remains the right of the individual and only concerns society by chance or accident. In Hawks' *Rio Bravo* (1959) the sheriff (John Wayne) refuses the help offered to him; Ford's Wyatt Earp, however, accepts it immediately. It is a fundamental difference: the first sheriff seeks to fulfil himself through his duty, the second thinks primarily about helping those around him.

. . . what a man's gotta do

At the same time Ford frequently shows us the dissensions and disagreements that divide communities, and his heroes act only in relation to the environment they live in. It is that environment that provides their task – a duty to fulfil for the good of the community; any personal vendettas are usually subjugated to the communal cause. The notion of having a task or a mission takes precedence over all personal considerations. This is especially true of *Rio Grande* in which Captain Kirby Yorke (John Wayne) puts his duty as a soldier before his marriage and family; and in *The Sun Shines Bright* (1953), in which an old Southern judge (Charles Winninger) risks his reputation in

Above: Judge Billy Priest (Will Rogers) and other veterans of the Civil War evoke nostalgia for the Confederate States in Judge Priest *(1934). Ford remade the film as* The Sun Shines Bright *in 1953*

would impress itself on the reader' can be applied to certain Ford films like *Young Mr Lincoln* (a splendid evocation of the youth of the American president), it is certainly not applicable to most of his work, including the Westerns. In *My Darling Clementine* (1946), that legendary hero Wyatt Earp (Henry Fonda) is reduced to everyday dimensions; he has no exalted status.

A man's gotta do . . .

It is interesting to compare the socially minded motivation of the typical Ford hero with the personal motivation of the classic Western hero. The classic Western is chiefly built around a ruggedly individualistic vision of the world: Allan Dwan's *Silver Lode* (1954), with John Payne as a man trying to clear his name, and King Vidor's *Man Without a Star* (1955), with Kirk Douglas as a drifter motivated by revenge, are perhaps the most extreme examples of this. Strong feelings, often of physical or psychological violence, predominate; there is hatred, vengeance, rebellion and conquest. A cowboy is usually out to avenge his brother, his friend or his own honour; an outlaw tries to escape from his past; a gunfighter follows his will to kill; a man needs to prove he is not a coward or has to overcome the devil within himself. In short, the genre draws its dramatic force from a few powerful ideas: a confrontation, an opposition, a tearing away. From the films of Raoul Walsh to those of Delmer Daves, Western heroes pitch themselves into a battle by their own free choice. And it is a battle that will allow them to accomplish their purpose – but from which, if they survive, they will emerge permanently scarred. Even if there are no horseback chases or bloody shoot-outs, the dramaturgy of the classic Western is precisely structured and depends on a number of climactic moments.

With Ford, however, the essential motivation is looser, more attenuated, and rarely drawn around an individual emotion or a negative, destructive driving force like vengeance. What predominates at the heart of his Westerns are journeys and wanderings: the slow odyssey of a wagon train, the patrolling of a group of cavalrymen, the crossing of a desert by a stagecoach, or by a group of bandits on the run. Ultimately his films are all odysseys of groups – the stage passengers in *Stagecoach* (1939), farmers and their families escaping from the Oklahoma Dust Bowl in *The Grapes of Wrath* (1940), cavalrymen out on missions in *Fort Apache* (1948), *She Wore a Yellow Ribbon*, *Rio Grande* (1950) and *The Horse Soldiers* (1959), the Mormon settlers in *Wagonmaster*, Ethan and Martin Pawley (Jeffrey Hunter) searching for Debbie in *The Searchers*. Each group consists of several people who either belong to the same walk of life, or are brought together and bound by the same collective purpose. Ford is only interested in personal

Most of Ford's films are about men working for a common cause and sharing the hardships incurred. Above: John Qualen, Ward Bond, Jack Pennick, John Wayne and Thomas Mitchell toil on the sea in The Long Voyage Home.
Below: Welsh miners enduring a pit disaster in How Green Was My Valley, *with Walter Pidgeon and Oscar-winner Donald Crisp*

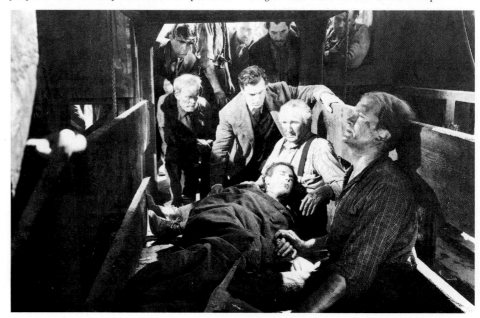

evokes it briefly and objectively, without any indulgence or lyricism; the swift shoot-out at the OK Corral in *My Darling Clementine* and the killing off of the outlaws who threaten the settlers in *Wagonmaster* are good examples.

Even the adventures themselves are non-violent in the way they progress; they are unfolded for us in a rhythm that is at once casual yet majestic. In telling a story Ford takes his time and works like a painter, rather than a strategist or a theoretician.

The true Ford hero has no need to use violence to prove himself. He simply does it, carried along by the collective ideal that leaves no space in his mind for doubt. Perhaps Ford's real heroes are the communities themselves: the unknown soldiers bringing peace to the West; the pioneers who are crossing the country to build new states; the inhabitants of

The story of Ford's films is a great saga of agrarian life: claiming or reclaiming, cultivating and enlarging territorial possessions.

Accordingly Ford's heroes take their character from the peasant, whatever their social origins. Heroes may be Irish peasants, farmers, Welsh miners, soldiers, whatever. In Ford's eyes the soldiers who run a territory in *She Wore a Yellow Ribbon* are involved in the same struggle as the Joad family in *The Grapes of Wrath*. And although the different communities in Ford's films are closed communities governed by their own rules, they are similar in that they share not only the struggles of life but its simple pleasures, too, like a dance, as in *Fort Apache* and *My Darling Clementine*.

The notion of possession accounts for Ford's passion for ceremonies. Celebrations, drunken festivities, dances, even funerals are the tan-

order to rescue a black boy from being lynched. In *My Darling Clementine* Wyatt Earp's vengeance on the Clantons for the killing of his brother is given much less importance than the dance in front of the church and the Shakespearian monologues of the travelling showman (Alan Mowbray). Earp is a supremely calm figure, not someone driven by a nameless hatred (as is the case of the Western heroes in the films of Anthony Mann).

Indeed, violence linked to the notion of a personal quest hardly exists at all in Ford's films. Killings, even woundings, are rare. Not a single Indian is seen to be killed or wounded in *She Wore a Yellow Ribbon*. In *Two Rode Together* (1961), Sheriff McCabe (James Stewart) fires only two revolver shots – the only gunshots in the film. Ford could never conceive a scene like the one in Anthony Mann's *The Man From Laramie* (1955) where Stewart's hand is maimed. Violence is never a goal in Ford's films or a means of self-fulfilment, but a duty or a last resort. When violence is inescapable, Ford

Above: in My Darling Clementine *Henry Fonda portrayed Wyatt Earp as a balanced, pensive peace-loving man. Right: a custodian of the West retires – John Wayne as Captain Brittles in* She Wore a Yellow Ribbon *with Harry Carey Jr, Joanne Dru and Victor McLaglen. Below: Travis (Ben Johnson) and Denver (Joanne Dru) in* Wagonmaster

a township whose chief aim is to establish a society of law and order – all those people who, whether consciously or not, have helped to build the United States and whose names and faces have been forgotten. And so it is their work that the films celebrate. This work may not be exalting; it is often thankless, seldom on a big scale, but it is stamped with a day-to-day heroism.

The homing instinct

Most of Ford's pictures are based on and perpetuate a theme that seems to haunt his last Western, *Cheyenne Autumn* (1964) – his elegy on the dispossessed Indians who seek to reclaim their ancestral lands – and that is the need not simply to build or see something through to its conclusion, but to arrive at the possession of a piece of land, a home or hearth, or perhaps simply a rocking-chair, which is exactly what is sought by Mose (Hank Worden) in *The Searchers*. There is also a need to fight against enemies and the elements to keep possessions in order to understand their complete value.

gible proof of the need to affirm publicly the ownership of a place, especially since it could be taken away at any time – as Lars Jorgensen (John Qualen) remarks in *The Searchers*.

The same motivation underlies Ford's fondness for landscapes that are immutable, notably the desert and rocky outcrops of Monument Valley, his favourite location. It is almost as if the film-maker shares with his characters the desire to possess these vast terrains in order to gain a profound appreciation of stability.

Even that antithesis of the Ford hero, Ethan Edwards in *The Searchers*, who can find no place for himself in stable society, is concerned with its continuation. In this fragmented, poignant film – the only one of Ford's based on a notion of individualism – Ethan sets himself against the ordered life and is seemingly involved in a desperate struggle to remain a loner, a rebel. After a hopeless search for his niece that lasts ten years, Ethan finally understands the uselessness of his revolt. He cannot bring himself to kill the girl when he finds her, tainted though she may be by living with an

Indian 'buck' and therefore a threat to white society. Because he is so concerned to preserve the wholeness of the homestead, he does not realize that the people who made it what it was, and thus its very nature, have changed. There is no place for him and after returning Debbie to the community he disappears, leaving the new generation represented by Martin Pawley to take over.

Exiles and nomads

Ethan is just one of scores of exiles that struggle to preserve society in Ford's films. Others include Irish and European immigrants who dream of gaining some sort of new birthright in America. In *The Man Who Shot Liberty Valance* (1962), restaurant-owner Peter Ericson (John Qualen) actually leaps for joy on hearing the news that he has earned his American citizenship. Ford's universe is also peopled by rootless characters who wander aimlessly – like the sailors in *The Long Voyage Home* (1940). Among these exiles there is even a tribe of Indians: the Comanches of *The Searchers* are Indians who have no territory;

they are constantly on the move. There is also the immigrant prizefighter (John Wayne) returning to his home town after killing a man in the ring in *The Quiet Man* (1952), and families put on the road by the effects of the Dust Bowl to look for new work in *The Grapes of Wrath*.

Other characters are exiled in different ways: the crazed white children and women in *The Searchers* who are refused recognition by their kinsfolk as they have been defiled by Indians. There are also the soldiers for whom the bugle song of retreat in *She Wore a Yellow Ribbon* and *The Wings of Eagles* (1957), or disgrace in *Fort Apache*, sounds a little like exile.

In Ford's films it is not only characters that may be uprooted but entire nations and historical periods. The director has often returned to moments when a social class, or indeed a whole race – in *Cheyenne Autumn* the whole Indian community is oppressed and exiled – is on the brink of extinction. Cheyenne autumn, Welsh twilight – these are both situations from which men and women are forced away to find new means of survival. In *How Green Was My Valley* (1941), industrial strife disrupts the working community and the idyllic family life of the Morgans in the Welsh village where they live at the turn of the century. The youngest son, Huw (Roddy McDowall), whose childhood provides the basis of the story, must finally follow his brothers and move on to pastures new.

Ford portrays people trying to remain faithful to themselves, and to their way of thinking, even when threatened by great historical upheavals. In this respect he may be a spiritual relative of the great Soviet director Donskoi,

Above left: an inaptly titled Belgian poster for The Searchers; *the film is less concerned with Debbie and her 'imprisonment' by Indians than with Ethan, who is a 'prisoner' of his obsession with finding her. Right: the killing of Liberty (Lee Marvin) – but not by Stoddard (James Stewart) – in* The Man Who Shot Liberty Valance. *Below: John Wayne and William Holden in* The Horse Soldiers, *one of Ford's poetic tributes to the US Cavalry*

Filmography

As Jack Ford: **1914** Lucille Love – the Girl of Mystery (serial) (prop man; possible credits for act; stunts; ass. dir); Lucile/Lucille, the Waitress (series of four films: She Wins a Prize and Has Her Troubles; Exaggeration Gets Her Into All Kinds of Trouble; She Gets Mixed Up in a Regular 'Kid Kalamity'; Her Near Proposal) (credited as dir. in some sources); The Mysterious Rose (act. only). **'15** The Birth of a Nation (act. only); Three Bad Men and a Girl (act. only); The Hidden City (act. only); The Doorway of Destruction (act; +ass. dir); The Broken Coin (serial) (act; +ass. dir). **'16** The Lumber Yard Gang (act. only); Peg o' the Ring (serial) (act. only); Chicken-Hearted Jim (act. only); The Bandit's Wager (act. only). **'17** The Purple Mask (serial) (ass. dir); The Tornado (+act; +sc); The Trail of Hate (dir. copyrighted to Ford, no screen credit; +act; +sc); The Scrapper (+act; +sc); The Soul Herder (reissued as short 1922); Cheyenne's Pal; Straight Shooting (reissued as short Straight Shootin', 1925); The Secret Man; A Marked Man; Bucking Broadway. **'18** The Phantom Riders; Wild Women; Thieves' Gold; The Scarlet Drop (GB: Hillbilly); Delirium (co-dir); Hellbent (+co-sc); A Woman's Fool; Three Mounted Men. **'19** Roped; A Fight for Love; The Fighting Brothers; Bare Fists; By Indian Post; The Rustlers; Gun Law; The Gun Pusher (reissued as short 1924); Riders of Vengeance; The Last Outlaw; The Outcasts of Poker Flats; The Ace of the Saddle; The Rider of the Law; A Gun Fightin' Gentleman; untitled one-reel promotion film for personal appearance tour by actor Harry Carey. **'20** Marked Men; The Prince of Avenue 'A'; The Girl in No. 29; Hitchin'

whose films were usually set in a period of social change or revolution. Generally the protagonists do adapt and overcome the crises they face in Ford's films, but they are often required to make costly sacrifices. In *The Man Who Shot Liberty Valance*, Tom Doniphon (John Wayne) kills the outlaw Liberty (Lee Marvin) but makes it seem as though Ransom Stoddard (James Stewart) has done so. For this

Above: Indian women robbed of their homes in Cheyenne Autumn, *based on the real tragedy of the Cheyenne. It was Ford's last Western and the last of nine films he shot wholly or partially in Monument Valley*

noble act Doniphon sacrifices the personal glory of the deed and the girl he loves to Stoddard, lives a lonely life and dies alone.

Ford's desire to celebrate collective effort in his later films was tainted with the cynicism of advancing years, and there are hints of bitterness. Between the winning simplicity of *Drums Along the Mohawk* (1939) – Ford's tribute to the spirit of pioneer America on the eve of the Revolutionary War – and *She Wore a Yellow Ribbon*, there is a great difference in outlook. In the latter Nathan Brittles reconsiders his existence as a cavalry officer and begins to question it, and also doubts the validity of his current mission to subdue the Indians even though he continues to pursue it.

Monuments to America

Ford's heroes age with his work. The last shot of *The Man Who Shot Liberty Valance* is of the elderly Ransom Stoddard crying: doubt and uncertainty are bound up with sadness. Perhaps by the early Sixties, the time of *Liberty Valance*, *Cheyenne Autumn* and *Donovan's Reef* (1963) – a kind of melancholic, sometimes comic, reflection on the past, set in the mythical paradise of a Pacific island – Ford had become aware of his own uprootedness and of his own peculiar state of being an exile within American cinema. Perhaps he also realized that the nature of his work would ultimately remain as unchangeable as his own Monument Valley, but that everything around him was crumbling and disappearing. But when he ceased making pictures John Ford left behind him several of his own enduring monuments to the building of a country: a few massive rocks left in the middle of a vast desert.

BERTRAND TAVERNIER

Posts; Just Pals. '21 The Big Punch (+ co-sc); The Freeze Out; The Wallop; Desperate Trails; Action; Sure Fire; Jackie. '22 Little Miss Smiles; Nero (uncredited add. dir); Silver Wings (prologue dir. only); The Village Blacksmith; The Face on the Barroom Floor (GB: The Love Image). '23 Three Jumps Ahead (+ sc). *As John Ford:* '23 Cameo Kirby; North of Hudson Bay; Hoodman Blind. '24 The Iron Horse; Hearts of Oak. '25 The Fighting Heart (GB: Once to Every Man); Kentucky Pride; Lightnin'; Thank You. '26 The Shamrock Handicap; Three Bad Men (+ sc); The Blue Eagle; What Price Glory (uncredited add. dir). '27 Upstream (GB: Footlight Glamour); Mother Machree (+ sound version 1928). '28 Four Sons; Hangman's House; Napoleon's Barber; Riley the Cop. '29 Strong Boy; The Black Watch (GB: King of the Khyber Rifles) (silent scenes only); Salute; Men Without Women. '30 Born Reckless (silent scenes only); Up the River (silent scenes only; + uncredited sc). '31 Seas Beneath (silent scenes only); The Brat; Arrowsmith. '32 Air Mail; Flesh. '33 Pilgrimage; Doctor Bull. '34 The Lost Patrol; The World Moves On; Judge Priest. '35 The Whole Town's Talking (GB: Passport to Fame); The Informer; Steamboat Round the Bend. '36 The Prisoner of Shark Island; The Last Outlaw; Mary of Scotland; The Plough and the Stars. '37 Wee Willie Winkie; The Hurricane. '38 The Adventures of Marco Polo (uncredited add. dir); Four Men and a Prayer; Submarine Patrol. '39 Stagecoach (+ prod); Young Mr Lincoln; Drums Along the Mohawk. '40 The Grapes of Wrath; The Long Voyage Home. '41 Tobacco Road; How Green Was My Valley. '42 Sex Hygiene (Army training short); The Battle of Midway (doc) (+ co-photo); Torpedo Squadron (private Army film not publicly shown); How to Operate Behind Enemy Lines (Office of Strategic Services training film for restricted showing). '43 December 7th (co-dir) (feature version for Navy; short for public); We Sail at Midnight (doc) (USA-GB: Ford possibly sup. dir. of American version). '45 They Were Expendable (+ prod). '46 My Darling Clementine. '47 The Fugitive (+ co-prod). '48 Fort Apache (+ co-prod); Three Godfathers (+ co-prod). '49 Mighty Joe Young (co-prod. only); She Wore a Yellow Ribbon (+ co-prod). '50 When Willie Comes Marching Home; Wagonmaster (+ co-prod); Rio Grande (+ co-prod). '51 The Bullfighter and the Lady (uncredited ed. only); This Is Korea (doc) (+ prod). '52 The Quiet Man (+ co-prod); What Price Glory? '53 The Sun Shines Bright (+ co-prod); Mogambo; Hondo (uncredited 2nd unit co-dir. only). '55 The Long Gray Line; The Red, White and Blue Line (short with footage from The Long Gray Line); Mister Roberts (some scenes only). '56 The Searchers. '57 The Wings of Eagles; The Rising of the Moon (Eire); The Growler Story (short). '58 Gideon's Day (GB) (USA: Gideon of Scotland Yard); The Last Hurrah (+ prod). '59 Korea (doc) (+ co-prod); The Horse Soldiers. '60 Sergeant Rutledge. '61 Two Rode Together. '62 The Man Who Shot Liberty Valance; How the West Was Won (ep. only). '63 Donovan's Reef (+ prod); The Directors (short) (appearance as himself only). '64 Cheyenne Autumn. '65 Young Cassidy (some scenes only); Seven Women. '70 Chesty: a Tribute to a Legend (doc) (+ interviewer) (shorter version reissued 1976). '71 Vietnam! Vietnam! (doc) (exec. prod. only).

Directed by John Ford, 1939
Prod co: Walter Wanger Productions/United Artists. **exec prod:** Walter Wanger. **prod:** John Ford. **sc:** Dudley Nichols, from the story *Stage to Lordsburg* by Ernest Haycox. **photo:** Bert Glennon. **sp eff:** Ray Binger. **ed sup:** Otho Lovering. **sup:** Dorothy Spencer, Walter Reynolds. **art dir:** Alexander Toluboff, Wiard Ihnen. **cost:** Walter Plunkett. **mus:** Richard Hageman, W. Franke Harling, John Leipold, Leo Shuken, Louis Gruenberg, adapted from 17 American folk tunes of the 1880s. **mus arr:** Boris Morros. **2nd unit dir/stunts:** Yakima Canutt. **ass dir:** Wingate Smith. **r/t:** 97 minutes.
Cast: John Wayne (*The Ringo Kid*), Claire Trevor (*Dallas*), John Carradine (*Hatfield*), Thomas Mitchell (*Dr Josiah Boone*), Andy Devine (*Buck*), Donald Meek (*Samuel Peacock*), Louise Platt (*Lucy Mallory*), Tim Holt (*Lieutenant Blanchard*), George Bancroft (*Sheriff Curly Wilcox*), Berton Churchill (*Henry Gatewood*), Tom Tyler (*Hank Plummer*), Chris Pin Martin (*Chris*), Elvira Rios (*Yakima, his wife*), Francis Ford (*Billy Pickett*), Marga Daighton (*Mrs Pickett*), Kent Odell (*Billy Pickett Jr*), Yakima Canutt (*Chief Big Tree*), Harry Tenbrook (*telegraph operator*), Jack Pennick (*Jerry, barman*), Paul McVey (*express agent*), Cornelius Keefe (*Captain Whitney*), Florence Lake (*Mrs Nancy Whitney*), Louis Mason (*sheriff*), Brenda Fowler (*Mrs Gatewood*), Walter McGrail (*Captain Sickel*), Joseph Rickson (*Luke Plummer*), Vester Pegg (*Ike Plummer*), William Hoffer (*sergeant*), Bryant Washburn (*Captain Simmons*), Nora Cecil (*Dr Boone's housekeeper*), Helen Gibson, Dorothy Annleby (*dancing girls*), Buddy Roosevelt, Bill Cody (*ranchers*), Chief White Horse (*Indian chief*), Duke Lee (*Sheriff of Lordsburg*), Mary Kathleen Walker (*Lucy's baby*).

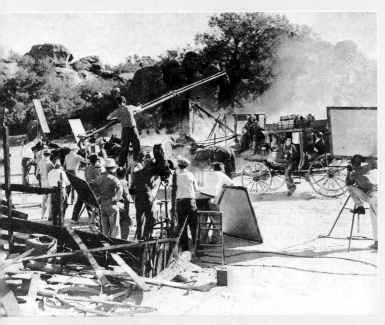

Stagecoach has often been credited with reviving the Western in Hollywood in the Forties. Rather, though, it coincided with a whole Western boom, appearing in the same year – 1939 – as *Dodge City*, *The Oklahoma Kid*, *Union Pacific* and *Jesse James*. Even so, when Ford tried to set up the film – his first Western since *Three Bad Men* (1926) – he found the genre was badly out of fashion.

He had bought Ernest Haycox's story, which he found in *Cosmopo-*

1

Apaches have broken out of the reservation and the telegraph wires have been cut. Nevertheless a varied group of passengers boards the stagecoach from Tonto to Lordsburg: Mrs Mallory, a pregnant wife going to join her husband, a cavalry lieutenant; Hatfield, a shady gentleman-gambler; Dallas, a prostitute run out of town by the 'decent' citizens; the bibulous and disreputable Doc Boone, who takes a keen interest in the samples carried by a timid whisky-drummer called Peacock. At the edge of the town they are joined by Gatewood, the pompous local banker. Riding alongside Buck the driver is Curly, a sheriff in pursuit of the Ringo Kid who has broken jail where he has been serving a sentence for a framed murder charge. Just outside town, Ringo himself joins the party (1). The stagecoach heads into Indian country, stopping shortly afterwards at the first staging post (2–3).

Above: John Ford – standing to the right of the boom-mike operator – filming Stagecoach

Initially, the group is strictly divided between the respectable and the disreputable, but the hazards of the journey temporarily blur the social barriers. Dallas and Doc Boone take charge of the sudden *accouchement* of Mrs Mallory (4). The Ringo Kid falls in love with Dallas, who is touched by his gallantry to her. The whole party is finally united by the Indian attack (5). The cavalry charges to the rescue (6), but not before Hatfield has been killed.

Arriving at Lordsburg, they go their different ways. The Ringo Kid avenges himself on Luke Plummer, the man who had framed him, and is reunited with Dallas. Curly, instead of arresting the Kid, connives with Doc Boone to speed the couple over the border. 'At least they're spared the blessings of civilization,' reflects the philosophic Doc.

2

'RANGE MEN . . . . .

CLAIRE TREVOR • JOHN WAYNE

in it. What's the difference whether it's played in the West or wherever?' He took it to RKO where even the powerful Joseph P. Kennedy could not persuade his producers to adopt the project. Walter Wanger, however, who owed a film to United Artists, was finally convinced. Wanger wanted to use Gary Cooper and Marlene Dietrich for the main roles but Ford insisted that it must be cast cheaply, so he hired John Wayne – whose career had so far failed to take off, and who was making five-day Westerns – and Claire Trevor, 'a helluva actress'. Ford surrounded them with fine character players: Thomas Mitchell and Berton Churchill, both stage-trained actors; Donald Meek, George Bancroft, Andy Devine and the cadaverous John Carradine. For every one of them, the role in *Stagecoach* was to prove the most memorable of his career.

Ford himself later drew attention to the faint resemblance of the story to Maupassant's *Boule de Suif*. The critic Welford Beaton was on a better tack, however, when he described the film as '*Grand Hotel* on wheels'. The essence of the story is the interaction of a little group of characters under the stress of a perilous journey.

The structure of the film is very formal. It divides neatly into eight carefully balanced episodes, of which the central and longest is the 24-minute sequence at the Apache Wells staging post with the birth of Mrs Mallory's baby, and the climax is the six and a half minutes of the Indian attack. The expository opening scene, set in Tonto, lasts 12 minutes, during which time every character is carefully and comprehensively introduced.

The characters are also exactly balanced; in one group are the respectable' people – Hatfield, Gatewood (actually an embezzler) and Mrs Mallory; in the other, the 'disreputables' – the Ringo Kid, Doc Boone and Dallas. Buck and Curly, outside the coach, stand aside, a sort of chorus upon the moral debate waged within the coach. The mild little whisky-drummer, too, has a detached function. It is he who states the simple moral of the film: 'Let us have a little Christian charity, one to another.'

The picture was made for $222,000 – $8000 under the assigned budget. The scenes in Monument Valley were completed in four days; the rest was shot on the Goldwyn lot. The Monument Valley days included the extraordinary stunt material staged by Yakima Canutt. Canutt related that after he had performed his most hair-raising feat – jumping onto the stagecoach's lead horse and then, in response to Ringo's rifle shots, falling first to the shafts and then to the ground, allowing six horses and the stage to drive over his prone body – he ran to Ford to ask if the cameras had caught it. 'Even if they didn't,' said Ford, 'I'll not shoot that again.'

At that time there were no specifically equipped camera cars, and ordinary automobiles were used for the amazing scenes where the cameras follow the chase at full speed. The cameramen found to their surprise that in keeping up with the horses they were driving at 40–42 miles per hour.

'I shot it pretty much as it is written,' said Ford, though Dudley Nichols was on the set throughout the film to write – or more likely to cut – dialogue as required. What is striking is the economy of the script. A broken half-line or two will often brilliantly illuminate a character or a situation. At the end, when the characters are returning to their own worlds, Mrs Mallory makes a hopeless attempt to prolong the brief contact with Dallas. 'If there is ever anything …' she begins awkwardly; 'I know,' says Dallas, understanding, but decisively acknowledging the unbridgeable gulf between them in the hypocritical, rigid society of their times.

Stagecoach stands alone for the epic quality both of its panoramas of the West and its human emotions. At the same time it permanently formed Western style. Ford was the first to make use of the spectacular topography of Monument Valley, and was to return to it many times again himself. The final shoot-out, which he had already used in silent films, and was to use again in *My Darling Clementine* (1946), has, since *Stagecoach*, become a cliché.

'It went back to what Wyatt Earp had told me. Wyatt was a friend of mine – in fact I still have his rifle in the corner of my bedroom.'

Ford has always stayed this close to his own West.

DAVID ROBINSON

litan magazine, for $2500. 'It wasn't too well developed,' he recalled, 'but the characters were good.' Producers he approached complained that people no longer went to see Westerns: 'Sure it's a Western, I said, but there are great characters

3

5

6

INDEX